THE POLICE IN HONG KONG

A Contemporary View

Allan Y. Jiao

D1546471

University Press of America,® Inc.
Lanham · Boulder · New York · Toronto · Plymouth, UK

Copyright © 2007 by
University Press of America,® Inc.
4501 Forbes Boulevard
Suite 200
Lanham, Maryland 20706
UPA Acquisitions Department (301) 459-3366

Estover Road
Plymouth PL6 7PY
United Kingdom

Library of Congress Control Number: 2006933310
ISBN-13: 978-0-7618-3634-6 (paperback : alk. paper)
ISBN-10: 0-7618-3634-9 (paperback : alk. paper)

∞™The paper used in this publication meets the minimum
requirements of American National Standard for Information
Sciences—Permanence of Paper for Printed Library Materials,
ANSI Z39.48—1984

Contents

Preface

This book is a comprehensive study of a police organization in Asia, the Hong Kong Police. Through a detailed examination of the practices and value orientations of this police force, I hope to inform the readers about an essential component of the criminal justice system in Hong Kong and the related social, political, and cultural conditions in the region in which the police work. As the first systematic inquiry of a Chinese Special Administrative Region police agency, this book includes descriptions and analyses of the Hong Kong Police's historical background, the 1997 handover, the changes and continuities, the structure and operation, the learning culture, the impact of the Bill of Rights, the street officer behavior, the management behavior, the crime problems, and the control of corruption and misconduct. The purpose of this book is to fill a void in criminal justice and police studies, as the Hong Kong Police has not been studied in a comprehensive manner by academics, to develop knowledge about police development in the region, and to advance understanding of police work in a changing society.

The examination of the police is essential for understanding the nature of government and the culture of society. The police are a law enforcement agency, have the most contact with the public, represent the most intrusive aspect of government, and their orientation often reflects the nature of the government. The police, therefore, provide a unique and meaningful insight to the inquiry of political influence on government bureaucracies (Bayley, 1985). Providing an immediate link between politics and citizens, a police organization often changes its strategies in response to changes in its political environment, affects citizen life, and provides feedback to the government it represents. The police in Hong Kong are no exception, as they represent the government and mirror the Hong Kong society simultaneously and their practice reflects the politics, economics, and cultures of the region.

The Hong Kong Police arouses special interest for academic inquiry because it is the only police force in the Chinese territory that has over one and a half century of Western colonialism. Policing in Hong Kong became a sensitive issue when the British and Chinese governments started discussing Hong Kong's future in the early 1980s: Would the Hong Kong Police be used as a political tool to continue Western influence or serve the interest of the mainland Chinese government? How would the Hong Kong Police enforce English laws in a Special Administrative Region that is geographically and politically a sovereign part of China? How would a police force that enjoyed questionable legitimacy during its colonial history build public trust in a new social, political environment? Would the Hong Kong Police be able to carry out their law enforcement mission and function as a professional police force? The issues faced by the Hong Kong Police, therefore, are significant; at the heart of the matter is the question, how a law enforcement agency constituted according to Western law enforcement principles due to Western colonization would function in a new political environment after decolonization.

The issues faced by the Hong Kong Police are unique politically because the end of the colonial rule resulted in neither Hong Kong's integration into the Chinese political system nor its own independence. After the region's change of sovereignty in 1997, Hong Kong has maintained its own economic, social, and political system under the "one-country, two-systems" formula. Hong Kong is a sovereign part of China, but maintains its own way of life. A crucial aspect of this arrangement is the implementation of the Basic Law of the Hong Kong Special Administrative Region (Chen, 1999). Political tension centers on legislation and law enforcement as they test directly Hong Kong's autonomy after 1997. The practice of the police as a law enforcement agency demonstrates the direction and development of the Hong Kong government in this new historical period as a part of China.

Due to this unique political arrangement, other former Western colonies' policing experiences do not have direct or immediate implications for the Hong Kong Police. Police problems in many former Western territories were caused by a breakdown in order associated with the strains induced by economic crisis, war, and the development of indigenous trade union and nationalist consciousness (Kuan and Lau, 1987:96). Hong Kong has not been in any general economic crisis, it is not a newly independent nation, and it has not returned to a political system it identifies itself with. Hong Kong policing, therefore, cannot be understood by inferences from other former colonies' experiences. For this reason, it is necessary to study the Hong Kong Police, a major public organization in Hong Kong, to clarify our understanding of a unique relationship between the police and their environment, a special case in government studies, public administration, and criminal justice.

Another significant rationale for studying the Hong Kong Police is its geographical jurisdiction. Hong Kong is the nerve center of a most dynamic economic region in the world, the Pearl River Delta. The Pearl River Delta region stretches from Hong Kong and Shenzhen in the southeast, to Guangzhou in the north, and Macau and Zhuhai in the southwest (Mitchell, 2002; Pritchard, 2002). Hong Kong is also considered the center of the "China circle" that connects with Macao, Taiwan, and the rest of China (Sung, 1997). Because of Hong Kong's geographical vantage and its close relationship with other parts of China, such a study should also contribute to our understanding of the sociopolitical situation in the rest of China.

The implication of such a unique historical background and geographical location is that a proud and rich Chinese culture can perhaps be reconciled with the widely hailed Western values of property rights, freedom, and democracy. As these general Western values are diffused widely in the Hong Kong society, Western law enforcement principles have also influenced heavily the Hong Kong Police. It is reasonable to assert, therefore, that the changes and continuities of the Hong Kong Police present a microscopic view of the complex political and cultural relationship between the West and China. For example, the effort for the Hong Kong Government to develop a Western style political system has been viewed positively by Western powers as a way to extend their influence, but often deemed critically by the Chinese government as creating chaos and instability in China. The study of the police role and function in such an environment should allow us to appreciate the multi-dimensional and ever-changing nature of the region, which is of great significance for understanding the rest of China. This study of the Hong Kong Police thus should help us keep abreast of the social and political development in the region.

Although learning about the Hong Kong Police cannot be separated from understanding the historical, political, and geographical circumstances of Hong Kong, the understanding of larger social environment alone will not be conducive to an in-depth comprehension of the culture and behavior of a police organization. Many nuances and details of police officers related to their values and mentalities would be lost in a broad brush of the government and politics in the region. For example, the Hong Kong Police cannot be understood accurately on the basis of the change of sovereignty and the police response to the 1997 transition alone, which would be overly narrow and superficial, as reported by many officers who participated in this study. The politics and police of a major metropolis like Hong Kong are deeply rooted in their own traditions and cultures that cannot be grasped explicitly by examining the events during the change of sovereignty only. The political and historical situations are transient, whereas policing in Hong Kong has been a constant, a function that has lasted over 160 years and the basic function of which has remained by and large, according to most officers interviewed in this study, unchanged after the handover. A detailed study of the Hong Kong Police is warranted to capture the fundamental human element in this police organization, which is likely to be missing in the broad analysis of the political development in the region. A microscopic examination of a large public organization should, reversely, also contribute to our understanding of the larger political and social environment.

As a large public organization, the Hong Kong Police can also be effective in influencing its institutional environment and changing and developing itself. At the very least, it should not be viewed as a completely passive, inactive entity, shaped only by external factors beyond its control. The police are not always on the receiving end in their interactions with the public and their parent government. The Hong Kong Police, in particular, has enjoyed a social and political status that is rarely matched by other major police organizations in the world. The role it has played in the society is perhaps far greater than these other agencies. Police organizations in other major cities certainly also influence their community life, but far less in comparison to the influence of the police in Hong Kong. The Hong Kong Police to a great extent is and represents the Hong Kong government itself. The greater reliance of the government and economy on the police in history and at present has led to this significant role. The Hong Kong government and economy, as Rabushka (1973:2) stated, "more than any other country in the world, approximate the classical economic notion of laissez-faire that postulates a limited role for government: law and order, contract enforcement, a definition of property rights, and perhaps defense against foreign enemies." This governmental arrangement means that the Hong Kong Police must fulfill one of the few most essential public functions in Hong Kong. The limited role of government and importance placed on the police have been attributed to Hong Kong's economic success by many people as, understandably, economic prosperity is not possible without law and order. The role of the police in the Hong Kong society and economy, therefore, should not be underestimated.

Furthermore, the Hong Kong Police, as one of the largest and often viewed as one of the most efficient and professional police organizations in the world, deserves to be studied in its own right. Two variables that stand out and contribute to the high respect of the international police community for the Hong Kong Police are low crime rate and low police corruption rate. The experience and development of the Hong Kong Police, therefore, are important to learn for the benefit of the police profession. It is well-known that Hong Kong, as a world-class city, has enjoyed tremendous commercial success. But a story behind this prosperity that has rarely been told is the story of the Hong Kong Police. The Hong Kong Police has experienced several major reforms from a colonial, paramilitary force to a more professionally oriented police force, from an authoritarian force with syndicated corruption to an organization that is more community-oriented and relatively free of corruption, and from a force that focuses on public order management to one that emphasizes service quality. Its experiences in developing and transforming itself reflect the many changes taking place in government in the rest of the world.

This book is based on an approach different from other works that often examine the politics, cultures, and economics of the region from a macro-sociological perspective; it is a detailed, empirical examination of the Hong Kong Police as a human organization as well as a political entity. The storyline of the book goes from Hong Kong Police's past and recent development to more specific areas of significance for the police profession. Chapter 1 provides the historical background and traditions of the Hong Kong Police as a British colonial force that carried the Royal title. Chapter 2 describes the role of the Hong Kong Police in the year of 1997 when the British rule ended and Hong Kong returned to China, a year full of intense speculations and concerns about the stability and future status of Hong Kong. With the narratives of the history and the year of 1997 completed, it is ready to provide an overview of the changes and continuities of the Hong Kong Police in recent years, which are covered in Chapter 3. From Chapter 4 to Chapter 10, seven specific topics of significance to the police in particular and the government in general are presented in detail. Chapter 4 describes the organizational structure and major operations of the Hong Kong Police. Chapter 5 provides a specific examination of the learning culture in the Hong Kong Police, i.e., its recruitment, selection, academy training, and in-service training. Chapter 6 discusses the impact of the Bill of Rights and other civil rights legislation on the police and their relation to the police's own cultural traditions. Chapter 7 and 8 provides a detailed look at the attitudes and behavior of street officers and management officers and their routine activities. Chapter 9 addresses the crime problems the Hong Kong Police face, including traditional crimes, vice, and organized crimes. Chapter 10 covers police corruption and misconduct and how these problems have been tackled in Hong Kong. The last chapter, Chapter 11, provides some closing remarks that wrap up the entire book.

To write a book of this nature requires first-hand data on both police management and frontline operations. Over the years, I have had a strong interest in the Hong Kong Police, collecting and reading information about this police organization whenever possible. Since the research for this book focuses not only on the historical and political environment but also issues conducive for understanding the value orientations and practices of the Hong Kong Police, including their organizational behaviors overtime, I have emphasized a systematic and empirical approach to studying the Hong Kong Police. I have traveled to Hong Kong several times over the past decade to observe its activities and interview its officers including a full academic year in 2001-2002. Ideally, I would have used both quantitative and qualitative research methods in collecting the data since a qualitative approach usually generates more in-depth knowledge, but sacrifices representativeness and generalizability and a quantitative approach is often based upon a more representative sample, but lacking in comprehensiveness and substance. Understanding the limitations of these approaches, I proposed to conduct both in-depth, personal interviews and a structured questionnaire survey with a random sample to the Hong Kong Police at the beginning of this study. The quantitative part of the proposal was rejected, however, on the ground that such a survey would be in conflict with the Force's own surveys.

The primary sources of information for this book are, therefore, qualitative, including first-hand personal interviews. Understanding the limitations of the qualitative approach, I do not claim that the officers I have interviewed are representative of the entire Hong Kong Police. The data generated from this approach, albeit inadequate, remains the best source of information available as far as this study is concerned. Analysis of the data follows the usual qualitative procedure of transcribing interview notes and organizing the data into themes and patterns that emerged during the fieldwork. The opinions of individual officers are presented extensively in quotes throughout this book because, although they may not be representative of the views of the entire Force, they are representative of the officers interviewed for this study unless noted otherwise. As I rely on the interview notes in presenting much of the materials in this book, I have also tried to minimize the limitations of this source by including information from on-site observations and documentary research.

In order to carry out this research successfully, I have taken advantage of both formal and informal channels. I am grateful to the Hong Kong Police for granting me the opportunity to conduct this study in a comprehensive manner. I am equally thankful to the many officers I was able to interview through informal and personal contacts. During the initial stage of this research, officials from the Service Quality Wing of the Hong Kong Police took valuable time from their busy schedule to discuss with me the specifics of my research plan. They met with me several times for many hours to help me hammer out a meaningful and organized research agenda. They provided also a great amount of verbal and written information during these meetings to familiarize me with the Hong Kong Police and lay the groundwork for my research activities. Two officers at the rank of inspector and superintendent from the Service Quality Wing were designated to serve as liaisons and coordinators for my research. These officers became my regular contacts in the Hong Kong Police who responded to my many requests and coordinated various research activities such as setting up interviews, arranging observations, and helping me search police archives.

The initial preparation and orientation sessions resulted in a more appropriate research plan and better procedure for collecting the data. The research instruments were made more specific to the police programs, levels of officers, and divisions in the Hong Kong Police. To avoid confusion, I was advised to follow the hierarchy of the Force, from the policy-making level to district operations and to the front-lines. As a result of these preparations, I was able to ensure that the methods and instruments were more acceptable and understandable to police officers in Hong Kong. I revised the original questionnaire I prepared in the U.S. several times and tailored it to different units and functions. All questions were worded as relevant and understandable to the officers as possible. Questions considered irrelevant, inappropriate, or unfamiliar to the officers were either taken off the lists or modified. For example, some of the questions were confusing and difficult to comprehend as they contained terms that are seldom heard of in the context of Hong Kong law enforcement. Such terms were rephrased or changed to those more familiar to the officers. After several mornings and afternoons of detailed discussions about the research questions, my questionnaire was significantly improved and various interview guides based on the questionnaire were created. I benefited a lot from this process as I learned a great deal from these officers, and was able to eliminate some of my own misunderstandings and misconceptions about the Hong Kong Police.

The question about the willingness of officers to answer questions truthfully has always been a concern in qualitative research. Whether the Hong Kong Police officers are forthcoming was not clear at the beginning. As time went on, I was better able to put the pieces together. As the research continued over an extended period of time, I was able to use a variety of methods and sources of information to triangulate the data. For in-depth interviews, for example, I used both formal interviews arranged through the Service Quality Wing and informal interviews set up by acquaintances and personal contacts. I interviewed both serving and retired officers; both sworn officers and civilian employees; and both insiders, those serving in the Hong Kong Police, and outsiders, those working in other public or private agencies that have frequent dealings with the Hong Kong Police. For observations, I used formally arranged observations such as ride-along with car crews and walk-along with foot patrol officers, pure observations of foot patrol officers in public places without the knowledge of the officers, and participant observations as an auditor or observer in a police meeting or a training session. I also used documentary research, including research in the Hong Kong Police Library, on the Police Intranet, and in local universities that keep collections of master's theses written by Hong Kong police officers. The length and depth as well as the variety of the research activities proved to be important factors for ensuring the accuracy of the collected data.

Most officers were quite open, frank, and enthusiastic in sharing their experiences and views. While there are various explanations for their candidness such as appropriately worded questions, interview skills, researcher personality, anonymity, and confidentiality, I believe that two factors stand out as most important. First, I am a complete outsider with no personal stake in the outcome of this study and my research focuses on general police issues for the sole purpose of advancing knowledge in policing. Officers understand that I do not represent any particular group in the Hong Kong Police or any local organization in Hong Kong. As a female inspector said, "Our tradition is receiving orders. We are a disciplined force. Officers don't talk much to us. So outside researchers can sometimes get more information." Second, the nature of this research appeals to the professionalism of the Hong Kong Police officers, many of whom consider it their professional duty to help an academic obtain a truthful and objective picture of the Hong Kong Police for the benefit of the police profession.

Overall I have interviewed over two hundred Hong Kong Police officers including patrol officers, sergeants, inspectors, senior inspectors, chief inspectors, superintendents, senior superintendents, chief superintendents, assistant commissioners, and senior assistant commissioners and many members of the public in Hong Kong. Although a significant number, the number of officers interviewed constitute about one percent of the Hong Kong Police. Also, due to the qualitative methods available for this research and the formal procedure used in selecting the officers, the views of these interviewees should not be construed as representative of the entire Hong Kong Police. I have, however, tried to minimize the methodological limitations inherent in the qualitative approach by covering as many police districts and programs in the Force as possible. Most of the officers I have interviewed and observed come from the Operations Wing, which covers the three territories (i.e., Hong Kong Island, Kowloon, and the New Territories) or six police regions in Hong Kong. They are from various division stations and units including Central, North Point, Wan Chai, the Emergency Unit, and Control and Command Center in the Hong Kong Island Region; Kun Tong, Wong Tai Sin, and Kowloon Bay Mass Transit Railway Unit (commonly known as MTR) in the Kowloon East Region; Mong Kok, Sham Shui Po, and Tsim Sha Tsui in the Kowloon West Region; Tsing Yi and Tsuen Wan in the New Territory South Region; and Tuen Mun and Yuen Long in the New Territory North Region. Other officers are from the Crime Wing, including Organized Crime Bureau, Commercial Crime Bureau, Criminal Intelligence, and Hong Kong Island Regional Crime Headquarters. Still others are from the Training Wing, including Police Training School and Higher Command Training; the Service Quality Wing, including Performance Review, Research and Inspections, Internal Investigation Office, and Complaints against Police Office (CAPO); Personnel and Recruitment Wing; Management Services; and the Police Headquarters. I have also interviewed some civilians and retired police officers who are working or used to work in the Operations Wing and Crime Wing. Outside the Hong Kong Police, I was able to interview some officers from the Independent Commission against Corruption (ICAC) of Hong Kong, government officials from the executive branch of the Hong Kong Government, and many members of the general public.

The changes and development of the Hong Kong Police can be examined from several theoretical or conceptual perspectives developed in previous police and sociological research. It is important to point out, however, before these ideas are laid out, that they have been arrived at inductively, after the data from the Hong Kong Police was collected and related analysis completed, instead of deductively, before the data collection began. I did not use the deductive approach, i.e., testing the applicability of certain theories or concepts for the Hong Kong Police because of the qualitative methods available for this study. More importantly, I saw the pitfalls of narrowing this study to tests of certain concepts and losing sight of the "big picture." As a matter of fact, several Hong Kong police officers warned me during the planning phase of this study against using preconceived ideas to guide my research and spoke about the importance of letting the data speak for itself. I realized only after examining all the gathered materials that several theoretical frameworks can be used to analyze the changes and development of the Hong Kong Police. These include Wilson (1972)'s concept of police styles (i.e., watchmen, legalistic, and service), Bourdieu (1990)'s concept of "habitus" and "field," Sackmann (1991)'s "organizational knowledge," Skolnick (1994)'s "law" and "order," Manning (1977)'s "dramatic metaphor," and the more general but related cultural and institutional perspectives (Brint and Karabel, 1991; DiMaggio and Powell, 1991; March and Olsen, 1984; and Meyer and Rowan, 1991) developed in previous organizational studies. While it may not be appropriate to use any one of these concepts separately for analyzing all gathered materials, they, in combination, fill some gaps in the analysis and facilitate the analytical process. The reasons why it is not appropriate to use just one of the concepts to piece together the gathered information should be obvious. The organizational context, the cultural traditions, the historical experiences, the institutional environment of the Hong Kong Police, to name just a few, are quite different from those of the organizations studied previously and having contributed to the concepts. They are used in this book, where appropriate, for the purpose of facilitating the interpretation of data and further developing our knowledge in policing. It is with this understanding that I have created a theme for this book, which is, broadly speaking, the police change and develop and eventually progress by counterbalancing various forces both within and outside the organization and by interacting with key groups or sovereigns in their institutional environment.

While the three different police styles Wilson (1972) develops, albeit in a very different organizational context, serve to conceptualize the changes and development of the Hong Kong Police, other concepts as mentioned above provide explanations as to why changes to different orientations actually take place. "Habitus" and "field," for example, help explain how police organizational knowledge interacts with the reality police face in the field in producing changes. "Law" and "order," representing two extreme police orientations, illustrates an inherent contradiction in modern policing and how it, overtime, may prompt the police to become more professionalized. The "dramatic metaphor" asks us to look beyond the images and rituals presented by the police to seek a deeper understanding of the motivations behind their change programs. Similarly, the general cultural and institutional perspectives force us to examine the interplay of different cultures (i.e., Western and Chinese cultures in case of the Hong Kong Police) and the impact of institutionalized practices on current police reforms. Admittedly, a few words like these do not do justice to the broader meanings and deeper connotations these concepts are intended for. Where they are used, therefore, they are meant to facilitate the analytical process and help us develop a better understanding of police changes and development. It is perhaps more appropriate to limit the use of these concepts, as they appear in this book, in this light.

As a monograph on the Hong Kong Police and its nature and culture using empirical data as sources of information, I hope that this book will satisfy the needs of both academics and practitioners. In academic areas, political scientists, social scientists, police scholars, China experts, and researchers in these areas should find the original data presented in this work useful. Professors and students in Political Science, Sociology, Public Administration, Asian Studies, Cultural Studies, as well as Criminal Justice and Criminology programs may use this book as a reader for any class that emphasizes an international or comparative perspective. For Criminal Justice and Law Enforcement Programs at the university level in Hong Kong, this book can be used as a primary text-book for classes designed to cover the Hong Kong Police. In the professional field, practitioners like government officials, public administrators, police executives, and police officers facing the challenge of changes in their political environment should benefit from reading the management strategies and organizational development experiences described in this book. This book, therefore, should be beneficial to academics, researchers, students, and practitioners alike.

Acknowledgements

My greatest debt is to the more than two hundred police officers in Hong Kong who have provided the most valuable information for this book during personal interviews and observations. The data they allowed me to collect is comprehensive, including not only tangible materials like structures and operations, but also intangible ones such as value orientations and personal views. These officers come from all units and ranks, including patrol officers, sergeants, inspectors, senior inspectors, chief inspectors, superintendents, senior superintendents, chief superintendents, assistant commissioners, and senior assistant commissioners. And they represent various units in the Operations Wing, Crime Wing, Training Wing, Service Quality Wing, Personnel and Recruitment, Management Services, and the Police Headquarters. I, not any of the officers, of course, bear full responsibility for all neglects, errors, and mistakes as they may occur in writing this book.

There is no doubt that without these officers' participation, this book would not have been written. I am grateful to the fact that many of them devoted numerous hours over a year-long period to help me collect the necessary data even though they owe nothing to an academic coming from outside Hong Kong. Not all of them, however, will approve of everything I have written in this book or the way the materials are presented. But I hope that they will take comfort in knowing that this book is organized on the basis of themes emerged from interviews and observations rather than my personal opinions. The views they have expressed, sometimes diverse and sometimes similar, are presented verbatim wherever appropriate and the activities they have allowed me to observe are described as truthfully as my senses allow. To protect the identity of the officers and to keep my promise of anonymity and confidentiality, I have avoided mentioning any of them by name or providing any information that might lead to their identification, unless the information used is already part of public record.

The Hong Kong Police were extremely accommodating and hospitable at all levels. The senior officers at the Service Quality Wing graciously accepted my plan to interview officers in various divisions that involve management and operations and different levels from senior assistant commissioners to street officers. They also honored my requests to observe foot patrol, ride in patrol cars, attend police meetings, participate in police training sessions, and be present at various police functions to obtain first-hand information about the Hong Kong Police. Both internal and public documents were made available to me including various police statistics and standard police reports. As much as I am grateful to the openness and helpfulness of the Hong Kong Police for giving me the opportunity to conduct this study, I have been equally impressed with individual officers' courtesy and professionalism. In addition to uniformed police officers, important information was also made available to me by the civilian staff from the Operations Wing and Crime Wing and retired Hong Kong police officers.

Although the analysis and writing portion of this project is largely a personal endeavor, I owe many institutions and numerous individuals for making the fieldwork and data collection part of this study possible. The United States Fulbright program provided me with a senior scholar award for studying the Hong Kong Police for a full academic year. The Department of Public and Social Administration at the City University of Hong Kong served as a host during my stay in Hong Kong, providing me with accommodation, office space, and research assistance where possible. The Department of Public and Social Administration also supported my participation in an on-going, in-house, research project on Public Sector Reform, a portion of which concerned the Hong Kong Police. Dr. Brian Brewer and Dr. Joan Leung organized ten police focus-group discussions for this purpose, and with the permission of the Hong Kong Police, I was allowed to be present during all these discussions and ask my own questions. Some of the students at the City University of Hong Kong were also engaged in research projects related to the Hong Kong Police. They shared their survey data collected at some police stations with me, which proved to be useful for crosschecking and validating part of my data. These students are Yik-yin Chan, Denise Chung, Ada Lai, Tsz-kin Lau, Gloria Leung, Thera So, and Steffi Tang. Many other faculty and staff at the City University, Hong Kong University, and Open University of Hong Kong provided valuable information or support for my research, including Anthony Cheung, Arthur Cheung, Maria Francesch, David Hodson, Ian Holliday, Raymond Lau, Linda Li, and Peter Lui. Senior officers from the Independent Commission against Corruption (ICAC) of Hong Kong, government officials from the executive branch of the Hong Kong Government, and many members of the Hong Kong public also made themselves available for interviews. Last, but not the least, my home institution, Rowan University in the United States, provided sabbatical leave for the academic year I spent in Hong Kong and has continued to support my effort in completing this book through course-load reduction.

1

The Colonial Past

The Hong Kong Police has a long and rich history that goes back to the mid-19th Century. Many of its earlier philosophies and practices remain discernable today in its thinking and activities. A brief look at its history at the beginning of this book, therefore, helps put our discussion of the Hong Kong Police in a historical context. Such a context is important especially for understanding the cultural traits and organizational knowledge of a major police force. The Hong Kong Police has experienced several significant transformations in history, following often the changes of the Hong Kong Government. Overall, according to Vagg (1996), the Hong Kong Police has experienced three major socio-political changes under the British rule, i.e., the colonial period (1841-1880), the administrative state period (1881-1980), and the democratic period (1981-1996). From 1997 to the present, the Hong Kong Police has been operating in its fourth period, the post-colonial period, which is marked by further democratic development and a more open society.

Hong Kong became a British colony because of the opium trade in the early 19th century. The enormous profits that were and could be generated by this trade directly motivated the British government's "seizure and colonization of Hong Kong" (Robushka, 1973:43). The sovereignty of Hong Kong was subsequently changed from the Ching Dynasty to the British Empire in 1842. It is hard to imagine today that any foreign government would be able to go to another country to force open its door for drug trade and if it did not, compel that country's government to sign an unequal treaty, and then take part of its land. Yet this was exactly what happened to China after Britain defeated the Chinese military in 1841. As an area established for opium trade or in today's words "drug trade," Hong Kong soon became "an unruly community of residents and crime immediately became prevalent" (Rabushka, 1973:43). Law and order was, therefore, a paramount concern right from the beginning of the colony. As Rabushka (1973:43) stated, the first urgent problem of the Hong Kong government was "to maintain minimal law and order and give protection for person and property" (Rabushka, 1973:43). Some examples that demonstrate this urgency are the Hong Kong government's building of a magistrate's court and jail in 1841 before building a home for the colonial governor, and legislation for establishing the police and court in the colony's very first year (Gaylord and Traver, 1994).

The early colonial government did not trust the local population and cited "internal insecurity, lawlessness, and proximity to China" as reasons for precluding a "viable representative government" (Rabushka, 1973:45). As a colonial police force, the early Hong Kong Police were "imported without seeking consent from the indigenous people" (Pang, 1999:123). Early police officers were recruited anywhere but Hong Kong. They came from England, India, Pakistan, and northern China. As one of the officers interviewed said, "My grandfather is from Wei Hai Wei, Shandong Province, which was a small British enclave in northern China." This recruitment practice resulted later in serous under-representation of Chinese in senor positions within the Police, the Legal Department, and the Judiciary. As English law and English language were dominant in Hong Kong's legal system, promotion of police officers was based on racial and linguistic lines (Gaylord and Traver, 1994).

The function of the police in a colony set up for the opium trade was clearly different from that of any police today. Policing in this environment could not focus on ordinary crime and law enforcement. Instead, the Hong Kong Police's priorities during the early days were control of the local population and public order. Its mission was to protect the person and property of the European merchants and maintain an environment in which they could profit. The police played a role in separating the local population from the Europeans for easier control. The Peak, for example, was off-limits to the Chinese until the 1950s. During this early part of the colonial history, the Hong Kong Police enforced both British laws and Chinese customary laws, the so-called "Two Track" legal system, the Common Law for the British and Chinese customary laws for the Chinese (Endacott, 1964). Early police officers were perplexed by the issue of whose law—both criminal and civil—the Chinese population should be subject to. Chinese law enforcement also created constitutional problems in matters such as access to the Supreme Court in England (Endacott, 1964).

Some unique factors in the early history of Hong Kong significantly influenced the initial development of the police. Hong Kong originally was not a colony for settlement purposes, it did not have a large or hostile resident population, and it was geographically a small territory (Gaylord and Traver, 1994). There was, therefore, no planning of a systematic nature for the policing function. As there was an influx and increase of the Chinese population, as more territories were ceded to the British Government, i.e., Kowloon and the New Territories, and as the trade continued to flourish, the colonial government became more concerned about law and order and a more systematic way of policing gradually developed. The Hong Kong Police developed mainly in a paramilitary fashion with the objective of controlling the local population. The function of the police for controlling the Chinese population is evident in Hong Kong's legislation during this period. Early ordinances concerning registration card, light and pass laws, registration of persons, etc., were directed at the

Chinese population. Anti-Triad ordinance was created to stamp out potentially subversive Chinese organizations, on the basis of two principles: first, the membership in Triad organizations was declared illegal; second, the Commissioner of Police served as the Registrar of Societies (Gaylord and Traver, 1994). The social conflicts in this early part of Hong Kong history were understandably mainly between the colonial police and the Chinese population. Crime control for the purpose of maintaining public order has since become a traditional Hong Kong police policy.

Many officers in the Hong Kong Police today view this early history as a humiliation to China. In the meantime, many think that it is an embarrassment to Britain. The lesson from this history for China is simply that a weak nation is bound to be bullied and controlled by more powerful nations. The Chinese history over the past three hundred years was full of such embarrassing episodes when foreign powers either defeated the Chinese military, or controlled parts of China, or divided up the country into different regions. The moral for Britain as well as other powerful countries is that a nation could be powerful militarily and economically, but lose the moral high ground and trust of less prosperous nations. This history, for example, has created distrust of Western powers among some Hong Kong police officers today and forces them to question the motives of Western leaders when they push for democracy, human rights, and the Bill of Rights in Hong Kong.

As the colony went through the transition from the colonial period to the administrative period, Sir John Pope Hennessy, the then Governor, saw a direct connection between securing the legitimacy of governance and the regulation of crime (Lowe and McLaughlin, 1994). He considered it vital that the local community have faith in the fairness of the criminal justice system and governance be premised on the rule of law rather than the parochial interests of British colonists (Lowe and McLaughlin, 1994). The Hong Kong Police, however, was created "to protect the interest of the colonists" (Pang, 1999:131), was superimposed from Britain, had to rely on coercion, and practiced a policy on the basis of nationality and political loyalty to Britain. As Brogden and Lau (2001:12) pointed out, racism was evident throughout the history of the Hong Kong Police until the last few years before 1997; racist policies were seen "in official pronouncements, in the ethnic composition of the force, in differential pay, and in its treatment of the local inhabitants." As a matter of fact, local inhabitants were recruited less in Hong Kong than even in other British colonies. Besides racism, another factor that explains this biased recruitment practice of the early Hong Kong Police is that Hong Kong was a very small territory on the southern coast of China. There was a strong fear among the colonial rulers that local Chinese might join forces with the mainland Chinese against the British rule. The conditions for colonial rule in Hong Kong, therefore, were different from those of other British colonies socially, geographically, and politically. After World War II, the local officers in the Hong Kong Police began to increase significantly. But the increase was not due to the change of racist attitude and reduced fear of the mainland, but to the drying up of recruitment sources from India and Pakistan, both of which broke away from Britain and became independent (Brogden and Lau, 2001).

During the administrative period (1881-1980), paramilitary policing not only prevailed but also was institutionalized (Pang, 1999). The police became highly centralized and militarized, and resorted to strong administrative control. They practiced a well-known "effective policing model," in which they focused on effective crime control and public order management (Gaylord and Traver, 1995). Under this model, the Hong Kong Police was given much wider powers than the United Kingdom police (Rear, 1971). As Alderson (1981:7) observed, "In many cases, colonial powers have had in the past to rely on strong and sometimes repressive police systems, backed up by considerable residual constitutional powers, although there have been many exceptions." In case of Hong Kong, the colonial rule resulted in greater police powers of arrest, detention, and search during the administrative period. For example, a police officer in Hong Kong could legally arrest any person without warrant if the officer reasonably suspected that the person might be guilty of an offence, however minor in character and whether or not the officer had seen such an offense committed. An officer could also enter on demand and search any place where any person to be arrested had entered previously or was believed to be present (Rear, 1971). The most important power that demonstrates the emphasis placed on public order management was that any officer could stop-and-search without warrant and, if necessary, arrest and detain for further inquiries any person whom he might find in any street or other public place who acted in a suspicious manner or whom he suspected of having committed or being about to commit or intending to commit an offence (Rear, 1971). For such police actions, the officers were not required to meet any standard of reasonableness.

The unusual powers and authority of the Hong Kong Police during the administrative period could also have been attributed to two other fundamental causes. First, the political and economic policy of the Hong Kong government, which "could be characterized as nineteenth century liberalism"(Beazer (1978:5), was a critical contributor. This policy stipulated "a limited role for government: law and order, contract enforcement, a definition of property rights, and perhaps defense against foreign enemies" Rabushka (1973:2). Such a policy resulted in Hong Kong "fewer government controls and restrictions on the legitimate activities of the private sector than any other country in the world" (Beazer, 1978:5). This governmental arrangement means that the Hong Kong Police must fulfill one of the most essential public functions and thus be given the power to do so. Second, such power was associated with the typical, undemocratic governing process in a colonized territory. As Beazer (1978) stated, Hong Kong was essentially under the bureaucratic rule of the governor and his civil service principals, which included the Commissioner of Police. There was the absence of an electorate (Rabushka, 1973); the process for public opinion to be represented by elected representatives was not available. The people of Hong Kong "could not and did not elect or appoint public servants or remove them from office" and their opinions were "seriously neglected within the legislative process" (Beazer, 1978:23). Moreover, both Britain and China were willing to maintain this status quo (Rabushka, 1973). In the end, although Governor Hennessy's v ision of a just and fair government governed by the rule of law was timely and insightful, paramilitary police practices with wide powers were unlikely to benefit from broad-based public support or legitimacy (Ng-Quinn, 1991).

As Hong Kong entered the 1960s, labor and pro-communist riots occurred occasionally, reflecting to a great extent some major social conflicts in the Hong Kong society. These riots continued to impact on the paramilitary development of the Hong Kong Police. As a result of some riots in 1956, procedures and training in dealing with riots were reviewed and tactical unit was formed. Riots in 1966 were triggered by the Star Ferry increase and then developed into protests against the police and the colonial government in general. In 1967, Hong Kong "suffered another wave of disturbances, a spillover from the Cultural Revolution" (Scott, 1989:96). The Hong Kong Police, staffed by this time with a majority of local officers, was able to control the pro-communist demonstrations. The doubt about local officers' ability to quell riots and their commitment to maintaining order, which was a myth at the time, was consequently dispelled. The Hong Kong Police was given the Royal title because of this new confidence by the British government. The successful suppression of these public unrests entrenched public order management as a top priority and paramilitary policing as a major strategy for the Hong Kong Police (Brogden and Lau, 2001). As Pang (1999:131) stated:

> Up to the Wartime, the colonial police was there to protect the interest of the colonists and to suppress the local people . . . paramilitary policing has been fully demonstrated to be effective and useful in the quelling of the urban unrest in 1956, 1966 and 1967. The real legitimacy for the use of semi-military equipment was achieved in the suppression of the 1967 disturbances, which was organized and supported by the communists.

Although the local officers enjoyed more trust from the British government and the Hong Kong Police gained the royal title, the police as a whole still suffered from the problem of legitimacy both in and outside Hong Kong. Outside Hong Kong, the Chinese government viewed the colony as created under duress and as a historical humiliation. It, therefore, did not recognize the legitimacy of the Hong Kong government, which to a great extent was represented by the Hong Kong Police. In Hong Kong, the local Chinese people did not view the police as legitimate due to two basic factors: one, the Hong Kong Police was imposed upon them by a foreign government; two, there was widespread corruption in the Royal Hong Kong Police. The public dissatisfaction with economic, social, and political issues often intensified with its anger toward the police, the most visible agent of the British government. In short, the Hong Kong Police was successful in suppressing public protests and maintaining public order, but failed to gain public confidence due to the lack of legitimacy. It is against this background that the Hong Kong government saw the need for change and started reform programs aimed at creating legitimacy and stability for the government. For the first time in Hong Kong history, the colonial government attempted to understand "the sources of discontent" and "what the protesters thought of their government" (Scott, 1989:87). Subsequently, the government-appointed Commission of Inquiry conducted widespread investigation into the causes of riots and protests.

In retrospection, there were underlying, intermediate, and immediate causes of public discontent toward the government and the police. The underlying causes lied mainly with "the established order," the "colony's political, economic and social structure," which created serious economic and social grievances and "formed the climate for protest" (Scott, 1989:91 and 94). The intermediate causes included "deficiencies in government policies" (Scott, 1989:94). And the immediate causes included direct confrontations on the street with the heavy-handed police (Scott, 1989) and scandals related to syndicated police corruption. As Pang (1999:Abstract) observed, up to the mid-70s, the Hong Kong people were distant from the police and perceived the police as "licensed rascals" who took bribes routinely. The public often felt being mistreated during stop-and-search, entry, seizure, and arrest, but found little channel to express dismay. A major police scandal was triggered by the escape of a corrupt police superintendent, Peter Godber, which triggered a huge public outcry and pushed the Hong Kong Police further into a legitimacy crisis. Due to these historical problems and poor confidence the police enjoyed before the 1970s, many senior officers in Hong Kong remain sensitive to the term "legitimacy" today. As an official from the Independent Commission against Corruption (ICAC) stated:

> The Hong Kong Police are sensitive to the term "legitimacy" for historical reasons. China did not officially recognize Hong Kong as a colony. And the Hong Kong government officials were not democratically elected. Why should they be viewed as legitimate? The issue of legitimacy was a sensitive one. The mere mention of the word touches some people's nerves.

As there must be light after a long darkness, these thorny episodes that lasted almost two decades eventually were turned into some more positive periods for both the Hong Kong government and the public. Since the mid-1960s, various government departments in Hong Kong began to review their performances. The Hong Kong Police started to seek legitimacy to balance their wide range of legal powers. It conducted an internal review of its relationships with the public in 1966 (Hong Kong Annual Report, 1966:153-4), created the Police Community Relation's Office and the Junior Police Call scheme, and rendered the Police Force more open and transparent. In the early 1970s, the community and the government developed the will to fight corruption and established the Independent Commission against Corruption (ICAC). The creation of ICAC is one of the most significant changes in Hong Kong history that has had a major impact on the Hong Kong Police. Changes also took place in other governmental departments. The Labor Department, for example, began to assess "a new and much more extensive legislative program" (Scott, 1989:95).

Many changes, however, were superficial occurring mostly in the area of public relations, image, and communications despite the need for a far-reaching structural and policy reform. The challenges for a deeper governmental reform were primarily due to the nature of colonial rule, whose goal was not to develop democracy, but to maintain control of an alien territory. The colonial government, for example, "was not prepared to share its authority or to establish alternative political bases at the local level" (Scott, 1989:96). The proposals to develop more power at and provide more resources to various municipal councils were met with serious difficulties. Britain, as a matter of fact, had put in great efforts to limit the emergence of democracy in Hong Kong. These efforts had a great impact on the administration of justice in the territory, resulting in a large paramilitary police force and an "assembly-line model of justice" that emphasized punishment (Gaylord and Traver, 1994:7). As recent history has demonstrated, it was not until the last decade, especially the last governorship, before Hong Kong's return to China that the colonial government started to introduce certain Western style democratic elements into the political system. As a Hong Kong police superintendent said:

> Chris Patten [the last governor] saw a need, and he rocked the boat. It had more to do with his personality. The governor before Patten stressed relationship between Hong Kong and China. . . . It's not a democracy. It's not totalitarian, either. Police stations were turned into fortresses in colonial days. Pattern's years were watershed.

As the Chinese-British Joint Declaration was signed in 1984, the Hong Kong people saw their future being decided by mainland China and Britain with little attention to their own interest. Also, the post-World War II generation, born and raised in Hong Kong with a stronger consciousness of civil rights, came off age by this time (Pang (1999). These two factors created a push for a more open and accountable government. The 1980s is, therefore, considered the beginning of the democratic movement (Vagg, 1996). During this period, the Hong Kong Police started the long and careful planning for the reversion of sovereignty to China. The first Chinese Commissioner of Police, Li Kwan-ha, was handed his baton in 1990 (Sinclaire and Ng, 1997). The police became more open and approachable and showed more willingness to accept public criticism (Pang, 1999). The investigation of complaints against the police came to be supervised by a statutory body the membership of which included elected legislative councilors. The change of the police in the 1980s, however, remained rather superficial and the police policies and programs were selectively and ceremonially presented to the public in a manner similar to what Manning (1997:35) described as the "dramaturgy" in policing. Some critiqued the police as adopting "the 'emperor's new clothes' tactics to conceal its primary role of law enforcement" Pang (1999:131). The message for changing the police was also quite mixed as the public demanded for reducing the police power on the one hand, but effective rather than procedurally legitimate policing on the other (Ward, 1989; Watson, 1989). Afraid of violent crimes, the people of Hong Kong were ready to give "their consent and personal safety to the hands of the police"

(Pang, 1999:131). In addition, the "horrendous armed robberies in the 1990s also provided a policy window for the police to further equip themselves" with a strong and powerful armory (Pang, 1999:131). The Hong Kong Police, therefore, continued to develop their paramilitary capability and put in great emphasis on public order management.

The administration of justice in Hong Kong during the democratic period (1980-1996) (Vagg, 1996) was similar to that in most major Western cities in terms of a series of stages (Gaylord and Traver, 1994), but seemed to have a more time-efficient and punitive orientation. The stages included entry into the system, the commencement of criminal proceedings for indictable offences and summary offences, adjudication and sentencing, and corrections. Like most Western cities, only one-third of all crimes were reported to the police and an even smaller proportion of offenders entered the system. The police had discretion to "divert juvenile and young offenders directly into police supervision rather than forwarding the case for prosecution in the Juvenile Court" (Gaylord and Traver, 1994:9). Juvenile offenders 14-21 years of age were also sentenced to and treated in more rehabilitative programs. For adult defendants, the criminal justice system clearly resembled "an assembly line designed to shuffle them quickly from arrest to conviction to sentencing" (Gaylord and Traver, 1994:9). An adult offender could not decide whether or not his or her case would be tried before a judge or a jury. The decision was supposed to be made by the magistrate, but in practice this decision was mostly made by or on behalf of the Attorney General. Adult offenders offered guilty pleas in nearly 90% of all cases appearing before magistrates and in nearly 60% of all cases that proceeded to the District Court. Adult offenders also received more punitive imprisonment and non-custodial sentences (Gaylord and Traver, 1994).

As Hong Kong entered the 1990s, a few years before the handover of sovereignty, the police were seriously concerned about both internal and external stability. Internally, the police management saw the need to stabilize the Force due to "a large outflow of police officers especially the police constable" (Chui, 1991:99). Ten years before the handover in 1987, for example, the Royal Hong Kong Police strength was 25,762, of whom 944 or 3.7% were expatriates. A year before the handover, the number of expatriates had dwindled to 500. Worried about their future or job prospect with the Hong Kong Police, many officers left "either for migration or for a better and more secure job in the private sector" (Chui, 1991:99). In 1995, Eddie Ki-on Hui became the second Chinese Commissioner of Police and was charged to lead the Force during the transition. As the shortage of manpower was believed to have hampered the efficiency of the Force and demoralized the rank-and-file, the police leadership endeavored to have fewer changes in order to retain police officers, maintain stability within the Force, and to attract new applicants (Chui, 1991). Externally, the police were acutely concerned about potential instability in the Hong Kong society during this transition. To maintain the stability and status quo of Hong Kong, Commissioner Ki-on Hui reassured "the public that the police on which they depended would continue doing their job in the old familiar manner. The less change, the better, was the philosophy" (Sinclair and Ng, 1997: Foreword).

The police, therefore, continued to emphasize their paramilitary role and public order management. In addition, they took up the border defense duty and prolonged training in military tactics within the Force (Chui, 1991).

The role of the police cannot be overemphasized for maintaining Hong Kong's political stability and economic prosperity during the transition in the run-up to 1997. But a heavy-handed police approach to maintaining law and order is likely to create more disorder than peace and stability. As a historically oppressive colonial force, the Hong Kong Police had to examine "the organiza-tion-environment relationship" before taking any appropriate necessary actions (Chui, 1991:101). In their effort to resolve the confidence problem within the Force and formulate strategies to meet public demand, the police administration walked a fine line between "the 'continuity' and 'change' elements" within the Force (Ho, 1989:96). The core police function that remained was public order management and the major contemplated change was the orientation of the Force from an authoritarian tradition to a more civil and service-oriented character. The training of police was, therefore, modified with a thrust in public service and well-drilled automations were not required the year before the handover. The new officers were expected to deliver service, to learn to "act towards people with courtesy, to be impartial, tactful, firm and polite. Discipline remained essential, but recruits had to learn to carry out their duties and gain public support" (Sinclair and Ng, 1997: 62). Many of these ideas would have been viewed as novel and even inappropriate in colonial Hong Kong, but they were believed to be essential for minimizing the police-public hostility during the handover.

To the extent that the colonial Hong Kong Police was characterized by a strong commitment to public order in both policies and practices, Wilson (1972)'s watchman style can be used here for analyzing the police orientation of this historical period. In the sense that "the police in dealing with situations that do not involve 'serious' crime act as if order maintenance rather than law enforcement were their principal function" (Wilson, 1972:140), the colonial Hong Kong Police fit the defining characteristic of the watchman style. Such a style was reinforced by "the attitudes and policies of the police administrator (Wilson, 1972:140). The motivations, characteristics, and consequences of this style, in case of the Hong Kong Police, are obviously quite different from communities Wilson studied. This style was developed purposefully rather than naturally to serve the interest of a colonial government. It was based on a paramilitary force with wide, often discriminatory, powers, and resulted in a legitimacy crisis for the police due to the detrimental impact it had on the local Chinese population. To alleviate the tension between the police and the public, the colonial Hong Kong government envisioned a more professional police orientation that focuses on crime and law enforcement. Related programs derived from such efforts are often presented selectively for public relation purposes. This phenomenon of selective presentation and symbolizations of behaviors is captured as "the drama of police work" by Manning (1977:27).

2

The 1997 Handover

1997 is the year that Hong Kong's colonial rule ended and its new status as a Special Administrative Region of China began. It was a year filled with intense speculations for the people both in and outside Hong Kong, bringing hope and excitement on the one hand and creating concerns and uncertainties on the other. It is exciting for the people of Hong Kong to enter a new era, but uncertain what this new era would actually bring. Because "Hong Kong is the established center for China's trade" and "the pivot of the economic integration of the China Circle," what the future might hold for Hong Kong would not only impact the life of millions of Hong Kong people but also have serious consequences for the rest of China (Sung, 1997:71). The impact, however, would be more political than economical since economic integration of Hong Kong with China started almost two decades ago and the region had already developed a strong economic relationship with the Pearl River Delta. The political relationship, at least in a formal and official sense, would not begin until the 1997 handover. The change of sovereignty and the subsequent development of the region in terms of its relationship with Beijing, therefore, would be of greater interest to many speculators. Furthermore, as the Chinese government was undergoing reforms of its own at various levels in its political system, the uncertainties of Hong Kong's future was closely connected with China's political transition rather than with its own (Naughton, 1997). Consequently, whether the "one-country, two-systems" arrangement would work ultimately "lies more in the political and social realms than in the economic realm" (Sung, 1997:71). The Hong Kong Police, with its mission to maintain public order and social stability, would bear the brunt of any uncertainties during the change of sovereignty.

Although the official local-central government relationship between Hong Kong and China would not begin until after the change of sovereignty, their relationship at the diplomatic level started in the early 1980s during Sino-British negotiations on Hong Kong's future. According to some former Hong Kong government officials, the Chinese leaders were very suspicious of their British counterparts as they consistently saw conspiracies from capitalist and imperialist powers. Chinese negotiators put the minimum on the table and were adversarial during the negotiations for any issues related to Hong Kong. The British negotiators were inexperienced with the Chinese world-view. They were unprepared in how to represent the interest of the Hong Kong people, either. Although supposedly speaking on behalf of Hong Kong, they did not take Hong Kong people's interest and political future seriously. Under the pressure from the Chinese government, the British made many concessions, creating great disappointment and frustration among many Hong Kong people. The people of Hong Kong subsequently saw the need to fight for their own future and took to the street in huge numbers. A city that was notorious for indifference to politics and civil rights became a politically charged territory overnight. In response to the demand of the Hong Kong public, the British government took a stronger position during later negotiations with China. Just a few years before the handover, the British colonial government in Hong Kong also changed its traditional stance and began "to encourage the development of democracy" in the territory in an attempt "to restrict, as much as possible, China's interference with Hong Kong's legal system after 1997" (Gaylord and Traver, 1994:5 and 39).

What did the year of 1997 mean to the Hong Kong Police organizationally and operationally? How did the change of sovereignty affect a police force that carried the British Royal title for many years? From the standpoint of an organizational study, the year 1997 serves as a departure point to gauge the changes and development of the Hong Kong Police and examine its adaptation to its new political environment. Cases as dramatic as this do not come along very often; the closest scenarios that police students examine usually involve police reforms implemented in some large municipal agencies in other countries. The understanding of the changes and development of the Hong Kong Police, therefore, may provide lessons on organizational development in general, particularly to those facing dramatic changes in their external environment.

The change of sovereignty, as a significant historic event, was expected to have a great impact on the Hong Kong Police as well as the society. There were many uncertainties and expectations concerning the role and functions of the police during the transition. Public opinion surveys in Hong Kong before 1997 (Chung, Tong, and Lui, 1992; Hong Kong Baptist College, 1993) reported a widespread belief that public order would decline, police corruption would increase, community would lose trust in the government, and the police would face serious problems as occurred in other former British colonies. Concerned about police corruption after the handover and potential negative impact of this transition, some outside critics demanded "that sweeping powers in the Hong Kong Police be curbed by 1997" (Lau, 1988a). Many others also anticipate that crime and violence would be out of control after 1997 and the Hong Kong Police faced "a possibly destabilizing return to Chinese rule" (Keenan, 1995:19).

An immediate question for many officers serving in the Royal Hong Kong Police was, what would be their future career status once the British control was over? The turnover of local officers and the exodus of expatriates who occupied many of the top brass and the related shake-up in the Hong Kong Police might have a destabilizing and demoralizing effect on the Force. The resignation rate of police personnel at the inspectorate rank and above had already seen an upward trend just a few years after the Sino-British negotiations began, going from 2.2% in the mid 1980s to 5.9% at the end of 1980s (*Ming Pao*, 1989). The 1989 student demonstrations and subsequent government crackdown in Beijing had obviously intensified this concern and sped up the resignations. To stabilize the Force and the colony, the British government designed a British Nationality Package to reduce the brain drain problem and encourage people to remain in Hong Kong (Wong, 1991). Full British citizenship was offered to many individuals in various key sectors across the territory. The Hong Kong Police benefited more from the British nationality scheme as more places were reserved for the officers. As a former Hong Kong government official and a police superintendent said:

> To a great extent, the Hong Kong Police represented the British government in Hong Kong. British nationality was offered to all officers at the inspectorate level and above. Other officers could still apply with special reasons and about 10% got it.

> The British citizenship was offered to 50,000 Chinese families with quotas allocated in each civil service department. Due to the concern that officers in the Special Branch might not be able to continue to work as police officers after 1997, there was no quota for officers in that Branch. So British citizenship was not given just to the police, although all officers could apply and some police constables did apply and got it.

Whether the British Nationality scheme served as a stabilizing factor for the Hong Kong Police is questionable since other factors were also in play in the officer's decision to leave or stay, and not everyone chose to have a British passport. According to a small survey in the Hong Kong Police in early 1990s (Wong, 1991), among the 52 officers who returned the questionnaires, 24% would like to emigrate to another country and 33% planned to leave the Force before 1997. The key reason for desiring to leave was lack of confidence in Hong Kong's political future after 1997 as most feared that the door to emigration might be closed and that Hong Kong might become unstable after the handover. However, 90% of the officers did not plan to apply for the British Nationality Package and 84% planned to stay in Hong Kong. The reasons given for planning to stay were concerns in destination countries such as job opportunities and racial discrimination, and preference for living in Hong Kong (Wong, 1991). This result demonstrates to a certain extent that despite concern about Hong Kong's political stability, officers in general prefer to live in Hong Kong and the effect of the British Nationality Package on stabilizing the police force was quite limited. As some officers stated:

> I don't think that it's a stabilizing factor. Rather, other measures like retirement packages served as a better stabilizing factor. Why would one want a passport to live in a poor country?

The 1997 issue has shadowed the whole Force with a pessimistic attitude towards the future. Under the current political confidence crisis, people have a general motivation to seek for short-term gains in terms of salaries and other benefits. Since no one can be certain of the future development near 1997, it is natural for the staff to settle their claim when there is still a government in control. Some officers may be eager to early retire in order to get their pension before 1997 (Lee, 1991:93).

A crucial role of a police organization is to stabilize a society undergoing major social and political changes. To do so effectively, the police must first stabilize themselves. It is clear that the Hong Kong Police needed "dependable troops" (Keenan, 1995:19) and required careful management at this historical juncture. To prepare for the transition, the police engaged in a series of activities to address the concerns and uncertainties in the Force. A working group was set up to deliberate on the 1997 change of sovereignty as far back as in 1986. The planning process resulted in the appointment of Kwan-ha Li as the first Chinese Police Commissioner in 1989 (Brogden and Lau, 2001). The practice of appointing the Commissioner of Police from within the Force started since then. The Basic Law (a mini-constitution of Hong Kong) formalizes this practice by stipulating that after 1997, the Chief Executive in Hong Kong appoints Commissioner of Police from within the Force, subject to endorsement by the Beijing Government. Another initiative, training officers to speak Putonghua (the most common Chinese spoken language), began in the late 1980s in anticipation of the transition. The Hong Kong Government has been running such a program ever since. As 1997 was approaching, the Hong Kong Police stopped overseas recruitment for the entire Force. But manpower planning was conducted to ensure that officers leaving the Force before the handover would not create a succession problem (Hong Kong Police Review, 1997). The Special Branch in the Hong Kong Police, which was a British intelligence unit, was disbanded and all files kept by this unit were transferred to Britain before the turnover.

Apparently localization was a major issue for the Hong Kong Police before the change of sovereignty just like in all former Western colonies. Politically localization was a natural process for ending the colonial rule, representing a form of successful planning to ensure that local officers run the police before and after the handover, without unduly dependent upon expatriate officers. Localization was also believed to bring progress to police service in general since under colonial rule restriction was in place on the nationality of those occupying the very top police posts and favoritism was reserved to expatriate officers under the term of employments (Mah, 1993). By removing racial discrimination both in recruitment and employment practices, there would be more equal opportunities for all nationalities in Hong Kong to be appointed as civil servants to enjoy equal terms of services. No longer would it necessary to maintain an organizational structure based on distrust of local officers. The Emergency Unit, for example, was set up years ago due to distrust of local officers in Hong Kong to serve as an intentional overlap in responding to riotous situations. Its functions today are based more strictly on operational needs of the five land police regions in Hong Kong. Although localization represents a move forward in organizational development in the Hong Kong Police, the pace of localization was deemed unsatisfactory to some officers and there were still "barriers in promoting the policy like political factor, and availability of knowledge and qualified persons" (Mah, 1993:52). Many officers at the inspectorate rank and above, both expatriate and Chinese, hold foreign passports and so the "meaning of locals" was not clear-cut. The localization policy therefore might affect the morale in some segments of the Force.

The complexity and magnitude of the Force required that the Hong Kong Police take a proactive approach to tackling various issues related to the transition and increase both internal and external communications in the years leading up to 1997. As the former Commissioner of Police Eddie Hui stated: "We need to prepare for and deal with the many issues raised by the transition of sovereignty of Hong Kong. This involves clarifying and restating our future operational responsibilities and ensuring that information is communicated promptly throughout the Force as transitional matters are decided. Also related to transition, we need to retain public confidence by reassuring them that social order will be maintained throughout transition and beyond."

As the British colonial rule was ending, the Hong Kong Police embarked on a new relationship with the Chinese police, called the Public Security Bureaus (PSBs) in the mainland. Although relationship with the PSBs was not completely new, the Hong Kong Police increased its open contact and cooperation with the mainland police to address crime problems and organize cross-training during the transition. As some senior police officers stated:

We have lots of cooperation with the mainland both before and after 1997. Before 1997 it was in private. After 1997, we openly cooperate with the mainland. The first meeting between the Royal Hong Kong Police and Public Security Bureau occurred in 1979. . . . We have more communication now with each other to target crime problems. We have more exchange of information. We used to have more shootings by criminals from the mainland. Now because of our exchange of information and cooperation, it is easier for the offenders to hide in the mainland than in Hong Kong. Also, it is easier to rob in the mainland because there are more rich people now in the mainland. . . . We are doing much better after 1997 due to our cooperation with the mainland police in terms of recovering stolen cars, reducing robberies, and reducing illegal immigration.

I went to Shanghai and helped the police there with some training. I was very impressed. Their training program is not bad. They have more professionalism. They are also more open. They care about their image internationally. For example, they did not use to have hostage negotiation. Now they want to learn how to end a hostage situation peacefully. They have negotiators. They used to use force only.

New arrangement was made also for the relationship and communication between the Hong Kong Police and the People's Liberation Army (PLA) stationed in Hong Kong. In 1997, a PLA advance party, which comprised of key commanding officers of various ranks, was briefed on the organization and structure of the Hong Kong Police and discussions were held as to how the two disciplinary forces should interact in areas of common interest. A senior superintendent from the Operations Wing was designated as the Police/PLA Liaison Officer to deal with all matters concerning the Hong Kong Garrison. The first major accomplishment in the liaison work was the successful transition of over 5,000 PLA officers and 500 vehicles from Shenzhen to the nine military camps in Hong Kong. This was followed by a number of familiarization visits made by both sides. A notable one was a presentation to over 400 PLA officers on the structure of the Hong Kong Police and the law and order situation in Hong Kong, held at the PLA Naval Base on Stonecutters Island in September 1997 (Hong Kong Police Review, 1997).

After the handover, the Hong Kong Police was calm and peaceful. As a post-colonial force, the Hong Kong Police stopped its overseas recruitment in 1995, started localization policy of the Hong Kong Government according to the Basic Law, and changed its language and residency requirements. All officers are now required to be proficient in both English and Chinese and have permanent residence, i.e., residence in Hong Kong for at least seven years. The Chinese language includes two dialects, Cantonese and Putonghua, that officers should be able to speak well. Expatriate officers remaining in the Force should also be able to speak Chinese. They are required to sign up and take a Chinese language course offered by the Hong Kong Government and be tested by a panel of examiners. Many of them were able to pass the course even though their Cantonese remains awful. There is no such a policy, however, that requires that expatriate officers leave the Force. For those who did leave, their decision was personal and voluntary. The Force did lose some expatriate and local officers before 1997, but there has not been a succession problem overall. The Force had 27,588 sworn officers and 5,926 civilian staff at the end of 1997, as against the strength of 27,659 and 6,046 respectively at the beginning of the year (Hong Kong Police Review, 1997). As more expatriate officers left the Force, the Hong Kong Police increased its training, transfer, and assignment of Chinese officers to fill their posts. As some senior police officers said:

> 1997 does not mean that all expatriate officers must leave. No expatriate officers were forced to leave. Their leaving was all voluntary. If they leave, they were fairly compensated with retirement benefits. Some chose to retire early. There are still 200 to 300 expatriate officers with the Force.

> I guess there were about 150 expatriate officers who left the Force before 1997. I would say most of these people were either close to retirement years, or had some concerns about or were not sure what would happen after 1997. They went with a handsome retirement package. There are still about 300 expatriate officers in the Force today. The turnover rate in the Hong Kong Police is very low in single digit only. I would say 97 is a good push because some officers left making it possible for others to move up. It didn't make much difference for a force as big as this. There are enough talents to go around.

> More expatriate officers left as we approached 1997. The Hong Kong Police increased their training, transfer, assignment of Chinese officers to fill those

positions left by the expatriate officers very quickly and things went back to normal without ripples. After 1997, overseas recruitment has stopped. It is an internal police policy to stop external recruitment, not imposed upon the police by the Hong Kong Government. It's a natural thing to do so since we have returned to China. Another reason the overseas recruitment stopped is that we now have the language requirement that the officers speak Cantonese, Putonghua, and English, which overseas applicants are seldom able to meet. Also the Basic Law requires that one must reside in Hong Kong for seven years before seeking a civil service position. The Force does not have any problem recruiting locally as there are enough qualified applicants from Hong Kong. The Hong Kong Police can still recruit overseas officers if special expertise is needed that cannot be found locally and these specialist officers are hired on a contract basis.

After 1997, expatriate officers are no longer hired. . . . They introduced the British culture to Hong Kong. Hong Kong people fear expatriate officers, but they respect foreign officers more than Hong Kong officers. . . . As many of them left before 97, there were about 110 promotions of Chinese officers who may not be as qualified. There were more opportunities for promotion in 97 and 98, but not any more.

Besides the tangible changes in structure, training, recruitment, transfer of positions, etc., there have also been certain subtle or psychological changes since 1997. Many officers actually view such changes as more significant than tangible ones. As a chief superintendent said, the change of Hong Kong to a Special Administrative Region of China has had the greatest psychological impact on the rank-and-file of the Hong Kong Police. As a post-colonial police force, officers must view their operations and environment from a new perspective. Although there has been no direct pressure or influence from China, officers must think about China more now when developing their strategies and conducting their daily business. This is only natural since Hong Kong is now a part of China and there is more interaction between the national government and the Hong Kong government. As some Hong Kong police officers and a former Hong Kong government official stated:

I think that many police programs were politically motivated and linked to 1997. But, if you link the changes to 1997, the senior management doesn't like them. 1997 is such a sensitive issue that everybody denies anything has anything to do with it.

Do you find that the Hong Kong Police have more control over the public now than before 1997? I think they do, because I see less demonstrations and I think the police have more control over demonstrators like not letting some protesters get into the territory.

Hong Kong government can't make any mistakes. China attacks Hong Kong government all the time with Da Kung Pao, Wen Hui Pao [Hong Kong newspapers viewed as backed by the Chinese government]. Politicians read these papers and are very sensitive to them. China were like an opposition party. Hong Kong government always thinks about how Beijing will think. But no one understands the Beijing government because for many years they remained ignorant and were not interested in mainland politics.

Although 1997 is a historic year and its psychological impact strong, most Hong Kong Police officers do not see a significant effect on them personally and do not think that their day-to-day activities and their working environment have changed greatly because of 1997. The nature of police work has remained the same. There have been no major changes in their organizational structure, operations, and policies after 1997 under the new Special Administrative Region Government. Where minor changes did occur, they are superficial and limited to the elimination of titles and insignia that have a colonial connotation such as Royal, Crown, and British. The Royal title was removed from the name of the Royal Hong Kong Police, and badges of rank and uniform buttons bearing the colonial crest and the royal crown disappeared. The colonial flag came down the flagpole at the Police Headquarters, replaced by the bauhinia banner of the Hong Kong Special Administrative Region. Where significant changes have concerned, officers maintain that they have been developing and evolving over the past few decades and are not attributable to the effect of 1997. The change of sovereignty was overall surprisingly calm and uneventful. The following are some typical comments from officers about 1997:

> On the night of June 30, 1997, we changed our badges and insignia. Imagine how we felt at that moment. We had some officers stationed close to the border. Commanders and officers were all on high alert. High level of communication was maintained with the Police Headquarters throughout the Force. In the end, we just stayed in the buildings or on top of the buildings watching the firework. Most important thing is that the Chinese army and PSBs kept their promise and did not interfere with us.

> 1997 is incidental as far as the Force is concerned. The Force is run by the same people, the law is the same, procedural manuals are the same, general orders are the same, divisions are the same. There were only minimal changes such as the "Royal" titles.

> It is like the City has a new mayor, the Chief Executive. Everything else is the same. We have the same duties, same tasks, same people. Ninety-nine point nine percent are the same people. Yes, we changed our shoulder insignia. But there are no water-shed changes. Yes, we have more contacts with the PSB. But it is the same government, same currency, same T.V. reruns, etc. There are some minor changes that are not due to the change of sovereignty. Gambling issue has been in the back of the burner for years. It is not new. There have been changes due to global trends like community policing. . . . We continue to have overseas courses and we've got people coming here to study Triad. We've got financial experts. The Security Branch has changed a little bit and looks at different types of threats now. There is no surging crime wave. Triad is not more active. We've never had a large Triad problem to begin with. Legislation against Triad started a long time ago. Crime figures are actually down. Crime patterns have changed a little, but we can't connect patterns of crime to a certain date. There has been no dislocation.

Major changes happened before 1997. The Civil Service Reform occurred before 1997. We have EPP, the Enhanced Productivity Project. The government budget doesn't affect policing much. . . . 1997 is not a factor for change. Everything remains basically the same. . . . There has been no change in day-to-day operations prior and after 1997. . . . Maybe expatriate officers feel the change. . . . After 1997, we lost many expatriate officers. We don't think it's senior police administration's policy.

Actually, the year 1997 has not created as dramatic an impact on the Force as most have imagined. The transition actually occurred 15 years prior to 97 when the Joint Declaration was signed in 1982. . . . Most changes are not due to 97. The Force has become more effective and more efficient over the years as a result of its own evolution.

Even among those expatriate officers who remain in the Force, most have not seen changes directly related to the year of 1997. As some of them stated:

After 1997, things are calmer. Before 97, no one was sure where we were going. If we knew in 1995 things would be like this today, I bet the 150 expat officers who left would have stayed. I like to work in Hong Kong. We have more and better educated officers here now. I have lots of opportunities. I was chief inspector when I was 28 and superintendent when I was 35. I think it's better than UK. Rule of law was a major concern before 97 and we have the rule of law. I would not say we didn't change. But we change for the better. We are more modernized and more service-oriented.

The leaving of senior expatriate officers did not create a big problem. Actually, we got rid of lots of deadwood. I don't think we had the gap as officers who replace them function just as efficiently if not more. . . . After 1997, majority of expatriates have left. But we are left to do our work ourselves. People's Liberation Army never comes out. We never see them. My boss never gives me a hard time. My men are doing a good job. . . . 1997 is not a factor. Operationally we have not changed that much. . . . Senior officers continue to attend international conferences, liaise with all Asian countries, UK, US, etc. Overseas training remains. Some officers were educated overseas. . . . We did have Public Sector Reform, EPP. The demand has changed.

The uneventful 1997 and thereafter may be surprising to many outsiders but not to the police officers themselves. Some view the acute interest of outsiders in the impact of 1997 as politically motivated and reflecting a Western bias toward China. A senior police superintendent said, for example:

We used to be controlled by the British. No one dared to talk about politics in Hong Kong and no country said anything because Hong Kong was a British colony. No country wanted to offend Britain or the U.S. Now after 1997, Western countries started to watch Hong Kong very closely because now Hong Kong is a part of China and they assume China has lots of problems. I think they wish Hong Kong to be in chaos. . . . In the Police Force, we used to have someone from Britain to serve as the Commissioner, or other senior positions, who had no experience in Hong Kong whatsoever. Even the governor was someone from outside Hong Kong. No one said anything. It was not a democ-

racy. Now Hong Kong is a lot better, a lot more democratic. Then the Western-
ers started to pick on Hong Kong. This is politically motivated.

As any police organization, change is constant due to new needs, increased
demands, and change in the society. The Hong Kong Police is no exception.
While most officers do not see 1997 as a significant factor in changing the
nature of their work, they do see many changes in the Force in recent years.
These changes, they believe, are not necessarily or directly caused by the 1997
handover. As years go by, the police must develop new knowledge, be more
efficient, use new technology, and raise their service standard in order to do a
better job for the public. For example, officers are now encouraged to learn
Putonghua because more tourists from the mainland visit Hong Kong. The Force
has cut its manpower as it hires fewer officers now in comparison to the number
in previous years. But the cut should be attributed to Expanded Productivity
Program, use of technology, and the financial and budgetary situation of the
entire government, not to 1997. The Force has put greater emphasis on service
quality in recent years and has as a matter of fact raised its service standards in
general. But service quality cannot be attributed to 1997, either, and instead
should be regarded as part of the organizational development process. The Hong
Kong Police take service aspect of police work more seriously because the
police profession has become more service-oriented overall. Many domestic and
international challenges also require that the Hong Kong Police be more service-
oriented in its strategy and emphasis. As some officers commented:

> A good deal of conventional thinking supports the theory that the 1997 change-
> over of sovereignty in Hong Kong provided the principle catalyst for changes
> within the operating philosophy and practical strategies employed by the Hong
> Kong Police Force. . . . From an 'insiders' perspective . . . whilst 1997 was a
> significant date for the Hong Kong Police, as it was for the remainder of the
> community, its primary significance was a historical event which came at a
> time of already shifting emphasis and focus for policing in Hong Kong. Indeed
> this changing emphasis came in response to broader international trends in
> policing, evolving demands and expectations from within the local community,
> as well as the perpetually changing focus of the domestic and international
> challenges facing the organization (Lee Ming-Kuai, 2002).

> 1997 handover did not change anything directly in the police. . . . The change
> has been brought about by new philosophies in governing Hong Kong of the
> Hong Kong Government. The Hong Kong Government put more demands on
> the police, asking the police to do more things, provide more quality service,
> have more accountability, have higher efficiency. The Hong Kong society has
> also changed as the people are more critical of and complain more about the
> police. . . . Although it is true that the pace of change has picked up more in
> recent years over the past 22 years, the change does not have anything to do
> with 1997. Changes are on-going. It's a process. . . . Changes occur due to
> higher education of the recruits and the public sector as a whole and society as
> a whole. Changes are creeping in over the past 4 to 5 decades.

When I first joined the Force, there was no intra-communication. It's a disciplined force. We receive orders. Now we have Open Forums. I have Open Forums with my own men. We have more communication and we are more open. . . . The last governor initiated all these changes: public sector reform, service quality. . . . So 1997 is not a direct factor. . . . Over the last 5 years after 1997, the society has changed. In the past people were told what to do. Now people expect explanations. Police have to show more respect, be more open, more transparent.

Whether changes in the Hong Kong Police are caused by 1997 may be too narrow a question and improperly premised. It is, after all, not clear whether China influences Hong Kong or vice versa in many social, economic, and cultural arenas. The Chinese society has become much more open and Westernized than ever before despite the enduring political ideology of the Chinese communist government. Hong Kong is not only a sovereign but also a geographically inseparable part of China and the Hong Kong and mainland people have daily interactions. Such close connections and relationships are bound to influence their cultures reciprocally. The Hong Kong Police and the mainland Public Security Bureaus, for example, run cross-training programs and learn from each other on a regularly basis. As an officer stated:

There is no clear cut of 1997. It's more of a natural change. There is a change, but not due to 1997. The change is more about professionalism. We do have more connections with China now. It's a matter of China opening up, not because Hong Kong has changed. Counterfeits and credit cards now are printed in China and we need to work together to deal with these problems. It's a two-way influence.

As it turned out, the Hong Kong Police was able to manage a seamless transition and contributed to the stability of the region during this historic period. The police maintained the rule of law and international confidence. The prediction before 1997 that the police would be demoralized and corrupt did not occur. The rates of police corruption and misconduct and the work of the Complaint against Police Office (CAPO) remain unchanged. The troops remain stable and dependable. The exodus of expatriate officers did not create a vacuum in the Force. As some expatriate officers left the Force, the police increased the budget for overseas training from $7.012 million in 1997 to $7.718 million in 1998 (Hong Kong Police Review, 1997). The fear that there would be a crime wave after the handover did not materialize, either. The crime rate in fact saw a decrease instead of an increase. The overall crime rate for 1997 followed the downward trend in prior years and reached the lowest level in twenty-four years (Hong Kong Police Review, 1997). On the Chinese side, the People's Liberation Army (PLA) and the Public Security Bureaus (PSBs) have kept their promise and did not interfere with Hong Kong Police operations. A stronger and more professional relationship instead has developed between the Hong Kong Police and the Chinese Public Security Bureaus.

Hong Kong as a society continues to be an autonomous common law jurisdiction after 1997. There were 8,400 public assemblies and demonstrations recorded in the four years since the handover. Two hundred thirty-two criminal cases were submitted to Hong Kong's final court during the four years since the handover compared to only 56 cases submitted to British court during the four years prior. The Hong Kong Police continues to manage law and order according to Hong Kong laws. There has been no increased surveillance and repression of suspect groups in recent years. Although banned in China, Falungong is allowed in Hong Kong as long as it does not violate the law (*Ta Kung Pao*, 2001). There has been no change since 1997 in the operations of the Independent Commission against Corruption (ICAC). The speculations that mainland-funded companies would be subject to different rules and make it difficult for the ICAC to investigate did not occur. According to ICAC officials, they have prosecuted mainland companies without interference from the mainland. As Chen (1999:47) commented:

> The continuity of the pre-1997 legal system, including its laws, its judicial institutions and procedures, and, most important of all, the personnel who operate the system, has been maintained. The rule of law has survived. Indeed, the role of the judiciary—now the guardian of the Basic Law in cases involving constitutional judicial review . . . has been enhanced. . . . The Hong Kong community has proved to be vigilant in defending the rule of law and human rights. All government actions continue to be subject to a high degree of public scrutiny and potential public criticism. Freedom of the press, and freedom of association and demonstrations have continued to thrive. Civil society is alive and well.

After the handover on July 1, 1997, the Hong Kong people were able to breathe an air of relief as the political and social system have remained largely intact. As the mainland Chinese would say, Hong Kong people are able to continue their "capitalist" way of life. The continuity of Hong Kong's traditional system, however, has brought also frustration because just like before 1997, Hong Kong remains a non-democracy and the public remains unable to elect directly its political leaders. Although the Basic Law of Hong Kong, the territory's post-1997 constitution, sets the eventual goal of an elected executive and legislature, Hong Kong has not seen any major breakthroughs in changing its political system since 1997. As one Hong Kong academic put it, genuine change to Hong Kong's political system is "only possible through reform that will permit the community to participate in the selection of its government. Such reforms might mean returning the legislature by universal suffrage and permitting it to participate in the formation of the government (through the approval of contract principal officials) or through the return of the Chief Executive through a system of open nominations and universal suffrage" (Burns, 2002:5). Different views have emerged on the lack of political progress in Hong Kong. Some blame the Beijing government for stifling the development of democracy in Hong Kong by keeping a tight control over Hong Kong politics. Others blame the Hong Kong business elite who they believe fear a welfare state (Burns, 2002). Still others blame both. One commentator said, for example, that the local pro-China elite and Beijing government are major threats to Hong Kong's democracy as they have failed to see the need for the political system in Hong

Kong to evolve (*Washington Street Journal*, 2002). Such a political climate augers potential public outcry and presents a daunting challenge to the Hong Kong Police.

3

Change and Continuity

As I walked into the Senior Officers Mess at the Police Headquarters in Wanchai one Saturday morning, I saw some precious, memorable artifacts carefully kept along the walls. These are pictures, antiquities, shields, swords, old uniforms, emblems, etc. that clearly demonstrate a military tradition of the Hong Kong Police. The Mess is also a microcosm of the long, historical development of the Hong Kong Police: in a glance, one can see the change from its original title, the Hong Kong Police, to the Royal Hong Kong Police in the 1960s, and back to the Hong Kong Police again after the change of sovereignty. It also displays diverse cultural roots of officers who have served in the Force. Its menu, for instance, continues to highlight different ethnic cuisines: curry on Tuesday, Chinese on Wednesday, fish and chips on Friday, etc. I came to the Mess for a pre-arranged interview with two high-ranking police officers, who kindly showed me around the place before we sat down at a tea table.

Over the past two decades, there have been many changes and continuities in the Hong Kong Police. Among the two high-ranking officers and many others interviewed, some underline changes, some emphasize continuities, some focus more on recent development, and some prefer to take a long view of progress the police have made over the years. In this chapter, I will look at the development of the Hong Kong Police in recent years from three different perspectives. First, I examine the Hong Kong Police from a social and contextual perspective to describe the relationship between the society and the police. The social and contextual aspects examined include social and family conditions, crime and public safety situations, right consciousness and the rule of law, and the political and economic environment. Second, I employ a cultural perspective to analyze the values, philosophies, and orientation of the Hong Kong Police. And third, I use an institutional perspective to examine the historical traditions and current reforms of the Hong Kong Police.

Social and Contextual Perspective

The development and evolution of a police organization reflect in many ways the changes and continuities of the society. The examination of the Hong Kong society, especially those aspects relevant to the police, is necessary for providing the contextual information for explaining various practices in the Hong Kong Police.

Social and Family Conditions

Hong Kong has been dubbed the "City of Life." With skyscrapers and high rises spreading across Hong Kong Island and Kowloon peninsula, the city gives one a sense of euphoria and attracts tens of millions of tourists each year. Behind this prosperity is a population famous for its mobility as many Hong Kong people consider the city a place of transition rather than permanent residence. They live here as an option and are ready to move elsewhere once life here becomes undesirable. "This provisional, temporary state of residency and local affiliation has been remarked on as part of the Hong Kong ethos during its colonial era" (Hong Kong Transition Project, 2001:14). As Lo (1993:104) observed, "there was no cohesion for people living in a borrowed place on borrowed time." The physical mobility and the lack of sense of belonging remain true to a certain extent in Hong Kong after the handover, "even when Hong Kong's identity and national status have been fixed and its residents regarded as Chinese nationals" (Hong Kong Transition Project, 2001:14). This sentiment is not conducive to developing a strong sense of community, often considered indispensable to the practice of community-oriented policing.

Hong Kong is also a city with a huge income gap between the rich and poor. Although its average individual income is $23,652, which is considerably higher than comparable regions in Asia such as Taiwan and Singapore (whose average incomes are $13,114 and $21,817 respectively) (*Open Magazine*, 2001), many vulnerable groups such as children, young people, and low-income families are not sharing in the prosperity of the Hong Kong society. The majority of the population remains poor or low-income. For instance, 60% of Hong Kong people live in public housing. The problem may be worsened for these groups at times of high unemployment rate and stagnant economic development. In terms of social class, there is a rather weak middle class in Hong Kong.

The word "class," however, may not be appropriate for describing an individual's socio-economic background in Hong Kong. As some academics point out, Hong Kong is not a very class-conscious society. The word "status" might be more meaningful because the people are more status-conscious than class-conscious. It is also difficult to define class as income alone may not be an accurate indicator and housing conditions cannot provide a complete measurement, either.

In Hong Kong, the sense of hierarchy or status is clearly present. Such consciousness may have been intensified by the absence of a strong middle class. In many places in Hong Kong, for example, there seem to be a clear division between the higher and lower echelons for members of the society or social institutions. The affluent enjoy the club membership set up for the privileged few in certain hotels, resorts, and entertainment areas. Cafeterias for students and senior staff in universities are located in different areas or floors. Management officers and street officers in the Hong Kong Police have two separate police clubs and in many police stations, senior and junior officers eat in different cafeterias. The absence of a robust middle class and a clear hierarchy in many social institutions may create the idea among police officers as well as the public that people in different statuses deserve being treated differently, leading to discriminatory attitude and behavior toward the poor.

Hong Kong is a society where people do experience discriminatory treatment because of their race and ethnicity. The government and the public have yet to discuss discrimination openly as a social problem. Both government officials and members of the public have either denied that the problem exists or shown an indifferent attitude toward it (Home Affairs Bureau, 1997). Some think, for example, that it is those who are discriminated against that should change their behavior. As a member of the public stated: "Hong Kong should educate those who are likely to be discriminated not to act so differently from others. Most of those who are laughed at do not get laughed at for the color of their skins, but for what they do, like dressing strangely -- out of fashion, or simply wrapping their heads" (Home Affairs Bureau, 1997). This attitude has been critiqued as a part of a culture of denial and lack of government attention (Loper, 2001). Many Hong Kong Police officers also deny that discrimination exists and regard it as not worth paying attention to. Perhaps due to this general attitude, Hong Kong has only laws against gender discrimination, but no legislation against age and racial discrimination (Hong Kong Transition Project, 2001). Racial discrimination, however, "has adverse affects on individuals, individual companies, and the overall economic, social and cultural development in Hong Kong" (Loper, 2001:27). Hong Kong, as a civilized, modern society, should confront this issue head-on instead of allowing it to worsen.

In many other social areas, Hong Kong has made tremendous progress. According to the recent Social Development Index released by the Hong Kong Council of Social Services, health care, housing, education, security, and technology have all been improved significantly. The Hong Kong people are generally better educated and healthier than they were a decade ago. The overall Social Development Index in 2000 improved by 40% from that in 1991 (Lee, 2002). These improvements in the society should contribute to social stability and, therefore, bode well for the Hong Kong Police. But there are certain emerging problems in family life in Hong Kong similar to those in many industrialized nations that do not augur well for the police and the criminal justice system in Hong Kong.

More marriages end up in divorce and domestic violence rate has increased significantly in recent years. The Hong Kong Council of Social Services' research shows that the number of marriages per 100,000 adults dropped from 866 in 1991 to 554 in 2000. In the same period, the ratio of divorces to marriages increased from 16% to 43.4%. The number of reported domestic violence cases per 100,000 households increased from 1,072 in 2000 to 1,213 in 2001

(Lee, 2002). The number of cases of battered wives and husbands reportedly jumped 25% in 2002, as the Social Welfare Department recorded 3,034 cases of battered spouses in the year compared with 2,433 cases in 2001. Cases of family violence involving criminal offenses such as rape and homicide rose 28%, from 505 in 2001 to 647 in 2002. Homicide in families increased from 9 cases in 2001 to 13 in 2002, according to the Hong Kong Police (Moy, 2003). These problems indicate that family solidarity may be deteriorating.

Another family-related problem is suicide. According to Dr. Paul Yip Siu-fai, director of the University of Hong Kong's Center for Suicide Research and Prevention, Hong Kong's suicide rate is "somewhere in the middle" of the overall world suicide table, higher than that of Britain and the United States but lower than that of Japan and Singapore (Rosi, 2002). But in comparison to Hong Kong's own suicide rate in the past, it is clearly going up as more people in Hong Kong take their own lives than being killed on the roads. It is estimated that about 3 people commit suicide daily predominantly by burning charcoal in closed rooms or jumping from high-rise buildings. Figures from the Coroners Court show that there were 1,059 suicides in Hong Kong in 2001—650 men and 409 women—up significantly from 777 in 1997. According to Stephanie Kumaria, director and counselor of the Hong Kong Samaritans' Multilingual Branch, these figures may not reflect the true extent of the problem because for the coroner to record a death as suicide, there has to be a suicide note left by the deceased and there have to be definite suicidal indications. If these criteria are not met, the death is recorded as caused by accidents. Multiple factors have been blamed for suicides: economy, financial hardship, family problems, trouble at work, and unemployment for adults, and school pressures or family and personal-relationship problems for teenagers. Lack of communication and understanding are other speculated causes.

Although Hong Kong police officers still hesitate in or shy away from dealing with domestic abuses, the increased domestic violence and suicide rate may force the police and the legislature to abandon their traditional view that family affairs are private matters that the government should stay out of. There has been an increased exposure of domestic abuses in the Hong Kong media and increased awareness of the harms caused by domestic violence in recent years. As a result, the Hong Kong society has become more sensitive to this issue and the idea that one does not hang one's dirty laundry in public is also changing. To provide better legal protection to the victims of family violence, formal and more aggressive police inventions in domestic violence situations may soon be put on the legislative agenda.

Another painful family issue in Hong Kong that affects police operations is the so-called Right of Abode controversy. This controversy is a result of the 1990s trend for cross-border marriages. Many children and spouses of Hong Kong residents, due to the lack of the right of abode, are forced to live outside Hong Kong. Some Americans have called Hong Kong a heartless city because of this law. Many street protests and demonstrations have been held by those affected by this law and those who sympathize with them. The police have deployed a great amount of resources to manage these demonstrations. The

Right of Abode controversy over the children of Hong Kong residents also led to the first, very controversial reversal by the National People's Congress (NPC) Standing Committee of the decision made by Hong Kong's Court of Final Appeal in June 1999. The Hong Kong Government sided with Beijing against the Hong Kong Court. Concerned that 1.67 million Chinese children of Hong Kong parents might take up residence in Hong Kong if the Court's decision was upheld, the Hong Kong Government petitioned to the NPC to reverse the Hong Kong Court's decision (Starr, 2001). The Hong Kong society is in a conundrum between the need to protect family unity and the need to maintain societal stability and the Hong Kong police are often caught in the middle and blamed for its heavy-handedness in maintaining public order.

Crime and Public Safety Situations

Despite these challenges to the police, crime and public safety are two areas that have seen the greatest improvement in Hong Kong over the past decade, according to the Hong Kong Council of Social Services (Lee, 2002). Being one of the most crowded and most commercial cities in the world, Hong Kong remains at the same time one of the safest with one of the lowest crime rates. Different explanations have been offered for these enviable crime and public safety conditions including both socio-cultural and environmental factors. Observers often witness, for example, "the important contribution of family and group loyalty to the policing function" (Alderson, 1981:8). Hong Kong people are known for their values of conformity and pro-order outlook, ideas advocated by Confucius. The concept "utilitarian familism" (Lau, 1988b), which may be viewed as a diversion of Confucianism, has also been used to explain Hong Kong people's law-abiding behaviors. In terms of geographical environment, Hong Kong has been a small capitalist jurisdiction on the tip of the vast communist China, concentrated by a hardworking people, many of whom escaped from the communist rule and appreciate the opportunities to seek a prosperous life in a stable society. As an unknown observer put it: "China is the sea. Hong Kong is the lifeboat. People on a lifeboat do not want to break the boat."

Besides these cultural and environmental factors, more direct contributors to the low crime rate and high security include Hong Kong's heavy investment in private security, a pro-order government, and a severe police force. Hong Kong is a heavily guarded society in which security personnel are seen deployed on business premises ubiquitously. There are high walls, iron gates, or fences around businesses, public institutions, apartments, and residential complexes everywhere. It is estimated that for every police officer in Hong Kong there are six security guards. Such a large private security and guarding industry "suggests very considerable investment in crime prevention and loss reduction by private enterprises and individuals" (Newman, 1999:139). In 1999, for example, there were 722 registered security and guarding companies in Hong Kong employing approximately 160,000 registered personnel (Broadhurst, 2000). In comparison, for every police officer in Singapore there are two private security guards and there are about 200 security companies in Singapore that employ between 15,000-20,000 private police (Broadhurst, 2000 and Newman, 1999).

The phenomenon of private security industry in Hong Kong lends support to Bayley and Shearing (2001:39)'s observation that "Policing is changing today as profoundly as when Sir Robert Peel put the first bobby on the streets of London in 1829. The new model that is being constructed consists of two elements. First, the people who authorize policing have become separate from the people who do it. Second, the new players in policing are not part of formal government." In this new paradigm, the very concept of government, technically the state, becomes problematic. It is difficult to recognize government when policing is no longer done exclusively by the public police and when people who have been authorized expressly to police are not employed by government. The significant role played by private security in Hong Kong, the extent and character of the structure of private policing, their impact on the society, and the related role and responsibilities of the government all demonstrate the need for a stronger relationship between the private security industry and the Hong Kong Police.

Historically, the primary role of a colonial government and its police was to maintain order. Although this tradition originated from the need to develop trade and economy during the early colonial period, it has evolved and diffused to more general areas of social control and governmental regulations. Hong Kong has had over the years a tough pro-order government and the Hong Kong Police has developed a strong capability for policing public order. The government control and the police function tend to be stricter and more intrusive in general in Hong Kong. Firearm control, for example, is very tight and it is very difficult, almost impossible, to obtain a gun in Hong Kong. It is mandatory to carry personal identification and ID checking is conducted ubiquitously on a routine basis. Furthermore, what is significant in Hong Kong is that this social control system, albeit severe, is widely supported by the public. Combined with heavy private investment in security and supported by the general public, the Hong Kong Police can be highly effective in fighting crime and maintaining public safety.

Right Consciousness and the Rule of Law

The widespread support for public order management as well as values of conformity and pro-order outlook in Hong Kong should not be viewed as contrary to right consciousness and the rule of law. According to a survey conducted by the Hong Kong Transition Project (2001), many people in Hong Kong worried about loss of personal freedoms before the handover. Several years after the handover, this worry has been greatly lessened as Hong Kong people have continued to enjoy the same personal freedoms. There are, however, some concerns about certain specific freedoms such as the freedoms of protest, press and speech, and the rule of law. Concern about the rule of law, for example, rose in August 2000, and continued at the same level toward the end of 2001 with 23% respondents polled being slightly worried, 26% fairly worried, and 12% very worried (Hong Kong Transition Project, 2002). Part of the concern has been triggered by the Falun Gong controversy and the newly proposed National Security Law. While the vast majority of Hong Kong people are not involved in the Falun Gong movement, they view the police treatment of Falun Gong members as influenced by the mainland government.

The legislative proposal for the National Security Law was drafted according to Article 23 of the Basic Law. The newly proposed bill carries maximum life prison sentences for treason, sedition, theft of state secrets, and subversion. It has been a sticking point in Hong Kong since it was tabled to the Executive Council for discussion on February 11, 2003. While the government maintains that the bill is necessary to protect the territory's security, critics say it could erode fundamental rights and freedoms as well as restrict access to information. Since the law would give the government the authority to ban local groups with ties to any organization banned by the national government, rights groups and democracy advocates worry that the law could be used to silence anyone critical of the government in Hong Kong or in China and therefore would curtail autonomy guarantees for Hong Kong under the "one-country, two-systems" model of governing the territory. Both European Union and the U.S. Congress have criticized the law saying that it would compromise Hong Kong's autonomy. Many members of the general public in Hong Kong also fear that freedom in Hong Kong would be curbed and their lifestyles changed because of the legislation (Cheung, 2003). They participated in huge street demonstrations in May and July of 2003. On July 1, 2003, 200,000 marchers took to the streets to protest against this proposed legislation. Five days later, on July 6, 2003, half a million people took to the streets to denounce the law in the city's biggest demonstration since the 1989 Tiananmen Square crackdown. Nearly 1,000 police officers were deployed for the march, as well as 800 marshals, to try to prevent any skirmishes or violence (Chinoy, 2003).

Since the 1997 handover, human right issue has been watched more closely by critics both inside and outside Hong Kong. As pointed out in the Hong Kong media (Cheung, 2002), quite a few human right controversies have occurred in the territory in recent years. For example, Public Order Ordinance has been tightened to require "notice of no objection" for rallies and protests. A veteran protester was arrested at home for allegedly staging unauthorized protest. Seven advocates were convicted of causing obstruction in public place by chaining themselves to a flagpole outside the Fortune Forum. Activists were jailed for five months for shouting at police officers through a loud-hailer during a protest. The National People's Congress reinterpreted abode provisions in the Basic Law, effectively overturning the Court of Final Appeal ruling to allow an estimated 1.67 million mainlanders to come to Hong Kong. Police used pepper spray to disperse abode claimants protesting outside Central Government Offices. Raid was conducted in Chater Garden to clear right of abode claimants and reporters were handcuffed during the clearance. The Court of Final Appeal has upheld the law banning the desecration of national and regional flags. The Chief Executive Tung Chee-hwa has labeled Falun Gong as an "evil cult." Controversies such as these and subsequent demonstrations have created a great challenge to the Hong Kong Police. For a police force that has traditionally put great emphasis on public order management and public security, the increased public protests would require, at least from the police perspective, that they continue to train and deploy a large number of officers to effectively manage public order.

Political and Economic Environment

Social, family, crime, and human right conditions aside, the larger political and economic environment the police work in must also be examined to better understand the police function. The Hong Kong government has practiced the so-called "Administrative Absolutism" for years, a philosophy that government should undertake to provide only law and order, contract enforcement, and defense "excepting externalities and public goods" (Rabushka, 1973:44). Under this philosophy, the government had focused on performing several essential functions, i.e., law and order, taxation, and public works; had minimal interference in private affairs; and rarely departed from a "laissez-fair style of economic management" in history (Rabushka, 1973:47). An important reason for this practice is that as a British colony, Hong Kong was founded to create wealth for the British merchants and the mission of the colonial government was to secure commerce. Policing had become an essential governmental function to help achieve this mission by insuring "such conditions as were necessary for commerce to flourish, for example, the suppression of disorder and the settlement of commercial disputes" (Rabushka, 1973:44). This tradition has meant that the Hong Kong Police enjoy a more prominent place in the political and economic system and play a larger role in society than do most major municipal police agencies in the world. The duties of the Hong Kong Police, for example, include not only crime control and law enforcement, but also internal and border security, public order management, and illegal immigration.

With a mandate to protect the economic interests of the business people, the colonial government in Hong Kong had no agenda to open up the political arena and develop the colony's democracy. The government officials, for example, were generally elitist and authoritarian and seldom reached out to the people (Kuan and Lau, 1985; 1987). After the Second World War, Hong Kong's economy grew dramatically, the city became highly modernized, the living standards improved significantly, and the educational level of Hong Kong people was raised considerably. According to the modernization theory, the thirty years of post-War development had created certain characteristics in Hong Kong that should have led to more democratic political structures in the 1970s. But an authoritarian political regime continued, with only some minor liberalization of its governance style. As Sum (1989:80) suggested, the change of the Hong Kong government might "take the form of evolution from an early-modern to a late-modern form of colonial-bureaucratic authoritarianism in Hong Kong." As an archetypal organization in this government, the Hong Kong Police also exhibited an authoritarian and paramilitary orientation.

According to some Hong Kong scholars, the local population had acquiesced to this political orientation largely because of the temporary nature of the
colony itself and the belief among many Hong Kong people that they were
living in a borrowed place at a borrowed time. As Lo (1993:104-105) observed,
many local residents viewed Hong Kong as a place of transit during the colonial
period.

> The temporary nature of the colony thus obstructed the growth of any sense of
> belonging to the territory, let alone 'class consciousness' among the proletariat.
> With their bitter experience of China, the people were disciplined to work, not
> by any kinds of coercion or hegemony, but by their poverty, their relatives'
> starvation on the mainland, and the newly found material benefits, freedom and
> liberal atmosphere which they enjoyed under the new regime. These crucial
> factors were the primary source of working-class acquiescence to domination.

As China entered the picture in the early 1980s to discuss Hong Kong's
future in anticipation of the expiration of the colonial lease, the political
dynamics in Hong Kong started to change. With Hong Kong's return to China in
sight, the economic interest of the colonial elites looked less relevant and rights
and freedoms of the mass population became more important. But since the
preparation for the territory's handover was a long drawn-out process that lasted
fifteen years from 1982 to 1997, the new political dynamics became centered on
Hong Kong's relationship with China. According to Sum (1989:82), for
example, the entry of China had "the effect of fractionalizing the new middle
class" and reduced its strength in demanding for democracy. The political
situation in Hong Kong therefore has been highly dependent upon what happens
outside the territory and Hong Kong has hardly had its own politics because
China has been a constant factor. Despite the "one-country, two-systems"
arrangement, Hong Kong is a part of China and local politics continues to reflect
national politics. As a former Hong Kong government official stated:

> Real politics is about the nation, not about the City. What is inside Hong Kong
> is not life and death, what is outside is. Hong Kong people were not involved in
> local politics because they could not do much locally. Once the British and
> Chinese started to discuss Hong Kong's future, Hong Kong people started to
> realize that they needed to do something; because, otherwise, Beijing would
> decide their life for them. So the democratic movement is about how to main-
> tain Hong Kong's autonomy using democracy as a shield.

Consequently, the colonial history, the socialist China, and the Western
democratic values have combined to create a political landscape in Hong Kong
that is increasingly liberal but undemocratic. Over the past two decades, the
ordinary people of Hong Kong have increased their demand for government
service. The population in the territory has continued to grow and has brought
with it certain social problems not unfamiliar to other major metropolitan areas
in the world. In response, the Hong Kong government has been significantly
expanded and has shifted away from its traditional laissez-fair style of economic
management. Government policies have geared toward providing more public

services and partially away from protecting the dominant class. The government has also adopted more what Sum (1989:85) called "appeasing strategies in times of crises." These strategies indicate that the government has become more active politically than before. As a Hong Kong government official said:

> After 1997, new accountability system was used. Ministers were appointed like the chief executive's cabinet. The government moved from apolitical to personal control. It is more political now. The previous governors had no personal goals. Tung has a personal political agenda.

The Hong Kong people have also shown great interest in politics and are actively involved in demanding for a representative government. As indicated in the survey by the Hong Kong Transition Project (2001), they spend a large amount of time watching or listening to news and current affairs programs. Fully a fourth of the respondents spend more than 10 hours a week on such past times. And fully 9 out of 10 respondents read a newspaper on a regular basis. There has also been a growing concern about and dissatisfaction with the government. The source of worry and dissatisfaction are not in conditions of living, but in government performances, policies, and leaders. One theory is that the increased dissatisfaction is due to higher expectation of the government after the handover. Since more people in Hong Kong consider Hong Kong as their home and regard the government, once colonial and run largely by foreigners, as theirs as well, they have dramatically increased their expectations of the government as a whole (Hong Kong Transition Project, 2002). Consequently, the complaints against the Hong Kong Police have increased significantly in recent years.

Over the past few decades, the Hong Kong public has demanded changes of certain specific problems in the Hong Kong Police, particularly police corruption. In response to the public outcry against corruption and the changes in society in general, the Hong Kong Police began to commit itself to fighting corruption in the 1970s and developed a more service-oriented strategy in the 1980s to gain public trust and strengthen public confidence. Since the 1990s, the Hong Kong Police has expanded its services and programs well beyond the traditional focus on public order management. As a former government official stated:

> People in Hong Kong expected social conflicts to be solved. Social conflicts tend to be very specific. But there are no demonstrations on the street. There is anti-corruption movement. 1967 proved that Hong Kong people were not docile tools, it's a real community.

The changes in the political arena have not changed the fact that Hong Kong remains an international financial and business center, and that Hong Kong people continue to place a high premium on economic growth. Hong Kong is a city that gives one a sense of euphoria at the first sight; but deep down one senses a strong tension due to economic downturns. Recent survey indicates that pessimism about economic conditions have reached the highest level in a decade. Economically related issues dominate personal concerns (Hong Kong

Transition Project, 2001). Many ordinary and less educated people see no prospect in improving their economic conditions and feel trapped and frustrated (Hong Kong Transition Project, 2002). In the midst of these serious economic difficulties, it has been suggested that the government abandon its traditional policy of non-involvement in economy and market and that citizens change their short-sightedness and traditional mentality of making quick money. Instead of blaming the problems as influenced by the outside world, the government and people of Hong Kong should have a long-term vision with short- and mid-term strategies. Hong Kong should recognize its internal problems, such as poor training, high land price, and a civil service not able to adapt to a new world economy (*Ta Kung Pao*, 2001).

Economic worries are often associated with fears about social unrest. In Hong Kong, the concern about social unrest has been found to correspond to concerns about the economy (Hong Kong Transition Project, 2001). Recent surveys indicate that 76% to 67% of Hong Kongers from 1998 to 2001 worry about the possibility of social unrest in Hong Kong. Although the level of worry about social unrest has fluctuated, a significant number of people remains fairly and very worried. Many citizens fear that Hong Kong may see rises in social unrest if economy remains unimproved (Hong Kong Transition Project, 2002). The implication of this relationship for the Hong Kong Police is that public order management and social stability should remain as a high priority on the police agenda. Law and order should continue to be regarded as a fundamental condition for the Hong Kong economy. In addition, the Hong Kong Police, the ICAC, and the entire criminal justice system must continue to push forward their fight against corruption and internal transactions, as these problems are seen as threatening to Hong Kong's business and economy. Arguably, therefore, the traditional role of the Hong Kong Police in maintaining a stable economic environment remains.

Cultural Perspective

When it comes to examining changes and continuities of an organization, an outstanding issue is culture. Culture indicates the values and beliefs of members of an organization, which influence their daily practices. Social scientists have asked whether culture has changed, how it has changed, and why it has changed. Since an organization is an element of a society, its culture also hinges on the larger cultural context. The culture in Hong Kong has been known to be a mixture of Western and Chinese values. Hong Kong also has many diverse social groups, rich and poor, elites and masses, professionals and laypeople, etc., that have each maintained their distinctive values, customs, and traditions. Western values are clearly a part of the elite society, but their impact on the life of ordinary people is less certain. As a Western academic who has lived in Hong Kong for many years said to me, the British colonial rule was quite superficial and had only reached the top and the elites. Underneath this rule was the vast majority of local population that have maintained the Chinese language, culture, and traditions. There is no doubt that a language gap exists between the English-speaking elites and the Cantonese-speaking masses. There exists also a gap between the values of the elite, which are more Western, and those of the ordinary people, which are more Chinese or Confucius.

Like members of the Hong Kong society, Hong Kong police officers can also be divided into groups that have been exposed to different cultural traditions. But the Western culture in general and British culture in particular have had a far greater impact on the Hong Kong Police than on most other public and private organizations and the society in general due to the fact that the Hong Kong Police had been for 156 years a colonial force run almost exclusively by expatriate officers. For years, the Hong Kong Police served the interest of the colonial government and foreign merchants and recruited officers overseas only due to a distrust of local population. It is only in the last two decades before the handover that the Chinese officers took the majority of the senior police positions. Such a long history of British management means that the philosophies, principles, and programs of the Hong Kong Police followed many of those used in the British police. Local Chinese officers had to demonstrate their English language proficiency and identify with the Western culture in order to move up in the police hierarchy.

The Hong Kong Police culture, therefore, is more Western comparatively speaking. But the Western influence is not across-the-board. It is stronger in the middle and top echelons in the Force, but weak among the lower ranking officers. Many sergeants and street officers, for example, do not speak good English and are not familiar with Western values. It is inappropriate, therefore, to categorically describe the cultural traits of the Hong Kong Police as either Western or Chinese. There is also a difference between the formal and informal police systems. Officially, the Force has used the British system and the English language for years. Unofficially, a strong Chinese culture remains and the local officers communicate in Cantonese. In the following, I seek to further understand the organizational culture of the Hong Kong Police by using Bourdieu (1990)'s concepts of "habitus" and "field", examining the relationship between Western culture and Confucianism, and looking at the integration of different cultural values.

Cultural Concepts: Habitus and Field

Organizational researchers have used both internal practices and external environment to explain organizational culture. Bourdieu (1990)'s concepts, "habitus" and "field," describe the internal organizational characteristics and external structural environment. "Habitus" may be interpreted as shared values and beliefs formed by traditions and history of an organization. These internal cultural traits are further defined as "organizational knowledge" by Sackmann (1991:165), which includes organizational members' ideas of "what is," "how," "should's," and "why," which are "descriptive," "causal," "normative," and "assumptive" respectively in nature. "Field" may be understood as the external forces impacting on an organization. Both organizational knowledge and external forces exert an influence on organizational policies and behaviors.

Police culture has been explained as resulting from "an interaction between the 'field' of policing and the various dimensions of police organizational knowledge" (Chan, 1996:109). This interaction not only influences police orientations and behavior but may also produce reformed cultural dispositions.

The "habitus" and "field" of the Hong Kong Police include, in the most general terms, its traditional values and a new social political environment. The paramilitary training, internal security structure, Police Tactical Unit, and Criminal Investigation Division that focus on public order and crime control represent an essential part of the organizational knowledge of the Hong Kong Police. In the meantime, the organizational environment of the police has changed from a British colony to a Chinese Special Administrative Region. No longer a colonial force, the police are in the process of developing new values and attitudes and new organizational knowledge. Keeping abreast with the changed environment and trends in contemporary policing, the police leadership has envisioned a more service-oriented organization and engaged in reforming the police culture. This effort requires reducing the authoritarian tradition and institutionalizing a new spirit of service in the value orientations of the rank-and-file. The pace of this change has clearly quickened during the years leading up to the handover and thereafter. The Hong Kong Police therefore has been gradually evolving from an authoritarian and paramilitary force to a more service-oriented and community-oriented organization. The officers are becoming more conscious of procedural rights represented by due process rules and procedures. But due to the "habitus" of the police, this change process has not been straight-forward and there has been strong resistance from the rank-and-file who remain committed to public order and crime control as the goals of policing. The interactions between the traditional emphases for public order and crime fighting, the "habitus," and recent demands for accountability and legality, the "field," have continued to create tensions in the police effort to change from an authoritarian to a service oriented agency.

Western Culture and Confucianism

Questions remain as to what exactly is the culture of the Hong Kong Police. As a police force where the vast majority is Chinese, its culture may emanate from some elements of Confucianism. But as mentioned earlier, the Hong Kong Police has been greatly Westernized due to Hong Kong's experience as a British colony and the Hong Kong Police as an important part of the colonial criminal justice system. British colonialism, as Gaylord and Traver (1994:12) stated, "exported Western concepts of crime and criminal justice to much of its empire without regard for structural or cultural differences." The Western criminal justice system puts greater emphasis on supremacy of the law, with its notions of judicial independence, individual rights, due process, and the rule of law. Many related Western concepts such as individualism, liberalism, constitutionalism, and human rights, however, "often have little resonance" in other civilizations and cultures (Huntington, 1994:40). In this context, the local officers of the Hong Kong Police may experience some strain between their own traditional values and their working environment, i.e., between the Chinese concept of social harmony and the Western demand for procedural justice. In this situation, personal obligation and responsibility and social stability can be viewed as the "habitus," emphasized more in Chinese traditional values held by many local officers, while the due process rules and respect for individual rights can be understood as the "field," demanded more by Western justice principles. It thus can be seen in the Hong Kong Police the encounter of Chinese and Western policing philosophies, the mixing of two very different law enforcement traditions and principles (Endacott and Hinton, 1968).

The organizational knowledge of the Hong Kong Police undoubtedly includes certain basic elements of Western philosophies such as political neutrality and the rule of law. The police officers, however, are predominantly Chinese. As years go by, the few hundred expatriate officers currently serving will no longer be there due to the end of overseas recruitment. As the racial makeup changes, the value orientations of the Force may also change. Many local officers cherish conservative values of conformity and pro-order outlook although they do not attach Confucius label to them. Values represented by Confucianism put greater emphasis on moral and ethical governance as a defining feature of the Chinese culture is the culture of shame while the Western culture is more of a culture of guilt. The implication for social control is that the Hong Kong Police would integrate its law and order practices with the "moral force and the rule of reason" (Reichel, 2002:81) and strike a balance between strict law enforcement and informal mediation. Following this philosophy, local police officers would be more reserved, more personal, and group-oriented, but pay less attention to individual responsibility and accountability. Similar points were made by a Hong Kong police officer who once visited the New York Police Department and another who had experience working with "Guilau," a term used generally to refer to foreigners or expatriate officers in Hong Kong.

Unlike New York, the Hong Kong Police did not use the accountability-driven Compstat system because of cultural differences. When I presented these ideas to the management, we felt that the Hong Kong Police commanders may be uncomfortable about the drilling process, standing in front of their colleagues and their seniors.

Guilau are more open-minded, more willing to accept comments and feedbacks, more willing to express their views. Chinese are more reserved. We have less Guilau now. It's both good and bad. Guilau are good because they fight for benefits and appreciate different views. They are bad because they like empire building. You are not a member of their empire, you are out.

Another officer sees cultural differences in the degrees of dedication of officers and the levels of social control. The conformist behaviors and pro-order outlook of the Chinese culture perhaps encourage officers to do more and bring forth a stronger control in the community.

British officers are more arrogant and less willing to go the extra miles. Hong Kong officers are more willing to go the extra miles. In comparison to Britain,

Hong Kong has stricter gun control and I.D. card system. ID checking cannot be so well implemented in Britain. There is generally tighter control here. In Britain, you can never get away with the stop-and-search activities you do here.

The basic values of Confucianism, although clearly present in the Hong Kong Police, tend to be latent or held subconsciously. Confucius precepts have never been officially endorsed for training purposes in the Force. Most officers, as a matter of fact, deny the presence of or belief in Confucianism even though their behaviors demonstrate conformist and pro-order values. These latent cultural traits are clearly a result of the 156 years of British colonial rule, which denied the relevancy of Confucianism in policing and governance. One senior officer laughed when he heard the word "Confucius," as he had never heard the word during his years of service in the Hong Kong Police. He did not refute the fact that officers may be Confucius but regarded Confucianism as representing a political party or ideology that police officers should turn away from.

I have never heard the word "Confucius." Officers may not say they believe in Confucianism, but they have favorable views toward Confucius values. Most of them consider themselves independent politically. They are not allowed to join any political party.

A former Hong Kong government official and a senior Hong Kong Police officer commented similarly when asked if they had ever heard of Confucius.

Confucianism and the Ten Commandments are no different. No, I haven't heard it during my service. Modern society has nothing to do with it. It's dead. The Hong Kong government is very pragmatic. It's in the law, a matter of convenience.

Confucian ideas are hardly taught in Hong Kong. As far as I know, Confucius is taught only as a historical figure at two schools in the entire city. We in the Police Force don't train officers in Confucius doctrines. We emphasize the tactical side.

Some other officers view Confucian philosophy as representing only one of the multiple cultures in the Hong Kong Police, which should not be used to exclude others. They also believe that there are many reasons for conformist behaviors and pro-order outlook, not necessarily because of belief in Confucianism.

We don't emphasize a single culture. We've been exposed to many cultures, British, Indian, Pakistani, Japanese, Chinese, and so on. Officers bring their own cultures to the Force. There's no official endorsement of a single culture. No racism, no cultural divides. They call me "Guilou," meaning "foreign devil," but in a good sense. I even use the word myself, I order Guilou tsa (tea). We don't offend each other by these words.

It's more like the inertia of Civil Service Reform. We've been multi-racial; we have Sikhs, Pakistanis, Europeans, Chinese from different parts of China, etc.

It's not a homogeneous population. Our promotion is based on merits, not on race. We've always had women. We have less glass ceilings. We are an equal opportunity employer. We have two languages, English and Chinese; but we have different versions in Chinese. Recruitment encourages bilingual and tri-lingual skills.

There are many reasons for conformist behaviors and pro-order outlook. They may not be Confucius; they may better be explained by economic, social, cul-tural, and legal reasons.

Confucianism is apparently not a philosophy a Western power would em-brace since colonial rulers were committed to transplanting their own cultures and systems to foreign lands. The former British colonists and the top brass of the Royal Hong Kong Police naturally would not think of adopting Confucian precepts in policing and might even consider them irrelevant to police work. Consequently, most officers do not believe that the Hong Kong Police has had a Confucius tradition. It is equally clear, however, that a large number of local officers in the Force do hold traditional Chinese values, represented largely by Confucianism. Since Hong Kong is no longer a British colony, the Chinese culture, particularly the Chinese language, plays a more prominent role in day-to-day policing. As some officers observed:

The Police Commissioner [PC] used to be a foreigner. The boss of PC also used to be a foreigner. The past two PCs are Chinese. We used to use more English before 1997. After 1997, both English and Chinese are used. In daily business, we use more Chinese. Before 1997, Guilau dominated the police cul-ture. There used to be more empire building among Australians, British, etc.; Chinese, too. After 1997, the picture is different. We have less foreigners in the Force. Efficiency and effectiveness are better now.

English level is dropping in the Force as there are less and less expatriate offi-cers and in some meetings Cantonese is used because local officers think it is more efficient.

Integration of Cultures

Although Western values and Confucianism represent two diverse cultural traditions and have created strain sometimes among the officers, the integration or combination of these cultural orientations is more of the norm than excep-tions. Western law enforcement principles to a great extent have been assimi-lated into Hong Kong police practices due to many individual officers' back-grounds and experiences. Hong Kong police officers identify with the Western legal system much more than with Chinese socialist legal doctrines. The police culture in Hong Kong therefore can be best characterized as a mix of Western and Chinese traditional values. As some officers said,

Since the 80's, the Hong Kong Police have sent more than 50 officers to UK in an exchange scheme, called "Swap Cops." The cultural exchange raised the standards of the Force. Most of the swap cops have become senior officers bringing Western values to the Force.

The Hong Kong Police combines Western policing principles with Chinese traditional values. . . . I believe in the rule of law more than Chinese traditional values. The mainland Chinese legal principles are not applicable to Hong Kong. I have faith in the autonomy of Hong Kong as a Special Administrative Region of China. I don't think that Hong Kong people have a strong sense of history such as the Opium War.

This integrated approach is also reflected in Hong Kong Police operations. On the one hand, the criminal justice system in Hong Kong models after the Western principle of separation and checks and balances. The legislative, executive, and judicial powers are separated. The functions of different components in the criminal justice system are similar to those of any well-administered city in the West. The Bill of Rights of 1991 has increased the government's burden of proof requiring that the police follow due process rules and collect sufficient evidence. Police officers face increased challenges due to the Bill of Rights, which imposes restraint on the use of police powers and requires that they bear "the full burden of proof in criminal proceedings" (Cheung, 1996:153). As a result, many Hong Kong officers see that due process has been raised as an important goal in policing and basic law enforcement principles from the West have taken hold in the Hong Kong Police. On the other hand, the Hong Kong Police functions in a pro-order environment where public order and social stability are valued much higher than due process rules and procedures. The police have traditionally placed a great emphasis on public order management and an "effective crime control model" of operations. As Cheung (1996:153) has argued, the impact of the Bill of Rights on the Hong Kong Police is "only procedural, not substantive, and can be accommodated by procedural adjustment in related areas of police operation." In addition, the Hong Kong Police manages one of the world's largest youth programs, the Junior Police Call, to bring values of conformity and pro-order outlook to the younger generation. As a visiting officer from abroad and a local officer stated:

One of the most impressive innovations observed was the Junior Police Call program, introduced in 1974 to bring young people and the police into a closer constructive relationship (Alderson, 1981:7). . . . The police pay great attention to their moral reputation especially in dealing with young people.

There are certainly also police values and behaviors that go beyond cultural lines and reflect certain universal characteristics of the police profession. As some officers pointed out, for example:

Hong Kong police attitudes, cultures, and values are the same as police everywhere. . . . Police officers are conservative due to the nature of police work. When new legislation is being discussed, they look at it from a conservative perspective. Instead of considering how to protect citizen rights, they look at whether there are loopholes that may be taken advantage of by offenders.

Institutional Perspective

The changes and continuities of the Hong Kong Police can also be examined by the use of institutional concepts in organizational literature. The institutional perspective serves as a useful tool for understanding the politics and ceremonies that pervade much modern organizational life (DiMaggio and Powell, 1991). It allows a broader view of the environmental context in which organizations operate. Meyer and Rowan (1991) believe, for example, that organizations are driven to incorporate the practices and procedures defined by prevailing rationalized concepts of organizational work. Institutionalized techniques, policies, and programs function as powerful myths, adopted ceremonially by organizations to increase their legitimacy and their survival prospects. As Meyer and Rowan (1991) observe, there are three processes that generate rationalized myths. First, many myths are generated by particular organizational practices and diffused through relational networks. These myths have their legitimacy based on the supposition that they are effective. Second, many myths also have official legitimacy based on legal mandates. The stronger the rational-legal order, the greater the extent to which rationalized rules and procedures and personnel become institutionalized requirements. Third, organizations, though influenced by their institutional contexts, do play active roles in shaping those contexts. Powerful organizations would attempt to build their goals and procedures directly into society as institutional rules. In short, Meyer and Rowan (1991:49) argue that isomorphism with environmental institutions has some significant consequences for organizations: (a) they incorporate elements which are legitimated externally, rather than in terms of efficiency; (b) they employ external or ceremonial assessment criteria to define the value of structural elements; and (c) their dependence on externally fixed institutions reduces turbulence and maintains stability (1991:49).

The influence of the institutional environment on the decisions and actions of organizations is further explored by March and Olsen (1984). To them, institutions are neither neutral reflections of exogenous environmental forces nor neutral arenas for the performances of individuals driven by exogenous preferences and expectations. They see an organization's past policies, past outcomes, and the like as being institutionalized into structures, procedures, and practices, which endogenously shape members' interests and identities. Members are seen as being "co-opted" into the organization's beliefs and commitments, and "socialized" into organizational roles, norms, rules, aspirations, and expectations. March and Olsen (1984) further assert that political institutions are independent factors, political phenomena are closely associated with political institutions involved in the events, and political events are mostly the consequences of interactions between institutions. March and Olson's works demonstrate the complexity of organizational change.

Powell (1991:191-192) explores four avenues of institutional reproduction, which explain why institutions have the tendency to resist changes. These are: (1) the exercise of power—skilled institution builders who gain power from a system of control and reproduction will typically expend considerable effort to maintain their dominance; (2) complex interdependencies—institutional structures and practices are very much embedded in a network of procedures and programs, the altering of which involves high switching costs; (3) taken-for-granted assumptions—social patterns may reproduce themselves without active intervention when structures and practices come to be taken for granted; and (4) path-dependent development processes—organizational procedures and forms may preserve because of path dependent patterns of development in which initial choices preclude future options, including those that would have been more effective in the long run.

Traditions

Many of these institutional concepts are appropriate for understanding the influence of the Hong Kong Police traditions as institutionalized police practices have evolved through a long process of institutionalization. The colonial police traditionally were preoccupied with maintenance of social order and treated the prevention and control of crime as secondary (Anderson and Killingray, 1992). Paramilitary policing was therefore applied to Hong Kong early on while civilian policing model was used in England. The government and policing in Hong Kong were imposed and the local population in the colony was controlled with coercive force. The paramilitary foundation of the Hong Kong Police existed also in tandem with certain fundamental policing principles such as "policing strangers by strangers" in the early days. Because policing was not based on consent, the Hong Kong Police did not have to "face up to controlling those aspects of crime and disorder which often arise out of the very nature of Western democracy" (Alderson, 1981:8). The interplay between Hong Kong Police's early policing principles and its external environment has been one of the sources of institutional myths of the Hong Kong Police. For instance, the creation of the Emergency Unit was triggered by the 1925-26 general strike. The evolutionary thesis posits that paramilitary policing gradually develops into civil policing as more consent or legitimacy was obtained from the local population. The primary conditions for service-oriented policing were political stability and the availability of a separate military force that can be deployed to maintain peace and order (Brogden and Lau, 2001). In Hong Kong, however, the military barracks were not sufficient for peace and order duties in colonial time. The Hong Kong Police therefore has developed a strong paramilitary capability and a mentality for military operations among the officers. Public order management has eventually been institutionalized as a primordial mission of the Hong Kong Police. As a visiting officer from abroad and a Hong Kong police officer commented:

> The Force has considerable investigative and riot control capabilities. Military aid is a pronounced feature of illegal immigration control as well as providing a back-up for the police in extreme cases of disorder. The police commitment to riot control is an impressive and sophisticated example of quasi-military capability, commensurate with the need to govern a colony (Alderson, 1981:8).

> The Hong Kong Police still have a paramilitary capability. . . . The Hong Kong
> Police must be prepared. Unlike police departments in the U.S., they don't have
> any other forces to help them. They are on their own.

Most officers I have interviewed believe that their traditional practices focusing on public order and effective crime control remain and there have been more continuities than changes in their operational priorities. The paramilitary tradition and emphasis on public order have resulted in a heavily policed city. The fifth United Nations Criminal Justice System (UNCJS) survey (1994), for example, ranks Hong Kong the sixth highest in terms of police to population rate at 640 police officers per 100,000 population, well above Denmark (238), Canada (249), Australia (275), and the United States (300), and exceeding other Asian neighbors such as Malaysia (430), Philippines (155), and Japan (207) (Broadhurst, 2000). Hong Kong, due to its large investment in policing, was ranked also as one of the top spenders on criminal justice, exceeding troubled jurisdictions such as Northern Ireland (Newman, 1999).

Transformations

The strong traditions of the Hong Kong Police in public order management and effective crime control does not mean that there have been no changes at all. Some changes have occurred as part of a natural development process. Others have taken place due to interplays between the internal forces that constrain change and the external impetuses that induce it in a way demonstrated in the institutional perspective. For example, the Hong Kong Police originally vigorously rejected the idea of creating an independent body to investigate police corruption and organized the Anti-Corruption Branch (ACB) under the Criminal Investigation Division (CID). In response to increasing public demand for stronger anti-corruption measures, the police later separated ACB from CID and upgraded it to the Anti-Corruption Office (ACO). However, such a tactic was no longer adequate to meet the public demand in 1974 due to a huge public outcry sparked by the Godber corruption scandal. The Hong Kong Police subsequently conceded to the idea of establishing an anti-corruption institution independent from the police, the Independent Commission against Corruption (ICAC) (Jiao, Lau, and Lui, 2005). This concession could be interpreted from the perspective of "coercive isomorphism." As DiMaggio and Powell (1991) observe, institutional isomorphic change occurs when there is a severe problem of legitimacy. Since the Godber scandal reflected the problem of syndicated police corruption, it seriously undermined the legitimacy of the Hong Kong Police and eventually became the impetus for fundamental change.

When the pressure to change is of less magnitude than fighting corruption, however, the police would have less incentive to change. A case in point is how the Hong Kong Police meets the demand for better police-public relations and more community crime prevention. Following its paramilitary traditions, the Hong Kong Police developed certain anti-crime practices that are often described by critics as coercive or heavy-handed. This approach to crime control eventually led to the degradation of its police-public relations program, despite the importance placed on it by the Hong Kong Government (Jiao, Lau, and Lui, 2005). This process is similar to what Tolbert and Zucker (1996) refer to as "sedimentation." The institutional myth and the organizational knowledge of the Hong Kong Police are public order management and crime control, which have a residual effect on any new programs such as community relations. As institutional theorists have noted, an organization would defend its myth as much as it possibly can.

The change of sovereignty has brought immense pressure to the Hong Kong Police (Gaylord and Traver, 1995). As the old colony was fading, maintaining stability both within the Force and in the Hong Kong society became a top priority of the Force. The police needed to fill the management vacuum left by top expatriate officers and exercise strong leadership. They face the task of establishing a new legitimacy in post-colonial Hong Kong. The key question is what orientation the police should have and operate under in response to the changing political landscape. From the 1990's to the present, the Hong Kong police have been building its new political legitimacy as a part of China and yet remaining intrinsically intertwined with the West as they practice English laws in a Chinese society and operate in a legal system different from that of China. This new orientation revolves around a series of Service Quality Initiatives and the idea that the public are customers of the police. Confronting traditional police practices institutionalized in the past, the last colonial governor, Chris Patten, initiated this reform. As a former Hong Kong government official stated:

> Chris Patten accepted the reform ideas because he had an open mind and adopted whatever he considered good for Hong Kong. David Wilson didn't accept them because he considered them too political, that they were just things used to make him look popular. . . . They wanted to increase officers on the street. The program was only partially successful because the commissioner was conservative. The government didn't push the police as hard as other agencies due to the nature of police work. . . . The idea of customer service did not come from the private sector. It came from the government. The word "customer" is used, because there was no such a thing as Hong Kong citizen. . . . Since government is not like private business, people cannot go to the next door if they are not happy with the service they get. We simply make it clear what services each agency provides and the public can complain about the services.

The reform effort has been spearheaded by a new Service Quality Wing, headed by an Assistant Commissioner of Police, created with the goal to bring about a change in culture and work attitudes within the Force. The Service Quality Wing launched the Force Strategy on Quality of Service in March 1995 seeking to develop a culture that involved officers at all levels in continually striving for improvement to ensure that services provided by the Force were effective, efficient, and economical. This strategy is "best explained in terms of its component parts, namely: the Force Vision and Statement of Common Purpose and Values; Living-the-Values; Surveys; Consultancy Support; Customer Service Improvement Project; Staff Suggestion Scheme; and Best Practices" (Hui, 2002:169). Due to these initiatives, the Hong Kong police have placed greater emphasis on the quality of their service and on building a culture of service. As former police commissioner Hui (2002:168) stated:

To ensure that the organization and management of the Force responded to growing demands for its services from the public, and was able to properly justify the government funding necessary to provide that service, a series of reviews were conducted throughout the 1990s with a view to improving the quality of service given by the Force. The Force's long term aims were to develop a police force that is accountable, lives within its means, manages for performance, and is service-oriented. To achieve these aims, the Force has pursued a dual approach under the broad headings of Service Quality and Performance Management.

The dual approach has resulted in an appropriate financial framework for responding to growing demands for police services, greater accountability, and more management initiatives. The police management has reorganized the existing planning and management structures, including committee structure and program management structure; delineated responsibilities of decision makers; reallocated resources; and established performance indicators and performance-related bidding (Hui, 2002). Some other management initiatives include wider use of technology, more focus on human resource management, and better communication. Police managers have shown in recent years greater interest in developing their capabilities to manage and motivate officers. To ensure that officers promoted share the new force values, the police management has openly and explicitly included officers' knowledge of service quality and responsiveness to change among the assessment criteria (Kwok, 1999). A healthy lifestyle has also been promoted throughout the Force. Consequently, a service orientation has gradually emerged in the Hong Kong Police. As some officers stated:

We have become more responsive after 1997 in the sense that we make the public aware of what we're doing. The police from the top down are engaged in communicating with the public, the legislature, the community groups, and the media. . . . The Force is more transparent and more open. The management is more open. They change, they grow up, they know communication is important.

The Service Quality Wing reviews service, performs audit, helps the Force enhance service quality. . . . Change of silence culture has worked resulting from long-term training. . . . In the old days few people had contacts with the police. Now it's easier to phone up. The public can get answers faster.

There were more changes in the last five years than in the last two decades. The Force management has done a lot to improve its services in the last two decades. While change has occurred, mostly the change happened internally. There are many things you can affect internally but not externally. Many remedies exist internally but not externally.

The Hong Kong police have had lots of changes over the past 30 years. The police have become much more professionalized because of ownership of the problems. Officers, especially local officers are more committed to police work. There has been more problem-oriented policing.

Following are some more comments from officers interviewed that indicate the changes of the Hong Kong Police.

There is a change in culture. Police have more accountability. Our day-to-day operations and duties have not changed much. The nature of police work has not changed much. What have changed are people's values and attitudes and the demands of police work. Now we have more responsibilities. Officers have more responsibilities. A report now is dealt with by an officer instead of a detective.

Less socialization occurs among officers. Drinking after work is discouraged. Officers are told to go home to their families after work. . . . Great change in attitude has occurred toward drinking and driving, very harsh now. There is also a change of attitude toward drinking in the Force. Health and physical conditions were hardly considered in the past. Officers used to drink a lot, not any more. The Force promotes healthy lifestyles. It's a cultural change against drinking.

The Hong Kong Police have changed a lot culturally from a paramilitary force to a service-oriented force. Not sure why there are so many changes at the same time. We created a lot of new jobs for ourselves because of the changes. Whatever crimes are mentioned in the media must be attended to immediately. Whatever the public complains on paper must be dealt with immediately. We are doing a lot more work than we used to. We have a lot more paper work, too. . . . There are things in the Force that I couldn't even imagine when I first joined the police, such as communication, customer service, etc. It's like running a business now. We have put more officers on the street. We used to have the idea of self-sufficiency. Everything we do was handled by a police officer. We used to have police cooks, police truck drivers, etc.; now we use civilians. We used to be low profile; we have 500 officers in one district, more than half doing administrative work, crime analysis, public relations, planning, training, etc. Now we put more officers on the street.

We have some minor change in law. Presumption of guilt is no longer valid. For public order events, internally we have more guidelines to strike a balance between people's rights to protest and our duty to enforce laws. Before and after you confirm a suspect is a criminal, you have to be polite and use restraints. . . . Hong Kong people are more conscious of their rights due to education and media.

Some changes have occurred in their attitudes and behaviors toward the police over the past 20 years. Twenty years ago, when a person was stopped for search on the street, he didn't ask why; now they do. But 20 years ago, police were viewed as corrupt and now the image is better. Still, most people address police as Cailau [a negative term for police officers]. So overall, the image in people's heart is still negative.

Besides views of the police officers, members of the public have also observed changes of the police in recent years. There is a widespread perception that the Hong Kong Police have changed significantly in their attitude toward the public as officers they come in contact with demonstrate a highly professional and courteous manner. There are also those who believe that some officers do not treat people from different social strata in the same way. The following are some of the comments from the public.

> Their manner is totally different from the conduct of some police officers on the beat in the past. . . . the public no longer fear the police as they did in the old days, and I think they now deserve acknowledgement as Asia's finest (*Offbeat*, 2002a).

> Nowadays the police are better educated, very polite, and always willing to help. . . . I respect and support the police even though I received a speeding ticket once from them, because they are very courteous and highly professional. . . . I respect and support the police. The officers are very businesslike and polite. . . . However, officers may not be as nice when dealing with lower-class people or people in a poor area.

Why have the Hong Kong police been engaged in changing their culture and attitude? One answer is that police must keep pace with and respond to changes in the society. The Hong Kong Police has changed from a paramilitary law enforcement agency to a more service-oriented organization due to societal change that had really started more than twenty years ago. As an officer stated:

> The Hong Kong Police have become more transparent, participatory, and service-oriented due to the ever-changing need of society. The Hong Kong society has become more democratic. People are more educated since we had representative government. Since early 1990s we have more universities and more people can get a college education. . . . Service quality strategy is good. If I put myself in the shoes of the public, I wanted to be treated politely, without being shouted at. Also, we are a major international city, we need to be more polite and have a good image. So we have mission, values, like a corporation, a business. We promote healthy life styles, life long learning. Knowledge is important.

Another answer to the question is that police must have legitimacy in order to function effectively. Vagg (1996:124) proposed that police legitimacy comprises of "the legitimating accounts presented by the state, the extent to which those accounts command public acceptance, and the actual level of 'consent to policing' or 'compliance with police.'" He demonstrated that in Hong Kong these different types of legitimacy were not necessarily related to each other and that "both legitimating accounts and compliance and consent are likely to be affected by broader shifts in the nature of the state, particularly those shifts which highlight questions such as 'whose law?' and 'whose order?'" (Vagg, 1996:125). The broader shift in the nature of the state in Hong Kong is clear at this point: it has changed from a British colony to a Special Administrative Region of China. The Hong Kong Police must create a new legitimacy at this time of change although "creating legitimacy" is not how the police would describe the purpose of their change effort. The police prefer to say that the goal in building a new police culture is to maintain public confidence. The word "legitimacy" as used by Vagg therefore is paraphrased as "public confidence" or "public support" and understood as such as far as the Hong Kong police are concerned. For example, former police commissioner Eddie Hui (2002) indicated that the Hong Kong Police had worked very hard for many years to maintain the support of the people of Hong Kong. In his statement of future strategic directions he said: "we need to retain public confidence by reassuring them that social order will be maintained throughout transition and beyond." A former Hong Kong government official also saw the importance of community relations for the police at this time of transition.

> The accountability system is new. . . .Police have become so liberal, tolerant after 1997, communicating all the time. . . . If they don't, they will lose public support. They are very smart. Hong Kong people cared about law and order. Hong Kong police have a bad record of beating for confessions. Officers know they need to balance due process and crime control. Top police people know they need community support. Community relationship is very important. Also, officers are more educated now and more comfortable talking to the public. Balance to community policing to both.

Consistent with the service orientation and community policing philosophy, the current police policy states that only under emergency situation would the Force exercise paramilitary character and on a routine basis the police would place top priority on cooperation to enlist community support. The efforts of the police to adopt a service orientation, however, have been critiqued as being "rather superficial" because of the continued priorities given to institutionalized "real" or "core" policing duties such as public order management and tactical activities (Lau, 2002:19).

Limitations of Reform

The Hong Kong Police was created originally to protect the colonial regime and manage public order. Crime control was not a priority. The transformation occurred when the police engaged themselves in changes to professional law enforcement and later to a service orientation. The paramilitary traditions of the Hong Kong Police, however, have always been influential in the later stages of the police development. When the Hong Kong Police incorporated the law enforcement function into its mission in the 1970s, it adopted a paramilitary crime control approach. When Chris Patten's customer-based public service reform and the Force Service Quality Initiatives were launched, the Hong Kong Police's paramilitary rituals and practices undermine the effort to build a service culture (Lau, 2004).

Due to its origins and the developed structures and processes such as the Emergency Unit, the Police Tactical Unit, and quasi-military training, there has been great resistance to the transformation to a service-oriented organization. The police officers remain committed to public order and crime control and view these duties as more important police work. Taken-for-granted assumptions are clearly evident in the officers' ready acceptance of these traditional police duties and the effect of institutionalization on the mentality of organizational members can be seen in some officers' inimical attitude toward the Service Quality Initiatives. This Hong Kong Police experience illustrates how the institutional environment affects the practices and behaviors of a major police organization and its responses to external challenges.

In Brint and Karabel's (1991:338) view, much of institutional analysis focuses on "institutional form and functioning" to the point where "institutional origins and transformations" is overlooked. The Hong Kong Police provides a rare case that encompasses origins (i.e., the process of institutionalization), transformation and resistance to transformation, form (i.e., structures and processes, etc.), and functioning (such as the shaping of police mentality). The Hong Kong Police traditions have been institutionalized into basic values, beliefs, goals, and attitudes. The rank-and-file officers' anxieties over the Service Quality Initiatives can be attributed to the institutionalized paramilitary traditions. All officers in the Hong Kong Police, for instance, undergo Police Tactical Unit (PTU) training and serve in the PTU at least twice during their career with the Force. Through PTU deployment, which often involves group patrol and militarized tactics such as sweeps and searches, officers develop a sense of power and a strong public order mentality. As an officer stated, PTU training and deployment constitutes a police officer's "baptism" into the Force (Lau, 2004:9). A police officer is thus effectively socialized into the traditional values and practices of the Hong Kong Police through his or her PTU experience.

A Brief Comment

The Hong Kong police are at a special time and a special place. They have been engaged in community policing and are committed to building a culture of service. This change may not be directly triggered by 1997, but is clearly associated with the development in the Hong Kong society and the field of policing in recent years. Conceptually, the Service Quality Initiatives are similar to the service style illustrated by Wilson (1972), but represents a new stage of development rather than a style of policing in the context of Hong Kong policing. They are an ambitious reform program, rationally conceived and politically insightful, but require a sweeping change of police character and an institutional transformation. In addition, this strategy demands new budgetary allocation and substantial investment in training the officers. A reform of such magnitude and complexity naturally is confronted with challenges and obstacles of various kinds and calls for application of knowledge in organizational change and social relations. In other words, adaptation to external environment must be accompanied by internal institutional development. If not, the reform may bring more bureaucracy instead of meaningful changes. The Hong Kong Police, therefore, has not only responded to changes in the society, but also has been actively involved in an organizational learning and development process to expand the officers' horizon, promote new policing philosophies, and support best practices in consistency with the changed political environment. The challenge ahead lies in how to balance the demand for public order and for legality in police behavior, for effective crime control and for procedural legitimacy (Skolnick, 1994).

4

Structure and Operation

The Hong Kong Police is one of the largest police forces in the world with 26,659 police officers and a budget of HK$11.3 billion (US$1.5 billion) (see Table 4.1). Hong Kong is a small jurisdiction geographically, but has a growing population that stands at 6,882,600 in 2004 (Census and Statistics Department, 2005a). With a police-population ratio of 1 officer to 258 residents, Hong Kong can be ranked as one of the heavily policed cities in the world (Jiao, 2002). In addition to its regular police strength, the Hong Kong Police also has 4,077 auxiliary officers, who play a supporting role for crowd management, key point defense, manning of command and control centers, and station defense (Hong Kong Police Review, 2004). The Hong Kong Police is not only responsible for traditional duties such as law enforcement and order maintenance, but for border security, counter smuggling activities, and internal security as well. In this chapter, I provide a description of the overall organization and major operations of the Hong Kong Police based primarily on information collected from first-hand interviews and observations. Because the purpose here is to achieve a general understanding of a large police organization, I will not delve into detailed analyses of crime problems, street patrol activities, and managerial issues. These and related areas will be covered in detail in separate chapters later. Where these issues are discussed, they are intended to assist illustration of the general structure and practice of the Hong Kong Police.

Changes over the Years

Like any large police forces in the world, the Hong Kong Police has experienced many changes in its structure and practices. The Force has expanded in size and grown in complexity over the years due to both a natural development process and various external pressures. Like many Western colonies in the world, the Hong Kong Police developed a paramilitary structure and public order emphasis early on both to defend the colony from the Chinese mainland and to control the local population. The fear of communists and associated civil

Table 4.1 The Hong Kong Police Strength

Junior police officers (Constables and sergeants)	24,079
Senior police officers (Inspectors and above)	2,580
Total officers	26,659
Police/population ratio	1/258*
Civilian staff	5,034
Auxiliary police officers	4,077

* It would be 1 officer to 224 residents if auxiliary officers are included in the ratio.
Source: Adapted from Annual Hong Kong Police Review 2004 and information released by the Census and Statistics Department of the Hong Kong Government (2005b).

disturbances led to the creation of the Emergency Unit in 1927 and the Anti-Communist Squad around the same time. This Squad became the Special Branch, which was headed by a deputy police commissioner and reported directly to the colonial governor. The Special Branch consisted of two wings—the Intelligence Wing and the Security Wing. As China was unified by the communists in 1949 and labor unions in Hong Kong became more influential, the District Watch Force, originally set up by wealthy local businessmen, was summarily disbanded and absorbed into the Hong Kong Police for fear of communist infiltration. In 1995, two years before Hong Kong's return to China, the Intelligence Wing of the Special Branch was disbanded and all sensitive data was transferred to Britain (Brogden and Lau, 2001). As one of the retired officers recalled:

> In Hong Kong, a small group of police officers were involved in politically sensitive work in a unit called the Special Branch. They dealt with political issues with a bearing on security. It was disbanded in 1995, later replaced by the Security Wing.

Besides certain enduring features such as the paramilitary structure and emphasis on public order management, there have been also certain progressive reforms aimed at higher efficiency and greater effectiveness. Directed by the then governor, for example, the top police management structure was reviewed in 1992 by Coopers and Lybrand Management Consultants, following a similar review conducted a decade earlier. It was recommended that changes in the command structure be made to accommodate new functions and responsibilities, "to secure improvements in value for money", to strengthen and redefine the roles of the main resource commands, and to allow more autonomy and decentralization (Coopers and Lybrand, 1992:ii). In 1997, the Force revised its planning and resource allocation machinery with the introduction of program management. This involved aligning the activities of the Force into six program areas: crime prevention; crime control; public order; human resources management; management services; and finance, administration, and planning (Hong Kong Police Review 1997). Despite these reviews and realignment, many officers view that the organizational structure and major operations have, by and large, stayed unchanged for many years. As a senor police officer and a mid-ranking officer stated:

> There was not much need for the Hong Kong Police to adjust its organizational structures, operations, policies, and officer training under the new Hong Kong Special Administrative Region Government.

> There has been no change in structure since I joined the Force in 1988. I know the Force was expanded in the 70s and 80s. But the structure has stayed the same. We have different police operations managed by different program managers, Director of Operations, Director of Crime and Security, Director of Management Services, etc., at the senior assistant commissioner level. These senior managers coordinate police operations at that level at their meetings.

Police Structure

The Hong Kong Police Force is currently organized into the Police Headquarters, five land regions including Hong Kong Island, Kowloon East, Kowloon West, New Territories North, New Territories South, and one Marine Region. Each region is divided into a number of districts, each of which has primary responsibility for providing police services in its area. Most districts are in turn divided into divisions, which are usually based around a single police station. There are altogether six regional headquarters, twenty-one police districts, and fifty-one police divisions in Hong Kong. The Police Headquarters is located in Wanchai, Hong Kong Island. This structure means that the Hong Kong Police consists of four levels: the Force, regional, district, and divisional. While most officers interviewed agree that the division is the basic unit, some officers add the subunit as the lowest or fifth level under the division. Factors such as population, crime rate, and geography are considered in determining how areas are divided. If Bayley (1985; 1992)'s categorization of police forces is used, which is based on dispersal of command, number of forces, and stated locus of control, the structure of the Hong Kong Police can be described as a centralized single system.

A formal and hierarchical structure is clearly in place in the Hong Kong Police. There are altogether fourteen ranks in this hierarchy including four top senior posts, six middle management ranks, and four frontline positions. The four top senor posts are the Commissioner, Deputy Commissioners, Senior Assistant Commissioners, and Assistant Commissioners. There are two Deputy Commissioners that cover Operations and the Management; five Senior Assistant Commissioners that assume Directors of Operations, Crime and Security, Personnel and Training, Management Services, and Finance, Administration and Planning; and seventeen Assistant Commissioners in charge of the

Support Wing, Operations Wing, Police Regions, Crime Wing, Security Wing, Training Wing, Personnel Wing, Service Quality Wing, Information Systems Wing, Planning and Development Branch, Administration Wing, and Finance Wing. The six middle management ranks are Chief Superintendent, Senior Superintendent, Superintendent, Chief Inspector, Senior Inspector, and Inspector. Finally there are four ranks at the street level including the Station Sergeant, Sergeant, Senior Constables, and Constables. There are seven to eight officers under each supervisor.

The top cop in Hong Kong is the Commissioner of Police (CP), who is a uniformed officer. He is appointed by the Hong Kong Government, which has control over the prospects for advancements above the rank of Senior Superintendent. The British tradition that emphasizes non-political involvement has been emphasized in the selection of the Commissioner and other top ranking officers. The promotions and personnel issues for officers below the rank of Senior Superintendent are controlled by the Commissioner. There is no influence in this process from a police union because Hong Kong Police officers do not have their union in the traditional sense of the word. They are members of several Staff Associations who cannot participate in any political activities or join any trade unions. They play a negotiating role with the police administration for issues mostly related to police benefits. As stated by some senior police officers and Lee (1991):

> The Commissioner of Police is a professional officer, a career officer, accountable to the Chief Executive of Hong Kong. The Commissioner is a civil servant, he must be politically neutral, as part of the British tradition. . . . Our Commissioner comes from the Force due to a natural process. Even without the change of sovereignty, there would be a Chinese police commissioner. We are structurally para-military. We are not political. Rules are expected by everybody.

> In Hong Kong, the retirement age now for members of the disciplined forces is 55.5. The senior officials including the Commissioner of Police can extend it for two years to 57.5. Age for retirement for members of other civil service departments is 60. Age is a mechanism to keeping the term of the Commissioner in less than 5 years or so because it would be a miracle to have a young officer to go through 13 ranks to become a commissioner. So age will limit their length of service as Commissioner of Police.

> The Hong Kong Police are not allowed to have union or be on strike. Police officers are civil servants. All civil servants are required to be politically neutral. They cannot join political parties. Union has never been an issue for the Hong Kong Police. The police by law are not allowed to be a member of a trade union. They are the only disciplined force in Hong Kong. They have staff associations. They can't take industrial actions.

> Since the work nature of the Police Force is very sensitive to the political aspect, the government must keep a tight control on the Force, which often leads to a deprivation of the right of the police officer. Besides that the officers' request to change the chairmanship of the PFC was turned down, their request to

set up a Committee of Inquiry to deal with the disagreement on the pay matters, has been ignored for a long time since the pay dispute in 1988. It is believed that the Government is not willing to abandon her power on a third independent party in controlling the Police Force (Lee, 1991:93).

The Hong Kong Police operations, both crime and patrol, reflect also the structure of the Force. At the Force level, the most serious crimes, cross-regional crimes, and cross-border crimes are handled. At the regional level, major crimes in the region and cross-district crimes are investigated. According to the police personnel classification, there are only five or six officers working as full-time administrators at each regional headquarters. Most officers at the regional level are either in the crime units or engage in special service operations including the Mass Transit Railroad (MTR) and Magistracy, which conducts search and provides escort of prisoners. The district level probes crimes confined to the local district. And the divisional level manages routine cases and misdemeanors. In the area of patrol, the Police Headquarters has Special Duty Units and Search Cadres that do patrol work; each of the six regions has its Emergency Units (EU), Police Tactical Units (PTU), and Traffic Units; each district has District Traffic Teams and Special Duty Squads; and each division assigns officers to walk the beat. As an inspector stated:

> Regional level can mobilize more resources like the state police in the U.S. Regional level has uniformed officers on foot patrol too, those wearing the blue hats. There are Traffic Unit, EU, and PTU at the regional level. PTU patrols on foot. The difference is, at the district and divisional level, officers patrol by foot, deal with minor traffic and crime problems. At the regional level, officers deal with specific problems, have special duties, and handle more complicated cases. Regional unit officers can also cross district boundaries and have equipment that district levels do not have. For example, regional traffic unit can do speed check.

The local police in Hong Kong include districts and divisions. Most police districts have multiple divisions. Yuen Long Police District, for instance, has three divisions. An exception is Mong Kok, which is a single-division district and thus has a greater amount of administrative work. A local police division is usually headed by a divisional commander in the rank of superintendent. Under the divisional commander, there are usually three assistant divisional commanders, in charge of operations, crime, and administration respectively. Subunits, which can be defined as subdivisions or substations, are headed by station sergeants up to senior inspectors. I visited one of the police divisions in Kowloon East, which offers a glimpse of the structure of a local police division in Hong Kong. The Divisional Commander, who was in the rank of chief superintendent, had been in that position for eleven months. There were two branches in the Division, the Uniformed Branch and the Crime Branch. There was a total of 166 officers in the Uniformed Branch, including 2 chief inspectors, 7 senior inspectors and inspectors, 11 senior sergeants, 26 sergeants, and 120 police constables. The Crime Branch has a total of 40 officers including 1 chief inspector, 5 senior inspectors and inspectors, 5 sergeants, and 29 police constables. The Uniformed and Crime Branches at the divisional level are the beginning points of every police officer's service in Hong Kong. The police practice a rotation policy that requires all officers at all levels to transfer to different units regularly as a way to broaden their experience and increase the variety of their responsibilities. As a senior and a mid-ranking officer stated:

> Everybody goes into Uniform at the beginning. A PC [police constable] can move into a Crime Investigative Unit. We balance command and control and try to move officers back and forth between Uniform and Investigative Units. Once moved up to superintendents, they become largely administrative and managerial. Moving from Crime to Uniform may be viewed as a demotion as Crime Unit members view them as elites. But we are a large force. There are many opportunities. There are no threats.

> We used to copy British procedures. Now we have to have our own. We rely on generalists. We can go anywhere and take up the jobs. We have multiple skills. It has been like this since the colonial period. I go to all kinds of places without prior training. I was told I was a prosecutor; then I was a prosecutor. . . . Technological crime unit officers, Bomb officers don't rotate. They are the exceptions.

The local police structure reflects both a hierarchical relationship with the top echelons of the Force and a relative autonomy in decision-making at the local level. The Police Headquarters and regions provide general responsibilities and expectations to the local units, but a division can set its priorities in response to local conditions. An example of the local command discretion is a minor change in the shift work system: there used to be three shifts, ABC, and now there are four shifts, ABCD, in some areas where D shift covers any task assigned by a divisional commander. As some senior officers explained:

> On a daily basis, a divisional commander looks at the problems in his area and region and makes appropriate decisions. . . . At higher level, every other year, we have "away day;" we go away for a day or two, look at challenges at a more strategic level.

> Each divisional commander is responsible for both Uniform and CID. The Uniformed Branch maintains visibility; CID investigates crimes. Divisional commanders have discretion as to how to use resources. . . . Commanders are evaluated not purely on crime statistics. It's one factor. Local characteristics, building structures, demographics, officers themselves committed or not . . . are all looked at.

> It's mainly territorial policing: Divisional level deals with various problems according to local conditions. Different divisions may have different problems to deal with. Central Division's main responsibility, for example, is public order now because of the Right of Abode demonstrations. Then if you go to Kowloon City Division, the main responsibility becomes crime prevention, police visibility, traffic safety, etc. Divisional commanders determine their priorities. One is given the territory and deals with its priorities. He knows best

the problems in his area. He knows the local conditions. . . . As a divisional commander, if I need help, I can go to the district command.

Police Operations

The Hong Kong Police management has laid out clearly several operational priorities of the Force that cover uniform patrol, emergency response, use of technology, crime, and public relation. These priorities require that the police maintain a strong visible uniform presence; provide fast, effective response to emergencies and major incidents; use new technology, knowledge and equipment to enhance operational efficiency; strengthen the effectiveness of the criminal intelligence system; enlist public assistance and support in the fight against crime; and enhance the fight against cross-border crime and exchange police expertise through close and effective liaison with mainland and overseas law enforcement agencies. The police management has also determined three priorities of its own that cover technology, quality service, and human resources. First, it would emphasize application of new advances in technology to enhance management efficiency, improve communication, and develop knowledge-based management. Second, it would strive to provide quality service by improving customer service and facilities at police stations, reinforcing the service culture in the Force, and enhancing professionalism in all police dealings with the public. Third, it would endeavor to identify human resource issues in order to improve the standards of recruits, provide strategic and comprehensive staff training, promote a healthy lifestyle, and motivate and reward staff for their commitment and dedication. In the following, several major operations and related police policies are examined including emergency response, crime prevention, public order management, and the Service Quality Initiatives.

Emergency Response

Emergency response activities are directed by three Command and Control Centers in Hong Kong covering all six police regions. The Command and Control Centers are where emergency calls are received and officers are dispatched. Besides activities related to responding to emergency calls, these centers also have a strong police command presence. The ranking of these centers parallels that of the Regional Command. The Hong Kong Island Command and Control Center, for example, is part of a territory-wide police command system. This system is monitored via computer link at Headquarters Command and Control Center. The Center also plays an important role in coordinating the activities of patrol officers and specialists, who often request assistance from each other. Each Command and Control Center follows a two-tier system of operation: the Lower Command handles day-to-day, mostly routine matters, and the Higher Command, also called the Executive Facility, allows the Regional Police Commander to take over public disorders and incidents or disasters from the Lower Command (Briefing Note for Regional Command and Control Center HKI, 1999). In addition, the Police Headquarters can take over the most serious public disorders or disasters in the most unusual circumstances.

I visited the Hong Kong Island Command and Control Center in a Spring day in 2002. There are four superintendents who staff three shifts at the Center; each is in charge of the whole Center during the shift. There are four teams at the Center; each has twenty-eight civilians including six Operators and two Senior Police Communication Officers (SPCO). Each team also has an inspector, a sergeant, a police constable, and an additional relieving constable who works from 9 am to 5 pm. The total number of staff on each team is thirty-three. There is also a separate Traffic Team with its own three shifts; A and B shifts are staffed with two sergeants and C shift has one sergeant. There are altogether about 136 employees working at the Hong Kong Island Command and Control Center.

The Hong Kong police handle about three million 999 calls per year. Eighty -five percent of these are non-emergencies. In the Hong Kong Island Region, 999 yearly statistics from 1998 to 2001 indicates that although the number of

Table 4.2 Emergency 999 Calls in Hong Kong Island 1998-2000

Year	Number of calls	Number Requiring Response	Percent Requiring No Response
1998	679, 978	135,815	80.81%
1999	879,743	129,408	85.29%
2000	945,065	121,205	87.17%
2001	1067,494	125,679	88.23%

Source: Adapted from call statistics provided by the Hong Kong Island Command and Control Center.

calls had increased steadily, the number of incidents requiring police response had been relatively stable. In the meantime, the percentage of calls requiring no police response had increased from 81% to about 88% over the four year period (see Table 4.2). Most of the calls the police do not respond to are nuisance calls, which are differentiated from real emergencies calls. As a team supervisor stated:

> We have many dispute cases, domestic disputes, shop disputes, loss, misunder-standing, nuisance calls, inquiries, mistakes, alarms, burglary alarms, and false alarms. Alarms are classified into alarm 1 and alarm 2; alarm 2 covers alarms that are not real. Repeated false alarms are put in records. There are no fines for false alarms. The Divisional level determines if the alarm is genuine, by either sending a car or a foot patrol constable. Calls are classified into emergency and non-emergency cases. There are about 1000 emergencies per month. They handle about 350 incidents daily out of 2000 calls per day. Seventy-five percent are nuisance calls. Many sick person and accidental injury calls. If a person collapses, the call would be considered an emergency; otherwise, the caller is referred to ambulance.

We have false calls, abuse of 999 calls. We respond to most calls. . . . We don't have overload of calls on police constables on a regular day. We have enough officers to handle emergency calls unless there are major disasters. . . . All emergency calls are responded to. Fire, crime, accidents, etc., are responded to. Medical and Fire Departments handle calls differently. . . . We are doing a pilot scheme; sometimes we don't need to send an officer. The Fire Department can handle fire to save resources. . . . Eighty percent of 999 calls are nuisance, non-emergency calls. If it's real emergency, EU is dispatched. Whether an officer is sent depends on the calls. We may send an ambulance. We have lists of things we consider as emergencies or non-emergencies.

On a typical day, the Command and Control Center operates by receiving emergency calls for assistance from the public and dispatches resources to deal with problems. Most requests for assistance come through the 999 system and are received at a rate of about one every eight minutes excluding prank calls which come in abundance. The 999 operator, on receipt of an emergency call, types the information into a computer as an incident. The incident is then electronically routed to the Divisional Console, which deals with the area in which the incident has occurred. At the Divisional Console the Controller has on his or her Command Display Unit a list of manpower available and he or she uses the radio to task appropriate officers to the scene of the incident. An operator copies down phone numbers and reported addresses, and matches them to confirm accuracy of the addresses. On the computer screen can be seen a duty list of officers available, an incident list that has been responded to, and all 999 call records. One area on the screen is reserved for the operator to input the data and another area for tracking and checking status. Operators at the Center work a sixteen-day cycle. For example, one operator works four days on CCCC shifts, takes two days off; then works four days on BBBB shifts, take one day off; and then works four days on AAAA shifts, takes one day off. The schedule may be tough for new operators, but they usually get used to it in about two months. Those who cannot adjust to the schedule normally resign in about a month. Due to good salary and benefits and difficulties in the private economy, most operators stay on the job and many have worked at the Center for more than ten years.

As most functions at the Center are performed by civilians, sworn officers assigned there mainly play the role of a supervisor or manager, monitoring civilian operators' activities, providing solutions and guidance if necessary, and generally making sure that the Center is run smoothly. Officers at different ranks are assigned to the Center on a regular basis. Sergeants are usually assigned to work at the Center for one year and can extend their duty to two years. Inspectors are stationed at the Center for one year and superintendents half a year. While sergeants and inspectors are required to be proficient in using the dispatching system, superintendents do not need to have specific knowledge of it because they provide general advice and deal with major problems only. Superintendents do need to know how to check incidents in the system.

Rapid response is emphasized at the Command and Control Center and on the street. If more than three calls are waiting, the alarm at the Center goes off.

If waiting time reaches twenty seconds, the alarm goes off. Most calls are completed in one minute; some in forty seconds. Most serious calls may take two minutes to complete handling. Response time for street level officers has been written into the performance pledge of the Hong Kong Police. The police pledge to respond to all real emergencies in nine minutes. Foot patrol officers have been able to keep this promise and the Emergency Unit (EU) officers can respond even faster as they are able to arrive at scenes of most incidents in five minutes. Any response time over nine minutes is reviewed as to location, route, and traffic conditions. All emergencies require police response even though many of them turn out to be misunderstandings after the police arrive. As a Center supervisor said:

> Crime reports may be due to misunderstanding. But we still consider them as emergencies. After we respond, we often find out that they are not real emergencies. For example, sometimes persons being reported are not burglars or robbers, but debt collectors who look tall and big. Also we have lots of mentally ill persons; their own families would make the calls as they mostly live with them.

The Divisional Controllers have a variety of resources at their disposal. For minor disputes a patrol officer is usually sent, and for more serious incidents an EU car is dispatched, which is fully equipped to attend to serious crime in progress. In the Hong Kong Island Region, the EU has been able to arrive, since September 1993 when the performance pledge was announced, on the scene of any incident within four minutes on average. An initial response time of this speed for the first vehicle unit is augmented by the availability of an EU platoon that can be reformed and redeployed within half an hour to the scene of any disaster or disorder.

The EU is a highly efficient and highly trained unit with multiple functions and responsibilities. Although its primary responsibility is to respond to genuine emergency calls such as crime situations and major incidents at the regional level, it also engages in preventive patrol and problem solving. It can function as a quasi-militarized unit and close escape routes. It provides assistance to beat patrol officers where needed with their special skills and equipment. Following statements from two EU officers in Hong Kong Island provide a clear picture of their roles and responsibilities.

> There are eight police vans used in the four districts and one command car and one canine car. Each car has five officers, the commander, the driver, and three officers. The canine car has two officers. The eight cars cover the four districts. We carry different weapons from the beat constables: beat constables have revolvers; we have long-barrel rifles and shotguns. At any one time, we have four cars running in the Region. At the end of our shift, four cars will be in and another four cars will be out. So not all eight cars work at the same time. Officers work eight hours and forty-five minutes per shift. We handle 999 calls. When we don't have 999 calls, we do proactive patrol and be visible. We do preventative patrol in high risk areas.

We have just under 200 officers in EU in Hong Kong Island. We have three shifts, ABC. All units come back to the station to change over and turn in their equipment for the next shift. Officers work eight hours forty-five minutes per day and six days a week. They have one day off. Every two weeks, they have two days off. So on average, they work ninety-six hours every two weeks or forty-eight hours per week. This has been reduced from the previous fifty-one hours a week. If officers work overtime, they are not paid with money but will get off time. All officer schedules are planned one year ahead of time.

We are a regional unit, deployed to do emergency response to 999 calls. There are five land regions in Hong Kong so there are five Emergency Units. We have about 10,000 999 calls in Hong Kong Island last year. About 10%, or 1,000 of these calls are real emergencies. Real emergencies are defined as burglar alarms, burglaries, fighting, suspicious persons, robberies, thefts, etc. Eighty percent of these 1,000 calls, or 800 are handled by EU. That's about 66 emergencies per month in Hong Kong Island. We emphasize quick response. The regular beat patrol officers are able to respond within nine minutes. We can respond in five minutes.

One incident may require more than one car. Cars from other regions may be brought in to assist if needed. The Regional Command and Control Center dispatches the EU cars through the Computer-Assisted Dispatching System (CAD). The emergency information would come up on a screen and the computer knows automatically which car is closest to the emergency and the car is dispatched automatically. The Command and Control Center decides which calls go to the EU and which go to the beat patrol officers. The eight cars are numbered in a certain way so we know which district they are from. For example, we have Car 7 and Car 3 in one district. We have emergency equipment and bullet-resistance vests, army helmet, first-aid kit, life-saving equipment, snap-checking equipment. . . . We can close some escape routes. We have MP5, semi-automatic, revolvers, and anti-crime weapons.

We have 10 to 50 calls per shift depending on the day and situation. Each of the four districts has unique characteristics. Assaults, crimes, illegal immigrants, etc. We analyze the problems and we may deploy our cars to deal with different problems each week. We may focus in one area overnight. We do mobifix: stop at a fixed spots and patrol on foot. We do car-park checks, talk to watchmen, close the gates. When we are not busy, we support front-line officers. Since 1980, the time I joined the Force, high visibility has been our policy. We try to be visible as much as possible.

We have plans in place for different problems. We can put in lots of manpower to deal with a particular situation if needed. We can help the beat officers where they need the special skills and equipment. We are better trained in firearm, we have tactical training. We use bullet-resistance vests when dealing with incidents. We handle dangerous domestic calls. We work in teams, five officers on a car. One is in plain clothes; but he is not a detective, he is a uniformed officer in plain clothes. Sometimes we send our plain-clothed officer in a place first to see if there is any problem and we follow closely after him.

Crime Prevention

Crime prevention is a major operation emphasized at all levels in the Hong Kong Police from the Headquarters to the frontline. At the Force level, the Crime Prevention Bureau plays a significant role in educating the public about crime prevention. Officers from the Bureau promote the concept of crime prevention with both business premises and individual residences. They identify premises that are vulnerable to criminal attack and provide specific advice to their owners for target hardening. They offer this service to a broad range of government, commercial and residential premises. They also liaise for this purpose with various professional bodies representing the banking, hotel, jewelry, property development, insurance, security, motor vehicle, and property management sectors. The Bureau has continued to help refine the provisions of the Security and Guarding Services Ordinance and conducted annual inspections of licensed security companies to ensure that the quality standards imposed upon the industry are maintained. In addition, they have made advances in such areas as architectural liaison and computer security. For individual residences, the Bureau has provided education to the public about domestic security and juvenile victimization through its Crime Prevention Bus and the "Robotcop" (Hong Kong Police Review, 1997).

The Police Public Relations Bureau (PPRB) plays the role of a coordinator at the Force level for community crime prevention activities. The PPRB and Radio Television Hong Kong jointly produce two weekly television programs, namely Police Report and Police Magazine, on police-related subjects and a daily radio peak-hour traffic report program for the public. The PPRB also liaises with television, film companies, and police districts and provide assistance in producing police-related documentary series (Hong Kong Police Review, 1997). Under the PPRB, there are Police Community Relations Officers and Neighborhood Police Coordinators at the district and divisional level who regularly liaise with local schools and local community and administrative bodies such as Mutual Aid Committees, Area Committees, District Councils, District Fight Crime Committees, and Kai Fong Associations to explain police policies and priorities and to prevent crime.

At the street level, uniformed foot patrol officers, plain-clothes crime unit officers, and special unit officers such as Vice, EU, PTU, and Traffic all maximize their presence on the street. Technologies such as CCTV and situational crime prevention techniques as well as police intelligence are all utilized to contribute to crime prevention. Police officers interviewed unanimously agree that maintaining high visibility is a top priority of the Hong Kong Police. Besides walking the beat and being visible, officers routinely conduct ID check and stop-and-search for crime prevention purposes. As an officer stated:

> One of the traditional practices is having police constables walk the beat. Visibility is an effective crime prevention measure. Being highly visible is a goal in itself. The police are also given wide power and authority such as stop-and-search. The power to stop and search makes the police very effective.

The Hong Kong Police also runs various youth programs for crime prevention purposes. The largest of such programs is called the Junior Police Call (JPC) scheme, which serves as a bridge between the police and young persons to help the latter develop into healthy and responsible citizens. Apart from participation in crime prevention activities, JPC members are provided with a wide range of sports, recreational, and educational programs. The police also play an important role in treating juvenile offenders to help them reintegrate into the community and prevent them from recidivating. One form of rehabilitation for juvenile offenders developed in recent years involves the use of a shock therapy. Some officers who served in the Special Duties Unit has put together a physically and mentally demanding three-day "shock therapy" camp in which frequent and serious juvenile offenders are thrown together with police officers to complete an exceedingly difficult course. They have been running these camps over the last six years (Smith and Lawley, 2003). Another treatment program is called the Police Superintendent Discretion Scheme. It was put in place when it was recognized that having a juvenile go through the formal court process is harmful to the youngster and may leave him or her with a permanent criminal record. The scheme offers a diversion from the criminal processes by having the juvenile formally cautioned by an officer in the rank of superintendent or above. The scheme is usually applicable to first time offenders below the age of eighteen who must meet a stringent set of criteria before the police superintendent exercises the discretion (Chan, 1998). As Chan (1998:117-118) stated:

> The underlying assumption of the scheme is based on the notion that juveniles, not having the experience and maturity in life, for one reason or another, falls on the wrong side of the law. The society recognizes the hard-core criminals from those who were temporarily led astray through immaturity, lack of self-control and influence of undesirable peer groups and such encounters should not be treated as harshly as would be other adult offenders. . . . Once the juvenile has been cautioned he or she is released without any follow up aftercare, or he/she is referred to the Juvenile Protection Section of the Police Force, or directly or indirectly to a host of rehabilitation programs offered by the Social Welfare Department, the Education Department and the Non-Governmental Organization. . . . The success of the scheme relies primarily upon the behavioral change of the juvenile; he must realize that this scheme and its related program offer him only one opportunity to rebuild his life and to start afresh as if nothing had happened before. This opportunity is a sacred promise the juvenile must keep, and the breaking of it would mean consequences that are irreparable.

Public Order Management

As part of the colonial tradition, the Hong Kong Police has been highly concerned about public order. Historically public order management had been a top priority and it is not until the 1980s that crime and law enforcement were brought to the same level of emphasis. The apparent reason for this accent is the political environment Hong Kong was in. The colonial government feared that mainland China and her huge population could potentially cause great instability in Hong Kong. A significant influx of immigrants, for example, would create serious public disorder and threaten the colony's economy. And Hong Kong, as a small jurisdiction on the southern tip of China, did not have a sufficient military force to defend itself. The police, therefore, "became the state's 'reserve army' to maintain the legal order, to bring the masses into conformity, to protect the capitalist mode of production and to preserve the status quo" (Lo, 1993:105). A para-military capability, which the police regard as essential for public order management, was developed and remains one of the dominant features of the Hong Kong Police. And anti-illegal immigration has become a traditional public order management activity of the Hong Kong Police.

Anti-illegal immigration has taken center stage periodically in Hong Kong policing in history. Due to the high level of influx of illegal immigrants, the 1980 Immigration (Amendment) (No. 2) Ordinance was passed after consultation with the United Kingdom and China, which abolished the previous reach base policy that allowed those illegal immigrants (IIs) who reached the central part of Hong Kong to stay (Chen, 1988). This 1980 ordinance streamlined procedures for repatriation; required all persons aged 15 or over to carry their ID card or other proof of identity at all times and to produce it to the police on request; required employers to inspect the ID cards of employees and introduced a related offense, that of employing a person without a relevant identity document, which carried a maximum penalty of HK$50,000 fine or one year's imprisonment or both; and required in addition the production of an ID card for all transactions with government departments (except emergency services). These measures made illegal immigrants "vulnerable to detection at police checkpoints set up on a random basis throughout the territory," denied public services to illegal immigrants, and "had an immediate impact on the numbers of illegal immigrants arrested and repatriated" (Vagg, 1993:363).

Vagg (1993) also observed that the measures put in place for fighting illegal immigration has affected the population as a whole and had larger political implications. Hong Kong residents have been required to possess the ID cards since 1949 and to carry them at all times since 1980.

> Over a period of some 40 years, Hong Kong has gradually become a more vig-
> orously policed society. . . . Such cards and, more particularly, random ID
> checks on the streets have been claimed to help the police in apprehending
> wanted persons in addition to detecting illegal immigration, although there
> have been periodic arguments about the wider implications of such policing
> practices (Vagg, 1993:366-367).

The wider political ramifications can be seen in the "stop-go" government policy responses to illegal immigration in Hong Kong, a flip-flop between treating this problem as a social control issue and as a political issue (Vagg, 1993:369). The police therefore have been stringent in some periods in controlling population increase and restrained in others due to "foreign policy concerns" and "feasibility of repatriation" (Vagg, 1993:370). As a senior police officer stated: "Politics drove police emphasis on public order management."

Hong Kong is now a sovereign part of China. Continuing to treat Chinese citizens as illegal immigrants may sound illogical. But, due to "the one-country, two systems" formula, there has been no change in the Hong Kong Police in its anti-illegal immigration operations. As a matter of fact, the Hong Kong Police and the mainland Public Security Bureaus have improved their cooperation in this area after the handover due to the Chinese government's policy to keep Hong Kong a separate administrative region. The Hong Kong Police and the Guangdong Border Defense Bureau now hold joint anti-illegal immigrant operations regularly. Officials from both sides meet monthly to exchange anti-II intelligence and tactics. The Hong Kong Police deploys an average of 2,662 police officers per day in tackling illegal immigration (Hong Kong Police Review, 1997) besides the regular beat patrol officers who conduct random stop-and-search activities that target IIs. According to the police, most of the IIs come to Hong Kong to seek employment, mainly as construction workers or casual laborers. Some, especially those from Northern provinces of China, appear to be more prone to committing crime owing to language barriers and difficulties in finding jobs. It is estimated on the basis of current police statistics that the police make about fifty arrests of IIs per day, which is significantly lower than previous years. The police credit their increased cooperation with the mainland to the downward trend in illegal immigration, which has been occurring at an annual rate of 15% since 1993. The year of transition showed an even more marked decrease of about 23% when compared with 1996 down from 23,180 to 17,819 arrests of IIs (Hong Kong Police Review, 1997).

An important measure of the current emphasis of the Hong Kong Police on public order management is the policy that every officer must serve in the Police Tactical Unit (PTU), a unit charged with the general responsibility to maintain public order. As a senior superintendent stated:

> The career pattern goes like this: street police constables go to the PTU and then to EU or Traffic. So all EU officers have served in PTU. Every police constable has the chance to go to the PTU at least twice. All sergeants and in-spectors go there once. I have been to the PTU and EU once as an inspector and now I have been back to PTU and EU as a superintendent.

The PTU companies are often deployed in operations dealing with large numbers of people. They maintain the cordon and venue security during major ceremonies and perform crowd control during key public events. For example, in 1997, PTU maintained the cordon and venue security during the handover ceremony, protected the venue of the World Bank/International Monetary Fund annual meeting, and performed crowd control during the opening of the Tsing Ma Bridge and firework displays (Hong Kong Police Review, 1997). Officers from the PTU Companies are also committed to assisting the Correctional Services Department in case of prison riots and have been involved in various anti-illegal immigration operations. The training for PTU officers concentrates on teaching the concepts of internal security, anti-crime, and crowd control.

The importance of the PTU has become more pronounced due to frequent public demonstrations in recent years. Every year thousands of people turn out for the candlelight vigil to mark the anniversary of the Tiananmen student democracy movement (Starr, 2001). Two major demonstrations in recent years are the Right-of-Abode protests and the anti-National Security Law gatherings. The Right-of-Abode issue originated from a court case in early 1999 involving four mainland Chinese citizens whose parents are from Hong Kong and who sought Hong Kong citizenship according to a provision in the Hong Kong Basic Law, which states that children of Hong Kong citizens born outside Hong Kong have the rights of Hong Kong citizens. The Hong Kong Court of Final Appeal ruled in their favor. But the Chinese government called the decision "a mistake [that] should be rectified" (Starr, 2001:270). The Chinese position was that the National People's Congress (the NPC) has the sole authority to interpret the Basic Law. The Hong Kong Government agreed with the Central Government on this matter, citing a figure of 1.67 million Chinese citizens who are children of Hong Kong parents and who could take up residence in Hong Kong, and petitioned to the NPC to reverse the Court's decision. The Court eventually acknowledged the final authority of the NPC to interpret the Basic Law and reversed its decision. Although the reversal met with the approval of most Hong Kong people, "opponents criticized it as setting a dangerous precedent with respect to the independence of the Hong Kong judicial system" (Starr, 2001:271) and sparked a series of public protests.

These public demonstrations have resulted in many arrests and controversial police actions. For example, on May 24, 2002, the police arrested eight abode right seekers after two hundred protesters besieged the car of the former Secretary for Security, Regina Ip, for about an hour outside the Legislative Council. More than two hundred officers participated in this operation, where ninety of them were shield carrying. The public and protestors later criticized the police for inefficiency and illegal banning of protest. On the day after on May 25, more than 300 police and immigration officers removed fifty sit-in protesters in Chater Garden, a small square described by the media as a grave-yard of broken dreams on that day (Lau, 2002). Police Commissioner Tsang Yam-pui said that officers decided to clear abode seekers from the area because emotions were running high and there was a risk of further unrest (Lee and Lau, 2002; Lau, 2002). In addition, two reporters were handcuffed during this operation for crossing the police line. The public and the media accused the police of using excessive manpower and force in this removal operation and criticized them for interference with freedom of press (*Apple Daily*, 2002; *Hong Kong iMail*, 2002; *Ming Pao*, 2002; and *Oriental Daily*, 2002).

Such controversies and criticisms have not changed the priority accorded to public order management and the police belief in their mission to maintain a stable and secure society. As a matter of fact, due to the more frequent demonstrations, Hong Kong residents are now required to provide advance notice and seek prior approval from the police before engaging in street demonstrations that involve a large number of people. The Hong Kong Police has put greater emphasis on this aspect of police work evidenced by more collaboration and coordination in this area. Some programs such as the EU also function as an intentional overlap to provide better resources for public order management.

This does not mean, however, that the police have become more heavy-handed in managing public order. As some mid-ranking and senor officers stated:

> There were few demonstrations in earlier days. They were taken very seriously and restricted. Now there are demonstrations almost weekly and people have become desensitized by them.

> If there is a demonstration, every unit is involved. Public order used to be handled by the Uniformed Branch at the district level only. This changed in 1996 because public order was taken more seriously. So in public order management, many units work together. I wouldn't say we are more heavy-handed; we just take it more seriously. We have actually become more tolerant because we got more complaints and the police managers have to answer all the complaints.

> We have lots of teamwork, as we work with drug units, traffic units, and crime units as well as the regular beat patrol. Road network must be clear to allow the EU to function. We maintain readiness for major incidents like typhoons, rioting, gangs, violent protests. The Police Tactical Unit also supports anti-crime activities. Each region has one PTU. They work in groups of two to four officers. They handle public order problems such as protests and demonstrations. They have an internal security function. Hong Kong media tends to report staged protests. Some groups simply want to get their message out, get on the newspapers, get on CNN. PTU and local police handle lots of situations like that. PTU has special skills, like sweeping the hill for crime evidence, that the local police cannot do.

> Emergency Unit is one of the old hangovers in the Hong Kong Police Force. Officers in Emergency Unit operate in vehicles. The purpose is to mobilize or gather a riot unit quickly. They are not part of the Uniformed Patrol or Tactical Unit. It is an intentional overlap. In some ways, their duties have been minimized in recent years. Historically, the reason for the Unit is that the Force did not believe they could rely totally on local officers to deal with major problems. So officers were recruited from Pakistan, India, Shandong, anywhere outside Hong Kong, to form the Emergency Units. This practice continued until the 1980's.

The Hong Kong public also ranks public order management as a core police service and has given high marks to the police for this activity. In the 1999 Public Opinion Survey, for example, maintaining public order stood out as the most frequently mentioned area of service, taking up 25% of all responses and topping the list with 35% of those interviewed ranking it their most concerned service. Most respondents (74%) were also satisfied with crowd management in comparison to only 35% that were satisfied with community relations (University of Hong Kong, 1999). In the 2001 Public Opinion Survey, the public continued to maintain high confidence (73%) in the Force and gave positive evaluations on the police performances in maintaining law and order (73%) and public order (71%). Maintaining law and order and maintaining public order were also ranked as two of the most important policing areas (University of Hong Kong, 2002a).

The Service Quality Initiatives

As emergency response, crime prevention, and public order management represent major police operations on a routine basis at the street level, the Service Quality Initiatives mark the most significant effort of the police management in building a service culture in the Force. The Service Quality Initiatives, spearheaded by the Service Quality Wing (SQW), involve providing training, workshops, and seminars to the entire Force aimed at building a new character in the Hong Kong Police and raising the standard of service to the public. A serious commitment to these goals is demonstrated by a worship entitled Living-the-Values that has been provided to all members of the Force three times. Officers at all levels and units are expected to be more service-oriented, treat the public as their customers, provide high quality service, and raise the public's satisfaction level. A force that cares is the theme of policing in Hong Kong today. Images of officers rescuing people from drowning, protecting the animals, holding hands of children to find their way home, attending to the sick and infirm, etc., are openly advertised in television channels and public posters.

The commitment to serving the people has been vigorously promoted in three areas in particular, i.e., enhancement of the Complaints against Police Office (CAPO), improvement of police report rooms, and public opinion surveys. Key areas identified for the police to work on include working in partnership with the community to prevent crime, providing the public with a high quality of service, improving communications within the Force and with the public, and living the values the police have publicly declared to hold. In 1997, the police made the CAPO investigation of complaints more transparent by installation of audio-visual recording equipment in all CAPO interview rooms. At North Point Police Station, they initiated a project to improve police report rooms and the service they provide to the public. The report rooms at the station and the station itself have become the benchmark for all other report rooms, police stations, and services to the public in the Force (Hong Kong Police Review, 1997).

To identify areas for improvement and measure public and police views of the Hong Kong Police, the Service Quality Wing (SQW) has engaged the MDR (Marketing Decision Research), a private professional consulting agency, and the University of Hong Kong to conduct both external and internal surveys. The Public Opinion Survey is conducted biannually. It is a random telephone survey based on the residential telephone directory, in which 2,400 to 2,700 residents aged 15 or 18 and above were selected. Usually about 1,500 to 2,000 residents agree to participate in the surveys and are eventually interviewed, representing a 65% to 75% response rate. The Customer Satisfaction Survey is also conducted biannually, which solicits opinions from those members of the public who have contacted the police for help. About 800 members of the public who made reports to the police during certain weeks and months of the year are surveyed, representing approximately a 50% response rate. The lower response rate is attributed to no-contacts during the week the telephone interviews are conducted. Discounting the no-contacts, the response rate is as high as 94%. The Staff Opinion Survey is a yearly internal survey of 10% of the Hong Kong Police. A simple random sample is used for selecting all officers in the Force including regular, auxiliary, and civilian staff but excluding officers at the Senior Directorate level/Commissioner rank. Over 90% of the selected officers complete the questionnaires for analysis. As in all quantitative surveys, the type of questions asked, the way the questions are worded, and the way the question-naires are structured may all influence how respondents expressed their opinions in these surveys. Certain questionnaire items, for example, seem to generate consistently positive responses while others negative scores. The following presentation of these survey findings, therefore, should be interpreted with caution.

In the 1999 Public Opinion Survey, only 23% of the respondents considered the police to be of high transparency and 34% commented the police to be of high accountability. Perception of reporting facilities, integrity, and performance in crime prevention and detection received relatively low scores in most of the years surveyed. However, the 1997, 1999, and 2001 Public Opinion Surveys indicate that a majority of respondents (79%, 78%, and 84%) felt a strong sense of safety living in Hong Kong at least during day time. Most regarded the police to be efficient and professional in 1999. And respondents held high regard in terms of their confidence in the police (74% and 73%) although their rating of overall police performance was a little lower in 1997, 1999, and 2001. As for service quality, the public considered manners of police officers, stand against corruption, professionalism, conduct, and discipline as the most important service attributes (see Table 4.3).

In the 1997 and 2000 Customer Satisfaction Survey, a majority of respon-dents (87% and 85%) that had called 999 to contact the police considered that the standard of service provided by the central 999 console was good. Most of the respondents (74% and 70%) who called police stations considered that the service provided by the police stations was good. Of those who reported their cases in person at police report rooms, 70% and 74% thought that the service at the report room was good. Among those who contacted crime offices, the majority (81% and 74%) rated the standard of service as good. Satisfaction with police at the scene was also high, at 78% and 88% for the two years. Satisfaction with police follow-up communication regarding case progress, however, was rather low, at 56% and 33%. Taking into consideration all the contacts respon-dents made with the police, most (72% and 76%) of them considered the police standard of service good (see Table 4.4).

The Staff Opinion Survey is conducted to gauge officers' perceptions of the Force. The majority of officers participating in the 1999 and 2000 survey believe in the Force vision, but a much lower percentage share the Force values (see Table 4.5). Only 54% and 61% believe that the Force did a good job in demonstrating these values in 2000 and 2001. The 1999 and 2000 Staff Opinion Survey also indicate that 77% and 75% could cope with stress on the job, but a lower percentage were satisfied with their workload and job or had a sense of fulfillment. Many officers believed that they could keep up with or were prepared for the changes; but over 59% felt that there were too many changes and the pace of change was too fast. In terms of training, most officers expressed

Table 4.3 Public Opinion Survey of the Hong Kong Police

	1995	1997	1999	2001
Transparency	—	—	23%	—
Accountability	—	4.2	34%	—
Perception of reporting facilities	5.1	4.7(53%)	—	—
Integrity	4.3	4.7(53%)	—	—
Performance in prevention/detection	4.7	4.7(53%)	49%	52%
Sense of safety	—	5.2(79%)	78%	84%
Quality of the Force/police officers	—	4.8(62%)	—	—
Public order maintenance	5.3	5.0(66%)	69%	71%
Discipline	4.8	5.0(66%)	63%	—
Efficiency	—	—	70%	—
Professionalism	—	4.8	73%	—
Overall confidence	—	4.8(74%)	73%	73%
Overall performance	5.2	5.1(73%)	62%	66%

Source: Adapted from Opinion Survey on the Quality of Police Services: A Report (MDR, 1997); 1999 Public Opinion Survey HKPF: Full Report (University of Hong Kong, 1999); and Key Findings: 2001 Public Opinion Survey (University of Hong Kong, 2002a). "__" indicates items or statistics not available. Where a number is used, it indicates a mean score on a scale from 1 to 7.

Table 4.4 Customer Satisfaction Survey of the Hong Kong Police

	1997	2000
Dialing 999	87%	85%
Calling police station	74%	70%
Visiting report room	70%	74%
Visiting crime office	81%	74%
Contact at the scene	78%	88%
Contact with traffic unit	77%	—
Follow-up communication	56%	33%
Overall satisfaction	72%	76%

Source: Adapted from Customer Satisfaction Survey for the Royal Hong Kong Police (MDR, 1997) and Customer Satisfaction Survey 2000 (University of Hong Kong, 2001a).

the need for computer, operational, language, and managerial training, and less than 50% were satisfied with training in general. In terms of priorities, the officers rated handling emergencies and maintaining public order consistently higher than crime and community relations in the three years from 1999 to 2001.

Table 4.5 Internal Staff Opinion Surveys of the Hong Kong Police

	1998	1999	2000	2001
Belief in Force vision	—	82%	88%	—
Demonstrating Force values	—	—	54%	61%
Sharing Force values	—	68%	61%	—
Cope with stress	—	77%	75%	—
Satisfied with workload	—	66%	62%	—
Satisfied with job	4.2	70%	59%	69%
Sense of accomplishment	—	61%	53%	—
Keeping up with changes	—	90%	76%	—
Prepared to change	—	72%	67%	—
Too many changes	—	58%	69%	58%
Pace of change too fast	—	50%	60%	50%
Need for computer skills	—	92%	91%	—
Need for operational skills	—	91%	87%	—
Need for language skills	—	84%	84%	—
Need for managerial skills	—	86%	81%	—
Satisfied with training	3.9	45%	42%	47%
Handling emergencies	—	86%	82%	80%
Maintaining public order	—	74%	74%	77%
Preventing crime	—	61%	58%	66%
Detecting crime	—	60%	58%	66%
Community partnership good/public liaison	—	46%	42%	37%
Overall Force performance	—	64%	64%	76%
Satisfied with leadership	3.9	50%	41%	46%
Satisfied with internal communication	3.4	20%	24%	34%

Source: Adapted from Staff Opinion Survey Results 1998; 1999 Staff Opinion Survey: Final Report; 2000 Staff Opinion Survey; and Key Findings 2001 Staff Opinion Survey (University of Hong Kong, 1998, 1999, 2001b, and 2002b). Measurement is on a scale of 1 to 6 with 6 being the most satisfied.

Sixty-four to 76% agreed that the overall performance of the Force was good. However, less than 50% of the officers were satisfied with police leadership in general and an even lower percentage were satisfied with internal communication.

As a result of the Service Quality Initiatives, the Hong Kong Police have been engaged in a historic change from an authoritarian tradition to a service orientation. The "assembly line" justice of the criminal justice system is widely viewed as an approach of the past. Externally, more emphases have been put on public relations, service quality, and clients as customers. Internally, the police treasure feedback from Force members more and have increased their internal communication at all levels. Divisional commanders, for example, chair the Open Forums with officers under their commands regularly. The police also organize sports activities, team activities, happy hours, etc., to boost morale and reduce rank consciousness. Work-related communication is also emphasized to help officers obtain better information and enhance their performances. An internal communication system, the Police Intranet (the POINT) has been established for this purpose. The POINT covers all types of information about the Hong Kong Police including the Commissioner of Police's Office; Three-Year Strategic Action Plan; Police Manuals and Orders; Departments of Operations, Crime and Security, Personnel and Training, Internal Security, Administration and Finance, and Support; Regions and Districts; Transfers; and Crime Statistics. The POINT is maintained by the e-Police Team of the Information Technology Bureau. Police officers can access the POINT to get help on their work-related problems and enhance their knowledge about police policies and practices. For crime-related questions, for example, officers can go to the Crime Wing Services page, where they can find information about scene of crime, investigations, and special services. A long list of special services is available that officers at all levels can request including organized crime, Triad, terrorist involvement, vehicle crime, drug-related cases, financial crime, debt collection, child abuse, human smuggling, fraud, gambling, case management, finger-print evidence, offender profile, DNA profiling, extradition, deportation, Interpol notices, liaison with other Chinese territories and overseas countries, mutual legal assistance, duty visits outside Hong Kong, statistics, wanted persons, watch list, reward notices, surveillance request, and witness protection.

Some Analysis and Discussion

The Hong Kong Police presents a highly hierarchical and paramilitary structure in which the Police Headquarters is responsible for the overall management and coordination of the regions and districts as well as provision of central operations and support functions. Senior officers at the Headquarters develop territory-wide plans and core police strategies, regional commanders follow the territory-wide plans in developing their own plans, and district and division commanders execute these plans and determine their operational priorities according to their local conditions. Such a structure is similar to what Bayley (1985; 1992) describes as a centralized single police system. Most officers interviewed also see a clear command structure in the Hong Kong Police. As a senior officer stated:

> Our structure is determined by the chain of command and territorial reasons. Every region is autonomous. The Headquarters is responsible for making general policies, providing central command. . . . At the Force level, different departments make policies. For operations, we have a policy department at the Force level.

The Hong Kong Police has four main levels, i.e., the Headquarters, six regions, nineteen districts, and fifty-one divisions, and fourteen ranks. This structure suggests that the Hong Kong Police has a tall and centralized hierarchy. Despite the many reviews and realignments over the years, this basic structure has remained unchanged for several decades. The Hong Kong Police, for example, was expanded in the 1970s and 1980s and different operations came to be managed by different program managers such as Director of Operations, Director of Crime and Security, and Director of Management Services at the senior assistant commissioner level. But the basic structure has stayed largely unchanged and many veteran officers have seen more continuities than changes in the police structure since they joined the Force in the 1980s. The officers also do not see a need to flatten the organizational structure, although some view the district level as either unnecessary or creating inefficiency.

There are two different views of the police structure and related operations among the officers. Some believe that the traditional structure is appropriate and necessary for a large police force, while others consider it bureaucratic and inefficient. Some prefer that the police stay apolitical and thus structurally bureaucratic, while others see a bureaucracy characterized by many rules and procedures as hampering integration and coordination. Regardless which side might be right, a force as large as the Hong Kong Police must decentralize many of its daily operations. The local needs, crimes, and other problems often dictate the organization and operations at the street level. The basic operations are organized at divisional stations to serve the needs of the local population. The decentralized operations, however, must be consistent with the formal organizational structure and follow the directives of the senior command. They remain, therefore, subject to critique by those who believe in higher efficiency and better coordination. The following are some typical comments from senior and mid-ranking officers regarding the police structure.

> Yes, the formal structure is important. A force as large as the Hong Kong Police must have some structure first. Then, needs, problems, crimes, etc. may dictate organization and operations at the district level. . . . The current command structure is a result of police tradition. It would be difficult to eliminate the district level. Police have to change the whole command structure if the district level is eliminated.

> Hong Kong police operations are based on divisional police stations to serve local people, to be close to the people. They are in the community. . . . We are a 24-hour day, highly visible operation. Foot patrol can't be dispatched from the Headquarters. We have 19 districts plus the Airport and the MTR, and 51 divisions. It's difficult to manage divisions without districts. Districts fit in geographical areas. They are similarly aligned with the civil districts, making it easier to coordinate and liaise with local Government districts. Management sees no need to flatten at this point.

> The Force is well structured, very systematic. The problem is that a senior commander can destroy the whole system easily. If he sees a problem down at a far lower level, he can skip the ladder and ruin the chain of command. I had

lunch with a regional commander once. He asked if we had any concerns. If he sees a problem, he can intervene right there; he doesn't have to follow the chain of command. So whether the structure is good depends on the senior commanders. We are well structured, but it doesn't mean it's working. We have many departments; but we are all separated. Integration and coordination are poor.

There are four layers in the Hong Kong Police: Force, regional, district, and division. District should be eliminated. I am not sure why we have it. But I think maybe the top management thinks it's easier for them to manage. Instead of communicating directly with lots of officers, all they need to do is talk to five or six people. Too many layers cause information delay.

The major police operations described in this chapter, i.e., emergency response, crime prevention, public order management, and service to a great extent reflect the professional orientation of the modern police and recent police reforms in many countries throughout the world. Some of these can be regarded as core police activities and tasks required by the police profession and driven by police traditions while others are demanded by a changing society and a community policing movement that has been developing in the international arena over the past few decades. While the Hong Kong Police considers all these areas their priorities, it puts a stronger emphasis on public order management. Such an emphasis can be attributed to a combination of factors such as police tradition and public demand. From an institutional perspective as elaborated in the previous chapter, public order management has not only been institutionalized into the basic goal of the Hong Kong Police, but also has been demanded by its external environment (Jiao, Lau, and Lui, 2005). Consequently, regardless of the real need for public order management, the Hong Kong Police continues to put great emphasis on this aspect of police work.

The Hong Kong police officers hold high pride in their professionalism and crime control capabilities. This orientation should not be understood as equivalent to Wilson (1972:172)'s legalistic style, in which a police officer tends to "handle commonplace situations as if they were matters of law enforcement" and "is expected to take a law enforcement view of his role." But since the 1970's, the legalistic orientation has received increased attention and emphasis in the Hong Kong Police, induced by the need to fight corruption and create a more professionalized force (See Chapter 10). The values inherent in the legalistic style have gradually taken on greater importance in the mindset of individual officers. Many of them indicate that they believe in Western-style law enforcement and political neutrality. They do not favor a social role for the police and they view moral preaching or shaping social development antithetical to the police function. Due to this stronger law enforcement orientation, they tend to focus less on service and community relations with the exception of youth-related programs. Their involvement in the youth and community programs, if any, is strictly for crime prevention purposes. In the youth programs organized by the police, for example, the officers emphasize crime prevention and better understanding of and support for the police. As some senior officers stated:

We are a very professional police force. We hold our heads up with any other police force in the world. We deal with problems other forces can't deal with. Police mirrors the society. It's a "can-do" police force. . . . We do not change the number of arrests because court and prison are overloaded. It's first of all not a major problem. If it is a problem, they should go to the Government to find more resources, not complain to us. We have to enforce the laws.

The Hong Kong Police do not have an overall policy for imposing moral mandate and shaping social development. We don't do any moral preaching. But we have Junior Police Call, youth programs, to bring young people to the police, to have more understanding of the police. So we have less crimes. Not for preaching, not for social development, just for more understanding and more support.

One of the institutional factors impacting on police practices is the crime situation. Because Hong Kong has a very low crime rate (See Chapter 9), the police resources that have to be allocated to crime control including terrorism and organized crime in many Western cities can be put in crime prevention and service-related activities in Hong Kong. At the very least the police administration enjoys greater discretion when it comes to determining what police activities should receive greater emphasis. Consequently there has been a stronger emphasis on community relations in recent years. As some senior officers stated:

The police on the one hand want lawfulness and on the other hand want to reduce fear of the police. They enforce the law and at the same time want to gain public trust. Thus there has been big investment in public relations.

The Hong Kong police prioritize various police functions through consultation with members of the Force. There is an internal mechanism. The question is, to what extent should the public have an impact on these matters? There is a process. . . . What Hong Kong public demands depends on what public is asked. Pressure is usually from the District Councils and Fight Crime Committees. They always want the police to do more, to be more visible, to provide better security, to have more stringent law enforcement.

The service style, according to Wilson (1972:200), is prevalent in communities where "the police take seriously all requests for either law enforcement or order maintenance . . . but are less likely to respond by making an arrest or otherwise imposing formal sanctions. . . . The police intervene frequently but not formally." Wilson further states that this style tends to be found in communities that are homogeneous, middle-class, where values are largely shared and crime is under control, and "the police will be freer to concentrate on managing traffic, regulating juveniles, and providing services." Hong Kong is obviously quite different from the communities Wilson studied and does not have a strong middle class; but it is a relatively homogenous society both in terms of the population and social values and the crime rate is extremely low. The Hong Kong Police also takes both law enforcement and order maintenance seriously. Whether the police are more or less likely to make arrests or impose formal sanctions is difficult to compare, however. There are, to a certain degree, certain elements that exemplify the service style in the Hong Kong Police, especially during the current push for service quality. Openness and trust, customization, continuous improvement, and professionalism are, for example, some of the organizational principles of the Hong Kong Police. Officers are encouraged to use social and communication skills, be courteous and respectful, and engage in life-long learning and development.

Although the Hong Kong Police has invested substantially in the Service Quality Initiatives, the service style as elaborated by Wilson (1972) should not be used to characterize the Force. Service quality is an area that does not fit the traditional police structure and operations and, therefore, remains a challenge for the police management. There seems to be a gap between police management and street officers regarding this aspect of police work. Police management strongly believes that effective policing comes with strong public confidence and genuine reduction in police misbehavior. Significant resources have been allocated for training officers on good behaviors and respect for the public. While the police leadership accepts the dual responsibility for reducing crime and improving service quality, street-level officers tend to find it difficult to reconcile these two aspects of police work in their day-to-day operations. As some officers pointed out, the police must fight crime and enforce the law, but these activities are often incompatible with the concept of service or the customer orientation. As service quality is emphasized, some officers may choose simply to do less to avoid complaints. Even among officers who believe in the importance of service, they still do not see Service Quality Initiatives as a straightforward process. As important as service may be, it is the police that eventually prioritize various police functions within the Force. And it is difficult to determine the extent to which the public should be involved in policing matters. In short, the effort to build a new culture of service and respect remains a challenge due to the fact that this is an area incompatible with the traditional police mandate. The police in other words change when the changes do not conflict with their core values and traditions. Where changes are against their core knowledge and principles, they are less likely to materialize.

The institutional perspective may shed some light on why the Hong Kong Police has only limited success at introducing the Service Quality Initiatives. These initiatives can be interpreted as the manifestation of a police organization's tactic to acquire resources and protect its domain (Mastrofski, Ritti, and Hoffmaster, 1987). In the changing environment of the Hong Kong Police, the police leaders have taken the initiative to make the changes themselves rather than being compelled by their sovereigns to adopt institutional forms and practices antithetical to their core values. Many rank-and-file police officers, however, see the Service Quality Initiatives as cosmetic or illegitimate police work. Some also fear that the strong emphasis placed on service quality would take away their authority and may even cause them to lose legitimacy in the eye of the public (Crank and Langworthy, 1992).

The Hong Kong Police traditions have been institutionalized into some of the basic values, beliefs, goals, and attitudes among the rank-and-file officers.

Their anxieties over the Service Quality Initiatives can be attributed to the institutionalized paramilitary traditions. As described in Chapter 1, the paramilitary traditions of the Hong Kong Police were institutionalized when it was a police force that the colonial regime relied on for public order management. These institutionalized myths have always been influential in later stages of its development. For example, its law enforcement function is characterized by a coercive crime control approach. Its paramilitary rituals and practices continue to undermine the prospect of a service culture. The change of the Hong Kong Police environment from a British colony to a Chinese Special Administrative Region has not had a significant impact in altering these institutionalized values. The only viable approach, it seems, is for the police management to make substantial changes to the contents of the socialization process for individual officers in order to develop the culture of service.

5

The Learning Culture

One of the recent developments in the Hong Kong Police is the cultivation of a learning culture and knowledge-based practice. It is clear from interviews and observations that such a culture and practice is permeating throughout the Force from recruitment and selection, to academy and in-service training, and to police policies at the senior management level. The police believe that the building of this culture must start with recruitment by putting a strong emphasis on higher education. In Hong Kong, applicants for police jobs can apply for both entry and inspector positions: those with a high school diploma usually apply for the constable positions; and those with a college degree can apply for inspector positions directly. Recruitment of these officers from outside the Force is referred to as "open recruitment."

Recruitment and Selection

Police recruitment in Hong Kong is a like a campaign that is carried out continuously throughout the year. The police believe that to maintain the quality of officers, it is crucial to increase the size of the application pool and raise the exposure of the recruitment programs to the public. The Force has a Public Relations Bureau that is actively engaged in publicizing these programs. It makes recruitment announcements on television, radio, and newspapers, and reserves regular TV time for the Hong Kong Police. Mini-career exhibitions, window displays, MTR station posters, and briefs in District Offices are also used to communicate recruitment messages. In addition, recruitment officers organize career talks regularly with youth organizations, at schools, and universities to enhance the chances to meet targeted groups (Chan, 1989).

On a warm Spring afternoon several years ago, several officers from the Hong Kong Police went to a local university to give a recruitment presentation to potentially interested students. They organized this event through the University Career Development Office. About sixty students showed up. A Senior Inspector from Selection and Vetting, the Recruitment Group of the

Hong Kong Police began the presentation by telling the students that the Hong Kong Police was established in 1844 and is one of the oldest police forces in the world. It now has 28,000 uniform sworn officers with thirteen layers in the police hierarchy from the entry constable to the Commissioner. He told the audience that they were recruiting about 30 inspector positions and 570 constable positions for the fiscal year and introduced the types of work these new officers would be expected to do. Their jobs, as he said, typically involve patrol and law enforcement duties at the divisional level, as directed by their supervisors, and a few might be responsible for administrative duties. The Senior Inspector explained that an inspector is usually in charge of a patrol subunit, a vice unit, or a district unit. As there are regional, district, divisional, and subunits, the subunits can be regarded as the most basic unit in the Hong Kong Police.

The students were told that police officers in Hong Kong have a diversified career path and a variety of positions to take. Every four years, police constables change districts for corruption prevention purposes. Every two and a half years, police inspectors change their districts. Due to the variety of police duties and responsibilities, students from all academic disciplines are welcome to apply for the inspector positions. Some students' concern that their university majors may be incompatible to police work is not justified. The more important thing in police work is common sense and the desire to help people. During the talk, a realistic picture of police work was portrayed to dispel some myths the students might believe. As the Inspector said:

> I have been in various posts, dealing with different challenges. If you like different challenges, consider us. Don't just look at the salary. You won't enjoy it if you don't want to be responsible for the society and if you don't enjoy helping people. Interest counts. . . . Our training is strict. We prepare recruits with real personal experiences. . . . There are many routine matters, trivial calls, dull days. I once responded to a call after a man who was cooking soup got locked out and called the police for help. . . . The job is not as dangerous, not as many injuries as in construction, sales.

Short videos were then shown to the students providing them with a visual image of the Hong Kong Police. In one video, officers were shown drilling in the rain, doing tactical exercises, receiving 999 calls, saving a drowning child, patrolling in speedboats, flying helicopters, and making a landing by ropes from helicopters. Another video portrayed a positive image of the Hong Kong Police by airing positive comments from the public about safety in the city despite its crowded street, dense population, high rises, and congested traffic. It also showed certain police activities such as police training, emergency response, traffic control, crime analysis, marine patrol, and helicopter lift. After the videos, information about eligibility, selection, training, and application process was provided.

Generally speaking, all officers are required to be fluent in Cantonese and possess certain Mandarin and English skills. The minimum educational level for all officers has been raised and police job has become more competitive in recent years due to the larger pool of qualified applicants. Although police constables can enter the Force with a high school diploma, police inspectors must have a college degree. While open recruitment is conducted for police constables, both open recruitment and internal promotion are used for inspectors. The official theme of recruitment for them is "to be a leader." Inspectors, as a matter of fact, are depicted as the elites of Hong Kong society during the recruitment process. As some senior police officers said:

> We have higher education requirement. . . . In the past, we often set high education standards and then lowered them because we couldn't find enough qualified applicants. Now we can keep the higher education requirement because we have more qualified applicants. There are several reasons for this. First, there are more universities in Hong Kong, where students can graduate in three years; second, the economy is not good, which makes a police job more attractive; and third, the nature of the job is also attractive. The Force is the only government agency that didn't have an employment freeze.

> We review our recruitment activities annually. Because of fewer vacancies, our recruits' qualities are a lot higher. We are quite satisfied with our new recruits. For 1999-2000, 31% selected were college graduates. Each inspector was selected out of 82 applicants, all inspectors are degree holders, and their average age is 26. Each constable was selected out of 25 applicants, 72% of them are in matriculation and above, and their average age is 22. Overall our recruits now are better educated, older, and more knowledgeable.

> We have anywhere from 700 to 1500 that apply for inspector positions, 8000 apply for police constables per year. But we only have 300 to 500 openings. . . . We try to be open, fair, and impartial. We have selection criteria such as maturity, language proficiency, physical fitness, leadership and management skills, interpersonal skills, common sense, and determination. We don't consider sex, age, and race.

The recruitment program makes no distinction in hiring males and females except in physical tests, which are slightly modified for females. More female applicants have been attracted to police work in recent years. Today about 13% of the officers on the Force are female. Female officers are required for conducting same sex searches. Many female officers have also assumed leadership and management positions. In Hong Kong as elsewhere there has been a long history of differential treatment for female officers before they gain equal status as male officers. They have been armed as male officers since the end of 1994 and early 1995.

The recruitment and selection programs in the Hong Kong Police are reviewed on an annual basis and reflect changes in the field and society. The Police Training School also provides input and assistance in the selection process. Over the years, these activities and related police policies have been significantly improved. Due to the budgetary constraint and fewer vacancies in recent years, however, the Force has cut down the number of Recruitment Centers and focused more on target groups. The following are some typical comments from senior recruitment officers regarding the changes and challenges in recruitment and selection.

> We were first influenced by the military model. We then added human resources, and later academics. We emphasize leadership skills and law. We do a lot of research to develop our recruitment programs. We consider the inherent characters of police officers and create job designs. We aim to have a complete package from selection to recruitment and to end-users. The whole process is affected by supply and demand as we have Form 5 and matriculated levels of education requirement.

> Our challenge is retention when economy improves. We aim to retain people in high technology and information technology areas. Another challenge is related to Equal Employment Opportunity policy, disability discrimination. . . . Height and weight are considered discrimination. Our current policy is that we do not hire applicants who have family members with mental illness. A case of this nature is pending in court. We also need to do more outreach in our recruitment activities, with focus on targeted audience. At present 40% to 60% of the applicants do not meet our minimum requirement. We need to target the right people.

Police Training School

The Police Training School of the Hong Kong Police is located in Aberdeen, Hong Kong Island, adjacent to Ocean Park. Green pastures spread over the hilltops surrounding the School, projecting a sense of peace in a picturesque setting. This is where police constables and inspectors selected from open recruitment receive their basic training. Police constables receive 27 weeks of training in Chinese in a program called Recruit Police Constable (RPC) course and inspectors receive 36 weeks of training in English in a Police Inspector (PI) course. Male and female officers are put at par with each other and receive the same training. The training is stringent. Those who cannot make it usually leave in the first three or four days and overall about 4-8% drop out during training. In the process as well as in recruitment, the police look for career-minded people committed to the police profession, and seek to screen out those that are not.

The Basic Training Courses are given to new police recruits at the early stage of their career including law and procedures, practical exercises, police tactics, weaponry, foot drill, parade, physical agility, first aid, public order, personal development, etc. A balanced approach is used in covering subjects related to crime prevention and crime control, detailed instructions are provided on how to follow Police Orders and Procedures, and appropriate materials are covered regarding officer discretion and stress. As some police instructors stated:

> Crime prevention in its broader sense is preventive policing and this is done by every police officer who is engaged in patrol and anti-crime operations. Both crime prevention and crime control are included in the basic training materials. There is no conscious emphasis on either one aspect at the expense of the other

from the training perspective. . . . Basic training focuses on crime prevention; some elements are on crime control, involving both proactive and reactive components in a beat policing project. One of our training objectives is to teach the recruits how to apply Police Orders and Procedures to the work of police officers. Insofar as these concepts have been included in the Police Orders and Procedures, they will appear in the relevant training syllabi.

Traffic courses cover discretion. It's difficult to discuss it in basic training because new recruits don't have any experience, yet. Selective traffic enforcement involves warnings and different phases of enforcement. There are established procedures in respect to discretion and conflict. For possible conflict between the police officer and the public, trainees are taught to apply the principles of professionalism, compassion, dedications to quality service, continuous improvements, and being responsive to changes as stated in the Force Values. They are also taught to apply interpersonal and communications skills to management of the conflicts. In the basic training courses, such procedures and dealings with the public are taught by instructors and reinforced through experiential learning, namely, practical exercises.

To assist recruits in dealing with stress, lectures on stress management have been designed in conjunction with the Police Clinical Psychologist and are taught to every one of them in basic training. Stress management subjects and conflict management have become the latest developed subjects to train officers in exercising discretions and handling conflicts.

New subjects such as the Bill of Rights, equal opportunity, anti-discrimination, and communicating with the press have also been introduced at the Police Training School following new legislations and policies. Instructors make sure that all recruits understand the importance of following these new laws and policies. Since law enforcement has been a strong and traditional emphasis in police training, the School emphasizes the apolitical nature of police practices and the rule of law principle. The following statement by a police instructor demonstrates how the training program has responded to the new development.

Scrutiny by media and elected politicians is a normal phenomenon in a democratic society. The Force is apolitical and respects "civil right," "freedom of expression", and "freedom of press," and will balance the rights of others as well. . . . Police training addresses Bill of Rights, rule of law, media, what you can and cannot do with the media. Rule of law is one of our common purposes. Law overrides tradition. Once the law is passed, police follow. We obey the law and we respect the spirit of the legislation and we do everything to facilitate. . . . Since the Bill of Rights was passed, all police officers had been trained to observe the legislation and the changes that had been brought forth by it. We all understand the Bill of Rights is above all general law enforcement practice. One immediate result is the addition of the topic in the Basic Training Syllabi. Insofar as the Bill of Rights has been included in the Police Orders and Procedures, it will appear throughout the syllabi. Law and practices will cease if they are not in line with the Bills of Rights. Standards of proof, conviction, assumption of guilt, all have to change, making the police more professional.

Integrity and other Force values have received greater emphasis as part of the Basic Training in recent years. Apart from specific lectures devoted to discussion of Force values, police instructors instill these values in daily activities throughout the training programs. The Recruit Police Constable (RPC) syllabus has been reviewed and redesigned to reflect the common purpose and changing needs of the Force and the community (Clarence Ki-yun Tang, 1998), and to incorporate the principles of Force values and service quality. The new RPC syllabus is designed also to provide recruits with a foundation to build their career, to establish a training continuum, foster the concept of career and a sense of dedication, and develop a learning culture starting from recruit training. Although these concepts are similar in a way to the idea of ethics, the term "police ethics" remains rarely used in basic police training and is often understood in the context of rule of law. Following are some of the comments made by police instructors regarding these recent changes.

> We train police officers to view police career as a high calling, a respectable way of life. . . . In the C and P Division, we run three types of courses, namely, Promotion, Development, and Traffic courses. All these courses have been held traditionally to enhance police officers in carrying out their duties. Ethical and integrity training are not taught as separate lessons. They are being repeatedly brought forward to trainees through all relevant scenarios and topics. In the C and P Division, there are numerous occasions that these are being emphasized, such as ICAC guest lectures, discussions on police indebtedness, management and supervisory accountability, etc.

> Police oaths and values are reinforced in all modules since day one. Vision statement, common purpose, and values define the role and character of police and are reinforced during practice. The vision statement is a result of two years' consultation with the entire Force. . . . In police training, rule of law receives greater emphasis, not rule by ethics. Rule by ethics is not a common term used in the Force. Rule of law is considered the most important principle and police ethics should also place the rule of law as the bottom line of every consideration.

> They should develop the appropriate attitudes demonstrated by observable behaviors, correct skills, and up-to-date knowledge (ASK) necessary for their duties and responsibilities in the first two years of their service. They are expected to fulfill the Force Common Purpose and live up with the Force Values. They can use the Basic Training they received as a foundation for career development.

> We train police officer in accordance to our Mission Statement. Ethics is not taught to new recruits. Integrity and other Force values are continually reinforced in the Basic Training programs. All the Force values such as integrity, fairness, professionalism, etc. are equally emphasized in the Basic Training programs. We view integrity and honesty more important in our values. It's too

far ahead to teach ethics for new recruits because they have so many courses. We show recruits we care. We upgrade our service. We have performance pledges. Police authority is derived from legal power and respect. Integrity and ethics of officers are emphasized at all fronts though the term "police ethics" is not generally used by the Force. We always follow the Force Statement on Vision, Common Purpose, and Values. Due recognition and reputation will no doubt help us in maintaining public confidence in the Force.

The new training strategy follows a purpose-driven curriculum (PDC) in line with the Force Strategic Directions. Curriculum designed and subjects included aim to fulfill the Force Common Purpose and Values, commonly referred to as Force Values among Hong Kong police officers. Advantages of such a curriculum, police instructors believe, include a clear purpose of training, easiness for both trainers and trainees to follow, clear formulation of the assessment and evaluation system, and integration of the Force Values into each relevant subject. The Force Values form the base of training and the depth of subject content is dependent upon the level of trainees and their needs. There are three dimensions to the curriculum: major common purpose, major values, and major subject content. For example, for handling domestic violence incident, the major common purpose includes maintaining law and order, preventing and detecting crime, safeguarding and protecting life and property, and working in partnership with other agencies; major values include integrity and honesty, respect for the rights of members of the public, fairness, impartiality, and compassion in all police dealings, and effective communication internally and externally; and major subject content includes definition, police power and action, professionalism and compassion, basic intervention skills, liaison with other agencies, and notebook entry. All current 108 subjects have been updated and integrated with the Force Values.

The Police Training School provides not only basic training to new recruits at the early stage of their career, but also other developmental, continuation, and promotion courses during their two-year probation period. Tutor Police Constable Course (TPCC) and Inspector Continuation Training Course (ICTC) are offered after the new officers have gained some real work experiences in the street. They are brought back to the School to further familiarize themselves with their training and reinforce the knowledge they learned. TPCC provides four-weeks of tutelage to newly passed-out police constables covering communication, supervisory, and counseling skills. ICTC is a two-week course given to Probationary Inspectors six months after they complete their training at the Police Training School covering writing of police reports and staff and management issues in greater depth. These two courses have a long history in the Force, but the Recruit Police Constable (RPC) and Police Inspector (PI) courses have had a longer history. Police instructors also help constables in their probationary period with practice, training, and examinations for promotion purposes. During examination for promotion to inspector positions, candidates are required to write English and Chinese papers, take an aptitude test, give an impromptu talk, participate in a group discussion, pass physical fitness test, demonstrate reading comprehension skills in Chinese, and complete certain management and leadership exercises. In short, the staff at the Police Training School is committed to improving these training programs through evaluation, research, and technology and by adapting to changes in the society. As one of the instructors said:

> We need to do more evaluation of training. We talked to recruits and we checked with their supervisors to see if training is adequate. In view of increasing sophistication of the Hong Kong society, the personal qualities of the recruits in terms of problem solving and communication skills will deserve greater attention in the years to come. Police training must improve in pace with the development of the society. In this age of rapid technological advancement, the use of technology to enhance training effectiveness would also place very high on our priority list as long as improvement is concerned. We may see development in IT-enhanced training aids, more specialists/expertise in training management, and more resources allotted to training grants for life-long learning.

In-service Training Programs

The Training Wing of the Hong Kong Police is responsible for providing in-service training to officers newly promoted to inspector and superintendent positions. The Training Wing is located on the fifth floor in a commercial building on Hennessy Road in Wanchai, Hong Kong Island. Its programs concentrate on management training during the officers' first three years on the job. After three years on the job, they are considered capable of functioning effectively without further training. Overseas training is provided to officers beyond the rank of superintendent, which is budgeted regularly. Because of its focus on management positions, the in-service training defines to a great extent the culture and character of management officers. There has been a high demand for this training and the course is run six times a year. Frequencies of the program also depend on the number of vacancies. Prior to 1995, the Hong Kong Police had 12 to 14 promotions of superintendents and 12 to 14 promotions of chief inspectors. This number has increased afterwards and there may not be enough room for everyone to attend the training courses. The trainees are instructed to leave their normal duties in the hands of their deputies in the period they take the course and thus have an uncluttered mind during their training.

There are essentially three in-service training programs, the Junior Command Course (JCC), the Intermediate Command Course (ICC), and the Advanced Command Course (ACC) provided to officers newly promoted to the first inspectorate rank, to the senior and chief inspectorate rank, and to the rank of superintendent respectively. Some of the training is geared toward motivation and boosting morale by senior police administrators and some is concerned with use of computers, use of computer reports, management techniques, language skills, and communication skills. There are a number of special features to these training programs. First, the course is divided into modules. Various training modules have been used to fit what is needed including Communications, Human Resource Management, Stress and Counseling Skills, Negotiation Skills, Information Management, Resource and Financial Management, Strategic Management, Public Order Management, Contemporary and Practical Issues in Policing, Political Awareness, and Police Ethics. Second, instructors of these courses are diverse including academics, outside experts, and experienced trainers from the Hong Kong Police itself. They follow a planned structure in delivering the course but are prepared to set it aside to discuss aspects of what they and the trainees consider essential in their learning. The trainees may also take part in a videoconference with experts outside the territory. A practitioner-turned-academic from Australia, for example, once hosted the conference, during which he discussed future trends of policing. Third, trainees are given an opportunity to discuss with senior members of the Force aspects of the organization they consider important. The senior members may include, for example, the regional commanders and district commanders. This interaction between senior and mid-ranking commanders is not for window-dressing. As an instructor told a group of officers in an ICC class:

> This is not a welfare meeting. You are expected to discuss professional stan-
> dards and you are expected to be honest and open with your views. For some
> officers this may be the only opportunity you will have to exchange ideas in an
> open and frank forum with very senior officers in the Force. I hope you make
> the most of your opportunity. You will also have a chance to meet the Deputy
> Commissioner of Police (DCP), Management, on the final day of the course.
> Once again you will be given the opportunity to discuss aspects of your organi-
> zation that concern you. We will spend some time on the first day going over
> what matters you may wish to see raised. The DCP, Management, will take the
> opportunity to share with you his views on what makes a successful police
> manager at your own level.

I describe some of the typical modules used in the ICC program in the rest of this section to provide a sense of what in-service training entails in the Hong Kong Police, starting with Communications Module. Communications is one of the largest modules presented to the ICC students primarily to improve skills. According to the instructors, the module could include specific subjects such as Establishing and Maintaining a Force Image, Internal Communications, External Communications, Role of Police Public Relations Bureau (PPRB), Media Strategy and Interface, Effective Community and Public Relations, Presentation Skills, and Effective Writing Skills. The module can be divided into three different but inter-related parts, one concerned with external communication, one with internal communication, and one with presentation skills. First, the module is initiated on the first day by introducing trainees to skills they need in dealing with media encounters, both hostile and friendly. It provides them with an insight into how the news media works and advises them on how they may prepare for studio interviews, give impromptu street interviews, and deliver key messages and sound bites. Outside practitioners, including journalists and media specialists, are required for this element of the module. Second, a senior officer from the Police Public Relations Bureau follows this up the next morning with an explanation of the Force policy in regard to working with the media and the ways trainees as individuals can contribute to the positive image of the Force. A course instructor then starts a discussion on internal communications. For the rest of the day, the instructor introduces the trainees to the subject matter and helps them classify the communication process and analyse the strengths and weaknesses of each classification, concentrating on special issues within an organizational framework. At the end of the day, the trainees are expected to have developed a clear idea on how to communicate more effectively within the organizational framework.

Third, trainees spend a day developing more effective presentation skills with an outside consultant. The outside expert discusses with the trainees how to improve their communication style whether it is in a written or verbal format. Designed to complement any skills the trainees may have already learned in previous training, this course assumes the trainees are experienced communicators and seek to develop their skills for greater personal impact. It is recognized that an important component of personal communication is the art of persuasion. Commonly described as the art of getting someone to understand a trainee's position in an issue and then achieving movement from that someone's position toward the trainee's own without conflict, it is an important element of improving a trainee's own managerial skills. The aim of this section is to allow trainees to reflect on what a negotiation process is, what the skills associated with persuasion and negotiation are, how one should question and listen to another's view points, and how this process can be applied to the trainee's own situation. At the end of the period, they should have a better understanding on how to influence and inspire audiences. Finally, a short course is held with the aim of improving writing skills. A police instructor explained the Communications Module in this way:

> For the Communications Module, we emphasize service to the community. We are a force committed to providing a service of quality to the community we serve. An integral part of this ethos is transparency and accountability. It is therefore essential that we are able to get our message across, both internally and externally, in a timely, clear, and concise manner whether in written or verbal format. This is an area where, for historical reasons, some of our officers find a skill's gap. They view encounters with the media and other groups with hostility and suspicion, seeing them as a threat. Effective training would enable these officers to welcome such encounters as an opportunity to put their message across.

A related module, Negotiation Skills, examines negotiations with subordinates, with peers and senior management, with political and community groups, and with other government departments. It includes Consultation Process and Techniques, Preparation and Research for Negotiations, Principled Negotiations, Obstacles to Successful Negotiations, and Overcoming the Obstacles. The module utilizes simulation and role-playing exercises and requires private sector expertise.

The next module, Human Resource Management, is based on contemporary research and thinking on major management issues, particularly leadership, people management, culture, and change in large complex organizations. The module includes Human Resource Strategies, Career Development, Performance Management and Appraisal, Training and Promotion System, Personnel Wing, Occupational Health and Safety, Equal Opportunities Legislation, Sex Discrimination Legislation, Personnel and Succession Planning, Staff Associations, Consultative Committees (e.g. JCC and SCC), Welfare Mechanisms and Funds, Grievance Procedures, Leadership, Motivational Techniques, Police Culture and Sub-Cultures, Change Management, Reward and Sanction Mechanisms, Labor Legislation, and Stress Management. The Training Wing has deliberately gone out of its way to utilize speakers who are not part of the Force to give a different perspective on these issues. The focus is on exposing police managers to personnel issues and enabling them to manage officers effectively. As a police instructor explained:

> The fact that people are our most important resource is obvious. Unfortunately some officers have not been given sufficient training in or exposure to modern thinking and legislative requirements in this area. With higher education standards and expectations of our younger officers combined with greater transparency and our philosophy of "living the values," it is essential that this training gap is addressed. This is especially relevant in light of new legislation that makes it easier for aggrieved officers to sue the Force.

Human Resource Management Module is divided into several sections. The first is academic with some practical application. Academics and practitioners with a great deal of experience in Hong Kong cover this part of the module. The instructor looks with practical insights into human resource and people management theories and discusses their applications to situational problems associated with people outside the Force. This process is deemed valuable because it broadens the trainees' horizon by providing examples of best practices and insights into a culture different from that of the police. The trainees are then asked how these examples apply to their own situations. They also have the opportunity to discuss human resource matters with a regional commander, who helps them understand the concepts as applied to the Force. The second section covers issues that are currently important to the Force. For example, the Force Psychologist discusses stress that may lead to suicide and officer indebtedness and examines the current trends for these issues. As a corollary to this analysis, a senior officer from the Discipline Unit turns the coin over and discusses disciplinary issues. The fundamental dichotomy of welfare and discipline is therefore presented. In the third and final section, a course director from the Training Wing introduces the idea of culture and its importance, examines the history and culture of the Force, and addresses the relevance of police culture to other government departments.

A related but separate module, Stress and Counseling Skills, is used to enhance the skills taught within the Human Resource Management Module. It provides the trainees with a more practical approach to coping with the difficulties in managing people. It is designed to make participants aware of their own and others' stress, lifestyle, and emotional problems that may impact on their decision-making process. This module includes Conflict Management, Lifestyle Management, Emotional Intelligence, Stress Management Techniques, Critical Incident Stress Management, Counseling, Understanding Oneself through Psychological Testing, and the Myers-Briggs Personality Test Profile.

With increasing empowerment, autonomy, and devolution of authority, Strategic Management Module has proven beneficial to the Force. Its aims are to introduce to participants some of the strategic management tools and techniques. The course begins by looking at project management and how one could plan a long-term operation using techniques that have been used usually by project engineers. As part of the course the participants use computers in planning a presentation and are tested on the level of their computer skills. They then discuss the subject in a more academic environment with a professor. They pay a visit to the Hong Kong Jockey Club, where they see how the theory and practice are relevant to the outside world. At the end of the day they are expected to be able to reexamine their own management plans and suggest areas for improvement. This module includes related Computer Software Programs, Change Management, PEST Analysis and Environmental Scanning, Project Planning, Forming and Leading Project Teams, Resource Allocation, Decision making, Monitoring and Inspecting, Benchmarking, and Comparative Studies in the Private Sector.

Two related modules, Information Management and Resource and Financial Management are also used in the ICC program. Information Management Module provides trainees with knowledge about various sources and systems of information available to them. Trainees learn how to access the information and use it. The purpose is to ensure that participants are fully aware of the different sources and systems of information, have the ability to determine their validity, and take advantage of them in addressing their problems. The module includes Force IT systems, Overt Sources of Information, Covert Sources of Information, Data Privacy and Protection, Data Storage, Statistics and Methodology, Internet-Based Research Project, and Referencing and Bibliographies. External input from academics and IT experts is required for this module.

Resource and Financial Management Module has become increasingly important to mid-level commanders due to devolution of financial autonomy in the Hong Kong Police. For historical reasons, this area may be where the middle managers are weakest. The module is not intended to develop accountancy skills, but to provide a range of skills appropriate for management functions within the public sector. It includes Budget Management and Control, Management of Utilities, Management of DSOA, Makinsey Papers, DEC and FEMC Papers, the Tendering Process, VFM and Cost Benefit Analysis, and the Role of P and D. Most lecturers for this module are available within the Force and the Government. However, some outside input is utilized to ensure a balanced program.

Contemporary and Practical Issues in Policing Module is intended to familiarize participants with important local and international issues and update them on practical skills required at their rank. A course of this nature is not complete without the participants learning something about the organization they work for, particularly in relation to aspects of the job that relate to the contemporary issues the Force faces. For example, this course examines problems like youth crime and initiatives available to combat them, and asks trainees to debate whether a traditional approach is sufficient in addressing them. It also examines the impact of the terrorist attack on September 11, 2001 in the United States and the implications this event has for Hong Kong. The module therefore is flexible in taking into account the changing nature of the policing environment. It includes Technical Developments in the Field of International Financial Crime; Technical Developments in Computer-based Crime; International Terrorism and National Security Issues; International Crime Trends and Groups including Russian "Mafia," West Africans, and Yakuza; Local Triad Activity; Local Crime Issues; and Workshops in Practical Training Issues such as in conducting ID parades and video interviewing.

A related module is Public Order, one of the major issues the Hong Kong Police confronts. The vast majority of trainees have a role to play in public order management at their rank. Due to the importance of the Police Tactical Unit (PTU) in public order management, this module seeks PTU input. The module is divided into two parts with PTU providing an update as to current world problems and an assessment of whether they are relevant to Hong Kong. Coupled with this is a presentation by a senior officer experienced in public order problems, who discusses the role of the trainees in these events and the problems officers are facing on the ground.

Political Awareness Module is also related to contemporary issues but focused more on the political aspect in policing. It is based on the idea that the police must be seen to be apolitical but not politically naive. It is designed to enhance knowledge of the political and constitutional environment the Force operates in. A professor in China Studies from a major local university covers the module. He or she normally speaks for about one and a half hour, provides an overview of the political environment of the Hong Kong Police, and allows plenty of time for questions and discussions. The participants examine the political arena in Hong Kong, particularly on the growth of the political parties, and the political framework of China. The module includes Government and Civil Service Structure, Local Political Environment, National Political Environment, Chinese Political Environment, International Political Environment, the Executive Council, the Legislative Council, Non-Government Organizations (NGOs), Political Parties, and Kai Fongs (Neighborhood Associations). To address the increased cooperation between the Hong Kong Police and the Public Security Bureaus in mainland China, a one-day trip to China is organized also for the trainees, which includes a visit to a police division in China, usually in the neighboring Guangdong Province. This trip has always been an enjoyable experience for the trainees as police officers at the Public Security Bureaus are excellent hosts and are open to discussion.

Police ethics has gained more importance in recent years and has been developed into an important module. Over the years, the ICAC has been a major contributor to various command courses particularly in the area of police corruption. Recently the ICAC has acknowledged that corruption within the Force is no longer the problem it once was. As a result lectures delivered by ICAC officers have tended to digress to the subject of malfeasance while still discussing corruption within an international context. Feedback from the trainees suggests that the ICAC lectures are poorly received and are not particularly focused on subjects they consider important. To address the ethical dilemmas the trainees face in discharging their supervisory responsibilities, the Training Wing officials surveyed international best practices and believed that the solution lies with the introduction of a police ethics module. The aim of this module is to raise awareness of the subject and have officers discuss in a group setting various ethical dilemmas. The module includes Definitions of Ethics, Fundamentals of Ethics, Importance of Ethics for Police Work, Practical Issues Faced by Police Officers, the Ethics-plus Decision Making Model, and video demonstrations. It is practical in its focus and uses up-to-date case studies from Hong Kong and overseas to highlight ethical problems and techniques for solving them. The module may also cover Police Culture and Sub-cultures, Internal Investigation Office (IIO), Complaints against Police Office (CAPO), Independent Police Complaint Council (IPCC), Independent Commission against Corruption (ICAC), Legal Context, Disciplinary Process and Proceedings, Sexual Harassment, Racial Discrimination, Whistle Blowing, and Supervisory Accountability. The following comment from a police instructor indicates the ideas behind the development of this module.

> There have been changes in the ICC and ACC training. At present I am developing an Ethics Course. Ethics used to be covered by a speech given by an ICAC official. The anti-corruption speech compares rates of corruption in Hong Kong with New York, London, etc. We found this speech that focuses on corruption inadequate in recent years because corruption is no longer a serious problem. But we do have malfeasance, double benefits . . . that may be better addressed by an ethics course. . . . I think an ethics course can help raise awareness.

Consist with the ideas of an ethics course, the police instructors emphasize the Force values throughout their training activities. Many of them indicate that the greatest influence on police training in Hong Kong over the past decade is Civil Service Reform initiated by former Governor Chris Patten. The reform has resulted in more emphasis on values, service, and accountability in training along with Robert Peele's community policing principles. Among the values promulgated, the instructors tend to view professionalism as the most important. Higher professionalism, including better protection of civil and individual rights as written in the Bill of Rights, represents a major change in the Hong Kong Police. This change demonstrates a stronger preference for Western policing principles rather than traditional Chinese values. The Chinese police emphasis on a teaching function, a moral mandate, or social activism is essentially absent in police training in Hong Kong. The training activities do not involve the use of informal occasions or opportunities such as meetings and holidays to reinforce Force values, either, as commonly seen in mainland China. Certain Chinese values such as protecting community interest and maintaining social harmony are viewed as important; but they do not receive greater emphasis in police training today than in the past. The level of emphasis on crime prevention and problem solving in police training remains also essentially the same as in the past. The police instructors do place greater emphasis on the service aspect of police work and believe that ethical training may be an effective measure for producing more responsible police behaviors. The following statements reflect some typical views among police instructors regarding changes in their training practices in the past decade.

> Compared to Royal Hong Kong Police, we talk about laws and procedures more; we talk about protection of individual rights and freedom according to the Bill of Rights more. But it does not mean we do it more. . . . Compared to Royal Hong Kong Police, Hong Kong Police places greater emphasis on efficient and effective crime control and we place greater emphasis on accountability and quality of service.

> The Bill of Rights of 1991 had more influence on training in 1991 and 1992, not much now. The change of sovereignty does not have much of an influence. Traditional Chinese values do not have a constant influence. Civil service reform has an influence.

> Values emphasized include openness, integrity, and professionalism. . . . Hong Kong police training does emphasize service aspects of police work; but it's less clear in moral aspects of police work. . . . I think ethical training is the most effective in producing responsible police behaviors. Disciplines only tell them what will happen if they don't follow the rules.

Personal Observations

Due to the openness and generosity of the Police Training School and the Training Wing of the Hong Kong Police, I was able to attend some training sessions and personally experience the courses provided to the officers. As an outsider, I was initially afraid that my presence would disturb the participants or create a nuisance to their routine training activities. But this concern quickly dissipated after I saw a high level of openness, candidness, and participation among the trainees in the training sessions. Their friendliness to and acceptance of my presence made me feel at home and the instructor's introduction of me as an academic interested in learning the inner workings of the Hong Kong Police put me at ease. In the following I describe several ICC training sessions I attended.

The first class is called the Myers-Briggs Personality Type Index (MBTI), offered at the Police Training Wing located at 500 Hennessey Road, Causeway Bay, Hong Kong Island. There were 13 participants in the course including 9 male intermediate commanders (1 of whom Caucasian), 2 female intermediate commanders, 1 commanding officer from Custom and Excise, and 1 civilian staff. MBTI is used as part of a human resource management approach to give officers an opportunity to become involved in examining how they approach decision-making in their daily life and an understanding of their own innate personality. By doing so, it helps them gain a greater understanding of the differences between themselves and others and allows them to analyze such issues as why conflict occurs, how best to approach team-building, how best to communicate on an individual or group basis, and how best to fit within the organization.

An internal instructor went over MBTI-related theories in the morning and provided practical exercises in the afternoon. He began by briefly introducing MBTI's origin and its application in private business companies. He introduced personalities and profile types and made sure that participants understood these concepts. For example, he used left-handedness or right-handedness to illustrate the innate habit or forced behavior. As he explained, "We prefer to use either left or right hands even though we can do with both hands." He went on to explain more complicated concepts and their relationships, i.e., extraversion and introversion and their need for each other for balance, senses and intuition and their need for each other for balance, thinking and feeling and their need for each other for balance, and judging and perceiving people and their need for each other for balance. He then provided a brief summary, "We don't use them equally well. We prefer one over the other. The theory suggests that we keep our preferences all our life. We do explore and understand other sides. But we don't change our preferences." All together 16 personality types were explored. With these concepts, the participants further discussed the psychological dimensions of police work. They got along with one another very well and worked harmoniously throughout the course.

The second class is called Human Resource Management and Communication, held at the Police Officers' Club located at a waterfront in Wanchai, Hong Kong Island. The same group of officers attended this class and a police instructor led the discussion of practical management issues as part of the training in the morning. Three senior police commanders also joined the class to communicate with the trainees and assist them in their learning. All three were female with a great deal of managerial experience and insight on the Force. They clearly articulated their thoughts and expressed their management principles. As part of the design, the class was divided into three groups and each senior commander joined a group. The purpose of this arrangement is to allow the participants and senior commanders to have direct communication and conduct open discussions. The objectives are to identify problems encountered in human resource management and internal communication and understand what the trainees as Chief Inspectors should do to address them. Through exchange of ideas, participatory management is realized.

In the class, the participants were given a chance to express their feelings of the problems first and were then asked to identify causes of the problems and what they could do to address them. Organizational metaphors were used to facilitate the discussion and presentation of the problems. The senior commanders also gave their views of the problems and commented on the presentations of the participants. One organizational metaphor used was the drawing of a tiger put up by the instructor and the trainees from each group were asked to explain the meaning of the drawing. The instructor used their explanations to make the point that people interpret the same picture in different ways and the same organizational problem in different ways, too. Problems associated with human resource management and communication were further discussed. The participants were then asked to draw a picture of their own with pencils on a piece of paper to represent problems they saw in the Force. Different pictures were drawn to represent various problems such as lack of manpower, lack of money, poor communication, bad communication, poor management, organizational rigidity, and gap between leadership and rank-and-file. Everyone was then asked to draw a larger picture on a larger piece of paper. Two pictures from each group were selected and posted on the wall for further discussion. One of the pictures indicated the lack of communication and how information was filtered out through the multiple layers in the police hierarchy. The participants discussed the causes of the problem as people, multiple layers, and trust. Culture was mentioned also as a problem. To address this, the Force should promote a learning culture and encourage officers to ask questions. As everybody joined the discussion, the atmosphere in the class became quite lively. The instructor then took a moment to provide his own take on the issue:

All immediate supervisors should do their jobs. For example, sergeants should solve their problems at their level with their power. . . . Filtering itself is not the problem. You should filter. If everything is passed on, the top rank will get the wrong message. But you should filter in the right way. Problems should be presented in a well-thought-out manner. It may be necessary for some problems to be filtered out. And when this happens, when a problem is not communicated, you should go back to the originator and explain why the information is not delivered to the higher rank.

Two other pictures selected for discussions were a ship and flowers. The ship was ready to go with smoke coming out of its chimney; but it was not moving because its anchor remained at the bottom of the water. The picture, as explained by its creator, represented opposing forces to progress. One of the senior commanders provided a brief comment on the picture and then asked the class, "What are exactly the problems?" A trainee responded, "One major problem is no trust." The senior then asked, "Why no trust? What are the root causes?" The discussion moved on in such a manner. The picture of flowers showed how some of the flowers were watered and others not. As explained by its creator, it described how valuable resources were taken away by new programs. Some trainees also interpreted the picture as indicating the lack of support from the Force. The senior commanders disagreed with this view. One of them said: "The Force gives us enough support to grow. The Force actually gives too much water. Why do we complain so much? Why don't we ask ourselves what we ourselves can do?" They also provided specific evidence to illustrate their points. There were many important posts, for example, that had been filled in the Force. The instructor then joined the discussion by pointing out the need for the trainees to look at the whole picture.

The session then continued with more discussion of the intermediate commanders' difficulties and more feedback from the senior commanders. One senior commander, in addressing the problem of complaints from subordinate officers, said, "If you allow the complainants to deal with the problem, they will do it. But don't give the assignment to one person, create a team. They will survey the situation and come up with solutions." The second senior commander said, "Time is a big problem. I got to use my time wisely. I can't talk to every member of the 400 officers in my division. The second thing I care about is attitude. If one goes to the Open Forum with the wrong attitude, he won't get anything out of it. He will just come and go. The third thing is the system: commanders should create the system for solving problems. If you have time, attitude, and system, you should be ok." The third senior commander added by saying that there was a need for more inter-unit communication besides communication between layers. The instructor then joined the discussion by asking the participants to go beyond traditional thinking, be creative, and think what they themselves can do.

The last part of this session involved group discussions on how to solve the problems and presentations of discussion results from each group. One officer representing a group said: "We need 'trust,' 'people,' and 'culture' to solve the problems. To create 'trust,' we need acknowledgement, feedback, and documentation, and find out what can and cannot be done. 'People' means that everybody has to play his or her proper role. 'Culture' needs to be changed from blame to learn and from word to action." The instructor then provided his input: "Let your subordinates know your plan. Let them know they have a role in your plan," and discussed how to get everyone involved. The three senior commanders also provided their feedbacks. One of them said, "Trust is easy to say, hard to do. How far can you go with trust? There are also multiple layers of trust; your immediate supervisor is one layer, your immediate subordinate is another. And there are multiple areas of trust." An officer representing another group presented several problems as causing the lack of trust such as culture, conflicts, different values and agendas, and layers and discussed his group's view on how to address these problems. In the area of culture, this group believed that the police should build a positive culture by setting objectives, changing performance evaluations, setting examples, having more regular supervision, and appointing good middle-people between layers. The senior commanders again responded and provided feedback to their ideas. One of them said, "What's the meaning of building culture? Is it building culture or personal style? Culture is very personal. When I was a divisional commander, I went out on a beat and learned the problems first-hand. You should go out and do the same and earn respect."

The third and fourth class are related to public order management and internal security in Hong Kong. Public Order Management was held at the Police Officers' Club in Wanchai, and Internal Security at the Training Wing in Causeway Bay, Hong Kong Island. The format of these sessions was different from the other two just described in that experts in related areas spent most of their time presenting the subject matters. A senior female commander from the Police Tactical Unit (PTU) covered public order management issues. Since there are many international events in Hong Kong, the potential for demonstrations is always there. She introduced the role of the PTU in internal security, crowd management, anti-riot, and routine and emergency operations. She introduced basic training, physical training, firearm training, and tactical training for officers in the PTU. Overall, their training includes 20% basic knowledge, 22% physical skills, 18% anti-crime tactics, 11% range and weapons, and 29% others. She also informed the participants of the organization, execution and deployment, and tactics of those groups usually active in anti-globalization activities such as environmentalists, labor activists, human rights groups, and anarchists, and police tactics in handling them.

A government official from the Security Department made a presentation on internal security issues to the class. He focused on possible disasters that could occur in Hong Kong and strategies for preventing and managing them. He went over the Government's preparedness in tackling various threats and its development of basic plans for emergencies. He underscored the concept of "effective emergency management," which involves preventive and mitigating action; good planning; testing, exercises, and drills; and review and revision. The basic principle for the Hong Kong Government's emergency response system is that operational command and coordination responsibilities are vested with emergency services and supporting departments and the Government plays a monitoring and supporting role. The Commissioner of Police is responsible for operations related to terrorism. A "Three-Tier" response system was adopted in 1996 to ensure appropriate response. Tier One involves emergency services operating under their own commands. The lead departments are Police and Fire services supported by other departments (e.g., Government Flying Service, Civil Aid Service, Social Welfare Department, etc.). Tier Two involves monitoring by the Security Bureau of development of the incident and progress of the responding departments. The operational aspect of the response remains the same as in Tier One. Tier Three, the highest tier, involves the direct participation of the Government for supporting the emergency response operations. He also discussed the three phases of emergency response, i.e., the rescue phase, relief and recovery phase, and restoration phase. In deliberating internal security issues, he encouraged the trainees to ask the following questions: "Are we prepared? Are we prepared for the future? Are we overconfident? Are we complacent?" He emphasized the important role of commanding officers in emergency operations: "If a police manager is absent and the organization collapses, there is something wrong with the management. In Hong Kong, the police are structured independently at different districts. Therefore, if there is an earthquake or a major incident in one area, the police will still survive as an organization."

The fifth class is on Stress and Suicide. A Police Psychologist from the Psychological Services Group of the Hong Kong Police covered the topic and discussed how to handle stress and prevent suicides among police officers. He opened the session by saying that stress management was one of the most important parts of a police officer's career. He introduced the psychological services his unit provides and told the class that Force psychologists provide law enforcement oriented mental health care and organizational liaison. Their services are voluntary, confidential, ethical, evidence-based, responsive, and proactive. He then discussed the problem of suicide, which is often related to personal life management, relationship, work, physical and mental health, and childhood. He went into detail about 24 suicide cases in the Hong Kong Police. Among them, 8 officers committed suicides by shooting (33.33%), 7 by burning charcoal (29.17%), 5 by jumping from height (20.83%), 2 by hanging (8.33%), 1 by jumping from platform 1 (4.17%), and 1 by inhaling town gas (4.17%). Possible causes for these suicides include indebtedness (11 cases, 45.83%), love affair (3 cases, 12.50%), work-related stress (3 cases, 12.50%), serious physical illness (2 cases, 8.32%), depression (1 case, 4.17%), being under corruption investigation (1 case, 4.17%), and criminal offense (1 case, 4.17%) and unknown (2 cases, 8.33%).

The Police Psychologist then explained the prevention strategies used in the Hong Kong Police. The Force relies on a priority assessment system, through which police psychologists and welfare officers are on constant suicidal alert for high-risk officers. Formations where these officers work are involved also in providing necessary assistance. The Force Psychological Services has conducted research on suicide cases regularly since 1980, developed a checklist for suicidal behaviors, and reinforced the Syllabus on Suicide Awareness. On a more routine basis, police psychologists and welfare officers promote their services, provide family education, and conduct training on stress management. The training is provided to officers of different ranks with 13 entry points, including counseling, helping of peers, and special briefing. Pamphlets on simple living, evils of gambling, peer pressure, etc. are often distributed. According to the Police Psychologist, more than 300 officers seek help from them every year and 55% of them are self-referrals. He pointed out the importance of support network, respect, and compassion for fellow officers. Finally, he discussed psychological screening and psychological competency.

A flip side of stress management and welfare support is Police Disciplines, the topic of the sixth class. A senior commander responsible for disciplinary offenses in the Hong Kong Police provided a lecture on this issue. He first introduced a variety of disciplinary offenses such as absence, sleeping, insubordination, intoxication, malingering, making false statement, unlawful exercise or unnecessary exercise of authority, willful destruction or negligent loss of government property, conduct to the prejudice of good order, and conduct calculated to bring the public service to disrespect. He then covered different disciplinary awards including caution, reprimand, service reprimand, forfeiture of pay, reduction in rank, order to resign, compulsory retirement, dismissal, and suspended punishment. He went on to discuss certain specific prevailing issues in the Force such as officer indebtedness. He emphasized the fact that the Force has a clear policy on indebtedness including administrative instructions on management of indebtedness, supervisory officers' role in disciplinary action, bankruptcy, police order ordinance, and interdiction policy.

The seventh and the last class observed is Leadership, provided by a dynamic and experienced outside consultant. The consultant started the class by discussing the basic law of listening, which includes listening, speaking, and communication. He emphasized that listening is a two-way street, from A to B and from B to A. He then asked the participants what names they liked to be called, what jobs they liked, what colors they liked, and what animals they liked. He had each participant provide a quick explanation to each of his or her preferences in a pre-determined amount of time, usually within one minute. He then asked two officers to make a brief statement about one of these subjects and asked the class to recall what these two had just said to see if and how much they could remember. He then asked, "If you don't remember, why? Why do you remember only part of it?" After some interactions on these points, he went on to discuss more complicated concepts such as scanning the environment, scanning the officers, situational leadership, and people management. The last part of the class was on change. He pointed to some of the changes taking place in the Hong Kong Police: "We look at education more seriously now. We treat arrested persons as our customers. Service Quality Wing was created. We encourage healthy life styles. Culture change with values: efficiency, quality, and accuracy." He then showed the class a short video called "Winds of Change," a cartoon that illustrates how two groups of people deal with changes differently. When the video was over, he explained: "You should ride the change and control the change. Face 'crisis,' which in the Chinese character means both danger and opportunity. Facing the winds of change, there are the predictors of the inevitable that expect the worse and do nothing and there are the pursuers of the possible that try every available means."

Other Learning Programs

The learning culture cannot be created simply by formal police training courses. It needs to be fostered also through other police and non-police programs. Ultimately, the idea of learning should be diffused to as many aspects of police work as possible. Following this principle, the Hong Kong Police has created an incentive program at both the Force and station level providing support to officers' educational effort. As a divisional commander said, "We have over 100 people at the station, all eager to learn. . . . We now provide more support for self-improvement. We have subsidies for police-related college programs and courses."

Police officers not only attend local university programs in Hong Kong but also take advantage of relevant ones overseas. In a warm Spring evening a few years ago, I was invited to attend a graduation ceremony for a dozen or so officers who had just completed their master's degree from Charles Sturt University in Australia. The police program at Charles Sturt University is practical in its orientation and has proven to be relevant to Hong Kong policing. The ceremony was held at the King House Mess at the Police Headquarters on Arsenal Street, Wanchai, Hong Kong Island. I arrived at the location at 5:45 pm and the ceremony commenced at 6:00 pm. The academic procession was led in by pipers in Scottish costumes with all invited guests standing. One officer told me that the tradition of Scottish pipers has been passed down because some Scottish officers in the very early days of the Hong Kong Police brought the pipes with them to the Force. The proceedings were opened and guests welcomed by the Head of the Graduate School of Policing at Charles Sturt University. After faculty members and Dean of the Faculty of Art gave their brief speeches, the graduates were presented to the Dean. A Senior Assistant Commissioner of Police, Director of Personnel and Training, delivered the key address. A representative of the graduates spoke on behalf of all the graduates. He expressed his gratitude for those who supported them to reach their educational goal and joked about how he himself got involved in graduate studies.

Two incidents prompted me to pursue a master's degree. One had to do with a drunken driver. I asked the drunken driver to do a breathalyzer test, a blood test, a urine test, and a walking test one by one. Before each test the driver gave an excuse for not taking the test, "I have asthma, I can't take the breathalyzer test; I have anemia, I can't take the blood test; I have diabetics, I can't take the urine test; I'm drunk, I can't walk. . . ." I talked to my supervisor about it. He said, "You need vertical thinking." The second incident was about President Jiang Ze-ming. President Jiang was driving a car in Hong Kong with his driver. I stopped the car for speeding. After I checked them, I reported the incident to the Command and Control Center. They asked me, "Who is in the car?" I said, "This person is so important. I don't know who he is because President Jiang is his chauffeur." I again talked to my supervisor about this, and he again told me that I needed vertical thinking. I didn't know what it meant, and the concept prompted my desire for graduate education.

As the ceremony came to an end with recessional Scottish pipe music, guests and graduates enjoyed a little drink by the bar. Afterwards, they had a sit-down dinner served with salad, chicken, salmon, and apple pie. While they were enjoying the dinner, a costumed piper walked down the aisle between the dinner tables a couple of times continuing to play the Scottish music. Toward the end of the dinner, several officers spoke informally on their experiences with the Force in regard to education. They pointed to the change that the Force had made from matter-of-fact thinking to conceptual and abstract thinking and how this new thinking requires graduate education. The police have come a long way in the area of higher and graduate education. In the past, police officers had to justify their educational effort and explain to their supervisors why they wanted to have an education, answering questions like, "Why do you want to get a master's degree? How does that make the rest of us look?" There has been a significant change today as education is valued by the management and most rank-and-file members. This does not mean, however, that there is no more resistance within the Force for officers working on their graduate degrees as those who do not have a college or master's degree may see a gap between them. As the evening was coming to a close, several speakers were telling jokes and making humorous remarks bringing laughter frequently from the audience. There was more drinking and chatting after dinner. The entire event was seamlessly organized. Despite the humors and laughter, it was a very formal and orderly evening.

Looking Ahead

The Hong Kong Police has been committed to a learning culture as part of an overall police reform strategy. This culture in essence embodies the use of cutting-edge training curricula, promotion of knowledge-based practices, and support for officers' educational effort. To maintain the most advanced training programs, the police directors at the Training Wing are actively engaged in updating, revising, and developing their training courses according to changes in the field and new knowledge in the profession. The Intermediate Command Course (ICC), for example, has been completely revised and now incorporates a modular approach by which the chief inspectors' perceived training needs are addressed. This modular approach introduces topics subject-by-subject over a three-week period. Each module is designed to be presented on its own to those with a perceived training need. In some ways the instructors are also experimenting with this course in an attempt to gauge the quality of each module. Training modules developed in such a manner are primarily based on new information in contemporary management and human resource research. Geared to opening the horizon for the trainees, they are above and beyond the traditional content for in-service training and reflect the police effort in cultivating a new learning culture.

From the instructors' standpoint, officers' training needs are paramount. They aim to meet their expectations so they will return to their formations with plenty to think about and be able to perform their tasks more professionally. To measure the trainees' progress, a written assessment is made upon each trainee at the end of the course as a final report. In this evaluation, the course director interviews all trainees on an individual basis to discuss what is achieved on the course. As the report is exhaustive and emphasizes trainees' inputs, they are expected to contribute and keep an open mind on all aspects discussed. The trainees' inputs as to how well the aims of the modules are addressed are taken seriously. Many of the courses are redesigned on the basis of feedbacks from the trainees. As a police instructor stated:

> We used to have more police related topics, about 70%, that cover crime, Marine, child protection, anthrax, EOD, etc. We use inside experts for these courses, which are inexpensive. We only had 30% topics related to management. . . . Trainees have more difficulties in management. Feedback shows they want more management related training. So we switched the percentages. Now 30% are police related and 70% are management related covering leadership, motivation, team building, group dynamics, human resources, appraisals, feedback, communication skills, presentation skills, etc. Outside experts, financial people and civil service people are brought in for some of the courses.

Specific courses are also evaluated regularly to determine needs and popularity. One of the recent evaluations of ICC modules indicates the following order of popularity based on percentages of responses: Communications (96.4%), Human Resources (94.6%), Public Order (88.5%), Ethics (85.5%), Information Management (82.3%), Stress and Counseling Skills (77.0%), Resource and Financial Management (76.7%), Contemporary and Practical Issues (75.8%), Strategic Management (70.6%), Negotiation Skills (69.3%), and Political Awareness (69.3%). Although the ICC participants have different comments about their learning experiences, they all seem to agree that they have been exposed to a variety of subjects and teaching styles due to the diverse backgrounds of their instructors. As an ICC trainee and instructor commented:

> The training programs are all in the right direction. I attended the intermediate command courses. Contemporary leadership and management skills are taught in the command courses. Outside people come in, give us lectures, give us broad perspectives. . . . I had also computer training, participated in Work Improvement Teams, Living the Values, and Public Satisfaction courses.

> It's hard to label the orientation of the training. I bring Western culture and my students are Chinese. They are more reserved. I think in general police training combines Western policing principles with Chinese traditional values. . . . In police training, I try to encourage open-mindedness, discussion, questioning, etc. . . . We emphasize a collaborative and participatory leadership and management approach. We are all part of a team, we should not be adverse to different ideas, and we do not emphasize an authoritarian style. . . . I believe that those trainings that use a combination of theories and practices, exercises, and shared experiences are more effective.

Besides the training courses the Training Wing provides, the Hong Kong Police has engaged in inculcating an organizational culture of learning and service. The Service Quality Wing has been spearheading this effort by providing a one-day workshop called Living-the-Values. This workshop has been offered three times to all members of the Hong Kong Police at the time of this study and has been credited to increased communications in the Force. Some officers, however, view training programs focused on culture and values as irrelevant to police work and desire more practical subjects such as language skills, computer skills, identity breaks, beat creation, large scene management, and government finances and budgeting. Some officers also sniff at the fact that some officers take courses for promotion purposes only.

To move to a higher level of knowledge and learning, the Hong Kong Police has been developing a Knowledge-based Program and has established recently a Research Division and a Police College. Because knowledge-based practices represent a cultural change, officers associated with this initiative are responsible also for selling and marketing the program within the Force. The success of the Knowledge-based Program may eventually depend on the extent of officers' contributions and consumptions of police-related knowledge. As an officer who has been involved in developing this program said:

> Forget about communication. You have to sell the program. You have to market it. You have to let people see the benefit of the program, that they can actually get something in return. When they see that, they start contributing because they feel they can get something out of it. Then the knowledge about police work, good experiences, best practices, problem solving lessons, etc., can be developed. We then will provide information to officers and get feedback and get the program going.

A Brief Comment

The learning culture in the Hong Kong Police as displayed in their various training, educational, and knowledge-based programs can be further examined from a cultural perspective. Organizational researchers have used both internal practices and external environment to explain organizational culture. Bourdieu (1990)'s concept "habitus," interpreted as shared values and beliefs within an organization, and Sackmann (1991)'s "organizational knowledge," including organizational members' ideas of "what is," "how," "should's," and "why" may form the basis of this learning culture. "Field," as external forces impacting on an organization, also affects the learning culture. This culture may ultimately be reformed through an interaction between the various elements in the "habitus" and the "field." The organizational knowledge, as far as the Hong Kong Police is concerned, includes, in the most general terms, the paramilitary training, police tactical training, and internal security emphasis. The external forces include, at the very least, the change in the Hong Kong society and the political transition from a British colony to a Chinese Special Administrative Region. From this interaction, a more advanced learning culture may emerge in the Hong Kong Police. In the meantime, the strength of "habitus" may present itself as an obstacle to the creation of a new culture or become a source of tension in the process.

The training programs in the Hong Kong Police can also be looked at as a result of interactions between and integration of Western and Chinese cultures. On the one hand, Western law enforcement principles are clearly emphasized in the training curriculum. Some officers are sent abroad for training and some others obtain their bachelor's or graduate degrees from overseas. On the other hand, as the training programs put a strong emphasis on public order and security management, it can be deduced, aside from the fact that the colonial paramilitary tradition remains strong, that Confucian values of conformity and pro-order outlook also have a significant influence on police training.

6

Rights and Obligations

One of the important recent developments in the Hong Kong Police that demands a separate examination is the police officers' view of human right. Human right is a Western concept that has taken "root in the Constitution of the United States in its Bill of Rights and in France in the Declaration of the Rights of Man" (Davis, 1995:169). Rooted "in the Age of Enlightenment and notions of social contract," human right is considered inherent in humanhood, as under the natural rights doctrine, independent of the state and government (Davis, 1995:169). It was introduced to Hong Kong when Hong Kong adopted the Bill of Rights Ordinance in 1991. As other Western concepts of crime and criminal justice, it was exported to Hong Kong due to British colonialism "without regard for structural or cultural differences" (Traver and Vagg, 1991; Gaylord and Traver, 1994:12). How this concept has been received by the Hong Kong Police as well as the Hong Kong society could demonstrate how Western values and Chinese culture diverge and converge, a subject that transcends cultural and national boundaries and is of global significance.

When right is discussed in the context of Hong Kong, a false premise is sometimes used that Hong Kong already was a democracy under the British rule. In fact, Hong Kong was not. She had enjoyed certain human rights protections under the common law; but "this tradition had not been codified in any meaningful way, though Britain had acceded to the international human rights covenants on Hong Kong's behalf" (Davis, 1995:169). The Joint Declaration of 1984 and the Basic Law of 1990 were the first two documents that included some basic democratic elements promised to the Hong Kong society. Hong Kong human rights movement, therefore, started with the 1984 Sino-British Joint Declaration, which not only guarantees "a plethora of rights associated with the liberal tradition, but it also aims to ensure judicial enforcement in the common law tradition, along with various associated democratic and capitalist elements" (Davis, 1995:170). The Joint Declaration was later developed to become the Basic Law of Hong Kong of 1990. "The presumption of innocence" clause was written into the Basic Law passed by the Third Plenum of the Seventh National People's Congress in April 1990. Article 87 provides, "Anyone who is lawfully arrested shall have the right to a fair trial by the judicial organs without delay and shall be presumed innocent until convicted by the judicial organs" (Yu, 1995:112). Then in 1991 came the International Covenants on Civil and Political Rights and the Bill of Rights, the adoption of which occurred only six years before the end of the British rule and the territory's return to China.

Since the Hong Kong government did not introduce certain democratic principles until the last few years of the British rule, there have been different explanations and speculations for this belated change of government policy. Some believe in a "conspiracy theory," as some Hong Kong academics put it, that a democracy movement would make Hong Kong indigestible to the Chinese government after its return to China. Some interpret the last-ditch attempt by Britain to create democracy as a measure "to restrict, as much as possible, China's interference with Hong Kong's legal system after 1997" (Gaylord and Traver, 1994:5). Others believe that the last British Governor, Chris Patton, was simply a staunch conservative determined to do what was right for Hong Kong with no regard to any political ramifications. Regardless of the motivations, democracy was good for Hong Kong, the Hong Kong people welcomed democracy, and the colonial government might have allowed an openness that was inevitable.

The Hong Kong people were ready for democracy in the 1980s due to economic, social, and political development in the region. The democratic movement in Hong Kong, as a fairly recent phenomenon, occurred largely due to the demand of the Hong Kong public and the impending change of the political environment. As the Bill of Rights Ordinance was passed, which incorporates the language of the International Covenant on Civil and Political Rights, the public in Hong Kong responded favorably to the increased protection of human rights. This support, some argue, demonstrates that the concept of right is not "alien" to Chinese (Ng, 1995:69). As a former Hong Kong government official stated:

> In Hong Kong, programs tend to be maintained over a long period of time. Housing, education, police. . . . They are all important. It's a rich government with resources and public will. Today's Hong Kong government is more concerned for individual rights because society insists on democracy and civil rights. Mistakes have been made in the Hong Kong SAR; but it's not worse than the 70's. . . . The machinery is getting better incrementally.

Because due process rules and procedures in the Bill of Rights were newly enacted and represented a departure from the past, the Hong Kong government needed to identify and revise prior laws that were inconsistent with the International Covenant for Civil and Political Rights. A Legislative Council Committee was formed and identified over 50 laws that might be in conflict with the Bill of Rights. A freeze period of one year, which was later extended to two years, was provided in the Hong Kong Bill of Rights for certain laws such as those relating to the powers of the Independent Commission against Corruption (ICAC) and the Hong Kong Police to be reviewed and brought in line with the Bill of Rights (Wu, 1995). This process of review and reform by the government, however, had been slow while the court was already required to follow the standard established in the Bill of Rights, creating conflicts between the executive and judicial branches.

The Bill of Rights of 1991, based on the International Covenant on Civil and Political Rights, imposes due process rules and procedures on the Hong Kong Police. It is required that the police no longer use the presumption of guilt in handling cases such as drugs and corruption. For example, in June 1994, a government case "concerning the presumption of possession of drugs was thrown out of court for violating the Bill of Rights" (Wu, 1995:192). As cases such as these tarnish "the image and credibility" of the police, the Hong Kong police "have imposed upon themselves a moratorium on a number of laws which they fear to be unenforceable" (Wu, 1995:192). As Hodson (1994) observed, the Bill of Rights and subsequent judicial decisions resulted in amendment to police powers from three courses of action: a formal review of legislation, a judicial decision, and self-imposed restraint.

With the Bill of Rights of 1991, the Hong Kong society has become more right-conscious and demanded more control of police authority. More people have started to complain about mistreatment from the police and voiced more loudly against police abuse. As the Bill of Rights requires that the Hong Kong Police follow more due process rules and procedures, the consciousness of citizen right has also become stronger among the police officers. As much as they complain about increased legal and procedural restrictions, most officers do not consider the Bill of Rights as fundamentally in conflict with their general law enforcement practices. As reported by many officers during interviews, the police today have more respect for individual rights compared to the Royal Hong Kong Police. They are committed to the Bill of Rights and enforcement of common laws. As a result, the police have become more civil, more accountable, and less authoritarian in recent years. As some officers commented:

> The Western legal principles have already taken hold in Hong Kong. Western practices are legitimated in the Hong Kong society. We don't need to balance Western law enforcement principles and the Chinese traditional culture. The Hong Kong Police is unique in the sense that it has integrated various values in its colonial police history.

> Even if we know one is the offender and is bad, we still have to collect evidence and follow all the laws and procedures. We need to know what power we have, what laws and restrictions we can impose. Citizens know their rights more now. We have more explanations to do.

In the Chinese cultural tradition, however, one's rights are often juxtaposed with one's obligations or duties. Rights are considered a dispensable part of human nature and are treated as a creation of the State. This tradition classifies different rights as separable rather than a coherent whole. The welfare rights and political rights are separated in mainland China, for example, with greater emphasis placed on the former. Economic developmental concerns, sovereignty, and collective interest are also viewed as the foundation of rights (Information Office of the State Council, 1991). The rights limiting the State are thus a lower priority and the State interests often supersede individual rights (Edwards, Henkin, and Nathan, 1986).

A case in point is the reactions to the proposed National Security Legislation. This bill is based on Article 23 of the Basic Law. But it is controversial due to two opposing views representing two different cultural traditions and values. Those who oppose it cite the damage it will inflict on rights and freedoms and those who support it argue for the importance of civic responsibility and national security. Critics say that it could erode fundamental rights and freedoms as well as restrict access to information. Both legislative protests and massive street demonstrations against the Bill have occurred. When the bill received its first reading in the Legislative Council on February 26, 2003, pro-democracy legislators staged a walkout and the Security Secretary Regina Ip was sprinkled with shredded paper. The lawmakers also burned a giant copy of the proposed bill outside (Shamdasani, 2003). On July 1, 2003, Hong Kong had the biggest rally, estimated at 500,000, since her return to Chinese rule as a massive crowd filled Hong Kong's streets during a six and a half hour march against the law. Demonstrators feared that the new law would give the government similar powers to suppress dissent that exist in mainland China. However, supporters for the law say that the proposed bill is necessary for protecting the territory's security and the legislature is required to pass it under Article 23 of the Basic Law. The Hong Kong government also supports the passage of the law and claims that it will not infringe on individual rights and freedoms. Mr. Tung Chi-Hua, the Chief Executive of Hong Kong, said in his first policy address of his second term in January 2003, for example:

> Following our return to the Motherland, ensuring national security has become the natural and basic civic responsibility for each one of us to observe and practice. The SARG has stressed all along that the enactment of legislation under BL 23 is meant to protect national security. It does not undermine in any way the preservation of the characteristics of Hong Kong as an open, pluralistic and cosmopolitan city. It will not affect the basic rights and freedoms we now enjoy. Nor will it undermine the SARG's compliance with internationally accepted norms of behavior. This is the fundamental principle behind the whole legislative proposal.

Reflecting these two opposing values, the Hong Kong Police may develop a human rights model in their law enforcement practices that is more or less a hybrid of Western and Chinese cultural traditions or a combination of liberal and conservative values. On the one hand, the police accept the supremacy of the law, with its notions of judicial independence, due process, and rule of law. The Hong Kong people favor the many protections of freedoms and individual rights. Their reaction to human rights does not lend "support to the view that this 'Western' concept is alien to them, that their 'rich culture' prompts them to support postponing the protection of rights until Hong Kong is richer or more socially stable" (Ng, 1995:70). As Davis (1995:180) also stated, "The recent human rights developments in Hong Kong certainly undercut the argument that universal human rights standards and processes have no application in an Asian context." On the other hand, the police officers, facing a series of issues ranging from stop-and-search provisions and identity-card checks to police powers in relation to demonstrations, complain that the striking down of the presumptions of guilt would leave them fighting crime with one hand tied behind their back (Vagg, 1996). When it comes to law and order, the Hong Kong people are also "conviction-minded, favor a strong police force, have little real use for the presumption of innocence, and think rather less of the rights of foreigners than the rights of locals—just as people in England do" (Ng, 1995:70). Regarding the two sides on the issue of rights, Ng (1995:69-70) further stated:

> The heart of the popular debate is rather the classical question—what are the limits of the rights enshrined, and how does one balance the freedom of the individual against the good of the community?. . . . The deepest concern so far expressed is the effect on law and order. . . . will the power of the police be so curtailed as to make it difficult for them to enforce the law? Will it mean guilty people will be let off unpunished?

Many officers hold the view that rights and obligations should be balanced. To do so, they believe that members of the public need to be educated about their duties to abide by the law and support the police. They maintain that as there has been an increased and stronger awareness of individual right and personal freedom, there has been a corresponding decrease of sense of civic duties and obligations. As an example, many officers say that there has been a significant increase of public complaints against the police in the past decade. They associate this increase with the increased demand for democracy, the Bill of Rights, and a stronger consciousness of individual rights. As an officer said:

> It was easier before. There are more civil rights now. There's nothing wrong in demanding for more rights. But our job has become more difficult. We have to satisfy everything citizens want. Some citizens are unreasonable. Some things aren't police business. We can never satisfy citizens 100%. . . . We have lots of pressure on the job. Lots of resources are wasted dealing with unreasonable requests and complaints. Each case takes us as long as three months to complete investigating. During this time we feel the stress working on the street. Some people just want to challenge the officers and cause trouble. We should give reasonable human rights and reasonable democracy. Citizen education is not as good as in Singapore.

It seems that in Hong Kong today the police have maintained an approach that would enable them to conform to the Bill of Rights without sacrificing their core law enforcement duties. On the one hand, the Bill of Rights has increased the government's burden of proof requiring the police to follow due process rules more closely and collect more sufficient evidence. Police officers have faced increased challenges due to Article 5 of the Bill of Rights Ordinance, which imposes restraint on the use of police powers, and Article 11(1), which requires full burden of proof in criminal proceedings on the side of the police (Cheung, 1996). On the other hand, the Bill of Rights' impact on police work has been largely "procedural, not substantive, and can be accommodated by procedural adjustment in related areas of police operation" (Cheung, 1996:153). As a police officer stated: "There was initial concern about these due process rules and procedures; but there was no difference in reality." The courts have also "shown a somewhat conservative streak, with some reluctance to adopt the more liberal foreign precedent, such as, for example, that embodied in such doctrine as the American exclusionary rule (a rule that provides for the exclusion of improperly obtained evidence" (Davis, 1995:178).

As Hong Kong becomes more democratic, the Hong Kong police may experience a tension between due process restrictions and their own traditional emphases on public order. The law requires that the police follow due process rules and procedures and protect civil rights, which are clearly demanded by an increasingly right-conscious society. Order, however, requires that the police control crime and maintain security, which have been an organizational prerogative of the Hong Kong Police. The tension between these two elements has been commonly observed in policing democracies. As Skolnick (1994:6) explains:

> The ideology of democratic bureaucracy emphasizes initiative rather than disciplined adherence to rules and regulations. By contrast, the rule of law emphasizes the rights of individual citizens and constraints on the initiative of legal officials. This tension between the operational consequences of ideas of order, efficiency, and initiative, on the one hand, and legality, on the other, constitutes the principal problem of police as a democratic legal organization.

To address this tension, the Hong Kong Police need to balance competing and often conflicting interests between an increasingly democratic society and a police cultural disposition to maintaining order. The increased interaction between legality and order may also exert an influence on the values and attitudes of Hong Kong police officers, despite the fact that the police operations have remained by and large unchanged. The following are some typical comments from the officers in this regard.

> The Bill of Rights of 1991 had a big impact on the Hong Kong police and police behaviors in general. Police were given wide powers. The Bill tried to make sure that police do not abuse those powers. Powers were defined in greater details. As a result, police were more careful and more sensitive about how to use information. Many presumptions of guilt were changed.

> Hong Kong citizens changed a lot in terms of their consciousness of their rights and their attitudes and behaviors toward the police. Hong Kong people in general are more aware of their civil rights. But as long as they observe their rights, we don't have a problem. . . . We have to be more careful, observe longer, have probable cause, and we cannot randomly stop people.

Everybody should follow the procedures, have a miniscule level of complaints, asking the question, "Is it proportional and appropriate?" Officers must balance rights of culprits and public.

The police overcame the initial impact of the Bill of Rights. They respect the Bill of Rights. The Bill of Rights does not have much effect. A little effect on the psyche of the officers as many feel they have too many things to worry about now. You may infringe this or infringe that. But Day-to-day operations have remained about the same.

The Hong Kong people are more conscious of their rights because of media and education. They are more suspicious about what officers do now. It's not that they know exactly what rights they have. It's like they think they know, or they think they have more rights than they actually have. Of course, we are talking about less educated people. Everything is human right now.

The police also have a different perspective on human rights, seeing encroachment upon rights more due to criminality than to police actions. They believe that they would be more effective in protecting civil liberties if they are allowed to be tough on crime. As Hodson (1995:9), a former Assistant Commissioner of the Hong Kong Police, said:

> Although I appreciate that it is not a concern of the Bill of Rights, we see a significant threat to human rights coming from criminal activity. Burglary is without a doubt an invasion of privacy; on a personal level, gang rape must be about the ultimate invasion. If you are in debt to loan-sharks there will be restrictions on your liberty; many victims are driven to prostitution, drug running, and suicide. . . . As a result of our efforts to tackle these criminal activities, we in the police see ourselves very much as being in the business of looking after the interests of the individual and of protecting him from threats to his privacy, life and liberty.

The police believe that fair and unbiased policing is important, but in the meantime are concerned that there is a price to pay for every curtailment or restriction of their power. Some of the powers and their curtailments include identity check, search and seizure, and law on loitering. On the one hand, the police agree that they should not pass details of a person's criminal record over the beat radio to an officer conducting an identity check or search because of bias this may produce. "The fact that a person has a criminal record should not create the suspicion to justify a police officer carrying out a search" (Hodson, 1995:12). On the other hand, the added protection of individual rights creates a cost to law-abiding citizens as criminals would take advantage of the new opportunities provided by the civil right protection. For example, after the law on loitering was amended, Hong Kong police officers are less able to take action against people who loiter in such public places as outside schools and in the corridors of housing estates. The number of arrests for loitering subsequently dropped from about 420 per year to about 150. One of the costs for this was lost wallets, which rose by about 9% per year at a time when crime rate generally was dropping in Hong Kong (Hodson, 1995). Although some may argue that the need to protect individual rights outweighs the cost of some individuals' monetary loss, the police believe that they and the public will not be able to afford the cost in many other cases if opportunities are missed for catching the offenders. Examples of such other cases are abundant including drug trafficking, money laundering, smuggling and extortion, theft and sale of nuclear weapons, and international terrorism. As Hodson (1995:14) and a street officer stated:

> We must keep our concerns about abuses of human rights and the abuse of power by the police in proportion so that we are able to tackle the real threats that exist in the real world.

> Who need human rights? Criminals do. Do you need human rights? No, because you don't violate the law. Police deal with criminals, offenders. . . . Citizens have rights and ask for explanations now. If arrest procedure is not right, offenders cannot be prosecuted.

The idea that rights are juxtaposed with obligations as reflected in the thinking of Hong Kong police officers can be interpreted as representing either the Chinese cultural tradition or a universal conservative police perspective. The Chinese culture emphasizes collective interest and individual duties; rights are often seen as a Western or foreign concept. The nature of police work also produces an inclination among officers to stress public good and citizen obligations. New legislations, new rules and procedures, that restrict police authority, therefore, are often viewed as beneficial to law violators instead of law-abiding citizens. Furthermore, the mission of a police organization to maintain public order and fight crime is inherently contradictory to the mandate to protect civil liberties and human rights. It is in this context that the police will grow and develop in democratic societies. Police officers must follow due process rules and procedures in their day-to-day operations. Although they may perceive that such rules and procedures reduce their ability to maintain law and order, police effectiveness is seldom sacrificed in reality because of these laws. Instead, the police usually become more professionalized in their law enforcement practices.

As Skolnick (1994) observed, the tension between the rule of law and the need to maintain public order has been a perpetual problem in policing a democratic society. As demonstrated in this chapter, the police in Hong Kong also experience the strain between society's due process restrictions and their own traditional emphasis on public order. The value system of Hong Kong police officers has been affected in this process also by their exposure to different police orientations, i.e., the traditional effective policing model and the new legality model. Clearly, the debate between crime control as the goal of justice and due process as the end product of the system will continue to influence policing in Hong Kong. If the rule of law can be understood as part of the "field," demanded by an increasingly democratic society, and maintaining public order as part of the "habitus," required by the police tradition, the police in Hong Kong must balance the competing and often conflicting interests between the "field" and the "habitus"(Bourdieu, 1990).

7

Street Officer

Police officers working at the street level on a routine basis include beat patrol officers, search cadres,[1] emergency unit officers, crime unit officers, and vice officers in Hong Kong. Street officers tend to have a different perspective from the management due to the situational context they are in and their role as street level bureaucrats. This pattern seems to be true in Hong Kong just as elsewhere. I have personally visited thirteen police stations all over Hong Kong to interview street officers and observe their activities. While I rely on the views of officers I have interviewed in presenting much of the materials in this chapter as well as the rest of this book, I do not claim that these officers are representative of the entire Hong Kong Police. A survey of a random sample of both junior and senior officers would be ideal in offsetting some of the limitations of the qualitative approach used in this study. I, therefore, proposed a structured questionnaire survey with a random sample to the Hong Kong Police at the beginning of this study. But unfortunately, this proposal was rejected on the ground that it would be in conflict with the Force's own surveys. Nevertheless, I have tried to minimize the potential methodological weaknesses inherent in this study by visiting police stations that represent a diverse array of police districts in all five land regions in Hong Kong.[2] Wan Chai Station, for example, is one of the oldest, where there are many businesses, hotels, and restaurants. Mong Kok Station is situated in the most congested and most crowded commercial district. The "new" Red Light District, according to the police, has moved here from Wan Chai. Kowloon Bay MTR Station covers part of the Mass Transit Railway system that runs through the five land regions. Officers working from an MTR Station do not serve a residential population and have less interaction with the public. With no report room of their own, they liaise with police stations located in corresponding geographical areas for case processing. Tuen Mun Station, located in the New Territory North Region, is far out from the business center of Kowloon and Hong Kong Island, which gives one a sense of relief from the smothering crowd and congestion commonly found in Hong Kong. And Yuen Long Station, even further out, is located in a district with about 30,000 indigenous residents. The indigenous people have maintained their own customs and traditions different from the majority of the population.

The structures of police stations are equally diverse. Some stations are as high as seventeen floors and others stand only four or five stories tall. Some have been newly remodeled; walking into them is like entering a three-star hotel. Others look run-down and decrepit. Police stations often contain a lounge, a T.V. set, a microwave, a bar, a dinning hall, a police club, and sleeping quarters with showers. Decorations of police stations are lackluster, painted or furnished mostly with white, blue, and gray colors. At Kun Tong Station, for example, the colors of the meeting room are mostly blue, gray, and white, with some margins painted black. The Tsim Sha Tsui Station has an oval table surrounded by twelve chairs in the meeting room. The door, carpet, and chairs are blue; the wall and a board hanging on it are white; and the table and cupboards light gray. The North Point Station is one of the most beautiful police buildings in Hong Kong, with a spotless and cozy meeting room that reminds me of a big-city law office in the U.S. At the Wan Chai Station, the sign "Video Recording Is in Progress" is clearly posted on the door and three officers are on duty in the reception area. Three chairs are put before the front desk for the visiting public and there are plenty of additional chairs and double-seat and single-seat sofas in the lobby area. Members of the public filing a report can wait in the area, which is air-conditioned and conservatively decorated with some live green plants. "Reporting Room" and "Interview Room" are right in the back of the reception area. A dining room, a club, and a barber shop can also be found in the building.

The officers I interviewed and observed are quite diverse, too, including beat patrol officers, search cadres, Emergency Unit officers, crime officers, and vice officers. Some are rookies and do not have a historical perspective of the Force; others have been on the Force for over twenty-five years and witnessed many changes. Some officers speak excellent English and Putonghua (Mandarin), while others speak Cantonese, the local dialect, only. There are both male and female officers present during all group meetings I attended. Female officers experienced more difficulty in earlier years; they were unarmed and assigned to cases that involved children, women, and domestic problems only. Later they joined the platoons and walked the beat. Now female officers occupy about 13% of the Hong Kong Police, are armed and posted in all units of the Force, including the Police Tactical Unit (PTU), often regarded the toughest unit in the Hong Kong Police; and they enjoy the same pay for the same jobs. As a senior officer said:

> There are three phases for women officers in Hong Kong. In the 1950's, the 1st phase, when the first woman officer was hired, she dealt with matters relating to women and children. In the 2nd phase, there was a wider range of duties and there were no particular posts that were designated as either for female or male officers. But female officers would not be armed. In the third phase, Equal Opportunity policy makes it possible for women to fill all kinds of positions. There were some very emotional issues about women officers. Some complained they were too small, they would lose their guns, they didn't know how

to shoot, they couldn't back up or help another officer, and so on. Some women officers argued that they were not hired to carry guns, so what the fuss? Then the policy was that whether women were armed was decided on the basis of the way women were recruited; if they were recruited as armed officers, they would be armed; otherwise, not armed. In reality, women officers never lost a gun, and they were better shooters than male officers. Then gradually there was a change of attitude toward women officers.

Most of the officers were open and frank. They were willing to talk and happy to see outsiders having an interest in their opinions. A few were a little more reticent apparently due to personality differences rather than fear or lack of confidence. They were not careful in choosing words or trying to hold back their views as they complained about the public, the media, the management, and sometimes even their fellow officers. They told stories, made jokes, and laughed heartily. They were friendly and got along well with one another, nodding to fellow officers' remarks, complimenting each others' viewpoints, and gently correcting incomplete or inaccurate information.

Most street officers are stationed at a divisional station, the basic police unit in Hong Kong. At this level, patrol officers work three shifts, called ABC while crime officers work 9 to 5. Patrol officers rotate shifts every week and change beats every three months. Frequent rotation, according to some police managers, allows officers to have a social life and meet different people. In some divisions, there is an additional D shift that usually runs from 9 to 5 and overlaps the day shift. Officers in the Emergency Unit (EU) are not a part of the divisional unit; they are members of a regional unit. But they work three shifts just like the divisional patrol officers. All other officers at higher levels in the police organizational hierarchy including district, regional, and Force levels do not do shift work unless major incidents occur. At the district level, for example, patrol officers usually work from 9 to 5. At the regional level, the PTU officers work from 9 to 5. At the Force level, search cadres and special duty units also work day shift only. As an officer explained:

> We have three shifts at the divisional level, ABC, for Uniformed Branch. But for Crime Units, it's 9 to 5. For district level and up we have 9 to 5 for Uniform and Crime unless Vice Squads are involved or Anti-Triad units are involved. It's the same for the regional level, which is usually 9 to 5, unless Vice and Anti-Triad units are involved. . . . In Wan Chai, we have 32 beats. We try to cover all the beat areas. Two officers patrol in pairs in buildings and at night. We may have two guys do two or three beats depending on the manpower we have. In bigger area that does not have much going on like the Exhibition Hall area, we have motorcycle officers. We had a man 10 days ago who took one officer's gun and tried to shoot him. We are more cautious and reinforce the manpower on patrol in certain areas. We double up.

Officers work 8 hours a day, 48 hours a week. They have on average three days off in every two weeks. Their working hours have been reduced from the previous 52 to the current 48 to provide them with better working conditions.

Each year, officers have anywhere from two weeks to 45 days vacation dependent upon their ranks and years of service in the Force.

Foot Patrol

Hong Kong is a perpetually crowded city from early morning till late at night. Usually up at 6:00 am, I left my apartment at 7:00 am and headed toward the MTR station, which took me to most police stations and, with some bus transfers, all over Hong Kong. I saw large crowds of people during early morning rush hours. Most people dressed casually, walking crisply to or from the station on their way to work. Subway trains arriving at the station were only seconds apart and were still not able to sweep up all the passengers standing on the platform. The first time I was in the MTR station, I was shocked by both the large number of people and the cleanness and orderliness at the station. All people need is a mass transit card called "Octopus" worth about HK$150 to go through the turnstile. Close-by, MTR customer service agents sell the cards and provide helpful directions. As I took the MTR, I quickly realized how convenient it is to ride in this modern transportation system. The directions are clearly marked in the train with electronic arrows and signals indicating where a passenger is, what the next stop is, and where one can transfer. There is even an electronic screen in the train providing passengers with major news of the day. As I looked around, I was equally impressed by the cleanness and freshness inside the train. There is no graffiti and passengers are frequently reminded through speakers that eating and smoking are forbidden in the train. The weather in Hong Kong is hot and humid most of the year, with occasional typhoon warnings that may or may not materialize. As meteorologists say here: "Signal 3 did not turn into Signal 8," indicating the loss of strength of the typhoon. When this happens, the day is usually quite wet and humid.

The vast majority of police officers walk the beat in Hong Kong. They do not find it difficult to familiarize themselves with the street and neighborhood conditions. They can locate an address easily because streets in Hong Kong are numbered from small to large by the use of informational technology and the Controller's system. Beat officers walk alone mostly during the day and in pairs at night. Three officers may walk the beat together in extremely busy areas. Search cadres serving as patrol officers at the Force level and dressed in distinctive uniforms also patrol on foot and can be seen at various locations in the city. While officers are on beat patrol, they walk in their area, stand at key junctures, and observe their environment. They occasionally jot down information in a small notebook or fill out a form while standing in a street corner, at a store entrance, or against a tall building. Patrol officers meet their supervisors usually twice per shift at approved locations. They have fifteen minutes break for lunch.

Beat officers perform a variety of duties. They receive and respond to all kinds of calls such as noise complaints, traffic congestions, domestic disputes, and shoplifting. Most of the calls are service-related and not viewed as police business such as environmental and sanitary conditions, land disputes, and debt collection. All emergency calls are responded to by the police in Hong Kong. The people officers contact and deal with in the street are mostly from local areas. Depending on the districts, there are both young and old people. But most tend to be younger, from 15 to 30 years of age, lower-class, and lower-educated, some of whom are suspects of criminal offenses. As some officers stated:

> We deal with younger people more, people from 15 to 30 years of age . . . lower class people . . . Triad members, new immigrants, etc. . . . . Environment and post determine who we deal with more. . . . Some troublesome suspects are active. They have no probation, only three weeks' tutor.

The types of problems officers handle depend on the area where they work. In a busy commercial district like Tsim Sha Tsui, they often mediate what they call "money disputes," disputes between consumers and business owners. In a district like Yuen Long, illegal immigration is a more typical problem; officers here make a certain number of arrests of illegal immigrants each month. In what officers consider unpleasant areas, they may come in contact with violators and criminals, those they describe as "lower-class," "bad people," or "drug addicts." In Mong Kok, for example, officers respond to more incidents because a larger number of "lower-class" people frequent the entertainment and night-life businesses in the area. Officers stationed in the MTR system, however, work in a confined, air-conditioned environment without many high-risk premises. But due to pocket-picking and indecent behavior problems, plain-clothes officers are deployed to detect offenders in the MTR. In general, officers frequently handle disputes, drug problems, youth crimes, and fighting. As some officers stated:

> We deal with many disputes, which are not dangerous. One officer can handle disputes. Robbery, assaults, burglary . . . need other units' support. Family disputes may take more time. . . . Many domestic disputes require a simple police presence and will go away. When police arrive, problems tend to go away. Citizens tend to use officers' presence to stop their problems.

> We respond to all requests and disputes. Disputes are mostly minor, but we still have to respond. Oftentimes they're disputes about prices. A person sees, say, a price of $64 but is asked to pay $100, gets into an argument, and the next thing that happens is one of them picks up the phone and dials 999. There is no minimum amount that says whether we should intervene or not. We take care of all requests.

> We try to neutralize parties in dispute, try not to side with anyone, and use a variety of means to deal with their problems. We have store visits, bar visits, and we stop gambling. We try to satisfy the public, ask what they need, help them, and solve their problems. We often just talk, comfort, and move on. Police can't do lots of things.

Officers also spend a great amount of time providing service to the public and building relationship with the community. As many people ask the police for help, officers can have anywhere from 10 to 30 contacts with the public on an 8-hour shift. They may answer questions about directions, provide simple information like the train schedules, or help a parent find a missing child in a shopping area. On a Saturday afternoon in Telford Garden Plaza, Kowloon Bay, two police constables responded to the request of a distressed woman looking for her five-year-old son. While they were walking to the center of the plaza, another constable appeared with the boy from the other side. Realizing that was her son, the woman became very angry and shouted across the square at the boy for not waiting for her. The two officers standing with her quietly reminded her: "Don't be so loud, please." As they finally joined together, the mother was still quite angry. In the meantime, the three officers gave the boy a hearty lesson: "You should listen to your mommy. Wait for her. Wait where she told you to. You made her worried and she thought you were lost or taken away by strangers. You must behave and listen to her . . ." They went on like this for about five minutes, with the boy standing with the officer who found him on one side, the mother on the other, and the two officers in the middle, before handing the boy back to the woman and resuming their patrol duties.

When officers are not occupied, they simply walk the beat, be visible, interact with the public, or engage in crime prevention activities. They are also vigilant in gathering intelligence. In determining what to do, they apparently can use lots of discretion. As some officers said:

> I wouldn't be active on the street simply because I want to be active. I wouldn't intervene without a reason. I intervene when I see something suspicious. Other times, I get to know the area, talk to people in the area. I can learn a lot about the area by talking to people. . . . We do security checks, building checks, high rises. . . . Unlike other places, we also do vertical patrol inside buildings. We check the security guards and make sure they are not sleeping. The guards are mostly pretty old and are supposed to watch the doors closely. We also have lots of back alleys besides major streets that need to be watched.

Officers follow some general principles for working in the street and use specific methods for approaching people. One of the principles is being visible. High visibility is believed to be a strong deterrent to criminal behaviors. Coupled with this principle is a routine street activity called "stop-and-search" conducted in the form of an ID check. Officers commonly view "stop-and-search" as an important method for crime prevention and can be seen checking IDs and questioning people at all hours in the street, in open-air markets, at subway entrances and exits, in and around port areas, etc. Like officers in land formations, officers patrolling the MTR system also put great emphasis on visibility and ID checks although safety, rather than crime, is a more important concern for them. As some officers stated:

> We walk more, be present more, and be visible more. . . . We spend 90 percent of the time being visible. . . . We check IDs. We spend more time preventing crime than arresting people. Uniform itself prevents crime.

There is no doubt that patrol officers can be seen just about everywhere in Hong Kong. As I walked in the street, I saw officers standing in key locations, keeping a close watch on people, or simply walking the beat. They are extremely polite and provide directions readily. In an early afternoon in Queensway, I saw an officer strolling through a shopping mall. Entering from one end of the mall, he walked slowly toward the other. Stores of all types on both sides of the hallway came into view and the place was packed. A young woman greeted the officer and started chatting with him. They walked at a leisurely pace together until reaching a bridge outside that connects with another building. The woman was then joined by a man and a boy. The man took a picture of the officer and the boy together. They then said "goodbye" and the officer started walking alone again. Around 9:00 pm in the evening one day in Ladies Street, Mong Kok, I saw three constables walking in the street. They then got into a quiet dark alley and stopped at a white car parked there. It seemed that they had been called to check out an illegally parked car. After inspecting the car and making some calls, they resumed their normal patrol duties. Around mid-afternoon one day in the MTR Kowloon Tong Station, I saw two police constables standing and watching people getting into and out of the station. They occasionally stopped people and checked their IDs. Within half an hour, they stopped twelve passengers including a young woman wearing long straight hair, two older men hauling bulky luggage, a middle-aged man dressed in shabby clothing, and two young men carrying backpacks. Before they stopped the young lady, they actually spread out to wait for her to get in between them as if she was going to escape. No arrest was made. Most of the people they stopped happened to be from the mainland with legal travel permits. Officers in Hong Kong seem to have a sharp eye on noticing mainlanders.

In a late morning in April, I accompanied a police sergeant from the Wan Chai Station on beat patrol. We walked in some busy streets with high rises first and then passed through a crowded commercial strip full of stores, vendors, eateries, and restaurants. Some streets were jammed with vehicle traffic and others crowded with pedestrians. We covered the entire District from the police station to the boundary that connects with the North Point District. As we walked, the sergeant told me that there are many traffic problems in the area, lots of illegal parking, lots of disputes, and many problems involving youngsters and drugs. Officers may use discretion in handling traffic violations by issuing warnings. As the sergeant quickly traversed the beat area, I found myself occasionally struggling to keep up. There was not a single incident during the entire walk, which lasted a little over an hour. As we headed back and entered the station building, I saw three civilians sitting in the reception area and waiting to make a report. The sergeant told me that most of the reports are concerned with losses due to pick-pocketing, which are seldom recovered. After we walked past the public area, the sergeant showed me the Station Report Room, Temporary Holding Cells, Equipment Room, Interview Rooms, etc. Four officers were eating box lunches elbow to elbow in a small office behind the reception area. The sergeant glanced at the officers and said to me ruefully, "Our officers have only a short time and a crowded office for lunch."

On any given day, in busy commercial districts at least, patrol officers are heavily deployed. Mong Kok, a district in Kowloon, for instance, is one of the busiest commercial districts in Hong Kong with large crowds from early morning till late at night. Many streets in the area are used as open-air flea-markets and are fully occupied by vendors of clothing, gifts, novelties, and electronic products. Inside the buildings on both sides of these markets are stores, eateries, and restaurants on the first floor and Karaoke bars, brothels, and massage parlors on the second or third floors. Due to extremely heavy pedestrian traffic, many streets are closed from vehicles. Officers from different divisions and officials from other government agencies are frequently seen patrolling and inspecting the area. On a Saturday afternoon in May, for instance, I saw two search cadres at the entrance of a commercial building, both busily filling out forms. At the same time, three beat patrol officers were walking past them. They walked faster than pedestrians, stopped at the intersections like everyone else, and waited for the light to change before crossing. Apparently used to walking in busy streets, they rushed past the pedestrians and squeezed through the crowds effortlessly. As they were hurrying toward the Mong Kok Station building, two other officers, one male and one female, were walking in the opposite direction. Unlike the three officers heading toward the station, they were taking their pace and walking slowly. Close to Lady's Street, three uniformed officials from the Hygiene and Environment Office were seen inspecting the area also.

To approach people, officers often use their experiences about people's manners and appearances. They may stop people because their clothing is out of place or the way they speak and behave is unusual. They usually have a reason or suspicion based on their past experiences when stopping people. They employ various methods according to their judgment of the context of an event: sometimes following the law and procedures, sometimes using morality and common sense, and sometimes simply making the best out of a bad situation. When there is difficulty in determining what to do, officers follow the law first, police order second, and morality third. They believe that they are primarily a legal force and secondarily a moral force. Although law and morality are both used, law is evidently used more for illegal activities and morality more for providing help to the people. The law does not recognize police discretion in Hong Kong; but police policy does. Following are some comments made by officers regarding how they approach people in the street.

> We notice suspects by their behaviors, eye contacts, facial expressions, time and location. . . . We check both nicely and poorly dressed people because both are suspect according to our experience.

> We use different skills in approaching different people on the street. To suspects, we need to have reasonable suspicion. We must put officers in a safe place. Our own safety and public safety are primary concerns. To the public, we are more polite and friendly. We conduct routine check of IDs of members of the public. Overall, we have three considerations: be safe, use common sense, and avoid complaints.

> We use common sense . . . moral reasoning, laws, experience, etc. . . . We enforce law more than ethics and morality. Also it depends on the location, experience, and education of the officers and members of the public. Experience

is important. Some of us don't have many years of service. That doesn't mean
that we've got less experience. We can be put in a very busy district and learn
many things in a short period of time that officers take a long time to learn in a
slow area.

I have worked for the Force for thirty years. I know how to deal with problems.
Younger officers may have more pressure due to lack of experience. Different
people react differently. . . . We have problems such as Triad, shop and customer disputes, fighting, and youth crimes.

Police officers in Hong Kong generally feel safe while on patrol. They do
not have the uncertainty and wariness that often accompany patrol officers in the
U.S. They do not show fear or nervousness in making street contacts and when
responding to summonses. One of the reasons for this is that, according to some
officers, they do not experience much violence on the street. Violent crime rates
are generally low and have become even lower in the past decade. Officers
consequently feel safer today. Another reason often mentioned is strict gun
control in Hong Kong. It is very rare for officers to confront weapons while on
patrol. Only about three to five officers are killed per year in the line of duty,
most of whom by traffic accidents.

Car Patrol

Officers on car patrol are a small minority in Hong Kong. They are members of the Emergency Unit (EU) and are responsible for genuine emergencies
and crimes. They engage also in proactive and preventive patrol when not
occupied with serious problems. EU officers, however, are not part of a local
division even though they work at the street level. They are members of a
regional unit because of their mobility and ability to cover an entire region. The
EU has traditionally functioned as an intentional overlap to beat patrol and
provides assistance to patrol officers when needed. As each police region is
divided into districts, car patrol is deployed by districts with two patrol cars
usually used in each shift and four officers in each car. Each region also has a
Traffic Unit that operates in a similar fashion but focuses on traffic problems
and uses both cars and motorcycles.

The EU Station in the Hong Kong Island Region is located in the Central
District. It is an old building built in 1946. As I walked into the station in an
early evening, I saw police vans for the EU and bikes for the Traffic Unit in the
lot. As the EU uses only vans that hold seven passengers, there are no American
style patrol cars to be found in Hong Kong. These vans, currently made by Ford
and soon to be replaced by Mercedes, are not like the family mini-vans commonly seen in the U.S., either, as they are longer and have a bigger trunk area
that holds all types of police equipment. All EU officers have received special
training and are equipped with special weapons. As an EU sergeant introducing
me to the standard EU equipment said:

We have an internal security function. So the equipment serves that purpose. Ammunition, 10 CS gas, tear smoke, 75 to 100 meters range fired from a pistol. We also have 10 CS we can shoot with a shot-gun through windows, and 2 grenades for tear gas, too. We have 6 Class B nuclear, chemical, biological suits in each car that can be used for anthrax. We have gas masks to go with the suits. Then we have spot light, night vision goggles, tactical goggles, cut resistance gloves, ropes, house entry breaking equipment, equipment that can open sliding metal doors, prier, toolset, roadblock with sharp nails that can flatten tires.

In the lot, the sergeant threw the roadblock equipment on the ground to demonstrate how it works and explained that there is only one such equipment in Hong Kong Island, the use of which must be approved by the superintendent in charge because of the potential danger it poses to the public. As he folded the roadblock back, he continued, "Then we have hydraulic breaking equipment, MP5 single shot, shot gun, shield for room entry, one radio to call for helicopter, life saving equipment, life buoy, and some extra rounds of ammunition."

At about 7:30 pm, the sergeant and I were joined by the EU superintendent, one plain-clothes officer, and two uniformed officers, one of whom was the driver. We got into the Command Car for the shift and started moving out of the station. As we crept past the narrow street of Lan Gui Fong, a famous upscale area on Hong Kong Island, we could see French, Spanish, Portuguese, and Tai restaurants, Karaoke clubs, and bars on both sides of the street. Caucasian men and women jam-packed the bars during early evening hours with glasses in their hands, chatting and laughing. The inside of the bar was clearly visible from the police car because the side of the bars facing the street was completely open in this warm, subtropical climate. Dressed in suits, many men apparently just got off work. Here and there blonde-haired women dotted the bar scene. With music playing in the background, patrons either sat at the tables or leaned against the bar counter. Some sat close to the sidewalk and others simply stood and drank on the side the street. There was a casual atmosphere in the place and a cavalier attitude toward drinking. The police simply had no business in pushing people inside because public drinking is not illegal in Hong Kong. As the car was crawling through the area, one officer said:

This is the more expensive area. Very few problems do we have in this area. There is no restriction on how late they can be open. You can stay as late as you want. If one closes, you can always find another that is open. So you can stay here for ever. There's no such crazy policy as in the UK that all bars must be closed at a certain hour. And because of that, we have less problems because people can take their time and drink and relax. They don't have to drink faster thinking the bar will be closed and they have to leave. And there are no large crowds at midnight because of closing time.

We stopped at the Wan Chai Police Station and sat down in the dining area to take a break. The officers ordered hamburgers, French fries, and coke from a McDonald restaurant nearby. Since I already had dinner, I had lemon tea only, a drink made by McDonald to suit the local taste. On one side of the wall where we sat there was a statute of Guan Gong, a popular ancient Chinese military general. His statute is commonly seen in restaurants and drugstores in Hong Kong as well as overseas Chinese communities. As a symbol for order for the police and protection for businesses, Guan Gong is widely worshipped and is believed to bring luck and fortune to those who honor him. While the officers were eating, they were all in full gear and maintained constant radio contact with the outside. As one of them explained, EU officers are not like beat officers who can take off their belts and relax; they must be ready to move in a moment's notice. Toward the end of the break, a call came in reporting a purse-snatching incident. A lady was apparently robbed after she withdrew some money from an ATM machine in a relatively quiet area on the East side of Hong Kong Island. A beat officer nearby had already been dispatched to the scene. An EU unit close to the scene was also on its way. The EU officers I accompanied were with the Command Car, which functions as a mobile command center responsible for coordinating emergency response activities. The Command Car immediately put on a siren in order to reach the scene faster. The use of the siren must be authorized by an officer at the rank of a sergeant. For the car to run through a red light authorization must be obtained first from a superintendent.

While the car was moving toward the scene, the plain-clothes officer maintained radio contact with the dispatcher and other responding officers. A female dispatcher could be heard providing a description of the suspect as a male about 28 years old, wearing blue jeans, possessing a cell phone, and having taken several HK$500 bills. As a junior officer listened, he recorded the information in a notebook. The officer manning the phone and the officer taking notes occasionally talked to each other and exchanged opinions about what was going on. In the meantime, the driver concentrated on driving and the sergeant listened and made decisions about what to do. They worked quietly and harmoniously as a team. Just before the Command Car reached the scene, a status report came in from the first EU Car that reached the scene indicating that the trail had turned cold. The case was immediately downgraded and no longer considered interesting. The Command Car slowed down and shifted to regular patrol. Cases such as this are not easy to solve unless officers happen to be at the scene immediately after the offense.

The Command Car was now cruising through Wan Chai. The commanding officers described the area as lower-class with many bars and restaurants. It used to be the Red Light District in Hong Kong; but most women now work in the gentlemen's clubs in the area and may serve as escorts when requested. The police are not particularly worried about individuals involved in prostitution because they generally do not present a serious problem. They are more concerned with drugs and fighting, which tend to cause more trouble. The use of psychotropic drugs among young people has been a major concern. Triad involvement, suspected in some bars and Karaoke, has also been a serious concern. Fighting could involve both local Chinese and expatriates and is often caused by drinking, girls, and rude manners such as staring. The sergeant and his unit had just arrested twenty-six people including five expatriates the night before for a fighting incident.

As the car was going through Causeway Bay, scores of attractive and brightly-lit shops came into view and wandering pedestrians were filling up both sides of the street. This is a busy shopping center with many name-brand stores such as the famous Japanese department store Sogo. Numerous people like to stroll around the area or hang out here till the wee hours in the morning. The sergeant said that the businesses here used to attract robbers from the mainland who would break the jewelry stores and take the valuables. The police therefore have beefed up patrol and conduct frequent inspections in this area. To strengthen surveillance, they are also considering installing CCTVs in such key locations.

Each month, the EU officers have some days reserved for certain special themes or activities. For example, they have Traffic Day and Anti-illegal Immigration Day once a month. A more regular activity is called Mobifix, a park-and-walk patrol method. As we reached the heart of Causeway Bay, the Command Car selected a busy and crowded juncture for a Mobifix. The EU officers parked and got out of the car, stood on the sidewalk temporarily, and patrolled a short distance, all the while keeping a keen eye on the environment. The purpose of this activity is to be visible and proactive and deter potential offenders at locations considered prone to crime and disorder. As the Command Car was parked for the Mobifix, officers from another EU car patrolling the area were already there. The commanding officer from this unit walked toward us, saluted to the superintendent, and briefed him about his unit's activities. The Mobifix lasted for about fifteen minutes before we got in the car and started moving again.

As the Command Car was heading to the East Side of the Island, we passed some "low-class" residential areas and quiet streets. In Hong Kong, it is often difficult for outsiders to differentiate a "low-class" from a "high-class" area as they often stand side by side. As I looked at some of the high rises, the sergeant quickly pointed at one of them as a public housing project and another virtually next to it as a private residential estate. There are also quite a few city blocks under construction. Looking at one of them, the superintendent commented that few places in the world are like Hong Kong where different parts of the city are constantly reinventing themselves by demolishing old buildings and erecting new ones. The land is so scarce and previous that no real estates are left abandoned.

Hong Kong Island is a geographically compact region. The Command Car can flip over the entire island in one shift. As the crew completed its patrol of the East Side, it was now heading toward the South Side to inspect a snap-check being conducted by local car unit. A snap-check is a roadblock set up for a short period of time during which the police conduct a quick check of all passing cars. The main purpose is to address the problem of illegal immigration. The South Side is an ideal place for this activity because the South Shore is an area many illegal immigrants (IIs) make their landing. There are also only three routes that actually connect the South Shore to Hong Kong Island. So it is easy to stop the traffic and find illegal immigrants by setting up a roadblock here. We arrived at the spot where the local EU team was doing the snap-check. The officers had their car parked on one side of the road and set up the roadblock to allow only a single lane to be used by passing cars. An officer stood by the open lane and flagged to each passing car for a stop. As a car slowed and stopped, the officer did a quick visual inspection of the inside to see if there were any suspicious persons and let the car go if there was none. Nobody was told to get of the car if there was nothing suspicious. The whole process from being stopped to leaving took less than ten seconds. As the area is relatively remote and quiet, the roadblock did not cause any traffic jam.

As the snap-check was being conducted, the superintendent, the sergeant, and the rest of the Command Car crew stood by on one side of the road and observed what was going on. It was about 10:30 pm and a Full Moon had climbed to the middle of the sky. The officers were in high spirit chatting and laughing. Looking at the Moon and the clear sky, the sergeant joked about the big bust they made the night before: "Maybe that's why we made twenty-six collars last night." They continued to talk a little about the weather before the snap-check was over. The check took about half an hour and altogether about thirty-five cars were stopped. None of the cars was searched and no driver or passenger was asked to step out because no one looked suspicious. When I asked what profile the police use to determine if a person is suspicious of being an II, the sergeant said:

> Taxis. IIs like to take a taxi and ask the taxi-driver to take them somewhere.
> We also look at the IIs' pictures we have in our records and develop an idea
> how they tend to look like. They tend to come from farther North than from
> Guangdong and they speak Mandarin. We once caught an II who'd stolen lots
> of building equipment from a construction site and he had those equipment
> hidden in the back of a car. . . . About 8% of the burglaries are committed by
> mainlanders. They tend to find a location where there is less private security, a
> remote area like here. Once there was a burglar from the mainland who got into
> a house in this area and the owner happened to be there. He confronted the
> burglar who ran away. We responded to the call, swept the hill, and found him.

On another night around 9:30 pm, I also saw a snap-check by a local EU car crew in Tat Chee Avenue, Kowloon. Six officers were involved in the check. One of them was standing by the EU vehicle, the driver was at the wheel, and the rest were by the street. After the roadblock was set up, the officer by the EU vehicle waved to all the cars passing to stop and checked inside quickly. Most cars were let go in a second or two. A few cars were directed to the side of the street for a more thorough inspection by four other officers. When this happened, the drivers and passengers of the cars would be asked to step out of their cars. About half an hour later and eighty cars stopped, the roadblock was ended and no one was arrested. Two of the officers were actually street patrol constables who resumed their beat patrol duties as the EU vehicle was driven away.

After the snap-check on the South Side in Hong Kong Island, the Command Car got on a free way and moved quickly westward. The Hong Kong Harbor and brightly-lit skyscrapers around it loomed in the distance. Having only a moment to enjoy the magnificent night scene, the officers looked straight at the

Harbor before making a turn into Wan Chai to do a rail-lane check. A rail-lane check is an inspection of rails behind certain buildings by officers walking through a back alley. It is conducted for the purpose of preventing burglaries and robberies as a burglar can climb up the rails and sneak into a residence easily and a robber likes to hide in a dark stairway waiting for their victims to come up. The EU officers walked through two narrow and dark lanes and checked all the rails in the back of the buildings thoroughly. The plain-clothes officer walked about ten meters ahead of the uniformed officers so as not to disturb any possible wrongdoers. The sergeant used a flashlight to check all the doors and windows. He told me that he once caught a burglar climbing up the rail in the middle of a burglary.

The rail-lane check marked the end of the shift during which the Command Car received eight emergency calls altogether and the officers were now ready to head back to the Central Station. At the station I was given the opportunity to observe the "pandemonium," as the superintendent put it, of changing shifts as many officers, getting on and off the shift, crowded the station at this time. Officers of a new shift were receiving a briefing from their commanding officers about events of the previous shift and instructions on what to focus on. Car crews ready to get off were busy completing paperwork, filling out forms and keeping records in their logbooks. All officers from the last shift must hand over their weapons at the end of the shift. Following a required procedure, commanding officers must look at each other as they take off and empty their weapons. The weapons on the car are supposed to have bullets put in them during potentially dangerous situations. At the time of shift change, all four car crews put their equipment on the floor and empty all the bullets. Each long barrel is also checked and tested individually to make sure that no bullets are inside. Commanders from the new shift examine the weapons and will not take them if they are not in order. The control of firearms is extremely tight even for police officers in Hong Kong. Most officers have never fired a single shot on duty in their entire career as police officers.

Since the EU has an internal security function, there are all types of weapons stored for this purpose in a highly restricted area at the station. In the less restricted equipment room, I was shown police radios, shields, tear smoke gas, weapons, etc. There were MP5s, shotguns, and many revolvers. Some of the weapons looked old while others quite new. Many equipments like radios were being recharged. As I was looking at some 8-inch long bullet-shaped projectiles, the sergeant explained to me that they can be fired when needed to the ground toward a crowd which will bounce around and hit legs of protesters. Because they are not accurate and may hit anything, the police will soon replace them with beanbags. There are also large boxes of weapons and equipment that are ready to be taken into an EU car for responding to serious problems anywhere in Hong Kong.

Once officers are off duty in Hong Kong, they are literally off duty. They are not encouraged to confront any offenders even if they happen to be witnessing a crime. In most occasions, officers are supposed to call 999 immediately to get officers on duty. They may use their discretion and intervene only when they are certain that they can handle the situation effectively. As the superintendent said:

> There is no need for officers in Hong Kong to be on duty twenty-four hours a day as we have several layers of officers always on duty. And off-duty officers can come to the station to be armed if necessary, which almost never happens. Officers can come from everywhere in serious situations like when mainlanders are robbing jewelry stores. . . . Twice I saw purse-snatching and theft right in front of my face when I was off duty. I made the decision that I could handle the situation and I made the arrests.

Handling Crime

Both Uniformed and Crime Branch officers handle crime problems and the divisional commander decides how to deploy them at the local level. It is generally a phased approach. Patrol officers handle the initial stage of the investigation, protect the scene, and give initial caution. If it is determined that a crime has occurred, they hand the case over to crime investigators. Crime investigators investigate the crime and interrogate the suspect. The Crime Branch officers at the divisional level investigate most of the crimes in their area while those in the Criminal Investigation Division at higher levels deal with more complex cases that often require more time and more expertise. Due to the budget situation in the Hong Kong Government, many crime officers have felt the pinch of budget cut. As one officer said:

> The Efficiency and Effectiveness Program (EEP) has an impact on crime officers. Detectives no longer have the kinds of allowances they used to have. They need resources to do investigations. But they don't have them. On top of that, they are under great pressure to solve crimes. Some of them just wish they could retire now.

Although uniformed officers do not play a major role in investigations, they are regularly briefed about criminal cases by investigation team leaders. They are directly involved in some special cases such as missing persons and death inquiries. They can also make arrests with the supervision of a sergeant, who in turn is under the supervision of an inspector. There is no specific statistics about the proportion of arrests made by patrol officers. But as first responders it is estimated that they initiate the majority of arrests. Common types of arrests include robbery, burglary, shoplifting, assault, fighting, illegal immigration, domestic abuse, drug-related offenses, juvenile offenses, and Triad-related offenses. Police officers in Hong Kong do not distinguish between detention and arrest. They are required to bring a suspect to the magistrate as soon as possible but not more than forty-eight hours.

Compared to Crime Unit officers, patrol officers play a more important role in crime prevention. Their activities in this respect are quite similar to community policing and problem-oriented policing in other parts of the world. They prevent crime by mediating parties in dispute, communicating with members of different groups, and educating the public about crime and safety issues. During the month of the Chinese New Year, for example, the police officers participate in a fortnight Community Service Festival in their local areas. They encourage residents to come to the local station to report problems. Citizens may also call, write, and send emails. The officers typically would survey residences where a problem has been detected, do follow-up visits of households victimized in the past, and organize anti-crime activities in target areas.

During a period from May to September 1993, five rape and attempted rape cases with young girls aged eight to twelve took place in a housing estate in Tin Yiu and Tin Shui, a new town area. The police analyzed the cases and found that the incidents occurred when young girls took elevators and were then taken under threat by the rapist to vacant flat where they were raped or sexually assaulted. One of the cases involved a victim who had cried out for help during the attack on the 38th floor and struggled with the rapist down to the 20th floor where the rapist ran away. Many neighbors heard the cry for help but nobody made a phone call to the police or intervened to help. It was apparent that the neighborhood relationship was weak. The weak sense of community and neighborhood relationship could be attributed to the fact that the residents had just moved in the area from various parts of Hong Kong and some were newly arrived immigrants. On the basis of this analysis, the police believed that a Community Awareness Program might help to solve the problem. They therefore utilized the rape and sexual assault cases as an opportunity to educate the residents in the new community (Chan, 1998).

Crime prevention is not only a routine police activity, but also a part of the community culture in Hong Kong. Many residential and business areas are walled. It is common to see gates to residential areas and apartment buildings locked up before midnight. Warning signs are posted conspicuously at business locations warning people about potential theft and criminal mischief. Such a culture allows the police to work closely with community organizations and private security to address their concerns. Monthly meetings, for example, are held with Mutual Aid groups, the members of which are elected by residents in their local areas. Regular contact is maintained with Kaifong Association, a general social welfare neighborhood organization all over Hong Kong. The police work closely also with private security on a regular basis. As uniformed security guards are invariably stationed at entrances to various places such as office buildings, apartment complexes, and schools, they are a major resource that the police rely on. They have a duty to provide formal surveillance, block access to property, watch for irregularities, and question suspicious persons. As a police officer said:

> To prevent crime, we target problem areas, patrol parking lot. . . . We have a high profile and try to be visible. We have vertical and horizontal patrol, inspect buildings, construction sites, vehicles, etc. We conduct stop-and-search. We work with owners' association, security guards, etc. Public Relations Officers and PCs work with and contact security guards to make sure they are doing their job instead of sleeping on duty.

One community organization that has a specific function in working with the police is the District Fight Crime Committee (DFCC). In the Tuen Mun Police District, for example, the police and the DFCC jointly organizes a crime prevention publicity campaign in which they remind residents to take measures to prevent crime during the Winter when the Chinese New Year takes place. The Hong Kong Police names this activity the Winter Precaution Campaign during which officers and DFCC members travel on an open-roof, double-decker bus in their districts distributing leaflets, gift packets, and scrolls; carrying crime-fighting messages to shopkeepers, residents, and villagers; and encouraging them to report crime to the police (*Offbeat*, 2002b). The DFCC was created in the early 1970s under the then Governor Murray MacLehose as part of the police reforms to upgrade the crime prevention and crime control function. It was first called the Fight Violent Crime Committee when it was established in March 1973 and was renamed the Fight Crime Committee in 1975. It then became District Fight Crime Committee (DFCC) in 1976. There are at present eighteen DFCCs, one in each of the eighteen administrative districts in Hong Kong. DFCC members are appointed by the Home Affairs Department with some cross-membership with the District Councils. The DFCC launched the Neighborhood Watch Scheme in 1985 to organize communal surveillance and provide information to the police. The police reforms in the early 1970s also resulted in the establishment of Police Community Relations Office (PCRO) at the divisional (now district) level (Brogden and Lau, 2001).

The police have also devoted significant resources to address youth crime. A prominent youth program, the Junior Police Call (JPC), was created in 1974 by the police to improve police-youth communication and mutual understanding and to gain the young people's cooperation against crime. Since 1974 over 800,000 youths have joined the JPC at one time or another and its membership of over 200,000 makes it one of the largest youth organizations in the world (Brogden and Lau, 2001). The School Liaison Officer Scheme was implemented in 1974, then taken over by the Neighborhood Police Coordinator in 1984, and again recreated in 1988 with the surge of youth crimes (Brogden and Lau, 2001). In addition, all police districts have Community Relations Officers who go to local schools regularly and organize after-school activities. Officers work closely with parents. They would, for example, call parents to pick up their children under sixteen after they take them out of disco clubs.

Although street officers in Hong Kong spend a large amount of their time on community crime prevention and problem-oriented police activities, some academics regard community-oriented policing in the Hong Kong a failure. This conclusion, however, is based largely on the instability of certain neighborhood police programs and the infrequent public use of them, not an overall assessment of the Hong Kong policing style and therefore may not be valid. The Neighborhood Police Units (NPUs), for example, has been evaluated on the basis of such criteria. The NPUs were introduced in 1974 and involved 1,406 officers by 1983 representing 5.8% of the total police strength. Each NPU area was divided into foot patrol beats with substations. However, the public use of the NPUs was scarce, the scheme was regarded as costly, and it was eventually discontinued.

The Neighborhood Watch Scheme (NWS) was launched by the DFCC in 1985 to organize communal surveillance and provide information to the police. But it met the same fate as the NPU scheme due to lack of participation. Consequently in 1997, the Home Affairs Department informed the Hong Kong Police that no plans were made to extend the trial to other districts. Besides practical issues such as instability and lack of participation, there are perhaps some institutional obstacles to developing community policing in Hong Kong. They include the paramilitary tradition of the Hong Kong Police, the socio-cultural environment of the Hong Kong society, the priority given to public order management, and the difficulty in implementing community policing itself like in many other countries in the world (Brogden and Lau, 2001).

Complaint

One of the common themes that come up during conversations and interviews with street officers is complaint. The complaint cuts both ways, both from and against the police. Officers say that citizens have higher demand on the police, are more critical about their work, and are less respectful to them in recent years. Members of the public are also more ready to sue the officers and there has been an increase in law-suits against the police. Many officers view the increased complaints and lawsuits as unreasonable demands from the public and claim that they have created more stress and pressure for them on the job.

Police statistics, compiled by the Complaint against Police Office (CAPO), corroborates only slightly with the officers' views. The complaint figures demonstrate an up-and-down trend over the past three decades (see Table 10.2 in Chapter 10). The first twelve years from 1974 to 1986, when CAPO first started compiling such statistics, saw the largest increase of complaints from 808 to over 4,000. In the next eleven years from 1987 to 1998, complaint figures decreased to below 3,000. Since 1999, the figures have gone up again fluctuating between a low of 3,083 in 1999 and a high of 3,833 in 2002. The number of complaints has increased in recent years, but not at a high level of the first decade when complaints were first recorded. Over the years, the number of police contacts with the public has also increased. The complaint rate, as measured by the number of contacts per complaint against police officers, has been relatively stable (Jiao, 2002).

According to a veteran officer, there are various reasons behind the complaints against police officers. Many are frivolous and used to vent dissatisfaction. Many are attributable to misunderstanding resulting from ignorance of the law and police policies. Some are filed because the arrested persons try to find a means to escape punishment or retaliate against the officers. A significant proportion of complaints, therefore, cannot be substantiated or can be regarded as false accusations against the police (see Table 10.2). Other contributors to the increased complaints include the generally higher knowledge and educational level of the public and the more open policies and channels for complaints provided by the government. Of course, police officers themselves also make mistakes; some complaints are clearly due to fault on the part of officers who are not conversant with the law or police procedures. Following are some comments made by officers regarding the increased complaints and lawsuits.

> There were a lot less complaints before. Now they sue for anything, even for not getting directions. Many complaints are trivial and technical. . . . They complain about not being able to get to their destinations fast. . . . Some people even complain when they see officers sitting in a restaurant for more than fifteen minutes. It's frustrating. We are humans. We have meals. Sometimes we eat more than fifteen minutes. . . . Some call the police simply because they need a witness to what's going on, some complain about noise, some about traffic accidents with no injury, many domestic disputes. . . . The "Quality Service" slogan backfires sometimes as one bad word may cause a complaint. . . . I got a complaint simply because I laughed when I saw a funny car a driver was driving. . . . Vice officers have less complaints and their job is less complicated because they don't wear uniforms. Uniformed Branch has to take everything.

> There are complaints about siring, about officers not dealing with traffic jams, about officers having bad manners, about being assaulted by officers, about officers not doing their job, etc. Many of the complaints show that the public doesn't know about police procedures. Like we have our siren on sometimes when there's an emergency and we turn it off when the emergency is gone. A member of the public may think that we were playing because it was not on the whole time and then complained about it.

> There are things that are not police job. The public doesn't know and sue the police for not doing their job. . . . Citizens call police for anything like water breaks. . . . We follow the procedures; but citizens can't keep up. For example, citizens don't know we are allowed to eat in certain establishments. . . . Stop-and-search causes most complaints, but it's the best crime prevention measure.

> New immigrants aren't familiar with Hong Kong law and give the police lots of trouble. . . . There are more problems from those immigrants who aren't too new and aren't too old, somewhere in between. Brand new immigrants don't cause much trouble. Neither do those being here for many years. . . . People are hostile to officers maybe because they had bad experience with police before, maybe they've been here for a while, gained legal status, and don't want to be treated as illegals anymore.

> We have many unreasonable requests from citizens. A case in point, we sometimes try to separate couples in dispute and then get sued for beating them. That's why we have the stress. . . . I had to restrain a man by holding his arm because he had a knife. Then I got sued for hitting him. . . . Some Hong Kong people are very selfish. If I'm screwed, all are screwed. When one is stopped, he wants others to be stopped, too.

As the officers perceive an increase in public complaints and lawsuits, they have also become more vocal about their dissatisfaction with the public. They complain about the increased demand and about the decreased respect and cooperation from the public. Here are some more comments from officers in this regard.

Citizens have more demands now. . . . We have more lawsuits now. The public knows the channel for lawsuits. . . . I'm not concerned as long as I'm doing the right things. I'm just stressed. . . . Most complaints are not valid. It's damn you do and damn you don't. We became passive as a result. . . . Citizens learn and know more things now. They sue more and have less respect for the police. . . . We are asked to be at the same level like American and British police, but citizens aren't at the same level. . . . Most complaints have no substance. We are doing a good job considering the stability and low crime rates.

The public doesn't care if you're a police officer any more. When I was a kid, I used to be scared of officers in uniform. But now citizens don't regard police as authorities. Police have to be very polite. Older people say "good morning," young people don't. . . . We don't have much challenge or pressure. Only problem is when we stop people, they may not cooperate. They don't know their obligations. We need to provide more public education.

The public has less respect for the police and is less cooperative to the police. . . . People will move aside for fire trucks but not for police cars. . . . They don't look at police officers as heroes as in the old days. There's also more demand for police because police are nicer now. . . . But we also need respect and understanding from citizens.

Public attitude toward the police is not as supportive as before. In recent years, the public complains more. We have to be more careful in doing our job. It's frustrating sometimes when we expect positive response from the public and don't get it. . . . We don't usually get cooperation from the public in the MTR. People are in a hurry under more time constraints. . . . It's hard to get information. They don't have to provide information. A fleshy woman may be an II; but she doesn't provide information, address, name to the officers.

Protesters shouldn't be against the police. People who want to have an assembly must inform the police of their intention and obtain permission first. But they don't always do. We must enforce the law. Why do protesters not cooperate with police? They know what they are supposed to do. Why do they have to confront the police? We're all for democracy. We're just there to ensure safety.

The media is not proportional in its report of the police. . . . Media only reports bad things. It never mentions good things officers do. . . . The media twists stories, they don't correct their mistakes, exaggerate police problems. . . . The police cannot say whatever we want; there are things police are ordered not to say to the public. But the public sometimes complains to the media and lie about what some officers say. The media doesn't do any investigation and take the public complaint as true and put it on the paper.

Due to the perceived increase in demand and complaints, many officers believe that their job has become more difficult overall. As some officers said:

The work used to be easier. Now we've more things to do. There's more pressure as there are more things to do and less time for family. There are more 999 calls. More people need help these days. . . . Public expectation is higher. Higher public expectation affects manpower. . . . There are more trivial matters that demand our time. We do more things and have less time for crime prevention. Some problems like smuggling is Custom's business; we should only handle possession and sales.

Not all street officers, however, view increased demand and complaints in negative terms. Officers that have a more neutral or positive position often have a different perspective in looking at these problems or are willing to put themselves in the shoes of the public. As some officers stated:

> Another reason citizens call us more is because they trust us more, we are more successful, we can provide more services. . . . Patience and tolerance are important. We need to have an eye for the detail and investigate the facts and have an accurate understanding of the situation. . . . Police policy emphasizes patience and tolerance. I am not really concerned about law-suits, I can't let the fear of lawsuits stop me from doing my job. Those who want to sue the police will do so no matter what we do and how we behave. . . . I offer to give information on lawsuits on site when there is a disagreement. . . . I don't have to be scared of lawsuits if I follow the procedures. As long as I'm doing the right thing and as long as we have the support, I'm not afraid of lawsuits.

> It's important to put oneself in the shoe of the public to understand public dissatisfaction. We were traveling in a European country once and were impressed by its magnificent buildings, beautiful sceneries, and special customs. However, our trip turned into an unpleasant memory when two impolite policemen intercepted us in a street one night and gave us a hard time with various excuses, hoping that we would give them money. This unpleasant experience gave me an opportunity to reflect on the role of police officers and public expectations for officers in Hong Kong (*Offbeat*, 2002c).

The street officers also have a lot to say about how complaints are handled by their supervisors and about the lack of support from police management. Many view the increased complaints as caused by behaviors of management officers. They complain about the way they handle public complaints and the lack of understanding from them. They wish to have more opportunities to air their grievances and that the senior-level officers listen to their concerns although they do admit that they will not be as open when talking to their higher ranks. Some believe that senior officers do know what they want, but turn a deaf ear. They generally expect more support and fairness from the senior administration as their job has become more challenging and the public is more demanding. They believe that top police officials should not always side with the public and outside suggestions should not always be accepted. Following are some comments in this regard from the street officers.

> Top management pays too much attention to complaint figures. They should look at the substance and content of the complaints. Reported figures and substantiated figures should be separated. . . . There are too many complaint cases. One phone call is a case. We should not be judged by complaints only. One area is bad does not mean other areas are bad. Citizens and management are too picky. . . . We like to have management support when we are doing the right things. But if our boss doesn't want to listen to our explanations, we will be

disappointed. . . . Management gives us the pressure by convicting us before examining the evidence. We should be supported if we aren't wrong.

Police constables may do less to avoid lawsuits because they don't feel they'll have the support and too many complaints hurt their careers. No matter which way it turns out, our upper level doesn't like complaints. We like to receive an order from our supervisor before we use force to avoid problems later on.

We don't have much pressure from complaints, more from the way the Force handles complaints because the Force doesn't always help or support us. We feel that the management doesn't like too many lawsuits and also we emphasize quality service. We're under the impression that the management picks those with less complaints for promotion considerations. . . . Complaints will hurt one's chance for promotion.

The police are too open for lawsuits. Other government agencies like the Fire are not so open. We've got lots of pressure from lawsuits. . . . Even if we did right, we still may get sued and the management is not behind us. So why do we work hard? It's better to avoid lawsuits by doing less.

I like to get more and better support from my supervisors. I have lots of pressure from the higher authorities and hope they loosen up. Sometimes it's the public's fault. Police job is more difficult because of more lawsuits, frivolous lawsuits that distract officers and take time away from doing our job. Officers aren't so scared of public complaints; it's the higher authorities that are more scared. Some newly promoted senior officers may not have as much experience or knowledge as their juniors. I don't think mid-management is doing a good job managing the lower ranking officers.

I don't like my supervisor to say "sorry" to the complainant when I'm not wrong. The upper and lower level management needs to listen more and tell less. Their attitude is important. Who would talk if you get a lesson after you talk? We need a straight upper management so we can be straight.

Street officers are stuck in between the police administration and the public and get squeezed. . . . Police officers beating citizens and citizens beating police officers aren't treated the same. . . . The police units that receive public complaints should educate the public not to sue if they don't have a good reason. . . . Media is not on the police side, either. We don't have much support from the management and administration when it comes to the media. . . . We hope they know what difficulties we have and how we work. Only when complaints come, they notice. We have to accept reality.

The frontline officers do not just complain about the police management. Many actually have a mixed view of the management as they are neither completely negative nor entirely positive about it. Some say, for example, that they like the management in general but not their immediate supervisors. Some say that there is more transparency in the Force now but less support. Many also understand and agree with their supervisors in the way they handle their problems and express an appreciation for improved quality of management officers. It is common to hear from the officers that the present management is more open and professional than previous ones. Following are some comments made in this regard.

> If we have pressure, our upper management has more pressure. We used to be a colony; the upper level had lots of power. Now we are not, the management has more pressure. . . . We have difficulty communicating with the higher ranks. That's why we have Open Forums. Open Forums are good for major issues, not for individuals' problems. We need to learn how to communicate better.

Officer Morale

The increased public complaints, frequent public disrespects, heavier workload, and perceived nonchalance from the police management seem to have taken a toll on officer morale. Many officers who have been on the Force for at least ten years say that their job was easier in the past and they used to enjoy more support. There is apparently a nostalgic feeling about the old days among some of these officers. The following comments demonstrate a recurring theme of officer morale.

> We had higher morale twenty years ago. We have lots of concerns and fears now. . . . We have more pressure during the transition, which affects morale. We have to do more with less manpower. . . . We do many things with the same resources. We need more resources.

> We don't get compliments sometimes for hard work and difficult cases. We have less initiatives to work than before. . . . There used to be more chances for promotions. . . . The morale is low for those of us on suspension when we didn't do anything wrong. Our salary is cut by half when we are on suspension. Even though the other half will be paid back if there's no problem, we still feel pressure working under investigation.

> We are getting better. We are providing better services. We are supposed to be happy. But we are not. It's easy to explain politically what's important. But we aren't clear about exactly what we're supposed to do. It's not like the more you do, the more you get. Everything becomes like, just to finish the work, finish the day, go home, and sleep. We don't have as much satisfaction as before. We make a good arrest; we're happy for a few days. But overall we have less satisfaction from work.

> We have lower morale due to less support. We hope for more respect and more support. . . . We aren't proud of being police officers any more. We don't want to tell people we are police officers. . . . Officers have less respect for the Force and less pride. . . . Police image is getting worse. The public knows we are scared. We are scared to work.

"Scared" may be too strong a word to describe the low morale among front-line officers. A more appropriate phrase might be "lack of incentives," which may result in passivity and trouble-avoiding behaviors at the street level. Around noon on a drizzling day in March, I saw two young officers walking the beat on

Hennessey Road in Wan Chai. A scruffily dressed Caucasian man with tangled gray hair was walking just two or three steps behind them yelling profanities. He was perhaps in his sixties, carrying a closed umbrella in one hand and a dirty brown-color bag in the other. He was shouting obscenities and racial slurs in both English and Cantonese to the two officers, "Stupid cops, fuck you, I'm gonna fuck you yellow dogs . . ." drawing attention from quite a few pedestrians. As he was cursing loudly behind the officers, the officers simply kept on walking at their normal speed without even turning their heads back. It seemed that they were trying to ignore this man. At the end of the block they made a left turn onto a smaller street and then sneaked into a narrow and dark ally, at which point the man finally stopped. He stood at the entrance of the alley with his head sticking out trying to see where the officers were going and continuing to yell obscenities for about a minute. All the time the officers didn't turn their heads around to make any reaction and all the time the guy cursed loudly and attracted attention from people on the street. I did not know what were the precursors to the cursing or what prompted the man to behave in such a manner against the officers. But I was stunned by the calm of the officers and their lack of action in confronting the man. I brought this incident up later when I met a police inspector. The inspector didn't seem to be surprised. He said, "Maybe the guy was drunk and he doesn't like the police. The officers didn't want to have any complaints. They didn't want trouble."

The reported incidents from the news media in Hong Kong also demonstrate a lack of respect or cooperation from the public, a significant factor contributing to low morale. In February, for example, a customer reportedly had lost his wallet while drinking coffee with friends at the Excelsior Hotel in Gloucester Road, Causeway Bay. He and his friends looked for the wallet and sought help from a waiter, but to no avail. After that, the victim called the police. Two uniformed officers were dispatched to investigate the complaint. But when they arrived, the security staff at the hotel ordered them to leave the premises (Lo, 2003). The blockage of police officers to investigate an alleged theft at the Excelsior Hotel came at a time when officers had their authority repeatedly challenged in the streets of Hong Kong. About two weeks earlier, a group of alleged Wo Shing Wo Triad members humiliated police officers when they were stopped for an identity check in Yau Ma Tei. During the incident, the apparently drunk young men intimidated the officers and one of them challenged an officer to a fistfight in full view of newspaper cameras. The standoff ended after police reinforcements arrived and the men agreed to hand over their identity cards. Eleven days after the Yau Ma Tei incident, the police were involved in another standoff while trying to arrest a group of ten men and two women suspected of involvement in a fight over a woman in a Sai Ching Street karaoke lounge in Yuen Long. The fight spilled onto the street before the police arrived. While being arrested, some of the suspects shouted abuse at police and threatened to give them a "hard time." The standoff ended also after police reinforcements arrived (Lo, 2003).

Officer Value

Complaints and morale issues aside, the street officers demonstrate certain typical values associated with the police profession. Many officers say, for example, that they joined the Force because they have a clear sense of justice and responsibility for the society. They are family-oriented, hold strong moral values, and believe in law and order. Despite the grumbling about the police management, many officers care about the police reputation. As an officer said: "Being an officer means law-abiding behaviors on and off duty because we represent the Force even after work." Similar to officers elsewhere, they embrace traditional law enforcement values but have a difficult time identifying with social aspect of police work. In a study that compares Hong Kong police officers with Hong Kong social workers (Cheung and Boutte-Queen, 2000:1617), for example, the police officers are found to be more conservative in protecting the family and express ambivalent feelings "about rescuing a child or preserving the family." They are also more punitive and revengeful, expressing strong "ambivalence about helping or punishing the perpetrator." Their professional role affiliated with the punitive system "may have contributed to these strong feelings." Many conservative and punitive values held by the officers are also consistent with the paramilitary traditions and institutional emphasis on public order management in the Hong Kong Police.

When discussing values, the officers often bring up the Force values the police management has been trying to inculcate in the rank-and-file since their promulgation in 1996. These values are listed in the "Vision and Statement of Common Purpose and Values," including the vision statement, seven objectives, and eight values, commonly referred to as "the Values" or "1-7-8" by the officers.[3] The officers say that the Force has put a stronger emphasis on these values in recent years. Divisional commanders talk more about legal and moral issues. And a workshop called Living-the-Values has been provided to all members of the Force three times. As a result, the value statements are now familiar to every officer. It is not clear, however, how much impact these values have on street officers especially when compared with their traditional values. Ideas along the lines of following statements, which are related to the Force values, are commonly heard from officers interviewed.

> The police have raised their standards, improved the quality of service, and adopted new values. . . . Every two months, we have discussion of different topics with seven or eight officers in each group supervised by a police inspector. . . . We are more polite now perhaps because of Quality Service policy. . . . 1-7-8 serve only as a reminder to us to be just and fair, a way to encourage us to do things we are already doing. They are ordinary principles for being a decent human being.

> Values set for the Force don't really matter to individual officers. Values are part of officers themselves and can't be imposed upon them. It's impossible to measure during officers' daily work who follow these values. If officers practice them, they may not be commended because only they know they are prac-

ticing them. What officers really care about are things more tangible like job security, support, promotion, and trust. Values are just theories. Practice is a different story.

We don't really put the Force values in our minds. The values advocated by the Force are just window-dressing. They are there for others to see, not for individual officers. . . . Officers rely on their own moral standards . . . 1-7-8 are what we were supposed to do from day one. They are nothing new. We have been practicing the same values all along. Different now is that they are put in writing and reinforce our sense of responsibility. . . . They keep talking about the values. They are only ideological education. I'm frustrated with them. We don't need to be preached everyday.

After 1997, new leaders push 1-7-8 to the top as an overarching policy. New police administration wants to make a difference. . . . 1-7-8 values are good, but it has become a show. . . . It takes serious communication to drive the message home. We do have communication channels, but they are channels only. . . . We try to reach out according to 1-7-8, but other agencies don't have these values. They don't understand why we go to them once a week. The values are just like the homework we have to hand in. . . . We should not make it a show.

Facing Change

Street officers see many changes both externally and internally in their working environment. Externally the educational level in the Hong Kong society has significantly increased over the past decade. Hong Kong is now a Special Administrative Region of China. More Mandarin-speaking tourists from the mainland visit Hong Kong everyday. There are also fewer illegal immigrants from the mainland. Due to these changes, many officers feel that there is a need to make some adjustment to their work routines. One officer said, for example:

We used to catch more illegal immigrants before 1997. We catch less now because it's easier for people from the mainland to come to Hong Kong and they don't need to cross the boundary illegally. . . . Maybe we should change the practice of stop-and-search for catching illegal immigrants.

Internally one of the changes is the increased number of college-educated officers who have more knowledge, possess better communication skills, and are better able to communicate with the public. But because of their higher education, they have developed a friction with many veteran officers. On the one hand, some veteran officers question the value of higher education for police work; some even think that it makes one unfit for police work. On the other hand, younger officers believe that new blood in the Force will eventually assimilate those who do not have the new knowledge. The Force as a result is experiencing a cultural clash between two groups of officers due to the education and knowledge gap. Those who have recently graduated from college, for example, may use a computer language that older officers cannot understand. As some officers commented:

Changes are related to use of computers, building police image, and service quality policy. . . . There is more technology. Crime reports are computerized. The Force encourages officers to get more knowledge and more training in new technology such as computers. Computer training is provided to all. . . . Experience is still important. So the new and the old must work together. . . . We used to focus on performance. Now we also emphasize knowledge and education. The Force is more computerized, has better equipment.

Another internal change concerns police management. Officers are overall quite positive about this change considering that the management has become more professional and efficient and has communicated more with the lower ranks. Some officers said, for example:

Internal communication has improved over the past few years. There is more communication between lower and higher ranking officers. Less hierarchy and better attitudes. In the old days, lower ranking officers' concerns seldom reached the higher level. . . . We have more transparency now. We can say anything.

The biggest change is management . . . DVCs [divisional commanders] now ask: "What difficulty do you have?" They communicate a lot more now with junior officers. . . . Officers in the same rank tend to get together, which is one of the problems. Now there are also inter-ranking officers that gather together.

Lots of changes have taken place in the past few years . . . rebuilding police stations, upgrading equipment, better uniforms, more communication with the external community, etc. . . . The management is not the same. They focus more on people than on machines. The promotion system is more fair than before. . . . The working environment is much more comfortable. There is more communication with the upper ranks. There has been more transparency and more interaction.

Not all officers see changes in the management in the area of communication and transparency as positive, however. As some officers stated:

DVCs talk about things we already know, big policy issues. Feedback is slow. . . . Open Forums aren't so open. We aren't talking. They may be aware of our problems, but they aren't able to respond to our problems. . . . Not much communication with upper management. We dare not talk or give suggestions during meetings with immediate management. Whoever talks a lot leaves a bad impression and may lose a chance for promotion. We need good reports from immediate management. It's rule by man here. Immediate supervisors are people, too. Theoretically, on paper, communication is better and promotion is more fair. In reality, not much has changed. I don't see a chance for management to really change.

There has also been a major change in the police in recent years in terms of its increased emphasis on service quality due to the Service Quality Initiatives. "Service Quality" has become a buzzword in the Hong Kong Police. In a broad sense, it means that the police will strive to improve their service for the public with civility and a customer orientation. They will do more things than before, some of which may not be viewed as police work by officers such as illegal hawking and illegal immigration. In a narrow sense, service quality means fifteen minutes' response time. Officers need to provide explanations if arrival time is more than fifteen minutes. Many officers believe that positive changes have taken place due to the Service Quality Initiatives. Their efficiency and quality of service, for example, have significantly improved in recent years and a service culture is taking shape in the Force. The following comments provide a glimpse of the impetus and effect of the emphasis on service.

> More emphasis is put on quality service after 1997 because the whole Hong Kong government has become more transparent. There're more changes, higher demand, higher qualification. We don't necessarily have more pressure. In the 60s and 70s, living standards were lower. Now we have more information, more knowledge, and more communication. We change to adapt to change in the society.

> In the old days, the police didn't project a very civil image in public, were more authoritarian, and could get away with it. The society has changed. The public has higher education and will no longer accept uncivil and authoritarian police attitudes and behaviors. They don't like the police tactics of control and threats or being rude. The police have become more civil and have more respect for civil rights. We are no longer just a force of order; we are also a force of service.

> We used to be more bureaucratic. Now we ask what extra we can do internally and externally. . . . Police enjoyed more power in the old days. Now we are more service-oriented. . . . The Force is more transparent today, more committed to serving the public. The district station has been remodeled to provide a better reporting environment for the public. . . . Our working conditions have been improved. . . . Police are treated like a business or a service that attracts customers, not like the run-down place in the old days. The public feels more comfortable.

> I don't see conflict between service and law enforcement. We have to enforce the law for protection of society. We protect society by being present. The public needs us. We provide quality service to some and law enforcement to others.

While many officers attribute the positive changes to the Service Quality Initiatives, some officers, especially those used to old practices, find it difficult to adjust to this change. Some view their job as having become more challenging and others find it difficult to balance service aspect of police work with law enforcement. The following comments provide a sense of these attitudes.

> In the old days, the police didn't have to be nice; now they have to be more patient. . . . It's true that in the old days the police were more authoritarian; but they also had a stronger deterrent effect. Now even kids don't fear the police and regard the police as ordinary servants. As a result, young people offend more. The public sometimes becomes the victim in the process. For example, some businesses mistreat customers and don't think the police can do anything

about it. In the old days, the presence of a police officer may mean that a bar owner will give some money back to a customer to end the dispute. But now, they won't do it because they don't think the police have so much power. In this sense, civilians are sometimes the victims of quality service.

It's easy to talk about quality service, but it's sometimes hard to distinguish politeness from being helpful. If you are polite to the offender, you can't help the victim. If you are helpful, you sometimes have to be aggressive and offend the offender. A very nice officer can't help very much. Being polite or not is not easy to distinguish sometimes.

Quality service means being polite and being helpful. "Upper levels" require this new style of policing and we suffer at the front-line. We are doing things other government agencies should do, court matters, illegal hawking, land disputes, family disputes, etc. They call, but they don't want police when police arrive and they don't press charges. If we do so many things, how can we be professionals? If service is pushed to the top, the main direction is wrong because our priority becomes not getting lawsuits. . . . We have quality service for others, but we don't have quality service for us. More workload and more demand have been put upon us. We do things used to be done by other agencies. Quality service is easier to say than do.

We have service quality. Service quality itself isn't bad. We agree we should be polite. But we are still police officers. We have to say "no" sometimes. We need to control, command respect. We are polite in investigating crime. But we get cursed and confronted all day. We aren't scared, just stressed. Quality service is hard to do. Everybody has different expectations. People are all different. We should solve their problems. Quality service is too abstract. Quality service and law enforcement are contradictory. We don't make it convenient for people. We stop people to check their IDs. We create inconvenience. Then nobody likes us no matter how nice we are. So quality service is hard.

Law and order and service must be balanced. . . . The police used to be more authoritarian. We should return to the old style. We need to focus more on crime control. . . . We responded to a domestic call. When we arrived at the residence, we couldn't get the door open. We talked with the husband who didn't let his wife out. It was the wife who called the police; but she wasn't injured. The man refused to open the door. We could only talk and tried to help the woman, but weren't able to get inside. If we took the man, he may sue us. Even if we wanted to help the woman, we couldn't. It's hard to balance law enforcement and service. Patience is like a test in itself. We must be polite even to a criminal.

We have more quality service to meet higher demand and higher expectations. We are challenged by the fact that we need to both provide service and enforce the law. To balance these two functions, we treat citizens with dignity even though we are enforcing the law. We give them protection and legal rights where applicable. We use discretion and don't intervene in every violation, every crime. But quality service policy confuses some officers because some police work doesn't involve service. . . . Most officers actually support quality service policy. We have satisfaction when we serve the needs of people and when we are able to help. It's the implementation part that causes lots of problems for the front-line officers. We have more pressure. We don't know who we are sometimes. We don't know what authority we have.

We do provide quality service. But no matter how good the quality of service is, we offend people. We are enforcers. We have to control ourselves and we have to protect ourselves. If there is a conflict between service and enforcement, we enforce the laws first; but we try to explain their rights also. If it's law enforcement, we try to satisfy service. . . . But you can never satisfy the public.

Quality service has gone too far. It's difficult for us. We are police, how can we have service quality? I respect you, but I have to do my job. . . . Citizens call police for too many things. We should educate the public at the same time as we push for quality service. We are also human beings. The management just asks us to do everything no matter what. If the society doesn't have police, it'll be chaotic. The police should have more respect. We are law enforcement officers. We arrest and investigate. We should go back to more traditional police practices. Service quality policy creates conflicts between management and front-line officers. We become servants on the street, have no respect, no power. Service quality reduces law and order's importance.

Impressions

Street officer behaviors in Hong Kong present a typical case of working under pressure at a time of change. From foot patrol to car patrol, from crime prevention to crime investigation, frontline officers serve as street-level bureaucrats representing the most direct contact the public has with its government. In return they may have become the target for venting dissatisfaction with anything that may go wrong with the government and experience first-hand many uncertainties and difficulties of a society in transition. The officers, however, have demonstrated a high level of professionalism and dedication at this difficult time and improved significantly the quality of service they provide to the public. Their complaints, excessive as they may seem, do not outweigh their commitment to the police profession and sense of responsibility to the society. The truth of the matter is: police officers tend to groan and moan as a way to release stress and pressure when given the opportunity to do so, especially in a setting that is anonymous and confidential. Hong Kong police officers are no different. Their frustrations should not be interpreted as a lack of professionalism or dedication. When they are out on patrol, investigating crime, or serving the public, they demonstrate a high level of professionalism and commitment that is easily observable.

The same can be said about officer morale. Although the officers complain about poor morale, how this low morale has affected their quality of service and productivity remains an open question. My impression based on personal observations is that the negative effect of their frustration on their daily work is insignificant. It is clear that the police officers are, by and large, able to continue to maintain their service quality and productivity. The sources and effect of the frequently-mentioned "low morale" need to be analyzed from a larger context in which officers work. Police officers work in a profession that is quasi-military in nature and often requires a firm stance toward the public. In such a working environment, they do not enjoy as much "democracy" with their management as those in other professions and frequently face public disrespect. The officers also routinely come in contact with the dark, ugly, and tragic side of society and may develop a negative view of the world as a result. This working environment is clearly a source of stress and burnout and could create a sense of disenfranchisement. These feelings, as frequently expressed as they are by the officers, could be better understood as occasional frustrations rather than a loss of confidence in their work. Nevertheless, the specific reasons behind officer complaints about low morale should be better understood for training and management purposes. There are at least three crucial factors that may have contributed to officer complaints about low morale. First, the adjustment to change both in the Force and in the Hong Kong society is an add-on to their routine responsibilities. Second, respect is an important cultural element in the Chinese society, the absence of which arouses a strong reaction from the Hong Kong police officers. Third, talking about low morale helps shift the burden of responsibility to the police management, from which the street officers wish to gain more support and understanding.

Another interesting officer behavior observed is their attitudes toward change. Change is a constant theme in all conversations and interviews with the officers. Two examples of this are Anti-II and EU operations. Anti-II activities are part of the colonial tradition. As Hong Kong is now a sovereign part of China, anti-II activities are used for the sole purpose of maintaining the arrangement of "one-country, two-systems." Government policies on IIs, as time goes on, may need to be adjusted because Hong Kong and mainland China will become more integrated economically, politically, and culturally. Moreover, the anti-II tradition seems to have created a bias against legal immigrants, which requires careful examination at a time of increased emphasis on civil rights and human dignity. As for the EU, its importance has been diminished due to several decades of peace and stability and a strong foot patrol presence in Hong Kong. Some officers view EU as a luxury that is no longer needed. Others, however, believe that the police must be prepared for the unthinkable and the security of Hong Kong depends on the presence of a strong para-military unit in the form of EU, whose rapid deployment, special military equipment, and specially trained officers may mean life and death during human and natural disasters. The intentional overlap and assistance provided to foot patrol officers remain essential in major emergency operations. As an observer, it seems that a correct balance has been struck between foot and EU patrol with the current size of the patrol fleet, which is extremely small in comparison to other major cities in the world.

Comments from many officers regarding the newly instituted Force value statements indicate that it may be unrealistic to expect such statements to have a significant, positive effect on officer behavior. Statements such as these are there to highlight and reinforce certain values and represent the stance of a large public organization. Many of the values such as integrity, professionalism, and law and order are consistent with the officers' traditional values and moral standards developed from their upbringing and socialization in the Force. In cases where the value statements come in conflict with their values and standards, they may create a certain level of frustration among the officers. Service quality, for example, is a new value introduced in recent years in response to changes in the Hong Kong society. It has been met with resistance from many officers in the Force. But resistance to service aspect of police work is a common phenomenon in the police profession and should be viewed as a natural part of the change process. As indicated from the institutional and cultural perspectives, the success of this process requires consistent and institutionalized effort in developing the individual officers as well as the organization.

Officer views of changes in the Hong Kong Police, particularly in regard to the Service Quality Initiatives, represent to a great extent the pain before the birth of a new culture. The police will inevitably continue to evolve and transform because what is taking place in the Hong Kong Police in terms of service quality is a part of the global trend in policing. The process is not meant to be easy or straightforward. Although the police management sees the need to change the culture in response to changes in the society, the balance of public and organizational interests are ultimately "seen in the decisions of officers in their day-to-day activities" (Langworthy and Travis, 2003:27-28). Street officers will struggle with the dilemma and sometimes contradiction between law enforcement and service, between tradition and reality, between habitus and field (Bourdieu, 1990), and between order and legality (Skolnick, 1994). They will always wear many different hats. They may be stressed occasionally. But they will eventually learn to adjust to their different roles as law enforcement professionals.

Notes

1. Search cadres patrol on foot; but unlike beat officers, they do not cover a specific area.

2. The stations include Central, North Point, and Wan Chai in the Hong Kong Island Region; Kun Tong, Wong Tai Sin, and Kowloon Bay Mass Transit Railway (commonly called MTR) in the Kowloon East Region; Mong Kok, Sham Shui Po, and Tsim Sha Tsui in the Kowloon West Region; Tsing Yi and Tsuen Wan in the New Territory South Region; and Tuen Mun and Yuen Long in the New Territory North Region.

3. The vision is "that Hong Kong remains one of the safest and most stable societies in the world." The seven objectives are: "Upholding the rule of law, Maintaining law and order, Preventing and detecting crime, Safeguarding and protecting life and property, Working in partnership with the community and other agencies, Striving for excellence in all that we do, and Maintaining public confidence in the Force." The eight values are: "Integrity and honesty; Respect for the rights of members of the public and of the Force; Fairness, impartiality and compassion in all our dealings; Acceptance of responsibility and accountability; Professionalism; Dedication to quality service and continuous improvement; Responsiveness to change; and Effective communication both within and outwith the Force."

8

Management Officer

Management officers are different from street officers largely due to their higher positions and longer experiences in a police organization. They may hold different world outlooks and values and see police problems in different lights. Management officers in the Hong Kong Police refer to those in the rank of inspector and above including both middle managers and senior administrators. Middle police managers include inspectors, senior inspectors, chief inspectors, superintendents, senior superintendents, and chief superintendents. Senior police administrators comprise assistant commissioners, senior assistant commissioners, deputy commissioners, and the Commissioner. This classification specifically excludes sergeants as part of the management because sergeants usually work closely with street officers at the frontline and share more similarities with street officers than with police managers. Many sergeants, for instance, walk the beat themselves and handle various street problems on a regular basis. Their functions and responsibilities differ significantly from management officers as a whole. As an inspector stated, there are two kinds of officers in the Hong Kong Police, the rank-and-file and the police cadres. The rank-and-file include police constables and sergeants who are generally referred to as JPOs (junior police officers) and there are about 20,000 JPOs in the Hong Kong Police. Police cadres cover those holding inspector positions and above and about 8,000 officers can be put into this category (see Table 4.1).

Managing Day-to-Day Police Operations

The police managers emphasize visibility, stop-and-search, response to calls, and order maintenance during their routine operations. Some of these activities involve beat patrol at the divisional level and others require coordination at the regional and Force level. At the divisional level, police commanders ensure that patrol officers stay highly visible in their respective areas, engage in crime prevention and problem solving, and provide quality service to the public. They believe that by being visible the officers can prevent crime and disorder in the community. They consider that the Hong Kong Police is doing an excellent job in community crime prevention. Some also believe that they should balance crime prevention activities with deterrence operations such as mobile patrol, rapid response, and arrests. As some police managers said:

> Officers in Hong Kong walk the beat and are highly visible. One extra officer is one extra prevention. . . . The Hong Kong police are already doing crime prevention at police stations, patrolling on foot, educating the public, and solving problems in the community. But we need more deterrence by mobile patrol, rapid response, and arrests. We need more members of the public and civilian organizations that engage in crime prevention.

Besides walking the beat and being highly visible, officers are given the authority to conduct stop-and-search, which is considered another effective crime prevention measure. The police commanders encourage the officers to stop and search but advise them to make decisions on approaching people based on suspicion and use care in the process. They consider it their job to make sure that officers stay active in the street. But many commanders trust that their officers will work hard out of their own initiatives. They commonly deny that they have quotas for stop-and-search. As some divisional commanders stated:

> Officers are stopping and searching people. It's one of the most effective measures. . . . They do it mainly due to their sense of duty. . . . We get complaints from people being searched. Officers need to explain why, be polite. . . . Officers are trained and guided on how to conduct stop-and-search. . . . There's no quota for stop-and-search. But officers get compliments. . . . They get compliments due to their sense of duty, not number of stops.

> I don't give figures like how many arrests, how many crimes, etc. You can focus on prevention. If officers don't have pressure, they can focus on prevention. If the public wants security, they need to give us some power. Police need to prevent crimes. Stop-and-search is a good crime prevention measure. They can only stop people who act suspiciously or have committed a crime or are illegal immigrants.

While some officers, according to police commanders, are active in the street due to their training, sense of duty, and pride, some other officers are just working day by day and are not motivated about their patrol responsibilities. They are not active either because they do not have a sense of career or they fear public complaints. A daily routine of a police commander therefore is to provide guidance and support to the officers, cultivate a sense of duty, and keep the officers motivated. As some divisional commanders said:

> I make sure that people who work for me work properly. I have to motivate them. My guys are under constant pressure to work twenty-four hours a day. I make sure that they have enough resources, well equipped. We try to upgrade the system for checking ID cards to show "Wanted" or "Not wanted." Our workloads have increased dramatically over the last ten years.

PCs are not motivated to be active on the street. They try to avoid complaints. . . . PCs work for money. Before 1997 the economic situation was good; you can make a fortune without much work. Nobody cared about morals or ethics. So a money culture has developed. People are so materialistic and so narrow-minded. In police work, we are so conviction-minded. We are not after the truth. Maybe if we go after the truth, we will be more motivated. . . . It's very difficult to instill a spirit of public service. If we are really customer-oriented, we should take this issue of truth and conviction further.

MTR runs through five regions. MTR is not an exciting district. I check with officers and make sure that they are motivated to work. Officers often do not feel they have an identity. We try to create a sense of identity for our officers. Another challenge is that I have to communicate with officers in stations away from the District Headquarters.

I would say officers are observant and cautious. But they are generally not motivated to be active on the street. They want to avoid complaints. Officers have respect for the due process. But they are cynical about complaints, about the media, and about the public. They believe that complaints against them are used often as a tactic to discredit the police.

Police managers take crime problems as a serious challenge and devote their time to it on a daily basis. For crime problems that have already occurred, they direct officers to work closely with related groups and to target specific locations and places. As break-ins go up, for example, patrol officers are instructed to increase their contacts with the watchmen and guards to make sure they are doing their jobs. But they do not consider that the police management is figure-driven and they are not held accountable simply by crime statistics. As some divisional commanders said:

Challenges include crime, law and order situation, burglaries, robberies, purse snatching, assaults, youth crime. Seventy percent of the population is below thirty in my District. . . . Public housing, potential hazardous incident areas. . . . Banks, hospitals, developments, population of 250,000, being an old division, drug addicts, street gamblers, long coastline, illegal immigrants landing in the area all present as challenges. . . . Some youths like hanging around 7-11, drinking, stealing petty cash.

Crime is number one issue I deal with. I have management meetings every morning to discuss crimes and do analysis. . . . We don't encourage elites syndrome, figures like arrests. We look at a particular area as a whole. . . . We used to be more figure-driven. Less so now. Some commanders may be concerned that if crime figures keep going up, they may be questioned for not doing their jobs. But they are not necessarily demoted. We are not as figure-driven as before. We should move away from the figure-driven policy. . . . We have less focus on crime partially due to the customer orientation.

Order maintenance activities focus mainly on special public events or incidents that involve a large number of people such as street demonstrations, civil disorders, transportation disasters, and natural disasters. Because demonstrations are more frequent in the Hong Kong Island Region, police commanders at the district and divisional level here find themselves routinely involved in managing such events. Public order incidents are rare elsewhere; but police commanders everywhere in Hong Kong take these events very seriously. If they do not have such an event, they regularly conduct public order training. If such an event does occur, it demands the most manpower and resources. Based on specific needs and requests, public order trainings and operations often involve multiple divisions and districts and various units at the regional level. As some police managers stated:

> The five EUs get together once a month. We look at our weapons, do tactical training. It may never happen. But we must be ready for major disasters, plane crash, natural disasters. . . . So we do training and run exercises, test communications systems, etc.

> Wanchai is the busiest station in Hong Kong. It's an old station. We have the Convention Center here. Public order issues often come up as there are many demonstrations. We follow Public Order Ordinance. There are people who break the law. I have to make sure that they don't get hurt, block traffic, or put themselves in danger.

> We often have special operations, traffic sometimes. . . . We respond to requests. We have marches, protests, petitions, school tours, sports ground activities. . . . They make the requests; we provide the service. We need to beware of everything. Right now, the Right-of-Abode seekers sometimes march from Chater Garden in Central to the Immigration Department in Wanchai. We have to be there. We take marches very seriously. What we do is if the march crosses two districts, we take over when the march gets our District, with the Tactical Unit covering the whole region.

Managing Administrative Functions

Most police managers handle various administrative, organizational, and personnel issues on a regular basis. Those in the rank of superintendent and inspector often serve as managers of a police division. While a superintendent serves as the divisional commander, inspectors are put in charge of the Uniformed Branch, the Crime Branch, and the Administrative Support Branch as assistant divisional commanders. In a police division in Sham Shui Po, for example, 2 chief inspectors, 3 senior inspectors, and 4 inspectors are responsible for the Uniformed Branch, which consists of 11 senior sergeants, 26 sergeants, and 120 constables. One chief inspector, 2 senior inspectors, and 3 inspectors are in charge of 5 sergeants and 29 police constables in the Crime Branch. A police manager also monitors the daily schedules, break times, overtimes, and leaves of their subordinates. Following are some comments by superintendents and inspectors regarding their work.

We are like a major corporation. We have our CEO, the Commissioner, and I am his manager. I tell them where I go for vacations. But so does a manager in IBM. We have our strategic plans and I follow and implement those plans.

I'm in charge of Operations. Another assistant divisional commander is in charge of Administration and Support. And another is responsible for Crime. A superintendent is in charge of the whole Division. . . . Supervisors randomly visit patrol officers or join them on patrol for about thirty minutes. Each officer can expect to meet his supervisor at least once a day on patrol. . . . Officers are not allowed to leave on evening and night shifts due to higher demand.

We used to have an inspector who graduated from the Police Training School in charge of a subunit. Now we emphasize sending experienced inspectors back to frontline operations and putting them in charge of a subunit. I am a senior inspector and I am sent back to be in charge of a subunit, which is one of the best positions in the Force.

Whenever my guys on the beat are hot and thirsty, I think they should just go to 7-11 or another store to get a drink. But the official policy is that on an 8 and a 3-quarter shift, an officer has one hour meal break, which can be divided into two, and fifteen minutes' break in first half and fifteen minutes in second half of the shift. So basically an officer is walking the beat for 7 hours. We stagger the handover and meal breaks so some officers are always on the beat. . . . We have designated places for officers to eat.

If we have overtime, we get time off. We don't get paid except the officers in CID. Those guys work very hard, always dealing with their cases, interviewing people. But with the government clamping down on budgets, they are also told to use time off and not get paid for overtime. But many of them can't take time off. With no extra pay for overtime, they don't want to work in CID. They want to be in Uniform, do your 8-hour shift, and finish the day. Less stress.

A significant amount of time is spent on administrative and personnel matters including human resources, policies, reporting, planning, and meetings. Most commanders believe that they are well resourced or have more resources than most places in the world. Some complain that they do not have adequate manpower to cover all beats and their officers are stretched. The personnel issues police commanders deal with often involve individual officer problems and complaints. They meet with the officers, communicate with them, pass on information to them, or refer them to other programs or units for further actions. An important part of a police manager's job is to develop officers under his or her command, including officer training, career development, and self-learning. As some commanders said:

I would say, very roughly, I deal with staff issues 20% of the time; policy writing and reporting, 20%; reviewing cases and policing, 10 to 15%; administrative planning, building planning, 15%; and the rest of the time dealing with people, meetings, etc. My chief inspector spends 80% of his time in the car and 20% of his time on administrative duties. We are an old station right in the middle of the village in Hong Kong, the Lan Gui Fong and Soho area. Soon they will demolish this building and turn it into a commercial and entertainment building.

Some of our officers have gambling debt or women's problems or a combination of the two. Maybe about 10% of the Force suffers from some psychological problems. When officers are in such a situation, the Force tries to help them recover by providing counseling services, treatment, and training. Their revolvers will be taken away. They will be put behind a desk to see if they will be ok. There are all kinds of procedures to protect them from being fired like judicial hearings. It takes a long time to get rid of a problem officer.

I handle customer relations, training, complaints and compliments, motivating officers, personnel issues, planning, career management, and self-learning. . . . We have the POINT, the internal information system. Messages get across a lot faster now because of computerization.

English is getting worse in Hong Kong. The CE [Chief Executive] actually talked about that. We need to improve the English language skill of our officers being an international city. English is the international language. We lag behind Singapore where almost 90% of the people speak good English. If we go to a bar, we can tell who is from Singapore because that person usually speaks better English and is more civilized.

In terms of salary, police officers in Hong Kong are paid a little higher than civil servants in other government departments (see Table 8.1). They are paid more, according to the police managers, because of the nature of their job, which is more demanding, and officers deal with more discretionary situations on a

Table 8.1 Monthly Salary Range for Police Officers in Hong Kong

Entry Point	Salary
Constable	
5 subjects at Grade E in HKCEE*	HK$14,670 - $20,995 (max.) (US$1,890 - $2,706)
3 subjects at Grade E in HKCEE	HK$14,240 - $20,995 (max.) (US$1,835 - $2,706)
Inspector	
Degree with a pass in examination	HK$25,480 - $53,675 (max.) (US$3,284 - $6,917)
Degree/Associate Degree/Higher Diploma	HK$24,810 - $53,675 (max.) (US$3,197 - $6,917)
Matriculation	HK$24,180 - $53,675 (max.) (US$3,116 - $6,917)

* Hong Kong Certificate of Education Examination.
Source: Adapted from *www.info.gov.hk/police*, retrieved in September, 2005.

daily basis. The higher salary as well as perhaps higher expectation of police officers also means that an officer cannot supplement his or her income through private employment without prior approval. And if approved, the work sought must be honorable, benefit the society, and not involve any conflict of interests. Officers can of course also increase their incomes through promotion to a higher rank. Police commanders say that various factors are considered in promoting officers such as number of arrests, compliments, sense of duty, and level of dedication. Some commanders see the promotion system as lacking in more objective criteria. Service quality, for example, should not be measured simply by the number of complaints.

Management officers as well as street officers rotate their positions regularly. Divisional commanders in the rank of superintendent usually rotate every four years and assistant commanders in the rank of chief inspector every two years. The divisional commanders interviewed at the time of this study had been in their position anywhere from eleven months to three years. Street officers change patrol beats every three months and police district every four years. Regular rotation is believed to benefit individual officers personally and improve the police organization generally because the officers gain a wider experience and develop a better career and the Force achieves better coordination and suffers less from corruption. Following are some comments by superintendents and inspectors regarding their experiences in this regard.

> If a detective is promoted to sergeant, he must go back to Uniform. He can apply to go back to CID subject to examinations. You have to serve in Uniform for two years before transfer. A Uniform inspector and a CID inspector can transfer to each other's positions. We want them to be exposed to different experiences, so different divisions can understand each other and work together better besides having better career development for individual officers.

> I used to work in a different district, where there are more demonstrations and many entertainment businesses. Here we have more elderly people in public housing and we don't have Karaoke. . . . As a new police division in a new town, it has less problems. But we still have lots of juvenile problems, problems related to social economy, and problems associated with transportation. They all influence our work.

> We are one of the busiest stations. . . . We have 24-hour businesses and attract people here because of the night-life activities here. . . . We have many crimes and juvenile problems. We also have an indigenous population in our District. The indigenous people have their own culture and customs. . . . Gambling is ok. . . . But law and order is the same for the indigenous population. Police officers treat them the same in law and order matters as Hong Kong citizens.

> Rotation and change of beats and shifts give officers a balance, variety, and even out workload. . . . The police change your job without changing your career. . . . And that's also what I like about the Hong Kong Police. . . . I like the working conditions here. . . . There are good opportunities for officers to find the right spot to develop and grow. Many officers have their right spots in the

Force. . . . As you can see, there are many careers for officers. . . . We have jumps in commanding positions in Hong Kong.

I used to work in Yau Ma Tai and Chang Sha Wan. I like the rotation between station operations and management. It's good for career development. . . . The policy is supposed to increase police officers' understanding of each other so they work better with each other. . . . I don't think it's fair for me to work in one station for ever.

The policy of rotation has been passed down from the Royal Hong Kong Police. Although most commanding officers see the benefit of this policy, some believe there are both pros and cons. It ultimately depends on the individual to view this policy either favorably or negatively. Those who enjoy their rotation experiences consider that the policy provides them with the variety and spice on the job. As years go by, they can build more relationships with various divisions and units, develop greater confidence in their job, and cultivate a holistic view of the Force. When an officer moves up all the way to the rank of assistant commissioner, for example, he or she often has been all over the police organization. One of the senior assistant commissioners interviewed has over thirty years' experience in the Hong Kong Police. He has had split experiences in Operations, Uniform, CID, Policy, and Management and thus been exposed to all types of police businesses. Officers like him are naturally in a better position to provide input on management decisions.

Those who do not enjoy their rotation experiences either have a bad time or see more drawbacks in this process. Some management officers, for example, were rotated for the sake of rotation without careful prior planning and consequently did not benefit from this experience. Some see this policy as an obstacle for meaningful changes in their districts or divisions. Commanders in some areas, for example, may not want to make waves or commit themselves to fundamental changes if they see themselves only as temporary managers of a division or district. They do not have a sense of belonging. Even for commanders committed to changes, they may face serious challenges and have to walk a fine line between an old culture and a reform program. As a senior inspector and a divisional commander stated:

I was transferred and was ready to go. Then I was told, "You are not coming here." I went to another station, and I was told again, "You are not supposed to come here. No one knows you are coming here." I asked the management and then was told, "You will go to the Command and Control Center." I was moving to three places before I finally came to the Command and Control Center. It shows that there is no planning by district commanders. What happened here to planning?

I think that the officers here had not been to other regions and this area has a different culture. The system was a bit loose: untimely submission of files, procedures not being followed closely, lax mentality, etc. Lower ranking officers tended to keep what's happening from me until some problems popped up. I had to tie up the loose ends. I had to let three officers go. . . . I'm aware of the fact that I was an outsider as I used to be with the Marine and I brought stan-

dards from the outside. I communicated my intention with the District level. I
tried to avoid dramatic changes and I tried to introduce changes incrementally.
I knew that they thought I didn't trust them.

Managing Changes

Police managers are in a better vantage point to see changes and development in the Hong Kong Police over the years. Many of them have personally
experienced the changes in such areas as anti-corruption, modernization,
professionalization, and service. After the anti-corruption years of the 1970s, the
police have been engaged in modernization with better equipment and technology. They have enhanced the efficiency of police operations. And more recently
they embarked on the Service Quality Initiatives and have improved their
services to the public (Hong Kong Police Review, 2000). The police are quicker
in responding to calls and better in informing and communicating to the public.
Email communication, for example, has sped things up significantly. Their goal
according to former Commissioner Hui (2002:168) is "to develop a police force
that is accountable, lives within its means, manages for performance, and is
service-oriented. To achieve these aims, the Force has pursued a dual approach
under the broad headings of Service Quality and Performance Management." As
some superintendents stated:

> Pursuit of excellence is one of our objectives. . . . The Force experienced great
> changes over the years. I came here in the 80s when the Force was in good
> shape. Pre-80s, in the 60s and 70s, there were lots of corruption. So the 70s'
> focus was anti-corruption and demanding for funding for the Force. The 80s
> were equipment years with modernization and pay rises. We have been well
> resourced since the 80s. . . . There are two boosts for Hong Kong's economy.
> One is 1949 when lots of people came to Hong Kong and put money here,
> which helped the economy. And then we have the booming property-market in
> the 80s, which brought in lots of money for the government. So we were able to
> receive more funding.

> 90s are the service years. We've changed our approach to police work. . . . We
> see the push for service since 1995 mainly due to the Civil Service Reform.
> We've reformed the government, become less bureaucratic, and we changed
> our attitude. Attitude is very important. The Police is a leading government
> agency in this reform. We emphasize ASK, attitude, skill, and knowledge. We
> emphasize leadership, training, so we understand individual needs, individual
> skills, etc. We emphasize communication more today. We can get our messages
> across the whole Force quickly through POINT because of IT change, informa-
> tion technology change.

The Service Quality Initiatives (SQI) started in 1994 along with the Civil
Service Reform under then-Governor Chris Patten. According to a former Police
Commissioner, in face of "the ever-changing environment and diversity of
demands made by the community," the police must serve "as a professional,
modern, caring force that is viewed with a sense of pride," "strive for continuous
improvement and be compassionate when dealing with members of the public"

(*Offbeat*, 2001). Many police commanders also believe that the Service Quality Initiatives represents a global trend and reflect the values and best practices of professional organizations. There are different ideas, however, as to the origin of the "service quality" concept. Some believe that it came from the private sector and others consider it from the government. Officers from the Service Quality Wing trace the origin to police consultancy, research, and experience overseas. Many police commanders believe that this policy is based on knowledge learned in the field of policing as well as understanding of changes in modern society.

A series of events had led to the implementation of the Service Quality Initiatives. The term "service quality" was first heard from the Commissioner of Police in 1994 and the Service Quality Wing was established in the same year. In 1995 the Commissioner put forward a Service Quality Strategy aimed at getting all members of the Force involved to improve efficiency and effectiveness and service both internally and externally. There are four essential elements in this strategy, namely, involvement, continuous improvement, three Es (i.e., efficiency, effectiveness, and economy), and the concept of customers. In 1996 the Vision and Statement of Values were promulgated after wide consultation with members of the Force. The police management obtained input from Force members and developed a focus on certain core values such as integrity, trust, and professionalism. In 1997 the police adopted and started to offer a one-day workshop called Living-the-Values for the entire Force. In 1999, the Service Quality Strategy was implemented. As part of this process, the Service Quality Wing endeavored to understand the Force and the community better and started collaborating with the University of Hong Kong to conduct three surveys: a yearly internal police survey, a yearly public opinion survey, and an alternate-year customer satisfaction survey, which involves those who have contacted the police.

The Service Quality Initiatives is a many-splendored thing and is based on the concept of total quality management. Part of it means that the police must provide better services to the public. The police have therefore refurbished the areas for crime reporting at many police stations to make them more comfortable for walk-ins. They have accepted an increasingly important role the public plays in policing and opened more complaint channels. Another part of it means that the Force is committed to improving internal management. Performance pledges have been created that describe the service delivered, performance standards, and monitoring methods. Performance audits are used to support the management process, provide checks and balances, and facilitate informed operational and managerial decisions. The police commanders have interpreted the concept of service quality in different ways. Some understand it as better public service, some higher professionalism, and some better law enforcement. As some of them stated:

> My definition of service quality is we provide service to the public according to their expectations. . . . Service quality means dealing with people in an efficient and courteous way whatever the need is. We try to communicate with the public more. We give officers advice: be courteous. . . . As police officers, we follow the law first. Service quality plays a supporting role to our law enforcement

duties to make sure that we enforce the law more professionally. So it's not a matter of relationship, it's two in one. Service quality can mean professionalism, integrity, fairness, and honesty in enforcing the law. Upholding the rule of law is service quality itself. . . . The last governor initiated all these changes: public sector reform, service quality. . . . We have to fight crime. Just that we do so more fairly with respect for human rights. It's the approach that is different, not the purpose.

Due to the Service Quality Initiative, public relation, communication, and a customer orientation have received a stronger emphasis in recent years. Internally, following the concept of "total quality management," the police have increased their communication at all levels. The management officers now communicate more, listen more, and seek more input from the lower ranks to provide a better working environment. Internal communication allows officers to not only provide feedback but also air concerns. Divisional commanders treasure feedbacks from frontline officers and hold open discussions called Open Forums with them regularly. Senior managers in the rank of assistant commissioner go to different divisions and districts to discuss officers' problems and learn about their achievements twice a month. The Commissioner of Police has lunch with officers from different formations once a month. As a result, the Hong Kong Police has been experiencing a major shift from a disciplined force to a service-oriented organization. The following comments from some police managers provide an idea about this change process and its impact on the Force.

> Service quality represents best practices learned. We need to have a cultural change. To do so, top commanders should lead by examples and get commitment from staff. We also have Performance Review, which has done a lot to change views of the media, the public, and quality of the officers. Officers wouldn't think of offenders as customers a few years ago. . . . We encourage staff participation. We have staff suggestion scheme. We have work improvement team by districts. Any officer can submit ideas to us, monitored by us. We have a data system in the computer to track identification and solving of problems. We advocate integrity and honesty.

> With twenty years' experience with the Force, I have seen many changes, values, and policies. The Force has changed from an autocratic and very disciplined force to a more consultative and open-minded force. . . . Workshops are used now in promoting values. I can make suggestions at the divisional level. There is more technology, better equipment, better deployment of officers, and better training that addresses officers' concerns.

> We changed from a paramilitary to service-oriented force. As the motto goes, "We serve with pride and care." We have more internal openness, which means more communication. I let them know what I do and what I want. . . . We were heavily influenced by UK as we changed from a paramilitary, regimented to a service organization. We have exchange programs with the UK force. Overseas influence is great. The change occurred mostly in the 90's because no urgent need existed in the 80's. Then we had Public Sector Reform. It's basically a change of ideas, philosophy, and outside influence.

Enormous changes have occurred. Quality service is emphasized both internally and externally. We are more service-oriented. Maybe we will be more decentralized, more academic, and have more discretion. I don't think officers' discretion is restricted in my District. We try to give them more decision-making responsibility. . . . Officers may use discretions for traffic violations if the drivers get the message.

We help the public understand the power of police search. During police stop-and-search, officers are trained to be courteous, quick, and helpful. The rate of complaints went down. We have performance pledge indicating what we do, why we are doing it, time-frame. . . . Police stations have become nice areas for people to report crimes, complaints, and enjoy some privacy. It cost a lot Force-wide; but it's important to have. Like going to a doctor, patients need a nice area and a nice receptionist. People need service quality.

We put greater emphasis on service quality and professionalism as a natural development process. . . . We are more customer-oriented. We explain to the public what we do. We as well as the Force are better than before. . . . We are crime fighters. We used to use more force. We now use more professionalism.

Regarding values, I treat a person the way I like to be treated. I tell my people to do this: treat them the way you treat your brothers and sisters. . . . I tell my guys, you have wide power, be proactive, don't be afraid. . . . I don't want my guys to be afraid in doing their job. . . . If you are doing your job professionally, if you don't use foul language, you have my support. . . . I interview all my officers at least once a year for at least twenty minutes. I tell them to do their job properly. There is so much experience you can gain here in a short period of time. My men are the best.

Management officers also experience challenges and difficulties in this change process and see the importance of honing management skills in developing their subordinates. Some officers do not have a strong concern for the public or do not take service to the public seriously. To change this mentality, police commanders try to develop a service culture. They view many of the training programs created by the Service Quality Wing useful for developing the rank-and-file. They also try to develop healthy lifestyles among the officers, boost morale, and reduce rank consciousness by organizing sports activities, team activities, and happy hours. They educate the officers about the changes and increased responsibilities that are traditionally not considered part of police work. They also admit that some weak performances are due to poor supervisions. The following comments from some divisional commanders indicate some of the lessons they learned and challenges they faced in this change process.

Now we are computerized. Many officers are not computer literate. Officers need to be trained. Some officers think there are too many changes over the past twenty years. Some officers don't think there are too many changes. Some don't care. If the front-line officers and divisional commanders don't buy the changes, the changes won't happen. Picking the right person is the key for success besides training, workshops, and communication.

Staff suggestion scheme is good. We suggested upgrading information technology. It saves us time and is accepted. Living-the-Values is also useful, which gives us a chance to speak our minds. . . . We have more responsibilities because we are paid higher. We do things that we may not consider police work. We raided a kindergarten once to inspect the place and count kids.

We have to do more self-learning. We want officers to spend more time with their family. Police officers now open the door for residents, refer them to appropriate agencies; older residents may need more service. We have to have new values. We have directions to follow. These directions ensure that officers know what to do. Living-the-Values workshops allow officers from different ranks to communicate with one another where rank-structure is not emphasized. We have annual dinner. But socialization between ranks is not common.

In the U.K. and U.S., people join the police because they want to serve the public. In Hong Kong, some officers join the force simply because they want a good job. We have to cultivate a concern in them by talking and communicating. Every Thursday, we have an Open Forum. I communicate to them about this concern. When you arrest someone, it's one of the public. You must have the spirit of serving the public. It's getting better.

Most officers today are of good caliber and doing a good job. For the minority of officers that are not up to the job and are not working as hard, there are several reasons. Some have worked many years without getting a promotion. Some have poor performance because they are poorly supervised as their supervisors just like to get by, follow the book, have a nice day.

Since divisional commanders are responsible for creating a service culture at the frontline, they face day-to-day challenges in this reform effort. While many of them understand the importance of this shift, they find it difficult to convince their subordinate officers. They find themselves spending more time talking about service quality or reminding the officers about expected behaviors. However, many of them feel challenged because they do not feel they have sufficient managerial skills and knowledge to work in a culture of service. Some typical areas of concerns include communication skills and officer development skills necessary for bringing about changes in line with organizational goals. As some police commanders stated:

I like to know how to improve internal communication, how to communicate better with the lower ranks. . . . We have different acceptance levels regarding the Service Quality Strategy. Different age and experiences are also factors. We are still adjusting.

Old culture is that you take orders, now you can give feedback. We are doing better in communication. Older officers need to have a bigger adjustment because they are not used to it. Younger officers are new and can accept service and communication easier.

They can never accept prisoners as their customers. . . . The biggest challenge for the divisional command is the transition from traditional policing to a more

service-oriented policing. The police now must emphasize service quality both
externally and internally. It's a challenge because this requires the police operate in a culture of service. The way how commanders work also has to change.

We try to be nicer, more polite, and provide more service. But we still get complaints because public expectation has risen. We tell officers not to worry much
about technical complaints. As long as PCs follow the procedures, are doing the
right things, they shouldn't worry about them. At the same time, we tell them to
avoid complaints if they can. We have about 10 to 20 complaints per month;
50% are technical complaints. . . . Quality service policy raises officers' awareness and sensitivity.

When I first joined the force, there's no intra-communication. It's a disciplined
force. We receive orders. Now we have Open Forums. I have Open Forums
with my own men. We have more communication and we are more open. But
police constables may not get the right message. They start to complain and
moan. . . . I give them every support if the officer is doing the job. . . . Police
officers have some discretion. There has been delegation to lower level. But
some men get the wrong message.

Several years into implementing the Service Quality Initiatives, there seems
to be also some mixed views of this strategy at the divisional command level.
Some think that the policy has gone too far because it is changing the nature of
the police, depriving police commanders of their autonomy and authority and
affecting police morale. Some think that it has not gone far enough as it remains
at the cosmetic or rhetorical level. Others believe that there needs to be a better
balance between public service and internal service. As some divisional
commanders said:

Quality service as a concept is good. But it's a little stretched. It's not realistic
to say all are clients. Some are clearly not my clients. So the concept is good;
but we should not go too far. There is lots of resistance within the Force against
it. We are more transparent, open, more tolerant, but less risk-taking.

It's stupid to invite the public to complain against the police, without telling the
public what's right or wrong. We talk too much about human rights. But if the
public does not work with the police, how can we serve them well?

I don't think the police have become more open. The Force has paid lots of lip
service. They have pretended to be more transparent. They try to tell the public
that. Internally, no changes. Communication is a sham. They impose their
views. They tell you something and then ask for your comment. Is this communication?

I wish to get rid of things that are not police business, get more support from
upper management, have higher morale, more resources. . . ... We don't need a
lot. Simple things can go a long way. But our requests are not responded to
quickly. Our quality of service has increased, but we paid a price.

Similar to street officers, some divisional commanders are also critical of the Service Quality Initiatives. They complain about the new emphasis on service, the lack of support from senior police administration, the increased workload, and the more critical public and the media. Some even question the overall value of the service strategy and the general direction of the Hong Kong Police. As some police commanders said:

> I joined the force in 1976 as a PC. We were so proud to be police officers then; we worn T-shirts with badges, we told people we were police officers. Now we don't do that anymore. I say I am a civil servant, a computer worker, etc., with a certain element of truth in them. The image is bad. I am not happy with the management; we go backward. Before 1997 we thought it was going to be good; we finally have a mother country. Now we are oppressed not by Chinese officials but by Chinese police management. We are ruled more by people than by laws. I would say 20% by law, 80% by man. Used to be 50% law and 50% people. Used to be more going by the rules.

> We were happier four years ago before the handover. We had more support from our seniors. We were defended more by our seniors. . . . We enjoyed more autonomy and discretion before. But now we have to do more things, follow more instructions. Look at those volumes on the shelf: there are more rules and instructions than ever. In other words, the police used to be more decentralized and now more centralized in terms of policy making.

> The Force has done lots of things like upgrading computers, remodeling police buildings and stations, getting new technology. But are these things what officers want? What I like to have is support. The Commissioner should stand up for the police sometimes. Some work should not be asked of the police, e.g., illegal hawking, counterfeit, unlicensed tutors, etc. . . . To a small degree, we are called to do the job of health and hygiene department. . . . The senior administration should be stronger to the media and tell them as it is. If what the media is reporting is not true, tell them so. Allow the police more time to do police work and get our dignity back.

> We have less power, less influence, diminished. We stand back pandering the media. We became soft as we move from force to service. I have not been restricted personally; others may have.

Another significant change that requires a new management approach is the general increase of educational level among the rank-and-file officers. Because of the higher education many young officers have received, they have a different attitude from the older officers without college degrees. Some police managers believe that higher education has created a gap between younger and older officers. Some also see a gap between college-educated junior officers and themselves. Issues have also been raised about whether higher education or the right personality is more important for police work. Because some management officers do not see a strong commitment from junior officers, they have second thought about higher qualifications and educational credentials. As some police commanders said:

Quality and education of officers, especially academic side of the Force, are higher. . . . New officers are more theoretical due to education. Not just new officers, but also old officers are taking courses. . . . When I joined the Force in 1972, Form 2 was enough; in the 80's, it was Form 3; and now it is Form 4 and 5. Internal procedures are streamlined. Service quality is better. . . . We still have sergeants who are old and experienced, but not academic. So there is a problem between old and young officers. We try to have them communicate with each other, have them chat with each other, organize social gathering, and provide training once in two months.

Officers have to work hard. I don't see college education makes a big difference. It's their personality that counts. They all have to work hard. The most important value is to have regard for the job, for the division, and for the public. That's my priority. Officer must have concerns and care.

We are getting better educated officers. The educational requirement has been raised. But in general the quality is not as good as in the old days in terms of sense of responsibility. Maybe it's a generational thing. This generation did not have to struggle to get where they are. They are more money-oriented.

The rank-and-file are well educated; but they aren't very committed. They do this just as a job, get paid, and go home. No sense of belonging, no sense of career. So when we ask them to be customer-oriented, they are upset. They don't want to accept these concepts.

Managing Community Relations

An important part of a management officer's job is to maintain good police community relations. The Hong Kong Police works through several available channels for this purpose including District Council, District Fight Crime Committee, and Kaifong Association. These community committees have been established in each district, whose members are either appointed or selected. Commanders at the district and divisional levels sit in the meetings held by these committees and invite their members for open discussions or "Public Forums" at their stations. Police commanders also pay regular visits to other local organizations such as housing estates and security companies to gather input from the community. In addition, each district has a Public Relations Officer designated to serve as a liaison with the community. And street officers are encouraged to interact and work closely with the community while maintaining their status as professional law enforcement officers. As some divisional commanders stated:

We work with District Fight Crime Committees, District Councils. . . . The district commander attends the District Council meeting. . . . Community committees can represent the community to a certain extent. We also have District Open Days when anybody can come. We can talk to parents and children. . . . I think that Public Opinion Survey provided by the Service Quality Wing is also important.

Our value is that we provide what public expects. We have a duty to do it. We have Public Relations Officers who attend functions in the community. I meet with community leaders regularly and ask them if there are any problems. . . . District counselors don't speak for all. Kaifong is there, knows what's going on. I have a police constable talk to them. When police constables walk the same beat for a long time, they also develop familiarity and relationship.

Police-community relationship depends on how we interact with the people. Different areas have different clientele and different, higher or lower, expectations. Community Relations Officer is the major link between the police and the community. We also have District Council and Fight Crime Committee. Each district is divided into sectors covered by police constables. We have police constables talk to shop owners. But we make it clear to PCs that they are not supposed to befriend local businesses or local residents. They are police officers.

In working with the community the police managers stress a functional approach. In other words they do not have a broad moral mandate and are not into shaping social development. Their attention is focused on addressing specific problems with specific measures. To address youth crimes and Triad activities, for example, the police maintain regular contacts with local schools, set up school teams, and organize youth-related programs and anti-Triad activities. Management officers also have specific expectations from the public. They expect the public to report crimes, serve as witnesses, provide information, and be reasonable in its demand. As some police managers said:

I hope citizens will report crimes, be cooperative, come forward to serve as witnesses, and be understanding to the police, not just blaming the police. . . . Citizens should actively provide crime-related information to the police. . . . Citizens need to know what they can ask, how much help they can get from police, how many rights police have. They must give, not just receive. . . . Citizens should be more active, show more respect, stop fooling with the police.

Although police commanders at the divisional and district levels interact with members of the community on a regular basis, they do not view maintaining community relations as a straightforward process. First, they see involving the community in police work and working with the community as a challenge. Second, they do not always have direct input from the community or know exactly what it wants. The community is not monolithic and it is difficult to balance different community interests. Members of a District Committee, for example, often have their own interests in mind and do not represent the majority of the residents in a district. Third, they see an overall change in the behavior and attitude in the public toward the police that makes it difficult for the police to work with the community. They have seen an increase in public complaints, a greater demand for police service, and generally a higher expectation of the police. As some commanders stated:

The challenge is to have involvement in the community, more informal sessions, seminars, etc. . . . We also try to figure out how to deal with community

members better. . . . It's easy to say that we should be sensitive to the community; but the community seldom gives the police a clear message as to what
they exactly want. Members of the public complain most of the time and are
very negative. They come to the police and tell the police what they want.
Some groups in the community are not very supportive of the police.

The Hong Kong society has become increasingly more sophisticated. The public demands fair and impartial law enforcement. We have to be right "the first
time and every time" just like everywhere else. Citizens should help us to help
you. . . . We had riots in the 60's, 80's; we dealt with them differently back
then.

A couple of years ago, public demand increased. The society is more democratic. Regardless of class, they know their rights. We have to provide better
service, provide a better place for them to come in. Station Improvement Project started two years ago.

Similar to street officers, some management officers complain about the
public for being disrespectful and uncooperative and the media for being biased.
They believe that the increased complaints and biased reports have taken a toll
on officer morale. Compared with the past they feel that they have less pride and
less initiative. As some management officers said:

Citizens in Hong Kong have changed. . . . They complain too much about trivial matters. We have more emergency calls, many of which aren't real emergencies They call the police when they cannot open their door. . . . I'm not
really sure how we can better educate the public about what are police problems and what are not. . . . We aren't all rotten apples. Most of us are good
officers. We used to have more pride. For example, we used to have our police
badge in the front of our wallet, but not any more.

I don't trust the press. I once gave them an honest version of what happened.
The next day they misquoted me. . . . The Nigerian man who was using stun
gun and accused officers of racism was eventually convicted and sent to prison
for eighteen months. But the news of him being convicted was published in a
small column in a corner of the paper, in sharp contrast to his accusations reported earlier. If he were not convicted, the news would have been on the front
page. . . . Many stories have been distorted by the press.

Due to the Service Quality Initiatives, the police have provided more channels of complaints for the public and the management officers are spending
more time processing the complaints. Handling complaints, however, is not
always a pleasant experience. Some commanders, like street officers, may try to
avoid complaints and thereby reduce their workload. As some police managers
stated:

Each time somebody makes a complaint, I have to write a report, and see the
complaint come to an end. I often see both sides are reasonable. And most
complaints are between one officer and one individual; there is no third party to
serve as witness. I explain to complainants if they don't understand police pro-

cedures. . . . And sometime I say sorry. And I write up the report. Once a woman was stopped because she was suspected of being an illegal immigrant. She turned out to be a local school principal. She complained fiercely and demanded a meeting with me. I met her and had to explain to her why she was stopped. Another time a granny complained about her granddaughter being stopped because she looked like an illegal immigrant. When the officer was checking the girl's ID, he asked the granny to go away. The granny was very unhappy about that. I had to explain to her that it's for protecting the privacy of her granddaughter.

Some bosses at divisional levels ask officers to avoid troubles and complaints. If they avoid troubles and complaints, they also reduce their workload. . . . The trouble may come from the boss, not always the public. For example, a driver who was a former police inspector was stopped in Causeway Bay for speeding. The PC wanted to give him a ticket. The driver said that he was the brother of a senior superintendent and he would complain. Then the sergeant let him go. This is sad. Another example, a group of taxi-drivers went to the police station to complain and were let go without being ticketed because the station sergeant didn't want too many complaints.

Although management officers as well as street officers grumble about increased public complaints, the actual number of complaints is well within the tolerable range. Most members of the public are also respectful of the police. Many police managers, especially those with overseas experience, are actually quite satisfied and enjoy working with the community in Hong Kong. What is different from the past is that the police management has been taking public complaints more seriously now. As some commanders said:

We have 100 to 200 stop-and-search per day in the entire system. . . . We have only two to four complaints a month. Most complaints are minor. Eighty-five percent are withdrawn, 10% informal resolution, the remaining 5% are technical complaints involving manners, stop-and-search, and some drunken complainants.

Management has taken complaints more seriously. Officers are so nervous about complaints that whenever upper management calls, they are afraid there might be another complaint. We have an officer who was actually praised in a letter of compliment. The Commissioner received the letter and when he called, the officer was very cautious, afraid it was a complaint. He did not say it was him first until he checked his book and he was surprised that it was a compliment.

I always say there's one test for police work: Can you walk on the street at midnight? I was visiting my relatives in London once and I saw two cars being burned simply because somebody was upset with his parking space being taken. I was driving through that street, saying to myself, "What country am I in? I wanted to get back to Hong Kong fast." Also, people in Hong Kong generally hold police officers in high regard. Once we are on the scene, people usually calm down and are obedient. In the UK, officers go to a bar to do something, they will take them on. Very seldom happens in Hong Kong.

Management Strategies

Officers in management positions employ various strategies in fulfilling their managerial and administrative functions due to their diverse personal backgrounds and different local conditions. One commander new to a division may choose to communicate more and understand the problems first before trying to rectify anything. Another may choose to set local divisional goals in alignment with Force directives and strategies. And another may focus on keeping a high morale by developing and supporting subordinate officers. Following are some comments by divisional commanders on their management strategies.

I made sure that I had all the information. Then I got hold of the supervisors and commanding officers and told them what I wanted. I brought some problems to their attention. . . . I used to be in the Marine and I was treated as an outsider. I knew I could be cut off from the bottom and not know what's really going on. . . . No matter what leadership style is used, it must be enjoyed by my men. I am a disciplinarian. . . . I prefer to start firm and relax later. I can't just follow my predecessor and be looked upon as just another superintendent. I spell out divisional priorities, have focus, set achievable goals. I then ask them to keep track of what they have been doing. . . . As I see the Station being improved, I give more allowances and make sure officers are enjoying their work.

I want to make sure that the officers leave the Station happy. I meet officers in informal occasions. There is more communication such as Q and A sessions. . . . We let them know what they are doing. We try to foster a sense of duty. . . . Station report was introduced earlier this year. But we don't want to give them red tape and too much paperwork.

For improvement, I must do the right things at my level in alignment with all the changes in the Force. . . . I am responsible for making sure that police order is followed. I make sure that citizens are treated courteously and served quickly. The Police Force is not a force of 1967. . . . Policing depends on experience, professionalism, and common sense. No matter how much knowledge one has, experience is still the most important. Tutor constables and sergeants also play an important role. Personal integrity, honesty, and professionalism are emphasized daily in police operations.

I need to make sure my officers are well versed about the law, understand civil rights and Force policies. . . . We emphasize values of professionalism, integrity, honesty . . . setting the scene that things are done openly. We tell officers to do the right things. We encourage officer initiatives. . . . There was an incident in Canton Road; officers in a patrol car saw four men in one taxi twice, stopped them, and found they were actually Customs officers. Mistake was made, but honest mistake.

Above divisional commanders, senior police management develops Force-wide strategies by conducting research on social, economic, political, and technological trends in Hong Kong as well as developments in the mainland.

Senior police managers regularly consult with major formation commanders and collate their views relating to challenges and opportunities facing the Force. They also examine models of policing in other jurisdictions (*Offbeat*, 2001). Looking ahead strategically, some police managers believe that the Hong Kong Police needs to prepare for the worst and adapt to changes in their environment. As some of them commented:

> I make sure that crime rate doesn't go up. . . . The Force should be prepared to move forward. . . . We need contingency plans and emergency plans and need to be prepared for major incidents. The Force needs to put one right person in charge of emergency and crisis situations. . . . There is not much difficulty in day-to-day operations.

> We have a long period of peace. The Force starts to relax a little. We don't get equipment we want fast enough. We don't have budget increase. In the 1990s, we had shooting, chaos, grenades, we didn't have problem getting what we wanted. Now there is no sense of emergency. . . . Robbery, deception, gun problem are more common now. Officers have to wear bullet-proof vests for certain calls. We need more professionalism, better recruitment, better support staff, and good and sufficient equipment. If we can't save ourselves, we can't save anybody. We have a long period of peace; but we must prepare for the worst.

> The establishment was set up ten years ago. So some changes are needed. Yuen Long was a quiet place ten years ago, but now a commercial center, and a lot more people live here. It has developed quickly and the Force has not responded to the urbanization of Yuen Long quickly enough. We need more resources and adequate manpower. We have to get approval to increase manpower. We don't have a good system to examine needs and respond to needs. It's a long drawn-out process. . . . I would suggest the Force reevaluate and calculate workload and manpower. It was done ten years ago. Things have changed.

Balancing Different Police Orientations

In a large organization like the Hong Kong Police, officers may identify themselves with different values and orientations. Many police managers, due to their vantage point, believe that the police should balance different police orientations. A commander at the divisional level, for example, may see the need to balance various police functions to achieve greater effectiveness for the division as a whole. This is especially true when police officers perform duties that represent diverse values and principles. A tension arising from such differences noted by police commanders is between law and order and protection of civil rights, as described by Skolnick (1994). The concept of discretion is often used in this context as a useful measure to balance them. As former Commissioner Tsang said (2002):

> Our main hurdle comes from a need to strike the balance in our approach to any given situation or incident. With this I refer to a full range of situations, en-

compassing trivial domestic incidents to large scale, headline making events. . .
. The use of discretion has a crucial part to play in our enforcement action and
it is a tool, which our officers are encouraged to use. . . . Perhaps nowhere are
the difficulties in achieving a balance more clearly seen than on the occasions
when we deal with public order events. In 2001 we policed more than 2000 of
these gatherings.

A related tension the police face is between law enforcement and service.
This conflict has become more significant in recent years due to the Service
Quality Initiatives and has become a sticking point among different groups in
the police organization, particularly between senior management and street
officers. On the one hand, most police managers see no conflict between these
two aspects of police work and expect the frontline officers to have the ability to
balance them. On the other hand, some middle managers and many street
officers find it difficult to do both in many specific police situations. Both senor
and middle police managers as a whole, however, recognize the challenge in
emphasizing service. But from their experiences they also see the challenge as
caused not only by a tension between law enforcement and service, but also by
higher public expectations. They believe that the Hong Kong Police should
respond to a changing society and develop an organizational character based on
the balance between law enforcement and service. This balance should be
reflected in all police functions, tasks, and individual officer behavior. The
following comments by some police managers indicate their views regarding the
relationship between law enforcement and service.

I don't see any contradiction between law enforcement and service. Officers
should be able to strike a balance by explaining what they do to the public.
They should be polite and have probable cause. We want consistency in law
enforcement. . . . We uphold rights and freedom of individuals. We also uphold
rights of community members who go about their daily business. We enforce
law, offer service, two core functions, deal with suspects, be polite. We serve
citizens, too. Law enforcement and service are not contradictory at all. Stress
doesn't come from the tension; it comes from higher expectations of the public
and the media.

I first try to manage my 300 officers. It's not easy to maintain the morale. The
Force is engaged in customer service; but many officers deal with bad people.
It's hard to convince officers to be fair and serve everyone, to balance law enforcement and service. They get complaints like bad manners, foul language,
etc. So officers complain, "Why do I have to do this?" So we tell officers to
treat innocent people politely. . . . We protect life and property, arrest criminals,
and provide services. . . . Law and order and quality service are what we have
to do. . . . It's difficult to balance law enforcement and service. I have to make
sure that officers know what they are supposed to do.

It's difficult to balance law enforcement and service. There are so many protests in Hong Kong. We require a seven-day notice for thirty or more people in
the procession for them to plan the march. We police our area if a march passes
through here. . . . All protests must be approved first. But some demonstrators

don't seek prior approval making our job very difficult. There are nine or ten protests that did not receive police permission since I came here.

The police managers also see ways the Force may use to enable the officers to balance diverse police orientations. Many of them believe that values and ethics such as professionalism and honesty are conducive to cultivating a sense of fair law enforcement and public service. They consider training and education programs important in helping the officers use discretion and communicate to the public. Police commanders also have an important role themselves in communicating to the rank-and-file about police professionalism, civil rights, and service for the public. As some commanders commented:

> Officers use professional judgment when there is a conflict. . . . More education and training are needed to better balance law enforcement and service. Officers must have the willingness to enforce the law and serve the public. . . . We have Mission and Values. . . . Professionalism is most important. We have to be seen as fair, we have to communicate more effectively, not necessarily open, but more effective communication.

> We have seminars where officers share experiences for handling stress and we emphasize the importance of professionalism. . . . We have discretion for some situations. We have Police Orders, degree of force policy, etc., where no discretion is formalized. . . . Every officer has discretion and has the same degree of authority.

> To balance service and law enforcement, officers must be vigilant even though they are providing a service. Values such as professionalism, right consciousness, and civil rights are important. Training and education are also important.

An Institutional Perspective

From an institutional perspective, institutional complexity, taken-for-granted assumptions, and psychological sunk costs, as well as rationalized myths and sovereigns (March and Olsen, 1984; Meyer and Rowan, 1991; Powell, 1991) are all relevant for understanding the challenges for balancing different police orientations. In the Hong Kong Police, the paramilitary traditions can be considered as having been institutionalized into premises, structures, processes, and practices. Frontline operational duties are embedded in these institutionalized elements. Many officers, therefore, continue to see their traditional public order and law enforcement duties as the core of their work. The institutionalization of the paramilitary orientation into the Hong Kong Police organizational structures and practices has resulted in a heavy-handed law enforcement approach. This approach in turn has nurtured rituals that are antithetical to the establishment of a service culture and created taken-for-granted assumptions and psychological sunk costs that hinder the formation of a police personality favorable to the service orientation (Jiao, Lau, and Lui, 2005).

The institutional perspective suggests that institutionalized values, rituals, and practices are often followed by organizational members without question.

The Service Quality Initiatives, as a new orientation, therefore, has not enjoyed widespread support from the rank-and-file of the Hong Kong Police despite the super-structural adoption of this strategy. Although the police administration may see no disagreement between law enforcement and service, the police management has experienced great difficulties in changing the police culture. Many officers also seem to have experienced serious stress between these different orientations. Added to the challenge is the perceived increase of public complaints in recent years, making many officers, especially at the street level, feel that they have lost respect and authority from the public. Instead of appreciating the significance of the service orientation at a time of change, many officers see the Service Quality Initiatives as a source of their stress on the job.

9

Crime, Triad, and Vice

The purpose of this chapter is to provide an examination of crime, Triad, and vice problems in Hong Kong from the perspectives of police officers. While different data can be employed to examine these issues and any single angle may prove biased or limited, the police view remains one of the most pertinent source of information because police officers deal with crime, Triad, and vice on a regular basis and thus occupy a vantage point for interpreting these issues. Views from members of the public are valuable for gauging public opinions; but they are not particularly useful for understanding police operations because members of the public seldom experience crime problems first-hand and their views are usually based on media coverage and personal speculations.

The police officers in Hong Kong generally do not see crime as an urgent or severe problem. The low crime rate and lack of violence in the city make them feel safe working in the street. But like any big city in the world, Hong Kong has its share of crime, organized crime, and vice activities, which plague some districts more than others. In the following, I examine these problems separately for the sake of organization. It is obvious that when the word "crime" is used, it refers to all types of crimes and illegalities including Triad and vice; and when the term "Triad" is used, it includes vice because profits for Triad groups are often generated from vice-related activities. Triad and vice are discussed separately, however, because police officers often talk about them separately depending on the cases that come to mind. The officers consider "Triad" as organized crimes and use the term "vice" to represent specific types of offenses such as drugs, gambling, and prostitution. They use these terms to highlight the types of crimes they deal with, not to distinguish them conceptually. They are certainly aware of the fact that they are not mutually exclusive.

Types of Crime, Triad, and Vice Problems

Crime   Perhaps because Hong Kong was a British colony, serious crime in the territory seems to resemble that in Western democracies more than in China. As Alderson (1981:7) observed more than twenty years ago, "Robberies, hi-jacking, kidnapping, and drug-trafficking indicate the level of both affluence and deprivation. Social cohesion is more fragmented. The cultural contradictions are greater." It is certainly true that serious crime such as robberies and burglaries exists in Hong Kong; but it does not represent the majority of the crime because most criminal offenses are trivial in the form of petty thefts, deceptions, overstay, and illegal immigrants (IIs). Most crimes are committed with a motive for material rewards. IIs, for example, are mostly economic migrants coming to Hong Kong seeking better economic opportunities. The material nature of the crime reflects the high commercial development and overall prosperity of the city. Many crimes, property-related or not, also mirror the youthful population, a largely adventurous, electronic, and computerized generation. Following are some comments made by police managers stationed in some of the most commercialized districts in Hong Kong.

> Out of fourteen crime complaints, I would say half are petty thefts, disputes, losses, etc. We have no major problems. If we have three burglaries in one day, that's major. . . . We used to have people from the mainland coming here to rob the jewelry stores and then escape to the mainland. . . . There are lots of trivial emergency calls, hoaxes, bomb scares, etc. Many dispute cases, domestic disputes, shop disputes, loss, misunderstanding, nuisance calls, inquiries, mistakes, alarms, burglary alarms, and false alarms. Robberies and burglaries are stable. But commercial crime and computer crime are on the increase.

> We have more robberies and burglaries mostly committed by young people. Mostly high school students and local residents are involved. We have more crime to deal with during the Summer when students are on vacation. Routine activity theory applies here for the thefts and burglaries that occur during high crime seasons. . . . We face many challenges including dealing with youth crimes, drugs, psychotropic drugs, illegal border crossing, burglaries, robberies, etc. We also have a good ethnic mix here such as the Muslim associations that we need to work with.

> We have many crime problems in our District. We have robbery and burglary, juvenile crime, mobile phone stealing, shoplifting, etc. . . . At our Division, we deal with many kinds of criminals. . . . We have 380-400 crime reports a month, including street crimes, robberies, burglaries, fighting, illegal immigrants, their hideouts, etc. . . . Illegal immigration is not our primary responsibility. The Immigration Department handles it. But when we check IDs, we also find illegal immigrants.

Triad   Triad is believed to have been heavily involved in corruption and organized crimes such as drug trafficking and illegal prostitution. As a feature of Triad operations, drugs and prostitution are run like businesses. An enterprise management process is used for prostitution, for example, from purchase (selection of women), transportation (transporting women to Hong Kong), to packaging (receiving training in Hong Kong), to marketing (advertising), and to sales (receiving guests). Women selected or induced into prostitution are trained in merger dorm rooms. If not willing, they would be put in solitude or beaten. The police estimate that organized crime groups provide as many as 40% of the women in prostitution and Mong Kok District is the base occupying about half of all illegal prostitution businesses in Hong Kong (*Ming Pao*, 2002). Women involved are clearly exploited by the Triad groups because most of what they earn go to their organizers.

One mainland Chinese woman in Mong Kok was from Zhuzhou, Hunan Province. She was nineteen years old and worked as a shop assistant in Zhuzhou. With the help of a "flat owner," she came to Hong Kong. She had no relatives in the city; but the flat owner arranged to get a 3-month permit for visiting "relatives" for her. She was trained to work as a prostitute after she came to Hong Kong. She had to work everyday unless she was sick. She was paid HK$100 for each customer she received. She could sleep only about five hours a day. It does not mean that she was always working; but she had to stay awake in case customers showed up. She never got the chance to see different places in Hong Kong. When she was not able to work during her period, she still did not know where to go because nobody would take her out.

Another Chinese woman, also nineteen years old, was from Yichang, Hubei Province. She was introduced to the business through personal connection while working at a restaurant in Guangzhou. Her friends introduced her to a man looking for girls like her. The man, nicknamed "Lautou" (Old man), was from Chiaozhou in Guangdong Province. He showed her where to go and how to get there and was received by organizers at the Hong Kong side of the border. It was the first time for her to be in Hong Kong on a 30-day travel permit. She reported similar underground vice activities in Guangzhou, which were treated harshly by the Chinese police as they would take all their belongings including IDs and collecting heavy fines from the organizers before releasing them.

Some organized crime experts in the Hong Kong Police regard Triad as a myth because there are many inaccurate or wrong perceptions of Triad both in Hong Kong and overseas. The misconceptions are often related to the impact and culture of Triad. According the experts, its impact is not as great as perceived and its culture is not as negative as portrayed. Triad groups and members are not rampant in Hong Kong. As a matter of fact, only about 3 to 5% of crime in Hong Kong is Triad-related. The following are some comments made by the police officers with extensive Triad experience.

> Triad originated in China in 1674 and had developed as an underground force until the Kuomingtong, the Nationalist, Period in 1911 and went underground again in 1940, 1945, 1949, and at present. Since China does not allow loyal opposition, Triad has existed largely as a disloyal opposition to the government in history. However, Triad-related crime occupies a small percentage, about 3.5%, of the total crime in Hong Kong. Triad should be demystified. To understand Triad, one should first understand the culture of Triad. People in the culture understand it and identify with it. Triad is not as bad as portrayed in the media.

> Organized and Triad crime figures are not always accurate. At street levels, many extortions and protection rackets exist. Rumor has it that Triad controls the MTR system. There really is no Triad influence on the MTR system. MTR

Corporation owns the system. There is little Triad involvement in the City Bus and Green Minibus routes where fares are fixed. There is perhaps some Triad involvement in Red Minibus routes where fares are not fixed, in informal parking areas, and in retail organizations.

Vice   As in many major cities in the world, vice activities in the form of drug trade, gambling, underage drinking, and prostitution are commonplace in Hong Kong. They nevertheless do not present a serious problem for the police. Police officers tend to view them as nuisances rather than law enforcement matters even though they hate such activities on a personal level. Among the different vice offenses, drug stands out as the worst from the police standpoint because all other vice activities are not necessarily illegal. Drinking is more of a problem for foreigners as most people in Hong Kong do not drink or at least do not drink outside their homes. Gambling has always been a problem; it is going up in some areas but is not getting out of control. Prostitution has been a part of Hong Kong life since the beginning of the territory as a British colony. As some police officers stated:

> Drinking is never a serious problem in Hong Kong. We don't have law forbidding public drinking. But even though it's not illegal to drink in public, you almost never see public drinking. . . . May be because it's not illegal, it's no longer a thrill. Some people do illegal things simply to test the law. What's also important perhaps is that Hong Kong people are never big drinkers in the first place. . . . Prostitution is not illegal, but exploitation of women and pimping are. If Triad is involved, for instance, prostitution becomes illegal. . . . In my opinion, there're three categories of prostitution, self-operated brothels, nightclub girls, and escort service. It is the last one that tends to be controlled by Triad and organized groups that smuggle and traffic women from other countries into Hong Kong. And the police are very serious about this type of crime. . . . Drugs has become less of a problem over the years because of a large police presence and possibly less demand. Today it's mostly the young people that have drug problems. Some young people go across the border, to Shenzhen, to buy and use drugs, because it's cheaper and easier to get drugs there. . . . Gambling is legal as long as there's no commission.

> Regarding drugs, we are not as badly hit as other areas. Treatment centers have more problems, although not very serious. . . . Waichai is different from other districts. There are people here all the time. People stay here after work, drinking and using drugs. We have some burglaries that are also related to drugs. Burglaries are often committed by drug addicts. . . . Among drugs, gambling, drinking, and prostitution, I hate drugs the most.

> Mong Kok District is the most densely populated. Night-life here is quite busy. Our station is also the busiest police station and has the highest crime rate and one of the highest crime reports in Hong Kong. We have the most vice. We have regular anti-vice operations. There are many prostitutes from the mainland. We hold them overnight when we catch them. . . . Prostitution is only one problem. It's a fact of life. There are too many for the police to handle.

According to the Hong Kong law, exploited prostitution is illegal and independent prostitution is not. But it is not always possible to distinguish the two. Women controlled by organized crime groups are less willing to talk to researchers or the police. Those working on their own are more willing to talk because they see the police as their protectors. Whether exploited or self-employed, women involved could be arrested for overstaying or violating immigration laws. Street solicitation for prostitution is also strictly prohibited. Other than these situations, prostitution is by and large legal and there are numerous brothels in West Kowloon. Often viewed as part of a decadent "capitalist" lifestyle by the mainland government, prostitution as a legitimate business has survived the change of sovereignty.

Besides brothels, nightclubs, escort services, and massage parlors are also commonplace in Hong Kong. Women working at a nightclub can serve as prostitutes and be taken out at a higher price. An escort service, as another form of prostitution, usually asks for HK$600 for an hour and HK$1,000 for two hours. Some offer discount if booked right away. Customers have Asian and European women to choose from. Massage parlors and saunas are not allowed to practice prostitution. But sexually explicit signs are sometimes posted on these premises with specific prices. In one case, a masseuse offered to have sex with her client, who happened to be a plain-clothes police officer, and was arrested. After she was convicted, the massage parlor appealed the court's decision. The appeal was denied; the presiding judge argued that massage parlors are public places and citizens are protected from harassment from prostitutes in such places as well as on the street. Although customers do not have a place to go inside a massage parlor as they do on the street, they deserve the same protection. The judge also differentiates massage places from hotel rooms, defining the former as public and latter private (*Oriental Daily News*, 2001).

As street walking is strictly prohibited, most prostitution businesses in Hong Kong, both legal and illegal, are indoors. Yellow neon lights on the street direct customers to these locations with explicit signs: "New Russian Girls," "Northern Mainland Girls," "Full Service," etc. Besides mainland Chinese and local women, there are females from different parts of the world working as prostitutes in Hong Kong as the advertising boasts of women from Europe, Russia, America, Brazil, Vietnam, the Philippines, Malaysia, Thailand, and Indonesia. Most of these women carry a tourist visa or travel permit.

A Karaoke nightclub operates differently. A customer is led to a small and dark room, where there may be a couch, a TV, and a coffee stand. A waitress would ask what drink and company one liked to have and provide them accordingly. The club charges customers different prices during different hours. The cover fee and hourly fee get higher and higher as time goes by from afternoon to evening and to late night hours. A hostess who serves as a company would play some games in the room or sing some songs trying to keep the customer longer in order to make more money. The hostesses are free to go after their shifts. But if they leave before their shift is over, they must pay for the remaining time, which is usually covered by their customers.

Shan Shui Po, Mong Kok, and Tsim Sa Tsui are districts located in Kowloon where prostitution business is rampant. Shan Shui Po prostitutes are the "low-class" and "low-cost," Trim Sa Tsui the "higher-class" and "upscale," and Mong Kok come in between. Old, run-down public housing buildings in Shan Shui Po contain many small residential units from which clothes are hung out the windows to dry. Lines of vending stands are set up on both sides of many streets. Some street-walkers can be seen standing behind the venders on the sidewalks wearing low-cut dresses and short skirts, smiling, but not talking. Men, older women, or pimps introduce them to passersby, and make sure that they are not police officers. A Thai woman working there was back and forth between Hong Kong and Thailand many times. All she needed was a passport. She was scared of plain-clothes officers and had a man checking out clients' IDs. Women like her are apparently engaged in illegal prostitution as streetwalking is prohibited and they do not have legal status to work in Hong Kong.

As one walks toward Mong Kok, the street becomes more crowded. More officers are also seen deployed in the area. Nathan Road as the thoroughfare in the area is full of retail businesses on both sides and many pedestrians walk on the roofed sidewalks. There is no sign of vice on this main commercial strip. But on the side of the street one or two blocks away from it appeared the yellow signs indicating prostitution locations. The streets here are narrow and usually closed from vehicular traffic due to large volumes of pedestrians. As Sinclair and Ng (1997:65) observed, vice rackets "flourish in the world's most crowded square mile, with an estimated 160,000 people in the high-rise environment." The uniformed police officers in groups of two or three standing in the middle of the street look like a small oasis in a sea of dark-haired people swarming about them. As I walked near the Mong Kok MTR station around 10:00 pm one night, I saw the streets packed with people, shopping, eating, walking, and looking around. Small vendors lined up the streets, selling small gift items, novelties, electronic games, shirts and pants, watches, toys, etc. Some food stands provided a quick bite, with cheap but tasty Cantonese food and cold drinks. No one was drinking alcohol in the street. Prostitution signs were everywhere with clear prices and descriptions: "Beautiful Northern Ladies," "Passionate European Women," "Gentle Soo-Hang Sisters," "Enthusiastic Malay Girls." There were also massage parlors and saunas in the area. Walking on the streets were mostly young people. But there were no street prostitutes soliciting sex. As I finished a pot of rice with beef and vegetable in a restaurant, I saw a young Chinese lady in mini-skirt popping out of a yellow-signed entrance with two men. One was walking closely beside her while another looking cautiously around. As I happened to be walking in the same direction toward Nathan Road, I saw the girl and the men moving quickly toward a mini-van parked by the road in which four or five other men were waiting. As the girl and the two men got in, they drove away immediately. What I witnessed may be a scenario where a woman was being transported from one location to another for prostitution.

Causes of Crime, Triad, and Vice Problems

Hong Kong is perhaps the most urbanized and most densely populated place on earth. Poverty that often results from such conditions apparently exists in Hong Kong. But there are hardly any ghettos and the common factors associated with crime such as high urbanization and overcrowdedness are seldom mentioned by police officers as problems. As a crime analyst of the Hong Kong Police stated: "Urbanization and overcrowdedness are not factors. Buildings are not abandoned here because land is too valuable. There is no graffiti in Hong Kong as people think this is home and they cannot move anywhere else."

Table 9.1 Monthly Average Income of Hong Kong Service Workers

Personal Service	HK$6046
Service Workers	HK$8488
Finance/Insurance/Real Estate Service	HK$9512
Clerical/Secretarial Workers	HK$10230
Wholesale/Retail/Trade/Leisure Service	HK$11628
Transport Service	HK$13386
Supervisor/Technical Workers	HK$17600
All service workers from craftsmen to supervisors	HK$10511

Source: Adapted from Census and Statistics Department of the Hong Kong Government (2005b) (See *http://www.info.gov.hk/censtatd*).

Although there are no large poor sectors in the city, poverty, especially shrinking income and economic downturns are often cited as causes of crime. The proportion of low-income population is high as 60% of Hong Kong people are in the low-income category, making on average a monthly income of HK$10,511 (US$1,401) (see Table 9.1). The median salary for professional and managerial positions is about HK$50,000 (US$6,666) (PayScale, 2005). The average annual individual income is about HK$180,000 (approximately US$23,000). The income gap between rich and poor is significant due to the lack of a robust middle class. Income gap and the economic condition are believed to have much to do with the ups and downs of crime rate. The police report that the majority of offenders who commit quick-cash offenses like pocket-lifting, purse snatching, thefts, and robberies are unemployed. Following are some officers' comments on the effect of economy and social environment.

Due to bad economy, high unemployment rate, there is more conflict in the society and more crime is committed. In the same way, bad economy causes family problems, juvenile delinquency, suicide, building jumping, etc. . . . There are more commercial crimes, deceptions . . . due to the recent economic downturn. Hong Kong is experiencing more bank robberies. . . . We had more armed robberies in the early 90s, which started to drop around 1993. Due to the Financial Crisis and economic problems, we have more property crimes. The 3% increase in crimes this year is related to economy and partially to poor parenting. Like in many families both parents work.

The correlation between economic recession and crime rate may very well be a perception of many officers because Hong Kong did not experience a significant increase in crime rate during the Asian Financial Crisis and subsequent economic downturn (see Table 9.2). The recorded crime rate has been relatively stable and, with the exception of 2003, has been lower than the years before the economic slump. There is no indication that public security has deteriorated in Hong Kong, either (*Ta Kung Pao*, 2001). Reported crime statistics, however, is generally not recognized as an accurate reflection of the nature and prevalence of crime due to such problems as underreporting and changing recording practices. Such statistics, however, can be more appropriately used as a rough estimate of crime patterns and direction of change in crime over time (Reichel, 2005).

Table 9.2 Arrest Statistics of the Hong Kong Police

	1989	1997	1998	2000	2001	2002	2003	2004
Violent crime	__	9303	__	9497	8435	8781	9080	9311
Burglary/Theft	__	13817	__	14858	14567	15099	16787	16838
Narcotics	__	4174	__	2859	3064	2903	2746	2712
Sexual offense	__	1050	__	991	777	753	872	1046
Immigration offense	__	2500	__	1929	1574	1022	694	599
Total arrests	43684	41714	40422	40930	38829	39665	42051	42991

Source: Adapted from Broadhurst (2000) and Hong Kong Police Review (1997, 2000-2004).

When examining crime rates, individual factors that have less to do with the socio-economic environment also need to be examined. Some officers believe, for example, that low education and problematic mental status cause people to commit crime. People commit crime for money, for revenge, and for love just like anywhere else. Officers blame also poor parenting for youth crime as some parents leave their children alone with hardly anything to do while they are at work. Many consider that a combination of factors such as bad family influence and negative social environment causes juvenile delinquency.

Although local people commit most of the crimes, some officers blame migrants from outside Hong Kong especially those from the mainland for the crimes. Police statistics shows that the number of mainlanders arrested for crimes had increased from 759 in 1998 and 774 in 1999 to 1,021 in 2000 and 1,265 in 2001. Figures from the Immigration Department reveal the number of female illegal immigrants and visitors from the mainland arrested and prosecuted for vice activities rose by 142%—from 1,458 in 1998 to 3,538 in 2001. The number of mainland inmates in Hong Kong prisons has soared over the past decade, from 4,656 in 1991 to 9,158 in 2001 (So and Cheung, 2002; *South China Morning Post*, 2002; *Ta Kung Pao*, 2002). The police report a range of crimes commonly carried out by mainlanders. One category is deception, for which 104 were arrested in 2000 and 129 in 2001. Another category includes burglaries and robberies where 126 mainlanders were arrested for burglary and 111 for robbery in 2001. And another is vice. There has been a clear increase of females from the mainland according to the Correctional Services Department. In 1991, of the 4,656 mainland inmates in Hong Kong prisons, only 708 were women. Ten years later in 2001, women made up 6,248 of the total 9,158 mainland inmates held, who were mostly involved in the vice trade. According to Chinese University Professor Lau Siu-Kai, the trend of more mainlanders coming to Hong Kong to commit crimes was an expected result of China's liberalization. The growing problem of migrants committing crimes is not unique to Hong Kong as the same phenomenon exists in Western Europe and the United States. Hong Kong and mainland governments need to work more closely together to adjust to different trends in people mobility to address the migrant issue (So and Cheung, 2002).

The police often say that the causes for Triad and vice hinge upon a demand and supply relationship because a market exists for them and a huge profit is involved. Triad and vice organizations serve as the providers and the individuals who frequent their businesses are the consumers. The relationship between them, however, is not simply based on a service provided and demanded. As a police officer explained, the motivation for organized crimes and vice activities is profit. But street level drug users seek drugs because of addiction or poor family and education. Females are knowingly or unknowingly involved in vice activities because of their need for money. The organized movement of women across borders for sexual exploitation creates many victims in the process just like elsewhere in the world. For example, a young woman from an Eastern European country typically responds to an advertisement for work abroad, signs a contract with a travel agency, and then is forced to work as a prostitute in the destination country to pay back the company that hires her (MacWilliams, 2003).

Police Efforts in Controlling Crime, Triad, and Vice

In a city with a very low crime rate according to Western standard, crime may not be seen as an urgent or critical task. Some officers stated, for example, that the police in Hong Kong have enjoyed such a low crime rate for so many years that they have become complacent about crime. But from an organizational and operational standpoint, the Hong Kong Police remains vigilant about crime and has committed significant resources to crime prevention and investigation. The number of police arrests over the years indicates that arrest activities have been stable (see Table 9.2). Although the number seems lower in 2001, the crime rate in the year is also the lowest since 1999 (see Table 9.3). Besides uniformed patrol officers, specific branches, programs, squads, and units in the Force are also responsible for tackling crime, Triad, and vice problems.

Crime   Organizationally, the Hong Kong Police designates specific branches to deal with crime problems at various levels. At the district and divisional level, crimes confined to the district and division including many

Table 9.3 Reported Crime Rates in Hong Kong

	1982	1989	1991	1992	1993	1994	1995	1996	1997	1998	1999	2000	2001	2002	2003	2004
Crime No.*	—	818	88659	84056	82564	87804	91886	79050	67367	71962	76771	77245	73008	75877	88377	81315
Crime Rate*	1667	1439	1541	1449	1399	1465	1493	1228	1038	1076	1122	1136	1085	1118	1297	1189
Detection Rate*	—	48	—	—	—	—	52	51	51	46	43	44	44	43	39	44
Homicide	—	107	92	108	86	96	73	77	102	66	63	43	66	69	52	45

* Crime no. in hundreds, crime rate per 100,000, and detection rate by percentage.
Source: Adapted from Broadhurst (2000) and Hong Kong Police Statistics (2005) (See *www.info.gov.hk/police*).

routine cases and misdemeanors are probed. At the regional level, major crimes in the region and cross-district crimes are investigated. At the Force level, the most serious crimes including cross-region crimes and cross-border crimes are handled. These various levels in the Hong Kong Police to a certain extent resemble the local police, state police, and the FBI in the United States but function as parts of a single police organization. As some police officers commented:

> Crime investigation is organized in a hierarchy. We have divisional crime units who handle routine crime reports that don't require too much experience and are not too complex. Then the regional units handle cases that are more complex and require more experience. Narcotics, Commercial Crime, Intelligence, Organized Crime, and Serious Crime Bureaus run across division boundaries.

> There are four levels of crime units, divisions, districts, regional commands, and the Headquarters. At the divisional level, officers respond to emergencies as the first responders. The situation is like a hospital. Patients check in at the hospital or in the emergency unit, and then are taken to wherever is appropriate. A criminal case is received or discovered at the street level and will then go to the chief inspector. It will go to the district commander if it is serious. If it is very serious, it will go to the regional level. The regional Crime Units are capable of handling most of the crimes. Only the most serious cases that affect more than one region and the public in general and for which there is public interest will be handled by the Headquarters.

> Crime Units gather crime intelligence, develop counter measures to deal with crime and prevent crime. In the process, they may recommend new legislations. . . . We seek information to find out how to tackle crime problems. The Assistant Commissioner of Crime chairs a Crime Committee that determines priorities in fighting crimes. There was a major review of crime operations in the 80's. Neighborhood Police Units in housing units phased out, the personnel were used to patrol high crime areas, task forces were formed like team policing in the U.S. The rationale is that Hong Kong is small. Police operations do not have to be decentralized.

> Each unit, each team has an inspector. Dependent on the levels, the team on duty takes responsibility for new cases. The regional level may also take new cases. Normally, divisional investigation teams have new cases. Commercial cases go directly to Commercial Crime Bureau at the Force level. Minor cases are handled by individual officers. Other more complicated cases by teams.

Crime statistics such as crime rates and detection rates are some of the key indicators of police performance (see Table 9.3). Crime statistics are important also for discerning crime patterns in various locations and the city as a whole. But since crime rates are believed to have more to do with economic and social conditions, they are not viewed as an appropriate variable for evaluating police performances. Crime rates in Hong Kong have also been quite stable for years making it outlandish to hold individuals accountable for them. Some officers therefore critique the use of crime statistics as a measurement of individual performances at the divisional and district levels. Some officers pointed out also that there may not be a connection between an officer's effort and the crime figure in his or her area. Crime statistics can be manipulated. Detection rates in contrast are believed to reflect the performances of detectives more directly. They should, therefore, be taken more seriously when it comes to managing individual crime investigators. As some officers commented:

> For managing crime investigators, individuals' detection rates are looked at more than crime statistics. For individual teams at divisional, district, and regional levels, crime statistics are not viewed as that important. But crime statistics, mostly detection rates, are important for the Headquarters as a whole, for the regions, for the districts, and for the divisions as a whole. Big bosses at the Headquarters do care.

> Crime problem is another major concern for me. I go through all crime reports everyday. Yesterday we had twenty-two reports. We look at crime statistics and identify crime trends. We also look at detection rates. But we are not really figure-driven. Crime rates have remained roughly the same over the past ten years. The boss does not reprimand commanders for slight increase or decrease of crime. . . . We are not number-based. We look at the context of those numbers. We used to be more number-driven twenty-five to thirty years ago.

> Crime statistics depends on the level where it is kept. Using crime statistics is unfair at the divisional level. For example, sometimes crimes happen between two shifts. If a resident is burglarized, he may not report it at the time the burglary occurred. Also we rotate divisional commanders frequently. So nobody owns a district. . . . Reported crime does not give us the whole picture. Lots of crimes are not reported and crimes can be displaced. For these reasons, I don't like the way they handle statistics. I think the idea behind statistics is false: if you compare statistics, you will take a passive role. You become dependent on statistics.

> People can manipulate statistics. Take pocket-picking, for example. Do you record it as loss or theft? Officers may ask the victim where he or she lost the money and can change it to a less serious offense. Minor assault, minor fighting, etc., can be reduced to non-events easily. Officers may also try to minimize their role and send people away. They can do lots of things to make cases disappear. They tell people to resolve their disputes, mediate between them, convince them that both sides are wrong, and ask them to go home and relax. Crime intelligence can be manipulated. When boss says, "I want intelligence." In a day or two, lots of intelligence come up. It's a game.

The police use different approaches to manage crime in their districts. They emphasize crime prevention by visible deployment of uniformed officers at key locations. They reinforce patrol of banks and jewelry and watch stores, for example, and call on such businesses to beef up their security. Fighting street crime and abuse of psychotropic substances among youngsters are two other priorities of the Force (*Offbeat*, 2001). Various anti-crime campaigns with anti-drug, anti-child abuse, and anti-youth crime themes are organized and publicized regularly. The police also try to strengthen their communication and computer systems and increase the number of video-equipped crime report rooms to facilitate crime reporting. They investigate the majority of the crimes reported. But since many trivial calls are made to the Command and Control Centers, responses to them can be a significant waste of police resources. The police therefore divert some of these calls in order to improve their efficiency.

As one district varies significantly from another, one can observe different policing styles in different locations. Some areas are proactive and some reactive. Some emphasize problem-oriented policing and some deterrence and visibility. Some rely on crime statistics for deployment of police officers and some the security guard orientation. While some districts are engaged in community-oriented policing, some officers view community involvement in police work inappropriate. They question the extent of public involvement in policing and prefer that members of the community work with the police when needed only because all they want from the public is information or intelligence. As some police officers said:

> The police have to be very responsive to crime. Intelligence to the police is like marketing. They have to know where the crime market is. . . . We do crime analysis at the district, regional, and Force levels, looking at crime patterns. Sometimes they are useful; sometimes they are not. The information is there. We use the information messaging system during briefings, which show robberies, thefts, and other crime problems in the last month, last week, or yesterday. We have lots of commercial and residential buildings in the area. Majority of burglaries occur in commercial buildings. We have more manpower in high-risk premises such as jewelry stores.

> We are passive, not proactive. . . . We follow the crime trends. We are still passive at the district and divisional levels. . . . We don't really check on tourists around here. But when we go to a bar, we see some people overstay, we will use discretion. There is not much space for illegal immigrants to hide in Wanchai. Officers can tell who are from here and who are from the mainland. You can tell by their eyes. We have Hong Kong eyes, mainland eyes.

> The crime units gather information from the media, have undercover operations, and seek information from members of the community. They work closely with District Fight Crime Committees and District Councils. Kaifong Associations and Mutual Aid Committees have lost popularity over the years. They are receptive to any information and investigate every crime complaint. They emphasize police-community partnership. They encourage crime prevention measures and building security. But they don't encourage private patrol.

> There are Crime Prevention Bureau at the Headquarters and Crime Prevention Officers at the district and divisional levels. There are publicity campaigns, crime prevention campaigns. Every officer has the duty to prevent crime. Winter Precaution Campaign involves anti-crime patrol in high crime areas, public education about crime, distribution of leaflets. . . . The rationale for Winter Precaution is that more people carry cash between Christmas and Chinese New Year and there is a higher crime rate around this time. . . . Visibility is a deterrent. It's a duty for officers to prevent crime. They do so because of training and sense of responsibility. Last year 48% arrests are made by patrol officers.

Our management decided not to use the Compstat program of NYPD because we felt culturally our commanders would find it very difficult to go through the grilling process used during Compstat meetings. We do have an Incident Mapping System that produces crime data for the frontline, divisional commanders, and the management. We do conduct crime analyses and target emergent problems. For example, when I was an Assistant Divisional Commander in one District, we reviewed crime statistics every day. When I first got there, there were thirty-two burglaries in one public-housing building. We reduced them to zero because I looked at the patterns, analyze the modus operandi, and targeted the problems according to what we found. We found that the time of the burglaries were mostly on Wednesday and Saturday, the two days when there was horse racing. Burglars use the money and spend it on horse racing. Some burglaries were committed by drug addicts to help them buy drugs and these people obviously have low skills in entering the residences. We also studied the stores that sold lottery tickets. We installed cameras in the elevators. We got Crime Unit and Patrol Unit together to target the problems and reduced the number to zero.

I used to think that the public knows nothing about crime and police work. We are the professionals. I was wrong. I have members of the public who came to me and complained about not seeing enough police officers and not feeling safe. I asked them why. They told me that during the time they go to work and the hour they come back, they don't see officers. So from 6:00 am to 9:00 am and 4:00 pm to 7:00 pm, we put all our available officers on the street. The public then feels safer and more satisfied.

Citizens should not be nosy; they should not be active. But they should provide information to the police, serve as eyes and ears, no more than that. Hong Kong is a crowded place; they can always see something. But nowadays many people don't bother even though all they need to do is pick up the phone. And that's all we want from them. It's not like in the U.S. where you have a place wide open, nobody around. In Hong Kong a crime happens, somebody got to see it.

Triad   Although Triad-related offenses occupy only about 3.5% of the total crime in Hong Kong, the police take them very seriously. They believe these crimes have an impact on the society and may cause serious damage to the economy. The strong concern about Triad is reflected by the resources devoted and attention paid to Triad and organized crime at various levels in the Force. At the Force level, the Organized Crime and Triad Bureau (OCTB) investigates most sophisticated and major Triad dominated criminal syndicates (Hong Kong Police Review, 1997). The units at the regional level investigate elaborate organized crimes, target major Triad activities, and conduct covert operations. The police at the district and divisional sections investigate locally committed organized crimes, target known Triad personalities, and inspect places frequented by Triad members. The police also organize periodic joint operations against Triad and organized crimes that involve multiple police units from different levels. In 1997, for example, seven such operations were conducted resulting in the arrest of 234 persons (Hong Kong Police Review, 1997). The only unit that is generally not active or less involved in Anti-Triad operations is the local Patrol Unit, which is responsible for regular patrol and crime duties. As some officers stated:

> We have a special unit to deal with Triad because it is difficult. Like small pox, they are not widespread, but bad. We use discretion, measure seriousness, give warnings to those under eighteen. . . . We follow the crime trends. We are still passive at the district and divisional levels. It may be different at the regional and Force levels, especially for drugs and organized crimes. . . . We have street undercover agents. We arrested twenty-nine traffickers last night that have Triad involvement.

The police are strict in dealing with illegal drinking, illegal prostitution, illegal gambling, drug problems, Triad activities, and illegal immigration because many of these offenses are sources of finance for crime syndicates. If crime syndicates are rich, they will create more difficulties for the police. These problems occupy a significant portion of police arrests.

Since Triad is a sophisticated social problem that goes beyond a single police jurisdiction, a successful strategy in dealing with it requires the support of the public and overseas law enforcement agencies. The police, therefore, have periodic public campaigns and work with other law enforcement agencies on this issue. They expect the citizens to come forward and assist the police in cracking Triad cases. They protect witnesses and have a witness protection program. But since Hong Kong is a small jurisdiction, witnesses often have to settle in other countries that have agreement with the Hong Kong Police. To target organized crime problems beyond the territory, the police collaborate with the Public Security Bureaus in the mainland and overseas police forces. They have significantly increased their cooperation with the Public Security Bureaus in drug enforcement and cross-boundary organized crimes in recent years. The Public Security Bureaus have recently also publicly acknowledged the existence of Triad in the mainland and demonstrated their commitment to working with the Hong Kong Police on this problem.

A campaign on May 8, 2002 in Mong Kok targeted Triad-controlled prostitution. Over 900 police officers including members of the Commercial Crime Bureau, Organized Crime and Triad Bureau, Narcotics Bureau, and Criminal Intelligence participated in this operation, during which detectives were sent over first to the locations with rental cars and forty busloads of uniformed officers then followed. Some officers were equipped with bulletproof vests and MP5 and about fifty detectives were wearing suits. They searched more than seventy locations and nine offices suspected of Triad involvement. As a result, the police claimed that they dismantled the largest cross-border prostitution ring and made 213 arrests including 18 core Triad members, 113 prostitutes, 43 persons working at the prostitution sites, and 21 involved in producing pornographic materials. Most of the prostitutes were from the mainland and some from Thailand and Vietnam. The police also froze HK$86 million's worth of assets. They believed that the Triad-controlled ring had been active for two years and accumulated HK$240 million in asset. With connection with mainland smugglers, the group recruited women from inland provinces and helped them enter Hong Kong either illegally or with two-way permits. The group was also involved in production and sales of pornographic materials and internet websites, magazines, pictures, and videos. It is estimated that the group made an income of about HK$10 million monthly (*Ming Pao*, 2002). This campaign was conducted with intelligence from and cooperation with the mainland police including Guangdong Province and Shengzhen City Public Security Bureau. Two hundred mainland public security officers were involved also in the operation across the boundary and made 41 arrests including 15 from Hong Kong.

Vice   Police officers in Hong Kong handle various vice activities such as underage drinking, psychotropic drugs, illegal gambling, and illegal prostitution. The main responsibility for targeting vice problems lies with the special units at the district and regional levels. Every district has a Special Duty Squad for drugs, liquor, gambling, and prostitution. The officers tend to view drug as the most serious vice activity, especially when youths are involved. To target this problem, they raid parties where young people were suspected of drug use. In the first seven months of 2001, increased police action led to a 77% increase in the arrest of people aged under 21 for narcotics offenses. As the former Commissioner of Police Tsang reiterated, "The fight against the abuse of psychotropic drugs, especially among youngsters, is the right move and will remain one of the Force's top priorities" (*Offbeat*, 2001). In addition, the Force has public education programs including mass media and advertising that target youths and warn them against the danger of drug involvement.

The police are strict with drug offenders, backed by tough legislation and heavy penalty against such offenses. They have developed an advanced crime analysis system that target drug problems. For serious drug trafficking problems, the police work closely with other law enforcement organizations. Over the years, the Hong Kong Police has developed a multi-agency approach in fighting against the drug trade. Due to the intensive law enforcement activities against drug offenses, the U.S. State Department removed Hong Kong from the major list of drug transit countries in November 2001.

On a routine basis, as elsewhere, undercover officers are deployed during drug operations. But Hong Kong police officers do not believe it is appropriate for themselves to be involved in sale and purchase of drugs. If it is illegal for a citizen to sell or buy drugs, a vice officer should not be involved in such activities, either, even if the purpose is to obtain intelligence. As a crime officer stated, "I see U.S. officers sell seized drug to informants and don't see any problems with it. I don't think police belong to the police if they don't see selling drugs as problems."

The police target illegal prostitution through both undercover operations and large-scale campaigns. During undercover operations, the police seek out owners of prostitution sites, persons who control and rely on prostitutes for living, and women who come to Hong Kong to practice prostitution illegally. The police use plain-clothed officers, called "loose snakes," in recreational areas, apartments, and unlicensed massage parlors, where illegal prostitution is suspected. "Loose snakes" are assigned to massage parlors as paying customers but would arrest the masseuses if they offer to have sex and close down their parlors as illegal businesses. Some closed locations would reemerge and the police would arrest the managers.

Multi-agency anti-vice campaigns often involve hundreds of officers in areas infamous for prostitution. The Hong Kong Police and the Immigration Department had such a campaign in West Kowloon on September 17 and 18, 2001. Altogether 223 agents searched 150 locations and arrested 275 female prostitution suspects and 5 male residents who overstayed their visas. The suspects were between age 17 and 45; among them, 126 carried single trip paper, 98 were illegal entrants, 15 carried Chinese passports, and 8 overstayed. Another 28 were Thais and Vietnamese. The 5 overstaying males were delivered to the Customs Authority. On May 11, 2002, 150 police and immigration officers carried out a major anti-vice operation in Mong Kok and arrested 76 suspected sex workers. Among them, 67 were two-way-permit holders, 4 held Chinese passport, 4 Thai passport, and 1 Indonesian passport. Many of the suspects came to Hong Kong as "sightseers" but were arrested for breaching conditions of stay. During this operation, the police also joined the CLP Power and the Electrical and Mechanical Services Department in removing electronic signs advertising vice services. The police said that the signs' cables could pose a danger to the public. In the first four months of 2002, 4,270 such signs were removed from buildings in Mong Kok and 80 people were arrested for displaying them.

Although large-scale anti-vice campaigns result in hundreds of arrests, they are routine police operations that do not indicate a deterioration of vice problems in Hong Kong. Such campaigns often boost the image of the police due to the strong stance they take and wide media coverage; but they may not have any lasting effect. Officers tend to have different perceptions about various police efforts in combating vice. Some believe that the police are tough and effective in handling vice in general. Some consider that certain vice problems such as drugs are taken more seriously than others. Some see vice being treated as a minor issue overall. Vice activities also create a mixed feeling for individual officers because it is not always clear what is illegal and what exactly the police are required to do in handling such problems. As some officers stated:

> Yes, we are strict with all kinds of vice activities, gambling, licensing, underage drinking, and drugs. For prostitution, there is a ready market and a willingness for female involvement. . . . Hong Kong police are not active and strict for illegal drinking. It's not a problem, except for some expats. We are active but not strict for illegal prostitution. We are active but not strict for gambling except when the media covers it as a problem. We are both active and strict for drug problems.

> Vice unit deals with drugs, gambling, and prostitution problems. Vice squads do decoy operations and undercover. Mong Kok prostitution exists because it's difficult to infiltrate. You got the whole building in prostitution, syndicated prostitution. But we have to follow the laws. I think they are controlled by Triad; they are organized prostitution. But there's no proof. I don't think it's

corruption. They are all organized. But the girls won't talk to us. They know
we always have decoy operations; but they don't know when and they don't
know who. And when we are there, they may not do it. The Force does not treat
it or think about it as a serious problem.

Police are a little confused about prostitution. There were mixed messages
about the sex industry from the community. The police prefer not to deal with
it. There were mixed messages about gambling, too. Due to changes in drug
problems, there is lack of clarity about what the problem really is. Customs
agents and police collaborate in dealing with piracy, which is extremely rare
nowadays. Patrol officers deal with public drunkenness, drunk driving, pornog-
raphy, and so on. Vice officers handle exploited prostitution, illegal gambling,
and narcotics trade. The public is not very hostile to exploited prostitution and
illegal gambling unless they operate in residential areas. They are more concerned with drugs due to their influence on children and family.

Working with the Mainland Police   An important part of the Hong
Kong Police crime operations concerns its relationship with the mainland Public
Security. Although challenges exist for their cooperation such as the lack of a
common legal system, the mutual interest in solving crime problems outweighs
their differences. There has been a stronger need for such cooperation due to the
increased flow of people between Hong Kong and the mainland after Hong
Kong's return to China in 1997. Many Hong Kong residents, for example, travel
to China for business or pleasure. As they are victimized in the mainland, they
may request assistance from the Hong Kong Police if they do not believe they
can get the protection they need from the mainland Public Security. Although
the Hong Kong Police's ability to handle a case that occurred in the mainland is
limited, it can maintain contact with the mainland police, obtain information
from them, provide assistance to them, and put pressure on them in solving the
case. Some crimes are also committed beyond a single jurisdiction and even
international in nature. They require the police from both Hong Kong and the
mainland to share information and intelligence.

According to the officers, the Hong Kong Police had developed a relationship with its mainland counterpart long before the 1997 handover. But its
communication and cooperation with the Public Security Bureaus have increased significantly in recent years. Their work together mainly involves cross-
boundary crime, intelligence, and training. Senior Hong Kong Police and
Chinese Public Security Ministry officials have recently discussed tightening the
policy of two-way permits for Hong Kong, considering the increase of crimes
committed by two-way permit holders. The Hong Kong Police proposed a
scheme to stop offenders from receiving two-way permits: by using a screening
mechanism with the mainland police, those with criminal records are not to be
allowed to come back to Hong Kong in a short period of time. Officials from the
two police systems also discussed cross-boundary crimes and firearms-related
crimes and cooperation in criminal investigation (*Ta Kung Pao*, 2002). Locally,
the Hong Kong Police works closely with Shenzhen City and Guangdong
Province. Hong Kong residents who are victims of crime in Shenzhen are able to
report the cases after they return to Hong Kong under a proposed system set up

with the Shenzhen Public Security Bureau. Hong Kong and Shenzhen police have liaison officers at the four border checkpoints and a hot-line for cross-border travelers. They have a referral system under which they can alert each other to crime reports in their own jurisdictions. They have also explored the possibility of linking the two forces' computer systems to speed up the tracing of firearms used in cross-boundary crimes (*South China Morning Post*, 2002). As some officers stated:

> We have worked with the mainland for a long time since early 80's due to geo-graphical closeness. I can pick up the phone and call before and after 1997 to the mainland and Macaw. It's about mutual learning and sharing. We work mainly in areas of crime cases, training, and cross-training. When Chinese Public Security Bureaus visit, we give them presentations.

> We used to have contacts on dealing with individual cases with the PSB. Now we have relationship also on management. We send officers to Beijing and PSBs for training. They have officers over here to visit and learn about our management process. They can get all the information they like. But they haven't attended our Command Courses because they are conducted in English. If they like to attend, they will be welcomed.

> The Hong Kong Police started liaising with the Public Security Bureau way back in 1979 although it was never made public. The first Chinese police delegation from Beijing Central Government came to Hong Kong in 1979. They were interested in Interpol. Since then the relationship slowly developed. Not long after, joint meetings were held on a regular basis once a quarter. There was considerable cooperation. But there was great difficulty due to the lack of legal framework. Now there are regular meetings with the PSB. Over the years, a close relationship was developed with the PSB.

The recent enhanced cooperation with the mainland has been largely due to a region-wide effort that includes China, Hong Kong, and Macao to combat crime, especially organized crime after Hong Kong and Macaw returned to China (Lo, 2001). The Hong Kong Police and its mainland counterpart have created joint programs to address specific crime problems, which have brought tangible benefits to both sides. For example, in 1997, their cooperation resulted in a 24% reduction in motor vehicle thefts; a high proportion of vehicles stolen in Hong Kong that ended up on the mainland were recovered and returned. Organized vehicle thefts and smuggling were reduced by 18.9%. During the year, 254 stolen vehicles were recovered, compared to 53 in 1996. Close cooperation also minimized the number of firearms entering Hong Kong, contributing significantly to the lower number of armed robberies (Hong Kong Police Review, 1997). In recent years, more international fugitives are using China as a bolt-hole to escape justice and are being picked up in Hong Kong. One of the main reasons for this trend is criminals' belief that since the 1997 handover from Britain to China, Hong Kong has become a part of China and a safe place to hide out. China's liberalization coupled with its lack of extradition treaties means suspected criminals wanted overseas—particularly ethnic Chinese—increasingly view China as a fugitives' haven (*South China Morning*,

2002). In reality, the Hong Kong Police remains in the common law system but now works more closely with China on criminal matters. The mainland police provide assistance to the Hong Kong Police upon its request to extradite criminals (*Ming Pao*, 2001). If the Hong Kong police "do not make such request, the Mainland Judiciary will handle the fate of the criminal elements" (Lo, 2001:7). The Hong Kong Police's internal communication system, the POINT, is a channel through which any unit can make request for assistance to the mainland Public Security Bureaus for investigation of criminal cases. District, divisional, and regional level officers in Hong Kong can make the request to the Liaison Bureau at the Headquarters for information from the mainland. As a police officer and an ICAC officer said:

> In 1989, 1990, and 1991, there were very high crime rates, which came down due to a key factor—the Hong Kong mainland cooperation. During the 80's, Hong Kong people exploited the border. When they committed crimes in Hong Kong, they would escape to the mainland. Then due to the relationship with the PSB, there was rendition arrangement although there was no extradition. As a result, China returned Hong Kong criminals who committed crimes in Hong Kong and escaped to the mainland. Hong Kong could not return criminals from the mainland if they entered Hong Kong legally. So each side did what it could. There was much cooperation, a reciprocity of good will. The PSB has not interfered in Hong Kong policing. At the same time, each side has lots of interest in what the other's doing.

> Hong Kong is actually safer than ten years ago. Crime is under control. Hong Kong used to have a car theft problem in 1989 and 1990. Now the situation is better due to work with the mainland. Cooperation between the Hong Kong Police and mainland police has been very good. They have stopped registering cars with right-hand wheels. Guangdong police have helped capture Hong Kong fugitives. All this happened when there is no formal repatriation of criminals in Hong Kong who committed crimes in the mainland and no repatriation of criminals in the mainland who committed crimes in Hong Kong.

The Hong Kong Police also passes on their experiences in fighting organized crime and drugs and gathering crime intelligence to the mainland police. As the Hong Kong Police intensified enforcement against organized crime, organized crime groups have moved increasingly to the neighboring Guangdong Province and the inland area, especially the Pearl River Delta region. They are involved in money laundering, kidnapping, smuggling, territorial expansion, hideouts, and corruption (Guangdong Police Studies Association, 2001). The mainland police, therefore, need assistance from the Hong Kong Police to deal with transnational and cross-border crimes. Due to better liaisons, both sides were able to solve some high profile cases and homicides. The mainland police, for example, have smashed a cross-border prostitution racket in Guizhou Province after receiving intelligence information from officers in Hong Kong. The racket had smuggled prostitutes to Hong Kong and a Hong Kong resident was among seven members of the racket arrested. During this operation, the mainland police said they had rescued nine young women who were due to be in the next shipment to Hong Kong. Women recruited are usually lured from a number of provinces with the promise of high-paying jobs in Hong Kong. But after they enter the territory, they are forced into prostitution, normally having to service up to ten clients a day to repay trafficking fees and the cost of their travel documents (*South China Morning Post*, 2002).

Perceptions of Effectiveness of Police Efforts

There is wide consensus that Hong Kong has very low crime rate. The overall crime rate for 1997 reached its lowest level in twenty-four years. In comparison with 1996, the overall number of crimes recorded dropped by 15% and, for the fourth consecutive year, there was a marked decrease in burglaries and robberies, down by 17% and 24% respectively. The number of bank, watch, and gold shop robberies dropped by 61%. The detection rate is 51.4%, which also compares favorably with other densely populated cities world-wide (Hong Kong Police Review, 1997). The overall crime rate has continued to follow the downward trend and has gone even lower in recent years (see Table 9.3). Crime rate in Hong Kong per 100,000 population is 1,667 in 1982, 1,448 in 1994, 1,493 in 1995, 1,047 in 1998, 1,118 in 2002, and 1,189 in 2004. Murder and violent crimes remain rare. Homicide for 1995, 1999, and 2000 is 73, 63, and 43 and most homicides are committed in a domestic setting; robbery for these years is 5,554, 3,640, and 3,433; rape is 103, 91, and 104; and wounding and serious assault is 743, 576, and 550 (Hong Kong Police Force, 2000). The low crime rates are especially conspicuous when compared to most industrialized countries. Comparative burglary rates show that just this offense alone in Australia (2,130), New Zealand (2,451), England and Wales (2,452), and Germany (2,936) exceed the overall crime rate for Hong Kong. In the U.S. a rate of 1,041 burglaries per 100,000 accounts alone for nearly three-quarters of the rate of all crime in Hong Kong. The burglary rate in Hong Kong was 223 per 100,000 and among advanced countries only Japan's burglary rate of 200 is at a similar level (Hong Kong Police Force, 2000; Mukherjee, Carcach and Higgins, 1997; Broadhurst, 2000).

The low crime rate may have contributed to a high sense of security in Hong Kong as shown in recent public opinion polls. In the 1999 Public Opinion Survey, 78% of the respondents found the city safe during the day and 37% felt so at night. In the 2001 Public Opinion Survey, the public indicated an even stronger sense of safety in Hong Kong as 84% felt safe at daytime and 59% felt so at night. From an institutional perspective, the low crime rate may reinforce the idea among Hong Kong police officials that public order management and effective crime control should continue to be emphasized. As the police selectively present these traditional strategies as responsible for lowering the crime rate, a phenomenon referred to as "drama in police work" by Manning (1977, 1997), the Hong Kong public can be expected to continue its support for such strategies, even though police actions alone are not likely to affect the crime rate significantly.

In fact, several factors are commonly mentioned as accounting for the low crime rate in Hong Kong, i.e., an environment highly favorable to natural and informal surveillance, cultural homogeneity, and high levels of public and private investment in policing (Broadhurst, 2000). High rises, dense population, small jurisdiction, and the structure of the Mass Transit Railway (MTR) system are some of the situational factors that help keep the crime rate low. Strong values of conformity and a pro-order outlook the public holds are some of the cultural characteristics. The heavy investment in policing is reflected by the ubiquitous deployment of police officers, the government's support for the police function, and a large presence of private security and guarding industry. For example, at a time when most government departments face a budget cut, there has been a 7% average increase in police expenditure in recent years, from HK$8,707 million for 1995 to HK$11,915 million for 1999 and to HK$11,892 million for 2000. Overall, a combination of a confined jurisdiction, the ethnic composition, and a pro-order public and government may have contributed to the low crime rate in Hong Kong. As an officer stated:

> Hong Kong has no urban problems. Hong Kong is orderly because of small jurisdiction, everybody knows everybody, ID cards, high visibility of patrol . . . similar to Singapore, which still has residential registration. We don't have residential registration, but we rely on IDs. Our system is based on the UK police; but UK doesn't have enough money to maintain high visibility. High visibility is expensive.

> The crime rate is low. There are several reasons for this. Hong Kong people concentrate on their businesses and on making money. It's already a small jurisdiction. On top of that, we have a very severe force. If we don't like you, we take you off the street. We take out the bad guys. . . . Crime rates are low because people in Hong Kong are law-abiding, have a pro-order outlook. Police do their best to make sure Hong Kong is one of the safest cities in the world as stated in the Vision Statement. We have achieved crime control with the service quality policy. . . . I think the Hong Kong Police ability in dealing with crime is better in comparison to the former Royal Force.

> The low crime rate can be explained by gun control, ethnic and racial homogeneity, tight territory and border control with few outsiders coming into Hong Kong. The population is local, and the police style emphasizes high visibility, strong presence, 9-minute response time, PTU unit, etc. . . . We have no graffiti in the train and low level of crime in the MTR because of short distance between stations and crowdedness. We don't allow people to hang around in the MTR.

Aside from the achievement talks, police officers do see room for further improvement. Internally, they express a need for more coordination. Crime Unit, Uniformed Branch, and Tactical Unit, for example, should work together more. The police need to break new ground in dealing with emerging and complex crimes such as white-collar crimes and commercial crimes. Regarding individual officers, they see the need for better training and greater incentives. The evaluation of crime officers can be made more objective and substantive.

Externally, they see the need for the police to further expand their work with the mainland Public Security Bureaus and overseas law enforcement agencies.

10

Corruption and Misconduct

The Hong Kong Police has been confronted with corruption and misconduct just like any other major city police in the world. Over the years, both the police and the Hong Kong government have taken drastic measures to address these problems. Consequently, the seriousness and magnitude of police corruption in Hong Kong have been significantly reduced since the 1970s. Bribery cases and officer involvement in vice, drugs, and organized crime, especially those that are serious, occur very rarely today and the police have been able to shift their attention to misconduct or malfeasance. While police corruption and misconduct in Hong Kong are not much different from other places, the police emphasis on malfeasance sets them apart from many major police organizations in the world. The tough official stance against officer debt and related personal financial management problems, for example, are seldom heard about in the field of policing elsewhere.

This chapter describes first the types of police corruption and misconduct in Hong Kong and examines their causes. Second, it looks at the internal police measures and external oversight mechanisms employed to address these problems over the years, particularly the Complaints against Police Office, an internal police unit known as the CAPO, and the Independent Commission against Corruption, an anti-graft body known as the ICAC, and their relationship. Third, it presents the views and perceptions of Hong Kong Police officers regarding the effectiveness of these measures. Lastly, a brief discussion of the future directions of the Hong Kong Police in its effort to fight corruption and misconduct is provided.

Corruption and Misconduct in the Past and Present

An officer with 35 years' experience with the Hong Kong Police once said that there were evil, abusive, corrupt officers just like there were brutal, animal-like criminals (Liu, 1988). Clean officers got ridiculed as stupid in the old days and treated like Frank Serpico, the New York City police legend of 1970s.

Moreover, police corruption was syndicated and institutionalized in Hong Kong before the 1970s. Syndicated corruption was linked by middle-ranking officers, the staff sergeants, who played a significant role in connecting vice businesses with their superiors in the Force. As they were close to the street and familiar with vice businesses, these officers were able to organize corrupt police activities. Their supervisors, mostly expatriate officers, either acquiesced or simply ignored the bribery when the money was offered to them. Expatriate officers became part of the culture, participated in corruption themselves, and were not able to discipline those under them. A culture of corruption developed and flourished, in which a whole police unit or even the whole station was "on the take." There were corruption syndicates, rent collectors, protection rackets, and the like. A high-ranking police officer would find it difficult to survive in this culture if he were to remain clean (Cheung and Lau, 1981). An ICAC official defined syndicated or institutionalized corruption in the following manner.

It has two features: A, involvement of "go-between," who is a middleman, often a Triad member, a staff sergeant; and B, degree of succession. The staff sergeant collected the money and put it in envelopes and in everyone's mailbox. Some say if lots of officers are involved, there is syndicated corruption. I don't think the number of officers is an accurate indicator of syndicated corruption. Degree of succession means that if a corrupt officer is gone, another will take his place. So the corruption continues.

There are several reasons for the rampant police corruption that existed in the early days in the Hong Kong Police history. These include the particular Hong Kong social and working environment. As a trading port, Hong Kong provided a context where vice activities flourished. Merchants, sailors, workers, visitors, etc., were mostly males and were not a stable population. Prostitution, gambling, and drugs became part of the Hong Kong life. Such an environment provided a fertile ground for police corruption. In addition, the police pay was low before the 1970s. Police officers depended on bribes from brothels and gambling clubs to supplement their income. The corruption was organized, syndicated, and a way of life (Brogden and Lau, 2001).

A clear characteristic in syndicated police corruption was the police-Triad alliance, which was tolerated by the then colonial regime. Some scholars suggest that the colonial government's tolerance of this alliance indicates that crime control was treated as a low priority before the 1970s. Because crime was not a major concern, its relationship with police corruption was largely ignored. Police protected vice activities in such areas as drugs, gambling, and sex in return for bribes (Sinclair, 1983; Traver and Vagg, 1991; Gaylord and Traver, 1995). Both police corruption and crime were highly organized as a result and a symbiotic relationship between organized crime and police corruption developed. This relationship led to many police and Triad frame-ups common before the 1970s. As Brogden and Lau described (2001:28):

While the police protected vice in return for bribes, they cooperated with the Triads to stage-manage raids on vice dens. Vice operators would hire people (mostly drug addicts) to pretend to patronize vice dens and the police would come in a raid to arrest them. . . . The police protected the syndicate's monopoly because it paid them huge sums in bribes daily. All bribes organized on a syndicated basis were collected every day in cash by the *machai*'s (subordinate gang members) of the "collector" who was a brother-in-arms of the local detective station sergeant.

Table 10.1 Corruption Reports against Police Officers in the Hong Kong Police

	1974	1976	1980	1990	1993	1996	1997	1998	1999	2000	2001	2002	2003	2004
Reported	1443	1119	523	475	614	576	512	560	507	602	513	565	532	435
Charged	_	_	_	_	_	32	13	22	11	14	8	18	16	10
Convicted	_	_	_	_	_	18	5	18	5	11	6	2	5	6

Source: Adapted from ICAC Operations Department Review (1998-1999), ICAC Annual Report (1999-2004) and ICAC statistics (2002).

Syndicated corruption no longer plagues the Hong Kong Police at present and is regarded widely as under control. Police corruption in general is a far cry from the past in terms of both number and frequency. According to the ICAC, the numbers of corruption reports against police officers from 2001 to 2004 are 513, 565, 532, and 435 respectively (see Table 10.1). The numbers of officers charged during these years are 8, 18, 16, and 10. And the numbers of officers convicted are 6, 2, 5, and 6. Serious corruption cases still occur and capture the headlines, but are extremely rare. When they do occur, they still demonstrate a high degree of complexity and symbiotic relationship between corruption and organized crime. One such case in recent years involves the detection of an illegal drugs refinery in Yuen Long, which resulted in the arrest of twenty-four suspects, including two former police officers who had allegedly arranged for protection of the drug enterprise. Five police officers were also arrested for allegedly shielding Triad gangsters in return for cut-price vice services and free meals (ICAC Operations Department Review, 1998-1999). Following are some comments from ICAC officials illustrating the corruption cases at present.

Corruption is connected often to organized crime and money laundering, involving computer crime and cybercrime. Financial investigation is particularly challenging. We used to go to people's home to search for money and gold bars. We can't find them there anymore. People would put money in an offshore personal account, an offshore investment account, in another country. It's much more difficult to investigate such corruption cases today.

I can confirm that organized crimes and corruption are often intertwined. Over the years, ICAC have investigated a wide range of organized crimes facilitated by corruption. Law enforcement officers and even members of the consular corps were found to be corruptly assisting drug traffickers and smugglers of various kinds (Kwok, 2001:2).

Tipping off suspects is another concern. In one district, a sergeant was considered doing a great job. When we told them that he was corrupt, nobody believed it. This sergeant tipped off the places involving vice all the time and receiving bribery. But each time, scapegoats were set up making it look like the sergeant did a good job. The sergeant was the only one receiving bribery. Team members knew about the scapegoat arrangement but weren't bribed. It looked like they were able to crack cases as scapegoats would go to court and plead guilty. We got a witness who testified against the sergeant and also team members who knew about the scapegoat arrangement. But since team members weren't bribed, they were accused of obstruction of justice. Eventually the sergeant was found guilty and convicted but team members were acquitted in a separate trial.

Some police officers also believe that a relationship exists between corruption and vice activities such as prostitution. In the "Red Light" District of Mong Kok, for example, hundreds of prostitutes work in small flats in large buildings. The area may be more appropriately called the "Yellow Light" District since yellow instead of red light is used for advertising prostitution businesses. The color "yellow" is also a symbol of pornographic publications and activities in the Chinese culture. As numerous women from outside Hong Kong work as prostitutes in the area, it is hard to believe that there is no connection between police corruption and organized prostitution. But to prove such a linkage is difficult. As a police officer said: "It's difficult to investigate prostitution in Mong Kok. The girls will not talk. Undercover officers find it hard to get evidence. Officers at the very low level may be corrupt. But no one knows where and when."

Police misconduct, which is based on complaint figures, was also commonly reported in the 1970s, especially after the establishment of the CAPO in 1974. According to CAPO statistics, police misconduct showed a sharp increase from 1974 to 1986 (see Table 10.2), which could have been caused by different recording practices in these earlier years. The annual number of complaints stayed steadily above 4,000 till after 1986. A decreasing trend in complaint figures had been observed for about ten years since 1987. From 1988 through 1995, the number of complaints fluctuated between a low of 3,084 to a high of 3,454. The figures went down below 3,000 in 1997 and 1998 and then up again fluctuating between 3,222 and 3,833 from 2000 to 2004. Most of the complaints and related allegations endorsed for investigation were either withdrawn or resolved informally. About 14% of the endorsed cases and allegations are substantiated on average (see Table 10.2). The vast majority of complaints according to police records are related to "neglect of duty" or "misconduct and improper manner" (Hong Kong Police Review, 2000). Besides such misconduct, an ICAC official sees malfeasance as an emerging problem that requires serious attention: "ICAC needs to look at malfeasance as the next area of concern, not just bribery. Public officials may be involved in practices that are not bribery but malfeasance that will benefit them after they leave office."

Table 10.2 Complaint Reports against Officers in the Hong Kong Police

	1974	1983	1986	1988	1994	1995	1996	1997	1998	1999	2000	2001	2002	2003	2004
#.cases	808	4241	4532	3217	3084	3454	3419	2937	2906	3083	3673	3246	3833	3384	3222
% withdrawn*		—	—	—	68.7%	66.7%	58.1%	46.9%	42.2%	—	40%	38.6%	40.9%	43.8%	44.1%
Informal resolution*		—	—	—	15.4%	17.9%	22.1%	27.5%	31.8%	40%	30%	24.4%	26.8%	24.5%	20.8%
Substantiated**		—	—	—	16.6%	11%	14%	13.6%	15.9%	16.7%	13.8%	12%	13.2%	14.5%	13.1%

* Of the number of endorsed complaint cases or allegations.
** Of the number of endorsed cases or allegations that were fully investigated.
Source: Adapted from CAPO Annual Report (1995, 1996, 1997, 1998, 1999, and 2000) and Hong Kong Police Review (2000-2004).

When asked about police corruption and misconduct, street officers tend to say that they do not have opportunities to be bribed these days. They believe that higher-ranking officers have more opportunities to be corrupt. Police managers including inspectors, superintendents, and assistant commissioners, however, cite a variety of corruptions and misbehaviors by subordinate officers, including bribery, Triad involvement, violations of due process rules, abuse of authority, gambling, and officer debt. Officer debt is one of the most frequently cited concerns and many police managers see a direct relationship between poor financial management and officer misconduct. Following are some typical comments from police managers regarding their concerns of corruption and misbehaviors by subordinate officers.

> I'm most concerned with subordinate officers receiving bribery, being in debt, unmanageable debt, and behaviors behind those debts such as gambling and prostitutions. . . . I'm very concerned with officers hanging around with Triad, drinking, bad manners with the public, abuse of power, abuse of force. . . . Anything that puts the Force in a negative light is a big concern for the top management; but we're concerned about it, too. . . . I'm concerned with deviant behaviors, insulting, verbal assault, gambling, and drinking. The Force has not managed gambling and drinking consistently. We have beer competitions, and we have all kinds of parties and gathering where officers can drink.

> There're still some lower-ranking officers who overspend and get themselves in debt, which is one of the most serious problems the police have at present. As a matter of fact, we have more officers having gambling behaviors, being in debt, and declaring bankruptcy in recent years. . . . One of the corruption cases we're most concerned with is obtaining loans from illegal sources. Obtaining loans over $2000 from places other than legitimate financial institutions or from friends is a violation of rules and regulations. Another problem is acceptance of advantage, cash, presents of financial value, etc.

> I'm concerned with the seriousness of the case, syndicated conducts, officers accepting or not accepting for doing or not doing something, unauthorized loans. . . . Those misconducts that are well-planned, have an adverse effect on the Force, Triad related, and known criminals related. . . . We deal with serious malpractice and misconduct such as obstruction of justice, beating suspects, assaulting prisoners, dishonesty, giving false statements, drink and drive, etc. . . . I'm most concerned with violations of due process rules and procedures in dealing with citizens and Triad involvement. . . . We are concerned with officer abuse of authority. We have bribery ordinance and code of discipline to deal with this problem.

Most of unmanageable debt cases involve lower-ranking officers. Senior police officers are seriously concerned about these cases because they believe financial problems impair officers' operational efficiency and may lead to other problems such as emotional difficulties and illegal behaviors. Indebtedness and associated gambling problem are described as a time bomb that may cause officers to commit corrupt acts and crimes. According to the police records, the number of indebted officers disciplined for having their operational efficiency impaired by their indebtedness went from 14 in 1999 to 11 in 2000 and then to 39 in 2001. The number of officers who went bankrupt rose from 27 in 1999 to 83 in 2000 and to 85 in 2001 (Lee, 2002a). Two hundred forty-nine officers were classified as unable to pay back debt in 2001, a 23% increase from the previous year. Among the 249 officers, 5% were due to gambling, 55% family and relative problems, 14% extravaganza and bad investment, and the rest major problems in life (*Ming Pao*, 2002). One officer committed suicide due to emotional and financial problems in December 2001 (*The Sun*, 2002). Three officers were allegedly about to perpetrate an armed robbery in October 1995 (Keenan, 1995). According to statistics kept by the Bankruptcy Management Commission, 41 cases up until the end of September 2001 were suspected of frauds and deception and were referred to the police for investigation, amounting to a total of HK$4.7 million (*The Sun*, 2002). Financial companies complain about officers suspected of frauds and send letters of complaint directly to police authorities on such cases. It was reported that more than twenty letters were sent to police authorities over a six-month period in 2002 demanding investigations of officer bankruptcy. One of these letters was published in a local newspaper (*The Sun*, 2002) and reads as follows.

> The above-mentioned person, XXX [name deleted by author], has borrowed a sum of HK$30,000.00 by way of loan arrangement from this company, Credit Limited on 30 August, 2001. Repayments are divided into 12 installments. Up to today's date XXX has paid three installments for HK$9,737.00, but has declared debtor's bankruptcy petition on 31 October 2001. We suspect that his voluntary bankruptcy proceeding within two months' time after obtaining the loan from us is obviously a deception and would like your authority to investigate this matter.

Other police behaviors such as gambling and drinking are taken less seriously unless they lead to officer debt or cause an officer to break the law. Police managers generally view gambling as a non-issue by itself. But when linking it to unmanageable debt or other misconduct, they raise their concern to a significantly higher level. Gambling is believed to be a common cause for unmanageable debt for certain officers. Some officers are also involved in illegal gambling. In the first week of October 1995, for example, twelve officers were allegedly involved with illegal gambling dens (Keenan, 1995). Drinking is not considered a serious problem either unless it causes officers to break the laws. A senior police inspector, for example, was charged with and pleaded guilty to driving under the influence seven times the legal limit. He was disqualified from driving for eighteen months, fined HK$7,500, and ordered to pay compensation and costs totaling HK$2,000 (*Hong Kong iMail*, 2001).

There are various causes for police corruption and misconduct today. Although corruption is no longer institutionalized, a relationship remains between corruption and organized crime. As stated by an ICAC official, corruption provides the air that organized crime can breathe. Corruption provides the means for organized crime and organized crime is corruption. Corruption and misconduct are also influenced by individual, personal, and cultural factors. An individual officer's financial difficulty and the human nature of greed can certainly cause corruption. Overuse of credit cards and unhealthy lifestyles can lead to officer indebtedness. In addition, peer pressure, colleague influence, language, etc. may cause officers to misbehave. Some officers abuse their authority and violate due process rules due to their racist attitude or insensitivity toward members of minority racial groups. Racism, albeit an uncommonly discussed issue in Hong Kong, does exist among certain police officers according to some Hong Kong civic groups. An African male, for example, was called with racial slurs and beaten up by several Caucasian officers according to a case heard at the District Court (*Hong Kong iMail*, 2001).

Mechanisms against Corruption and Misconduct

Mechanisms against police corruption and misconduct in Hong Kong come in different forms as in any civil and free society. They include the public and the media, the politicians and government officials, the laws and the legislature, and independent oversight agencies and the police programs themselves. They fall generally under two categories: internal measures that involve Hong Kong Police's own efforts and external measures independent from the police. Some officers prefer internal disciplinary procedures and regard them as more effective. Other officers see internal measures as time-consuming and unproductive and recognize the importance of external mechanisms for controlling officer misbehavior. Many officers believe in a combination of police self-regulation and public monitoring. As some police officers stated:

> To control and prevent corruption and misconduct, we need both internal and external elements. Internally, we need better recruitment, better pay and benefits, better values, and reinforcement of values such as integrity and honesty. Externally, we need anti-corruption laws and anti-graft agencies.

> The Bill of Rights has a great impact on policing. The government has become more open. . . . Then there is public scrutiny and mass media. . . . The public are more aware of their rights. People are more prepared to report corruption and complain about police misbehavior. Information and communication technology also make it easier for people to report.

Many officers, however, also complain about the public and the media for their lack of understanding of the police. They view the public as unsupportive and frivolous in their complaints. They find little reason to trust the media as they feel it is biased and interested only in airing the "dirty laundry." In reporting the findings of the Independent Police Complaints Council (IPCC) contained in the IPCC Annual Report 1996, for example, a reporter of a leading local newspaper exposed only the increases in the allegations of fabrication of evidence, neglect of duty, and impoliteness, with no mention of areas that were improved (Lee, 1997). Regarding the complaint substantiation rates, the media tends to focus on selected figures and question the validity of low rates (Sai, 1998). An editorial of a local newspaper commented, for example, "It is striking that, out of 5,052 allegations last year, 972 were resolved by informal resolution and only 113 were substantiated. . . . Is the system under which complaints are investigated properly constituted and operating effectively?" (Editorial, 1997a).

Among the various control measures, the officers tend to agree that those involving the efforts of the Hong Kong Police and the Independent Commission against Corruption are the most important. Both are professional law enforcement agencies and the officers hold them in higher regard than civilian oversight bodies. They respect the internal measures and programs put in place by the Hong Kong Police for disciplinary, investigative, and control purposes. They also respect the professionalism and independence of the ICAC as an external body for handling all police corruption cases and believe that it has a strong deterrent effect on officer misbehaviors. The following sections examine these internal and external measures in detail.

Internal Measures

Internally the Hong Kong Police has a zero tolerance policy against misconduct. Both tough disciplinary measures and preventative proactive strategies are in place for controlling police misbehavior. The reactive or punitive approach is represented by the disciplinary programs and complaint investigation activities. The proactive approach is exemplified by the cultural change programs and performance monitoring mechanisms. Several units in the Service Quality Wing are responsible for these functions. The following comments by a few officers provide a glimpse of the structure and operations of this Wing in regard to controlling police corruption and misconduct.

Our senior management is determined to fight corruption. The Commissioner often says that the Force will not tolerate any illegal behaviors. . . . We have Performance Review, Research and Inspection, and Complaints and Internal Investigation Branch. Performance Review is responsible for education and change of culture, which is a challenge for this Branch. It's always a challenge to win the hearts and minds of officers. We are a police force with fourteen police ranks and fifty civilian grades. It's hard to introduce changes. . . . We formulate strategies, implement action plans, and review best practices.

Research and Inspection is driven by management concerns. We conduct inspections after being directed by senior management. For example, we just inspected the Forensic Firearm Examination Bureau. We examined its workload, structure, charter, resources, etc., in light of three Es, efficiency, effectiveness, and economy. Some people don't trust inspections. They create hurdles. There are some dinosaurs that don't want to change.

We have Service Quality Strategy. We have surveys and feedback. Total involvement means more informal contacts and more discoveries of problems. We'll also have a knowledge management system that'll help us identify problems, set service standards, and conduct efficiency studies. I believe our Service Quality Strategy is a good mechanism for improving performance and controlling police malfeasance.

The "hard" or more punitive measures represented by the disciplinary, investigative, and supervisory activities are carried out by the Disciplinary Unit, Complaints against Police Office (CAPO) and the Internal Investigations Office (IIO). All officers facing court charges are generally referred to an internal disciplinary inquiry over related incidents. The CAPO and IIO, both under the Research and Inspections Branch, rigorously pursue complaints against officers or evidence of misdemeanors. The CAPO handles public complaints and IIO investigates internally discovered misconduct. There have been no major changes in the CAPO in recent years. A gradual growth of manpower has occurred and its standard has improved due to performance pledges. The growth, according the police, is related to more public complaints. At the IIO, the police also review their role in monitoring corruption and advise the management on prevention strategies. The Hong Kong Government has also considered the creation of an independent body for conducting complaint investigation. Many officers are against this body even though they understand its establishment is inevitable. A former ICAC officer also believes there is no need for an independent agency for dealing with police misconduct because the Ombudsman already exists. As some officers stated:

> At IIO, we are a focused, small unit of ten officers with background in CID. CAPO isn't independent now, but will be eventually. I personally don't think CAPO should be independent because it's more efficient when the most experienced officers, who are internal officers, conduct the investigations. Independent CAPO makes it political.

> In my opinion, the independent complaint body won't help much for solving the problems we have. They don't have the expertise for investigation and still need to rely on the police to get information. They would discourage lots of officers from doing their job as officers will only try to avoid problems. . . . Misconduct isn't a big problem. Corruption is more serious and therefore ICAC should be independent and complaint investigation should not.

The CAPO was established in 1974 and is responsible for investigating all complaints against members of the Force, including regular officers, traffic wardens, civilian officers, and members of the Hong Kong Auxiliary Police Force. It functions as a division of the Complaints and Internal Investigations Branch (CIIB), commanded by a Chief Superintendent directly responsible to the Assistant Commissioner in charge of the Service Quality Wing. The work of the CAPO is monitored by the Independent Police Complaints Council (IPCC), which comprises of professionals and community leaders appointed by the Chief Executive of the Hong Kong Government. Main functions of the IPCC include monitoring and reviewing the investigations of complaints conducted by the CAPO. A "lay observer scheme" has been established whereby observers attached to the IPCC can be present during interviews of both complainants and the accused without prior notification. Video interview facilities were introduced in every CAPO office in 2000.

Complaints against the police can be made in various forms, by mail, telephone, or walk-in at a local police station, where a sergeant sits at the front desk.

All complaints are passed on to the CAPO, classified into categories, and then distributed to individual units in the Force and investigated by experienced police officers. The CAPO publishes an Annual Report on complaint statistics. Section I in the report contains information about complaint trends at the Force and regional level, methods of complaints, relationship between number of complaints and degree of police activity, nature of complaints, informal resolution, and sub-judice procedures. Section II includes information about results of investigations and follow-up actions on complaints for all cases endorsed by the IPCC during the year under review. During 2000, members of the public lodged 3,673 complaints against the Police, some 19% more than in 1999. The IPCC endorsed 3,548 investigations, of which almost 40% were classified as "withdrawn" or "not pursuable," and some 30% were minor or trivial complaints settled by informal resolution. Of the complaints that were fully investigated, 13.8% were substantiated, leading to 48 police officers disciplined (Hong Kong Police Review, 2000). According to the CAPO's Annual Report (2000:II), its investigative information is used in the following manner.

> Upon completion of a CAPO investigation, the investigation file is sent to the IPCC Secretariat for examination. Reports are then circulated to IPCC members for their approval of the handling of the complaint investigation and their endorsement of the investigation findings. It is the Commissioner's stated policy to reduce the level of complaints and to this end, management information is provided by CAPO to all levels of command throughout the Force, to facilitate the identification of potential problems and initiate action to reduce and prevent complaints. This information takes the form of monthly statistical reports on new complaints received, quarterly reports on complaints received, together with the results of investigation, and the annual review of complaints against police. Each report provides an analysis of general and specific trends. Reports are also provided to Force management at Police Headquarters and on an ad-hoc basis to Police Commanders upon request.

The police have devoted significant resources for investigating complaints related to police misconduct. Elaborate rules and procedures have been established for handling police problems from abuse of authority to unmanageable debt. In case of officer debt, the police investigate if there are any violations of disciplines and may establish a disciplinary hearing committee to address officer bankruptcy. According to the Force policy, all officers filing for bankruptcy are subject to police investigation. Officers at the rank of inspector and below are dealt with internally; officers at the rank of superintendent and above are investigated by the Civil Service Disciplines Department (*The Sun*, 2002). Officers declaring themselves bankrupt can be disarmed, demoted, and sacked. From 1999 to 2001, more than twenty officers were put under criminal investigation after they declared themselves bankrupt. Disciplines imposed on these officers range from severe reprimands to dismissal with at least one being charged with failing to report his debt in full when borrowing money from a financial institution. Another officer was accused of imprudent financial management with the subsequent ruling that his problems had impaired his work efficiency (Lee, 2002a). Following are some comments from police managers on unmanageable debt.

> We have instruction from Headquarters on how to deal with unmanageable debt as a disciplinary problem. We have Disciplinary Review and we hold Disciplinary Tribunal to see if the officer is guilty. A superintendent is in charge of the hearing. It's a very time-consuming process. . . . We have CAPO and ICAC. Disciplinary actions will be taken against those who violate the values of integrity and honesty.

Tough disciplinary measures against officer debt have clearly put some members of the Force on edge. Some officers have called for a review of police disciplinary rules regarding officer debt and other personal life problems. The appeals come as many officers, having seen colleagues punished severely, are reportedly concealing financial problems to escape similar penalties (Lee, 2002a). One sergeant challenged police promotion ban imposed on him and claimed that he was being punished for his relatives' criminal records (Chow, 2002). Some police supervisors also see a negative effect of tough disciplinary actions on officers' initiatives. An inspector says, for example, that some officers may be reluctant to use discretion and will not take any chances while on duty due to concern of potential corruption charges or complaints.

Besides the disciplinary measures against corruption and misconduct described, there are internal procedures that are managerial in nature and are instituted partially for prevention purposes. Officers, for example, must switch duties regularly every two to four years. Vice Unit officers rotate once a year. For foot patrol, the supervisor and officer ratio is one sergeant to ten constables. For CID, the ratio is one inspector to five sergeants. Patrol arrangement varies by location and size of a district to allow for effective supervision. Although foot patrol officers usually work alone, they are almost never in isolation and are constantly under the public eye due to heavy pedestrian volume in most areas. Patrol officers work evening and night shifts in pairs and they enter buildings in pairs. In addition, supervisors meet patrol officers at least three times per shift, including random visits. Following are some comments made by police managers regarding public monitoring and police supervisory functions.

> Police constables work on the street. Supervisors and the public check and monitor them in a natural environment. An officer must be visible, walking the beat. He is to a great extent supervised by the public. Members of the public will call and complain when they see officers in an air-conditioned area for half an hour. And we deal with it.

> I joined the Force in 1972 and I see many changes personally. In 1974 ICAC was formed and the Force was improved. Service of internal staff is strengthened. Senior officers inspect officers. Front-line officers are supervised by inspectors. Front-line officers are made sure that they do their jobs. Officers contact supervisors at least twice per shift. Then there are random contacts.

In contrast to the "tough," "rigid," or "immediate" investigative, disciplinary, and supervisory measures represented by the CAPO, IIO, and police
management, the police also promote certain values such as integrity and
honesty and endeavored to build a culture of service among members of the
Force. Such activities are part of the "proactive," "preventative," or "long-term"
approach to controlling police corruption and misconduct. One of the areas
particularly appropriate for this approach is recruitment as many officers believe
that better recruitment is the key for preventing future police misbehaviors. In
this spirit, the Hong Kong Police has made certain changes in its recruitment
activities. The Recruitment Branch has increased its emphasis on prudence over
daring, "marking a turnaround" from previous years, "when it tried to entice
recruits with such swashbuckling images as marine-smuggling stings, gambling
raids, and shoot-outs in the street" (Keenan, 1995:19). Other areas highly
appropriate for the proactive approach include training and socialization
activities in the Force. In-service training programs and Living-the-Values
workshops have all been used to reinforce positive officer values and the spirit
of service. The police management has also integrated value training and quality
service ideas into a Healthy Lifestyle Campaign as part of the socialization
activities. Following are some comments by police managers regarding these
activities.

> The Police promote healthy lifestyles among rank-and-file officers. Gambling
> and drinking, for example, are discouraged. In Hong Kong, however, drinking
> isn't a big problem to begin with. Most Hong Kong people aren't big drinkers.
> Hong Kong people don't want to get drunk. They consider being drunk disre-
> spectful. . . . We promote healthy life styles by organizing healthy activities,
> Living-the-Values workshop. We have staff quarter club and family activities,
> and we provide counseling and education to officers.

> Police officers' behaviors are regulated more by good management than by
> group membership. We have formal training once a month for the entire Force.
> Designated staff design content of training. . . . Informal activities include rec-
> reational events, picnics, sports, after-work activities, and healthy-lifestyle
> activities. . . . Same rank officers or cadres at the same rank like to drink to-
> gether. Sometimes officers at different ranks get together. . . . We encourage
> interaction between senior and junior officers.

As described earlier, the police are determined to maintain a clean and honest Force and have been tackling police indebtedness vigorously. The police
management has also used the proactive approach such as the Healthy Lifestyle
Campaign to address this problem. The management recognizes that in the long
run building up a culture of prudent financial management and a healthy
lifestyle will be the best solution to unmanageable debt. As such, financial
prudence remains a major theme of the Healthy Lifestyle Campaign (*Offbeat*,
2002d). Commanders at all levels are vigilant in identifying officers with
financial problems early so that timely assistance including debt restructuring
can be offered. The Force Psychological Services Group also provides stress

management workshops for officers with unmanageable debts in order to alleviate their stress arising from this problem.

What happens to relationship between superior and subordinate officers when mistakes are made or rules are violated? To what extent do they share responsibilities? It is interesting to note that the Hong Kong Police is more individualistic than police in some other Asian countries such as Japan (Bayley, 1991) when it comes to taking blame. Officers are personally liable for their own acts and omissions. Consistent with one of the values of the Hong Kong Police, "acceptance of responsibility and accountability," individual officers themselves are held accountable for their mistakes. This value does not mean that superior officers are not accountable for the acts and omissions of their subordinates in any circumstances. Senior officers are held accountable when they know their subordinates' mistakes but choose to ignore them. Supervisors are expected to prevent misbehavior such as bad words and rude manners from becoming serious problems by issuing supervisory warnings. If an officer continues his or her misbehavior after the supervisory warning or other corrective measures, the officer him- or herself will be liable. The following comments made by officers in the rank of Inspector, Superintendent, and Assistant Commissioner shed some light on superior-subordinate relationship in the area of taking blame and indicate that sharing of responsibilities seldom occurs unless mistakes are made at the very low level in the police hierarchy.

> If I see an officer keep long hair, wear untidy dress, etc., I as the supervisor will give the subordinate the proper warning. Then I'm considered to have done my job. If I turn a blind eye, then I am responsible. . . . Majority of cases, senior officers aren't held accountable for behaviors of their subordinates unless the juniors are misinformed or did not receive the right instructions. I would say that less than 10% of disciplinary actions are against neglect of duty including failures of supervision.

> Senior officers usually aren't held accountable. But they should know their men. If some problems come up, they may be questioned, "How come you don't see a sign?" We've got stacks of procedures governing individuals by ranks and posts. So we don't have much sharing of mistakes. It's more individualistic. We're very rank-conscious. That's one reason there's a gap between ranks. . . . When a junior officer commits an offense, if we see management problem, if the senior officer is accountable, he will be held accountable. Sharing of mistakes isn't very common. We do accountability studies. CAPO does them. District and regional commanders can also do them.

> Who is responsible for mistakes depends on the situations and is related to supervision. Immediate senior officers are very often held accountable for behaviors of their subordinates. Depending on the types of mistakes, superior and junior officers share liability for mistakes. . . . Supervisors of problem officers may be called to explain why they didn't detect the problems. It's not a blame culture. If it's consistently happening due to supervisor neglect, then the supervisor gets blamed.

On paper, senior officers are held accountable for behaviors of their subordinates. But in reality, they are not. Only the immediate seniors at the Subunit level are accountable. Yes. If PCs have done something wrong, the Inspector, mostly a Subunit Commander, is accountable. No higher commander will be held accountable. Basically Sergeants up to Senior Inspectors only. Chief Inspector and below are governed by Police General Procedures; Superintendent and above are governed by Civil Service Regulations.

External Measures

The most significant external body for controlling police corruption and misconduct is the ICAC. The ICAC was established in 1974. Long before its establishment, the Anti-Corruption Branch (ACB) was created within the Criminal Investigation Department (CID) in 1952. Anti-bribery Ordinance was also passed by the Legislature before the emergence of the ICAC. Bribery, as addressed in the Ordinance, is defined as accepting advantages without authority, including material benefits, entertainment, etc. Several major police incidents and politically charged events led to the eventual creation of the ICAC. The most direct and original cause is organized police corruption, which reached its peak in the 1950s and 1960s. The public had grown extremely dissatisfied with the police due to their corruption and started to question their legitimacy and by extension the legitimacy of the colonial rule. In response, the government attempted to set up an anti-corruption body independent of the Hong Kong Police in 1960 and again in 1971. Both attempts failed due to vigorous opposition from the police. Against this background, the British government appointed Murray McLehose as the new governor in 1971. His appointment signified Britain's intent to change the governance style of the colonial government and establish the regime's legitimacy.

McLehose initiated a series of government reforms for this purpose, some of which directly targeted the Hong Kong Police (Lo, 1993). The Hong Kong Police was forced to separate the ACB from the CID and upgrade it to a semi-independent unit named the Anti-Corruption Office (ACO) under the command of an Assistant Commissioner of Police. "The strengthened ACO, with the reinforcement of a powerful anti-corruption ordinance, set out to fulfill its mission in 1971" (Lo, 1993:88). Given three years to produce results, the ACO showed much greater investigative determination than its predecessor. One significant success of the ACO was the discovery of a major corruption scandal involving Chief Superintendent Peter Godber, then Deputy Commander of Kowloon. As Lo (1993:89) describes:

> He was found to be in possession of assets equal in value to HK$4.3 million, approximately six times his total net salary from August 1956 to May 1973. . . . Before the charges, Godber was given one week to make representations. By using his position as the Deputy District Commander of Kowloon, he managed to flee the territory. His escape elicited mass public outcry. Young people rallied on the streets shouting the slogan "Fight Corruption, Catch Godber." Journalists fiercely attacked the incompetent government. Local politicians sharply condemned the scandal, which had become hot gossip in restaurants. Public pressure for the punishment of Godber mounted. The issue triggered the peo-

ple's discontent towards social inequality and injustice in the past years. Their hatred towards corruption and the invulnerability of British officials to the rule of law intensified their disrespect towards the colonial state governed by a handful of "foreign devils."

The Godber scandal not only reflected rampant corruption in the Hong Kong Police but also suggested that a colonial official could be above the law. Combined with other problems Hong Kong was experiencing at the time such as "bank runs, fare increases, youth riots, communist confrontations and student unrest," "the crisis marked a moment of profound rupture in the political and economic life of the colony" and "intensified the crisis of colonial hegemony" (Lo, 1993: 89, 91, and 106). Meanwhile in 1972, the management consultants McKinsey and Co. were engaged to look into civil service reform in Hong Kong. Their report revealed that a sizable portion of the community "hated" the police (Grant 1992:70). Hence, if the colonial regime was to successfully change its governance style, reform of the Hong Kong Police was imperative. MacLehose proceeded on two fronts. First, taking advantage of the Godber scandal, he set up the Independent Commission against Corruption (ICAC) in 1974 despite the Hong Kong Police's continued objection (Lo, 1993). Second, the Hong Kong Police was pushed to adopt several major reform schemes borrowed from the London Metropolitan Police. The ICAC operations currently follow three tough enabling ordinances: ICAC Ordinance, Prevention Ordinance, and Corruption Ordinance. The following comments from some ICAC officials indicate the historical urgency for such an agency and the tough nature of the Anti-corruption Ordinances.

> Commission of the High Court wanted ICAC created. Corruption of police was so rampant there was a need to have an independent body. You know what they say, "You either get on the bus or walk along the bus; but you never stand in front of the bus." It was time to create this agency. There were student demonstrations and mass protests. Officer Godber incident triggered it. The objective of ICAC was to enlist public support, create a better society, and better economy.

> The acceptance of advantage without permission of his authority is corruption. Officers will be mostly disciplined or cautioned. Such offense is prosecutable if it involves a senior getting gift worth more than HK$500 from a subordinate. . . . If it is within limit and with permission, officials can use some benefits. In civil service, one is not allowed to borrow money from subordinates and accept values of entertainment. Whether transaction of money is legal can be determined by the willingness of the giver. A civil servant's asset should not be disproportionate to civil service income. If there's any dispute regarding the legality of one's excessive assets, it's up to the Court to decide whether the disproportionate asset is legal.

The establishment of the ICAC reflected the public's detestation of corruption on the one hand and its acceptance of the government's coercive maintenance of public order on the other. Corruption control ultimately "helped transcend class conflict and unite capital and labor on the same front" (Lo, 1993:108). It enabled the colonial government to accomplish "part of its hegemonic functions" and "facilitated the dominant class bloc to dominate its subordinate and reestablish domestic order for capitalist production" (ibid). For these reasons, there has been a strong legislative backing and public support for corruption control in Hong Kong both in history and at present. The ICAC remains a well-funded independent anti-corruption agency today and its independence with a check and balance system is stipulated in the Basic Law. The following comments by some ICAC officials indicate the strong judicial and legislative support and executive privilege the ICAC enjoys.

> Landmark judgment from the High Court and Court of Appeals says that our laws are proportionate and rational considering the nature and importance of ICAC to fight corruption. . . . The power of the Commissioner of ICAC is derived from the Legislature, not part of Civil Service, who answers directly to the Chief Executive, similar to the Director of Audit. A number of committees oversee the operations of ICAC, appointed by the Chief Executive. It parallels the Intelligence Agency. The first Director of ICAC was actually from the British Intelligence Service. During the 80's and 90's, private complaints went up. After 97, public complaints also went up. But the ICAC has been able to handle them effectively.

The ICAC has practiced a well-known three-pronged approach to fighting corruption, i.e., detection, prevention, and education. This unique approach reflects three major functions of the ICAC: criminal investigation, corruption prevention, and community education. It has proven to be a useful model for corruption control for many of its counterparts around the world (Annual Report by the Commissioner of the ICAC, 2000). Following are some comments regarding the three-pronged approach from ICAC officials.

> ICAC's success depends on a three-pronged strategy: prevention, education, and deterrence. The three-pronged strategy helps build an anti-corruption culture. . . . Among the three elements, I think deterrence is the most important because I have seen well-educated officers and governmental officials involved in corruption. We once had a head of the Diplomatic Department of an African country arrested because he sold passports to one of our undercover agents.

> One of the success factors. . . . is our celebrated 3-pronged strategy which ICAC has adopted in fighting corruption. First, corruption prevention to improve on the system control; second, education, educating the public of the evils of corruption and to enlist public support. Third, enforcement and deterrence. All the three prongs are important but personally speaking, I consider deterrence most important. Over the years, I have seen too many examples of persons who are well educated, working in an environment of good management system, yet decided to become corrupt. For them, they have obviously calculated the risk and opportunity cost and considered that the risk is worth taking. For them, they can only be stopped through deterrence, which means an effective law enforcement to ensure they stand a high risk to be caught, coupled with stringent law and deterrent sentences, obviously in balance with the human rights (Kwok, 2001:2).

The three-pronged approach is only the outfit, what really counts is our coordinated effort. We work together, consistently. With information gathered from Operations, the Prevention Bureau designs strategies to prevent corruption, and Community Education Department uses the strategy to educate the public. We walk the same step with no time gap. For example, there are many police constables, not many sergeants. Some constables paid for sergeant tests. We arrested seven officers. We alerted the Prevention Department where recommendations were made. And then the Education Branch used them for education purposes.

Structurally, the ICAC is divided into three departments according to the three-pronged approach including Operations, Corruption Prevention, and Community Relations. The Operations Department is the investigative arm and the largest department of the Commission. The Head of Operations, who is also the Deputy Commissioner, is responsible to the Commissioner (Annual Report of the ICAC, 2000). Under the Head of Operations are two Directors of Investigation, one for the public sector and one for the private sector. There are four investigation branches and four groups under each branch covering various government agencies and private businesses.

The Corruption Prevention Department is responsible for identifying loopholes in the practices and procedures of government departments and public bodies. It provides management consultancies at the request of various agencies in the public sector. By way of assignment studies, which involve critical reviews of specific work areas, it helps identify problems and makes recommendations on how to eliminate or reduce corruption opportunities. The Department also advises private organizations, upon their requests, on ways and means to prevent corruption (Annual Report of the ICAC, 2000). It has developed reports on a wide range of topics on removing corruption opportunities. Reports issued to the Hong Kong Police recently include Police Vehicle Pounds: Work of Motor Vehicle Examiners, Handling Confidential Information at Regional Command and Control Centers, Massage Establishment Licenses, Police Driving School: System for Driver Examination, Routine Validation and Licensing, and Issue of Security Personnel Permits.

The report on Massage Establishment Licenses serves to illustrate the corruption prevention process of the ICAC. In Hong Kong, the licensing of massage establishments and the enforcement of license conditions are governed by the Massage Establishments Ordinance. The Commissioner of Police is the licensing authority and is responsible for enforcing the Ordinance. After a police sergeant was convicted for accepting free massage services and unauthorized loans from a massage establishment operator, ICAC agents from the Corruption Prevention Department reviewed the police licensing and enforcement procedures. The review showed that there were inherent corruption risks in the system as massage establishment operators had an incentive to bribe police officers in order to expedite the issue of a license or for advance warning of police inspections and raids. They recommended that supervision and control in the licensing and enforcement procedures be enhanced, guidelines governing the assessment of applications be laid down, and supervisory checks be conducted on applications that were approved despite adverse comments from police districts or neighboring residents. It was also suggested that supervisors of enforcement teams add targets to planned inspection schedules at short notice to reduce the risk of tipping off and police management provide clear instructions prohibiting officers from accepting entertainment from operators with whom the police have official dealings (Annual Report of the ICAC, 2000).

The Community Relations Department is responsible for educating the public against the evils of corruption and harnessing support for the ICAC. Great emphasis is put on moral education of youngsters in the early years of their life to arouse their awareness of the corruption problem. During the year 2000, for example, a series of programs were launched for cultivating positive values among young people. These included a cartoon series project, a youth website, several school-based projects for primary students, and a project for secondary students. A total of 110,000 secondary and tertiary school leavers were reached through face-to-face school talks (Annual Report of the ICAC, 2000). The Department has also involved the mass media, public sector, business sector, and Hong Kong Ethics Development Center in its education activities. In addition, it has developed a program for new arrivals, obtained cross-boundary cooperation, enlisted community support, worked with building management, run the ICAC Club, held clean elections education, and conducted ICAC Annual Survey.

The ICAC has enjoyed an unblemished reputation in the Hong Kong public. The three-pronged approach has been managed effectively and is widely regarded as a success. It is believed among many insiders that public trust, good management, accountability, and proactive investigation have contributed to its success. As some ICAC officials commented:

ICAC is a legal force. Its authority is based on legal power. But its success depends on public support and good management. We are effective because we have maintained public trust and confidence. We have more open management, two-way communication, and a mentor system. I meet my investigators every three months. We show we care. We want them to become part of our organization. Everybody contributes. The first generation of ICAC is reaching retirement age; we need to build a second generation of leaders and managers.

We are more elaborate, more transparent. We used to report only closed cases to ACOC (the Advisory Committee on Corruption). Now we report on-going cases. We are more accountable. We had to bring laws in line with the Bill of Rights. We follow due process rules, and we are careful of stay of proceedings caused by unduly long period of time in investigations.

Corruption cases are hard to investigate because they are hidden. Perception may not be accurate. We used to be reactive. We became proactive five years ago using more informants, under-covers, enhancing partnerships with the community, public bodies, and government agencies to the advantage of the ICAC and the agency. People don't like to expose their own corruption problems. We work with them to convince them that it is for their own good.

Some of the questions often asked about the ICAC are, who serve as ICAC agents and who watch these watchers? According to an ICAC official, members of the ICAC are recruited in a similar fashion as police officers. ICAC agents are similar also to the police in terms of salary and rank. They used to be recruited overseas due to a distrust of local agents. Officers who join the ICAC now are usually seconded from the Civil Service. As Hong Kong has eight universities, many agents are college graduates and all agents are required to have at minimum a Form 5 and above education. After they join the ICAC, they go through three years of on-the-job training. All ICAC officers are also on a two-year contract. The Commissioner of the ICAC can exercise his power to dismiss an officer with ACOC support. Officers with grievances can appear at ACOC and appeal to the Chief Executive and then to court for judicial review.

As an agency vested with extensive powers, the ICAC has a comprehensive system of checks and balances to ensure that its agents act within requirement of the law. For this purpose, the ICAC is guided in its work by four advisory committees: the Advisory Committee on Corruption (ACOC), the Operations Review Committee (ORC), the Corruption Prevention Advisory Committee (CPAC), and the Citizens Advisory Committee on Community Relations (CACCR) (Annual Report of the ICAC, 2000). The ACOC is the principal advisory body of the ICAC and oversees all the Commission's activities. Its membership includes the chairs of the ORC, CPAC, and CACCR who serve on ACOC as ex-officio members. It advises the Commissioner of the ICAC on any aspect of the corruption problem in Hong Kong. The ORC reviews work of the Operations Department of the ICAC. It found in 2000 certain common types of malpractice and misconduct including misuse of authority; neglect of duty; outside employment; and acceptance of gifts, loans, entertainment, and favors from persons of doubtful character or persons having official dealings. The ROC concluded that government employees misusing their position, though not amounting to bribery offences, has become a significant issue and saw the need to shore up discipline and ethical standards. The CPAC advises the Commissioner on the work of the Corruption Prevention Department. The CACCR advises the Commissioner on the work of the Community Relations Department (CRD). The Committee supports and gives advice on a number of CRD's educational activities aimed at raising the ethical standards of public and private sector employees (ICAC Advisory Committees, 2000).

An ICAC Complaints Committee was set up in 1977 to oversee the handling of non-criminal complaints against ICAC officers. This committee is serviced by a non-ICAC secretariat and consists mainly of members of the Executive Council and the Legislative Council. The Administration Wing of the Chief Secretary's Office is responsible for the Committee's secretariat duties. The terms of reference for the Committee are: (1) to monitor, and where appropriate to review, the handling by the ICAC of non-criminal complaints by anyone against the ICAC and officers of the ICAC; (2) to identify any faults in ICAC procedures which lead or might lead to complaints; and (3) when appropriate, to make recommendations to the Commissioner of the ICAC, or, when necessary, to the Chief Executive. Any person who has a complaint against the ICAC or its officers may write to the Secretary of the ICAC Complaints Committee, or complain to the ICAC at any of its offices in person, by telephone or in writing. In 2000, 44 complaints against the ICAC were received. This compared to 37 complaints received in 1999 and 25 in 1998. The 44 complaints contained a total of 116 allegations, the majority (59%) of which concerned abuse of power by ICAC officers and the rest was related to neglect of duties (22%) and misconduct (19%) (ICAC Complaints Committee, 2000, 2001). The following comments by an ICAC official and an advisory committee member illustrate the oversight of the ICAC.

Who watch the watchers? First, the Advisory Committee on Corruption (ACOC) chaired by an Executive Council member, consisting of Commissioners, business and community leaders provides oversight. They meet every six weeks and review cases that have been on going for more than twelve months or on bail for over six months. We can't close a case without the Committee's approval. Subcommittees of three members consider minor cases and cases that aren't pursuable. Each ten investigators deal with about fifty cases in Operations. Second, the Department of Justice has units monitoring internal investigation, misconduct, corruption, and crime related problems. Complaints against the ICAC are registered at the Department of Justice. Then there is the media. It's an elaborate system, lots of paperwork, a necessary evil to gain public confidence. We try to build a learning culture, a culture of sharing experiences, both positive and negative.

The ICAC Corruption Prevention Committee meets once a month, works on projects related to public and private bodies, issues related to funding of projects. We evaluate reports of the ICAC. We discuss the funding issues at the meeting concerning both government and private companies. ICAC also provides consultation to agencies regarding issues like procurement and tendering.

Police-ICAC Relationship

As two largest law enforcement agencies in Hong Kong that to a great extent check and balance each other, the Hong Kong Police and ICAC have had their share of tensions and frictions over the years. Because the original purpose of creating the ICAC was to root out police corruption, the police had open hostilities with the ICAC at its inception. Soon after its establishment, the ICAC prosecuted a series of organized police corruption syndicates. Its "zero tolerance" policy against corruption and a wave of arrests of police officers stunned the Hong Kong Police. Several thousand off-duty police officers responded by laying siege to the ICAC Headquarters, threatening a collapse of law and order. Faced with this large demonstration, Governor McLehose granted an amnesty for corruption offences committed before January 1977. Looking back, according to an ICAC official, there have been two schools of thought in Hong Kong regarding this amnesty. Some believe that it was justified and necessary considering the reality at the time while some contend that if the rule of law is to prevail, there should not be any amnesty for any police corruption. It is ultimately a matter of practicality versus principle. Despite the controversy, syndicated police corruption has since become history. A recent open police-ICAC friction, which was far less dramatic than in 1977, erupted in May 2002. The dispute was triggered by police protests over the high profile arrest of a Senior Superintendent, the deputy head of the Police Narcotics Bureau (Vines, 2002). The Senior Superintendent was alleged to have accepted advantages, including free prostitution services, from a nightclub operator for tip-offs on impending police operations against various establishments in Tsim Sha Tsui and Mong Kok, including nightclubs and karaoke lounges. Democratic lawmaker James To Kun-sun said it was a worry that such a senior officer could be linked with what appeared to be such a sophisticated graft syndicate (*South China Morning Post*, 2002). The Commissioner of Police and many rank-and-file officers, however, openly criticized the ICAC for the arrest stating that the ICAC abused its authority. A police statement said that the graft-busters should be "more circumspect" about publicizing arrests and that police officers were "deeply concerned" about other cases against colleagues in the previous year in which charges had yet to be laid. The statement, drafted by senior officers, was approved by the Commissioner of Police. The Commissioner also appeared before the legislators to discuss the row. He told the lawmakers that the ICAC had "seriously affected" the Force's reputation by the way it handled a senior officer's arrest. In a terse series of exchanges over the dispute, the Commissioner refused to admit the Police had done anything wrong in issuing a statement criticizing the ICAC after the arrest. He said that the police issued the statement after they found the background information the ICAC provided for them about the case did not support the agency's press release (Lee, 2002b). The police also informed the press that the number of corruption reports involving police officers had dropped by 14.8% from 602 cases in 2000 to 513 in 2001 (*South China Morning Post*, 2002).

In response to the police attack, the ICAC issued a statement saying that all arrests were made in strict accordance with the law. The Commissioner of the ICAC told the lawmakers that it was necessary to explain the arrest to avoid media speculation. The individual officers were not harmed in the exposure, however, he pointed out, because they did not name any suspects. According to figures from the ICAC, of the fifteen publicized cases involving the arrest of police officers from 1999 to 2001, twelve resulted in prosecution and three were pending further investigation or legal advice (Lee, 2002). The ICAC stated further that senior police management would be briefed if any of its members were involved in anti-graft operations and a report would be given to the police via the ICAC's Operations Review Committee for cases involving police officers but resulting in no legal action (Shamdasani and Lee, 2002a and 2002b).

In the heat of this confrontation between the police and ICAC, the Chief Executive also intervened by speaking to both the Commissioner of Police and of the ICAC. In the end the police objections fell far short of taking to the street even though they demonstrated strong solidarity in their protests similar to those in 1977. As the Commissioner of Police said: "Police are satisfied with the responses of the ICAC. The relationship between police and the ICAC is good and we will continue to cooperate with each other" (Shamdasani and Lee, 2002a). The Commissioner of the ICAC also said that the row had not affected their cooperation (Lee, 2002b).

Although there have been disagreements between the Hong Kong Police and ICAC as described above, they are extremely rare and cannot be used to characterize their relationship. After all, the police and the ICAC are both law enforcement agencies and are generally able to resolve their conflicts, if there are any, through existing channels. The recent police protests against the ICAC do not represent a widespread police hostility toward the anti-graft agency. Instead, they may very well be motivated by other concerns of police management such as low officer morale. According to media report, the police had been dogged by scandals around the time the row began. There had been reports of police officers being arrested or committing suicide. The police had been accused of using unnecessary force and means in dealing with abode seekers and in the high-profile arrests of activists who helped organize alleged illegal assemblies. Additionally, the police were facing an imminent salary cut along with other civil servants (Lau, 2002). When the police morale is low at a difficult time, police leaders may feel compelled to voice publicly their support for the troops.

On a routine basis, collaboration and cooperation between the Hong Kong Police and ICAC is the norm rather than exceptions. Over the years, they have adopted a coordinated partnership approach to investigating police corruption and to reducing opportunities for corruption. As a senior police officer commented:

> ICAC work with IIO in corruption investigation operations. We must give the cases to ICAC to allow independent and impartial investigation. An Assistant Commissioner of Police liaises with ICAC on the Corruption Prevention Committee. It is also regularly advertised on the mass media that the police liaise with the ICAC over safeguards against police corruption.

ICAC operational liaison with the police management has been enhanced at all levels through the establishment of the Police-ICAC Operational Liaison Group and by regular briefings provided by senior ICAC officers to various police formation commanders. The Hong Kong Police runs regular workshops on management issues for senior and middle-ranking officers that also invariably include input from the ICAC, particularly on the topic of supervisory accountability. One specific area of cooperation is in investigation of counterfeit credit cards. The manufacturing of counterfeit credit cards used to be a boom industry in Hong Kong. Largely due to the collaborative effort of the police and the ICAC, Hong Kong is no longer a desirable jurisdiction for such corrupt activities. According to the police and ICAC, these illegal businesses seem to have relocated to neighboring countries (ICAC Operations Department Review, 1998-1999).

Although the partnership approach for controlling corruption has been an official policy for the police and ICAC, an existing policy seldom translates itself into real actions and results. The police and ICAC both understand the importance of fostering a culture against corruption. Over the years, serious effort has been made to develop this culture, which in turn has become the foundation for police-ICAC cooperation. As stated frequently by officers of both agencies, a significant part of the success for controlling police corruption can be attributed to a partnership relationship between them. But more importantly, a partnership relationship built on a culture against corruption is far more effective than one on written policies. Following are some comments from ICAC officials that demonstrate this partnership relationship and the importance of creating a culture against corruption.

> Changing culture is most important for changing behaviors. A great reason for our success is that we have built an anti-corruption culture. . . . We have partnership with the police. Internally the police must be willing to work with ICAC. ICAC are more effective due to a partnership relationship. Agencies did not use to like ICAC investigating their agents for corruption. Now they realize it is in their own interest to fight corruption.

> I recommend a strong partnership approach. ICAC see great value of a strong partnership with other local and overseas law enforcement agencies. In the old days, when ICAC arrested a government official, this might not be welcomed by his head of department who would blame ICAC for bringing scandal to his department. "Don't air your dirty linen in the public" is outdated and can only encourage corruption. If the dark days of corruption teach us anything, it is that turning a blind eye to corruption simply will not do. Corruption will only grow bigger. We are pleased that heads of law enforcement agencies today have changed their attitude and are taking a proactive strategy to tackle corruption. Indeed, many of our most successful cases originate from their proactive approach or as a result of joint investigation (Kwok, 2001:3-4).

> Public comments made by police officials have changed dramatically over the last ten years. They used to say, "Only a few junior officers not well trained were involved." Now they say, "We have zero tolerance. We will do everything in our power to get to the bottom of it with ICAC." It is for the good of the agency. From an officer's perspective, corruption is a crime and hurts an officer's career. From the management's perspective, corruption is demoralizing and hurts the health of the organization.

> ICAC has existed for twenty-seven years. It makes sure that good police officers have the support and can move up. Good officers benefit from ICAC. That's why we can have the partnership approach. In the 1970's, ICAC was thought of as an agency that would hurt them. Those guilty of corruption did not like it; those who were clean did not like it, either, because both felt ICAC hurt their professional pride. This mentality is gone now.

Officer Views Regarding Effectiveness of Measures

It is apparent that a force the size of the Hong Kong Police has its share of corruption and misconduct. But compared with other big city police in the world, most cases seem to be quite minor and would not even be considered worth mentioning in the news media in cities like New York and London. Police officers at all levels and the public in Hong Kong also hold the view that syndicated police corruption no longer exists and corruption in general is under control. One superintendent said, for example, that police corruption is uncommon and corruption cases have decreased significantly over the years. In contrast, police misconducts in the form of officer debt and gambling have become a bigger concern for the police management in recent years. But these problems percentage-wise or Force-wide remain insignificant. A civilian member of the Advisory Committee on Corruption Prevention (ACOCP) in the ICAC said, for instance, that the Hong Kong Police has had its share of problems such as indebtedness and suicide; but their rates are very low.

Why is the Hong Kong Police able to control corruption and misconduct effectively? The police officers from various units and ranks have provided a variety of explanations. These include salary and benefits, job security, working conditions, lack of opportunities, education, training, officer quality, communication, professionalism, change of attitudes, values, morality, ethics, self-respect, police rules and procedures, laws, and the ICAC. Although these factors are all encompassing, they generally fall under five categories: 1) increased material benefits (i.e., salary and benefits, job security, and working conditions); 2) reduced opportunities (i.e., lack of opportunities for corruption and misconduct); 3) improved internal management (i.e., education, training, officer quality, communication, and professionalism); 4) an anti-corruption culture (i.e., change of attitudes, values, morality, ethics, and self-respect); and 5) deterrence (i.e., police rules and procedures, laws, and the ICAC).

These five categories are designed to achieve different goals and objectives, but all aimed at producing an effect on police corruption and misconduct. The first and fourth points, increased material benefits and an anti-corruption culture, are intended to create a long-term effect on officer behaviors. As part of the benefits, officers in Hong Kong enjoy several economical choices including police quarters, public housing, and free-interest loans. The rent for police quarters is only about 4% of an officer's salary, equal to HK$700 (US$90) per month for a junior officer (see Table 4.1). For public housing, the rate ranges from HK$1,000 to $3,000 (US$130 to $390) per month. Regarding the anti-corruption culture, as described earlier, both the Hong Kong Police and ICAC have been committed to building such a culture for many years. A culture against corruption consequently has developed in which the rank and file has a negative attitude toward corruption and holds a strong sense of police career. In the old days, for example, a saying that "Good men don't join the police" was commonly heard in Hong Kong. Due to a clean reputation of the Force today, a young person seldom experiences parental objection when making a decision to become a police officer. The second point, reduced opportunities, is aimed at having an immediate effect on officer behaviors by blocking opportunities for corruption. The situational crime prevention theory developed by Clarke (1996) provides an excellent explanation and rationale for this strategy. The third point, improved internal management, is clearly grounded in the idea of total quality management. The fifth point, deterrence, involves punitive measures designed for punishing and preventing corrupt and wrongful behaviors. Almost without exception, police officers and civilian ACOCP members regard the watchdog of corruption, the ICAC, as having the most significant deterrent effect on corrupt behaviors. Following are some comments made by police officers and civilian ICAC advisory committee members regarding these points.

I don't want to lose my career and a higher than average income for some trivial gains. . . . I would say that the reason we have less corruption is because of our higher salary, personal values, utilitarian values, and change in the society. . . . There has been hardly any corruption and less misconduct due to higher salary, more job security, and fewer opportunities to be corrupt. . . . We don't need to be corrupt. Corruption benefit doesn't equal salary. So what's the point of being corrupt? We don't have the opportunity for corruption, either. . . . We have less corruption because of higher salary and better benefits, more fair treatment, better personnel, better training, and ICAC.

We arrest lots of people and occasionally some of them may bribe officers. I guess some people will always be corrupt. But there aren't many opportunities to be corrupt for police constables. We have higher salary and more benefits. Citizens don't give much money nowadays. ICAC is also very effective. It doesn't mean it never crosses my mind—I still think about it sometimes.

Police officers received significantly higher pay in the late 70s as a measure to reduce police corruption. Now officers look at the opportunities and most would refuse to take them because they wouldn't think it's worth it—they'll lose a lot more if they lose their job and pension. . . . Salary, benefits, and methods of investigating misconduct all contribute to a clean force. . . . The reasons for decrease of corruption include better quality of police officers, better education, and better communication. There's less temptation for officers to be corrupt also due to better working conditions. The culture is also against corruption.

More importantly, a personal sense of self-respect, sense of justice, sense of morality are important in controlling corruption. . . . We have long-term vision and values. If corruptions occur, colleagues will say something and will stop them. . . . Anti-corruption culture has been created over several phases. Officers now will tell other officers not to do it. The culture is there. . . . There is no chance for it. Colleagues will talk. And we think about our family. It's not worth it.

Both Bill of Rights and rule of law and traditional morality and ethics are important. If everybody's ethical, there's no need for the Bill of Rights. Law works more quickly and efficiently. In the long run, morality and ethics are more important. Rat needs cat to deal with. But if there's no food, there is no need for cat.

ICAC is there. It's not worth the risk being corrupt. . . . There's no incentive to fabricate evidence. There has been major house cleaning for many years by both the police and the ICAC. . . . ICAC is very effective. It definitely has a deterrent effect. ICAC is independent, reporting directly to the Chief Executive, has special power, internal control mechanism, and high standards. ICAC employees are on contract and there is independent monitoring of ICAC. They are very serious. . . . Corruption isn't a big concern due to ICAC over the years. Everybody knows that if you are corrupt, it will catch up with you and then you're gone. Now we have some corrupt cases, but very minor.

Before the 70s, police problem was severe due to corruption. Station sergeants used to be the connecting points for the syndicated corruption. But not any more due to ICAC. Not a single area of the police has not been looked at by ICAC. Not a single stone has been left unturned. As a result, organized corruption is gone. Now only individual officers are involved; but corruption cases are very rare.

The system's improved over the years that minimized corruption. Let me give you an example. A friend of mine left a handbag in a cab and reported the loss to the police. My friend could remember only part of the cab number and the driver's name. The police were willing to help but couldn't access the system. Such a measure may be bad for people like my friend who lost things and who are eager to get information, but stopped lots of corruption.

Looking Ahead

The Hong Kong Police and the ICAC have made tremendous effort in controlling corruption and misconduct and, with solid government and public support, have had an impressive record in reducing police corruption. From the time the ICAC was created to the present, corruption cases involving the police have been declining consistently. The police have come a long way from the days of syndicated corruption and public distrust. Officers today can take pride in the fact that they can pursue a career in a clean and healthy organization. A recent Public Opinion Survey also indicates that the respondents have a strong confidence in the police (74%) with a mean rating of 70.0 on a 0-100 scale on overall police performance (University of Hong Kong, 2000). There has been a rise of police malfeasance cases in recent years, however. Many members of the public have grown increasingly more critical of police misconduct. According to the same Public Opinion Survey, about half of the respondents held the view that members of the Force take unfair advantage of their job position occasionally (42%) and frequently (7%). In terms of personal conduct, 27% were dissatisfied with the private lives of police officers and only 13% felt satisfied. Nevertheless, many members of the public, about 63%, remained satisfied with officer discipline, 58% satisfied with police willingness to offer assistance, and 50% with police manner.

Public opinions such as these may contradict with the fact that police corruption is under control and misconduct rate is well within a tolerable range because the public does not evaluate the police from a longitudinal or comparative perspective, and tends to judge the police on the basis of negative perceptions and media reports. The public opinions, however, do seem to coincide with the police management's concern for officer malfeasance. The police, therefore, have directed more attention to police misconduct in recent years. As a strategy, the in-service training workshop Living-the-Values has been used to address this concern as well as police corruption. The Force has been pursuing a value-based training program to promote integrity, professionalism, and quality service. It can be expected that the police will continue to stress these values in order to raise officer awareness of ethics and lower the number of complaints from the public.

As many officers claim to have suffered from a low morale in recent years due to changes in the society and within the Hong Kong Police, the police management has tried to walk a fine line between addressing malfeasance and boosting officer morale. To do so, the police need to strike a balance between strengthening public confidence and maintaining police autonomy. To strengthen public confidence, the police have continued to target officer misbehaviors such as bad manners and attitudes that cause public complaints. They can also be expected to accept the Independent Police Complaint Council (IPCC) for investigating police malfeasance—a key to strengthening public trust as the ICAC in history. To uphold police autonomy, the police have continued to give emphases to their law enforcement functions and their political neutrality and voiced criticism when the public and other government agencies such as the ICAC cross their boundaries in dealing with the police. The Hong Kong Police, therefore, can be expected to keep a balance between the public demand for a more open and transparent police force and the internal desire for traditional and professional police practices. To do so, the police are poised to sacrifice certain amount of police autonomy by accepting the IPCC even though many members of the Force view the IPCC "an unwarranted intervention of the police autonomy" (Sai, 1998:117).

The nature of police reform is such that the police seldom view the creation of an external oversight body for the purpose of improving police services as desirable even though it is inevitable. In the same way as the police rejected the ICAC in history, they have been successful in keeping the CAPO an internal function. Their success is due largely to the timeframe in which the IPCC was originally proposed, which was immediately after the 1997 change of sovereignty, when the priority of the Hong Kong Government was to maintain social stability and public order. Social stability and public order require first and foremost a stable and orderly police force. At a potentially chaotic historic moment, it was a concern that the IPCC, which grants the power of complaint investigation to an external body, would be damaging to police morale and, therefore, unacceptable (Editorial, 1997b). It has been several years since the handover and the Hong Kong Government has been able to maintain a stable and orderly society. The time may have come for the government to focus its attention on the service quality of the police.

The Hong Kong Police has made tremendous progress since the 1970's in its fight against corruption and misconduct. It can be expected that the police will continue the programs and strategies that have proven successful, many of which are looked upon as models by other police forces in the world. They can also be expected to forge ahead with new initiatives and break new grounds in raising the standard of their service. One of the emerging areas is concerned with social policies such as civil right protection and multiculturalism. At a time of economic downturns and major political changes, it is unlikely that the Government will consider any new policies that may affect the effectiveness of the Hong Kong Police. But, as the economy stabilizes and the democratic system matures, the Government will become more open and responsive to public demand. One of the yardsticks measuring the progressiveness of a police organization is its protection of civil rights and its sensitivity to diverse cultural groups. There has been a gap in this area in Hong Kong policing because many officers view socially motivated laws and legislations as only remotely related to their profession.

There is no question that the Hong Kong Police has made enormous stride in controlling corruption and misconduct. But with a commitment to improving social and cultural life in Hong Kong, it has the potential to advance to an even higher rank in police protection and reliability of police services (See Porter et al., 2000, 2004). Bias, bigotry, and racism, for example, have received scant attention from police management as well as other government agencies. There has not been any significant progress in anti-discrimination legislations in policing, housing, employment, business, and service industries in Hong Kong. The cavalier attitude toward these issues and the lack of legislation in these areas are not consistent with a world-class city that Hong Kong prides itself on being. Police officers, for example, often assume that people of a certain ethnicity or nationality are offenders or suspects. As Loper (2001:29) said, "In general, the most negative views are reserved for people with darker skin and people from developing countries, including mainland China." Frontline officers need to move away from their negative stereotypes of mainlanders, South Asians, South East Asians, and Africans. The police management can provide sensitivity and diversity training for officers to help them better work with people from different backgrounds. Such training can be integrated into the Service Quality Initiatives being implemented in the Hong Kong Police. It should start by making sure that police officers understand the significance of civil right policies and multiculturalism in contemporary policing to avoid the perception that the training is simply another moral preaching session irrelevant to their daily work.

From an institutional perspective, the concepts of isomorphic change (Di-Maggio and Powell, 1991; Meyer and Rowan, 1991) and "sovereigns" (Crank and Langworthy, 1992) are appropriate for understanding the Hong Kong Police experience in fighting corruption and misconduct and building a professional force. Coercive isomorphic change and normative isomorphic change are ideas particularly relevant to understanding the creation of the ICAC (Jiao, Lau, and Lui, 2005). As official enquiry into the riots in the 1950s and 1960s revealed widespread and syndicated police corruption, there was a deep antipathy against the police in the Hong Kong society (Scott, 1989) and a sizable portion of the community "hated" the police (Grant 1992:70). Against this background, the British government appointed McLehose as the new governor in 1971 with the intent to establish the colonial regime's legitimacy (Lo, 1993). As a major sovereign of the Hong Kong Police, the colonial government saw the need to reform the Hong Kong Police in order to successfully establish the colonial government's legitimacy. The ICAC was therefore set up in 1974 despite the Hong Kong Police's objection (Lo, 1993). After its establishment, the ICAC adopted an aggressive, proactive approach in investigating and prosecuting corruption syndicates. The police-Triad symbiosis began to disintegrate. Consequently, these changes in the institutional environment of the Hong Kong Police led to the importance placed upon professional law enforcement, previously a secondary priority.

The institutional perspective sees institutionalization as constraining change and emphasizes the role of external impetus in inducing change, with change being understood as a result of the interplay between these two forces. Although the Hong Kong Police originally rejected the idea of creating an independent body to investigate police corruption and kept corruption investigation an internal function for many years, it could no longer go against this idea in response to the huge public outcry in the early 1970s sparked by the Godber scandal. The police concession supports the notion of coercive isomorphism, which states that institutional isomorphic changes take place when an institution is suffering from a legitimacy crisis (DiMaggio and Powell, 1991). When the external pressure to change is of less magnitude as fighting police corruption, however, there would be more room for the police to maneuver. The status quo of the IPCC and police response to calls for addressing social equity issues may serve as such examples.

11

Lessons Learned

Several lessons can be gleaned from the contemporary experience of the Hong Kong Police. Broadly speaking, they range from the political and cultural to the structural and operational, to the organizational and institutional, and finally to the strategic and futuristic dimensions. The political and cultural lessons have to do with the global implications of a Western colony's return to Chinese sovereignty and how the inner workings of the police in this process illustrate the relationship between Western due process rules and procedures and Chinese values of conformity and pro-order outlook. The structural and operational aspects provide information on certain effective police practices that may have contributed to a stable society and low crime rate. The organizational and institutional experiences demonstrate the systemic development of a large police organization at a time of major social changes, including continuities of its traditional practices and transformations to a more service-oriented culture. The strategic and futuristic dimensions answer the question: how should the police develop internal and external strategies to confront challenges in their pursuit for excellence? To these different but related lessons we now turn.

Global Implications

As China entered the picture in the early 1980s in anticipation of the expiration of the colonial lease, the law and order situation as well as the political dynamics in Hong Kong started to change dramatically. With Hong Kong's return to the motherland in sight, the power and economic interest of the colonial elites appeared less important and rights and freedoms of the mass population became more relevant. The people of Hong Kong were more outspoken about their demand for democracy while many government agencies contemplated changes of their traditional colonial practices. From this historical perspective, policing as well as politics in Hong Kong has been significantly influenced by the change of sovereignty, a process that had lasted fifteen years. After 1997, the British colonial history, the Western democratic values, and the socialist China continue to exert a combined impact upon the political landscape in Hong Kong, which has become increasingly liberal but remained undemocratic. The nature of the police function in this context reflects this complex socio-political reality.

Throughout the colonial history, the Hong Kong Police has developed an emphasis on public order management. Western democratic values such as human rights and due process rules and procedures were not introduced to Hong Kong until China and Britain commenced their negotiation of Hong Kong's future. The Joint Declaration of 1984 and the Basic Law of 1990 were the first two documents that included some basic democratic elements promised to the Hong Kong society. The International Covenants on Civil and Political Rights and the Bill of Rights Ordinance in 1991 were adopted only six years before Hong Kong's handover to China. The Hong Kong people realized at this time that they had to fight for their own political future. They were ready for democracy and reacted favorably to the concept of human rights and the Bill of Rights. The society had become more right-conscious in general as more people complained against government mistreatment and demanded for control of police authority. The Bill of Rights Ordinance imposes due process rules and procedures on the Hong Kong Police and the subsequent judicial decisions have resulted in further amendment to police powers. The police, for example, are no longer allowed to use presumption of guilt in handling cases involving drugs and corruption. So the impending change of sovereignty and the public demand for more openness provided the impetus for the democratic movement in Hong Kong, a historic but fairly recent phenomenon.

As Hong Kong becomes more democratic, competing and often conflicting interests have become more pronounced between the public and the police. The increasing public demand for an open society and the police traditional emphasis on public order are bound to create a tension for individual officers. On the one hand, they must work within due process restrictions and on the other, under the mandate to maintain public order. Such opposing values commonly present themselves as a dilemma in policing democracies (Skolnick, 1994). But an additional cultural contradiction adds to the dilemma in Hong Kong because these opposing values can be viewed as reflecting Western law enforcement principles and Chinese cultural traditions when examining the Hong Kong Police. With the passage of the Bill of Rights, questions have been raised about its impact on the Hong Kong Police and its congruity with the Chinese culture of conformity and pro-order outlook. Unlike the Western concept of human rights, which is viewed as indispensable and inherent in humanhood, a citizen's rights are often juxtaposed with obligations and duties in the Chinese cultural tradition. The collective interest and individual duties are emphasized and rights are seen as foreign in the Chinese culture. Such a cultural tradition combined with the nature of police work may produce a police orientation that stresses public good and citizen obligation.

The police mission to maintain order and fight crime is also inherently contradictory to their mandate to protect civil rights. Police officers tend to view new legislations and rules and procedures that restrict police authority as beneficial to law breakers rather than law-abiding citizens. They see more encroachment upon human rights due to criminality than to police actions and believe that they would be in a better position to protect civil liberties if allowed to maintain their wide power. They are for fair and unbiased policing but are, in the meantime, concerned that there is a price to pay for every curtailment or restriction of their power. Sometimes they see too high a price to pay in instances where the police follow due process rules but fail to detect serious offenses such as organized crime and international terrorism. But, values and concerns aside, the police in Hong Kong understand they must follow due process rules and procedures as an important law enforcement principle. They must adjust, adapt, grow, and develop in a more open and democratic society. They have thus reevaluated their policies to ensure that their practices conform with the requirements of due process rules and procedures and officers be well versed with the changed laws and regulations. The gathered evidence from the police demonstrates that they have not sacrificed their effectiveness in maintaining law and order because of the due process rules and procedures. Instead, they have become more professionalized in fulfilling their law enforcement responsibilities.

Considering the diverse cultural values and their integration in the Hong Kong Police, I am tempted to characterize the Hong Kong Police as representing a hybrid of Western and Chinese values. To make some sense out of this amalgamation, the police have adopted an approach to balancing rights and obligations. They conform to the Bill of Rights without sacrificing their effectiveness. In other words, the police accept the Bill of Rights and follow the due process rules and procedures in their daily work; but they continue to emphasize the effective policing model. These two emphases are not necessarily contradictory to each other because the police see the Bill of Rights as having a procedural impact rather than a substantive effect on their daily activities (Chen, 1998). They have cultivated a strong awareness of due process rules and procedures and follow them in their daily work; but their day-to-day operations in maintaining order and fighting crime remain unchanged.

Despite the burden of disentangling diverse values and principles the police follow, there are many misconceptions about the Hong Kong Police that can be dispelled now. The Hong Kong Police is an apolitical professional organization and remains committed to law enforcement after the change of sovereignty. Operating in a Chinese Special Administrative Region, it has had no difficulty in enforcing English common laws and carrying out its law enforcement responsibilities. It is primarily a legal force with legal authority and secondarily a public service organization with a moral reputation. Although the issue of legitimacy plagued the Hong Kong Police in its colonial history, it has enjoyed strong public confidence since corruption was put under control in the 1970's. In their daily activities today, Hong Kong police officers follow the law first, police order second, and moral reasoning third. They support the rule of law and see it their duty to protect civil rights. Notwithstanding their Chinese cultural root, they have continued to develop themselves professionally and pursue excellence in serving the public.

The Hong Kong Police has transformed successfully from a British colonial force to a Chinese Special Administrative Region force. While its basic practices are rooted in the colonial police traditions, they are duly informed by both Western law enforcement principles and Chinese cultural values. The most significant lesson learned in this context is that a law enforcement agency that follows Western law enforcement principles can function effectively in a largely Chinese society. With the passage of the Bill of Rights, the Hong Kong police officers have a greater respect for and a stronger awareness of individual rights today than in the colonial past. Their acceptance of human right demonstrates that the concept of right is not "alien" to the Hong Kong officers and Western values of due process rules and civil rights can be reconciled with the Chinese values of conformity and pro-order outlook. The widely hailed Western values of property rights, freedom, and democracy can be integrated into the proud and rich Chinese cultural tradition. Ultimately, Western ideologies and cultures can be integrated or coexist with Chinese traditions and values. Such reconciliation and integration have implications not only for law and order but are of global significance for social and cultural transformations.

As the Hong Kong police officers experience the strain between their own traditional values and their working environment, i.e., between the Chinese concept of social harmony and the Western demand for procedural justice, it can be seen in the Hong Kong Police the encounter of two very different law enforcement traditions and principles. The organizational knowledge of the Hong Kong Police that has been developed in this context includes certain basic elements of Western policing philosophies such as political neutrality and the rule of law and the Chinese values of conformity and pro-order outlook. Although Western and Chinese values represent two diverse cultural traditions and theoretically create a heavy burden on individual officers, in reality, the integration or combination of these cultural orientations is more of the norm than exceptions in Hong Kong policing. The police administration is politically neutral but endeavors to build a strong moral reputation for the Force. The police management stresses a functional approach in addressing problems in their areas but devotes significant resources to building community relations. The police officers believe in the rule of law and, in the meantime, are committed to maintaining social and public order. The police do not have a broad moral mandate and are not into shaping social development, but engage in community policing and public service. The individual officers are responsible for maintaining good conduct while on duty and required to be prudent and ethical while off-duty. They are personally liable for their omissions on the job but are also held accountable for mistakes in their personal life such as poor financial management and unhealthy life styles.

Effective Police Practices

The Hong Kong Police experiences offer some valuable lessons for the police profession in general, particularly in the area of police management. It has grown, developed, and changed just like any other police force in the world. It has transformed itself in response to the changing time and environment from a colonial, paramilitary force to a more professionally oriented police force, from a force that focuses on public order management to one that emphasizes law enforcement and crime control, from an authoritarian force with syndicated corruption to an organization that is more community-oriented and relatively free of corruption. Its experiences in developing and transforming itself reflect the many changes taking place in policing around the world. In regard to specific police practices, the Hong Kong Police has been successful in achieving a low crime rate, in fitting its organizational structure with its daily operations, in raising its effectiveness and efficiency in its daily activities, in improving internal management in terms of both horizontal and hierarchical relationships, and in controlling police corruption and misconduct.

The Hong Kong Police has been credited as a crucial factor for the low crime rate and high sense of security in Hong Kong over the past decade. Widely regarded as one of the safest cities in the world, public safety has seen even greater improvement after the change of sovereignty. Various conditions, i.e., urbanization, dense population, overcrowdedness, and poverty that are often used to explain crime problems in other parts of the world do not present themselves as causes of crime here. Although poverty exists in Hong Kong just like any urbanized area, there are no ghettos and no sense of deprivation. Vice activities in the form of drug trade, gambling, underage drinking, and prostitution are commonplace but are not viewed as a serious problem by the public. After Hong Kong's return to China, the number of mainlanders arrested for crimes has increased significantly. But the overall crime rate remains lower than before the handover. In this working environment, the police officers generally feel safe while performing their routine duties. They do not experience much violence and do not see crime as an urgent or severe problem. With the low crime rate and high public sense of security, the police in Hong Kong are able to claim proudly that they have realized their vision "that Hong Kong remains one of the safest and most stable societies in the world."

Various factors have been used to explain the safety and stability of Hong Kong. As mentioned earlier, these include a strong public policing policy, heavy investment in private security, and a mixture of socio-cultural and environmental conditions. The Hong Kong Government has adopted a pro-order policy and supported the development of a strong police force. At a time when most government departments face a budget cut, there has been a 7% average increase in police expenditure in recent years. Gun control is extremely tight in Hong Kong and even police officers have to turn in their weapons at the end of their shift. The Hong Kong Police has improved its overall efficiency and effectiveness in dealing with the crime problem over the years. In Hong Kong today police officers can be seen ubiquitously, walking the beat, checking IDs, and engaging in crime prevention. There has also been heavy investment in private security. The extent and strength of the security function are far-reaching and have had a significant impact on individual behaviors. Culturally the Hong Kong people are homogeneous and are known for their values of conformity and pro-order outlook. Geographically Hong Kong remains a small confined jurisdiction that can be easily controlled. Situational factors like high rises, heavy pedestrian volume, and the design of the Mass Transit Railway (MTR) system create an environment highly favorable to natural and informal surveillance. It can be expected that the Hong Kong Police will continue to take advantage of these factors in maintaining its effectiveness for controlling the crime problem.

The Hong Kong Police Force has a highly hierarchical and paramilitary structure divided into four main levels, i.e., Force, region, district, and division. The Police Headquarters at the Force level is responsible for the overall management and coordination of the regions and districts as well as provision of central operations and support functions. Over the years, the police have been through many reviews and realignments. But this basic organizational structure has remained unchanged. Its personnel system includes fourteen ranks and the selection of the top ranking officers follows the principle of non-political involvement. Matching this structure and personnel are several operational priorities that cover uniformed patrol, emergency response, crime control, public order, and public relations. These priorities require that the police maintain high uniform visibility; provide fast, effective response to emergencies; maintain vigilance in crime prevention and investigation; maintain public order; and maintain public confidence in the police.

The basic police operations in Hong Kong are based on divisional stations and regional units to both serve the needs of the local population and address problems that extend beyond a division or district. The local police perform highly visible foot patrol operation in the community and respond to routine emergencies. Specific branches at the division, district, region, and the Force levels are designated to handle crime problems. These levels to a certain extent resemble the local police, state police, and the FBI in the United States, but function as parts of a single police organization making them far more efficient and effective. While police at all levels emphasize crime prevention by visible deployment of uniformed officers, they use different approaches to managing crime and serving the public in their districts. Some areas are more proactive and some more reactive. Some use problem-oriented policing and some stress police deterrence. Some rely on crime statistics and crime patterns for deploying officers and some adopt the security guard orientation. The responsibility for public order management lies mainly with the regional units such as the EU and PTU. Public order operations and related trainings often involve coordination and cooperation of multiple divisions and districts and various units at the regional level.

All police districts are engaged in community-oriented policing and committed to a partnership relationship with the community. The police work with the public through several channels. Local police commanders invite community members to their stations to have open discussions regularly; and pay regular visits to housing managers, security companies, and key local areas to gather input from the community. Each district has a Public Relations Officer designated to serve as a liaison with the community. Street officers walk the beat, stay visible, interact with the community, and provide services to the public while on routine patrol duties. They also work closely with community organizations and private security to address their concerns and solicit their support. Their activities in this regard are quite similar to community policing and problem-oriented policing in other parts of the world despite the fact that the Neighborhood Police Units and the Neighborhood Watch Scheme were both terminated due to instability and lack of participation. The difficulty in mobilizing the community and maintaining civilian participation has been a challenge to the Hong Kong Police just like elsewhere. But the discontinuance of certain community-based programs should not be used to determine whether the overall policing style of a police organization is community-oriented or not. The basic police operations of the Hong Kong Police demonstrate that it remains committed to a community orientation.

For combating serious crimes such as organized crime and drug trafficking, cooperation between the Hong Kong Police and the mainland and overseas law enforcement agencies has become a top priority. The police anti-Triad and anti-narcotics campaigns have increasingly involved cooperation with these other police organizations. Consequently, the Hong Kong Police has developed a multi-agency approach to addressing drug problems and cross-boundary organized crimes. An important part of this multi-agency approach concerns its relationship with the mainland Public Security Bureaus. The Hong Kong Police has been developing a relationship with its mainland counterpart since the 1970's, long before the 1997 handover. But the cooperation and joint programs between them have increased significantly in recent years. There has been a stronger need for such cooperation due to the increased flow of people between Hong Kong and the mainland. This new situation requires that the police from both sides share information, intelligence, and training. The mainland police have provided assistance to the Hong Kong Police upon its request to extradite criminals. The Hong Kong police officers can make request to the Liaison Bureau at the Headquarters for information from the mainland. The Hong Kong Police also passes on its experiences in fighting organized crime and drug trafficking to the mainland police. These two police systems' joint programs have brought tangible benefits to both sides.

The traditional formal bureaucratic structure is highly appropriate and necessary for a large police force to ensure that it stays politically independent and professionally focused on law enforcement. The basic police operations, i.e., emergency response, crime prevention, and public order management to a great extent reflect the professional orientation of the modern police and are regarded as core police activities. It is difficult, however, to define public relations as a core professional activity compatible with these traditional police operations. But maintaining good public relations is crucial for an effective police organization. To achieve this effectiveness, the police have decentralized many operations at the local level despite the bureaucratic structure and professional orientation of the Force overall. Provided that the decentralized police operations follow the general directions of the senior police command and do not threaten the formal organizational structure, the local needs, crimes, and problems often dictate the organization and operations at the street level.

Effective police structure and operations should be based on a cohesive relationship both among parallel units and among members in the same units. The police have several measures in place to make sure that officers in parallel units understand and cooperate with one another. One of these measures is regular rotation of officer positions, which benefits both individual officers and the police organization as a whole. It allows individual officers to gain a wider experience, have more variety and spice on the job, and develop a better career. It improves the police organization by ensuring that the Force have better coordination between units and suffer less from divisiveness and empire-building. Officers in horizontal units in the police hierarchy work cohesively with one another to achieve their common goal. On a daily basis, foot patrol officers, crime officers, EU officers, and PTU officers function as street level bureaucrats, maintain high visibility, engage in crime prevention, and maintain public order. They respond to service calls, handle disputes, inspect known crime locations, and intervene in youth problems. As Crime Unit officers investigate crimes that have occurred, beat patrol officers focus on crime prevention. They prevent crime by mediating parties in dispute, communicating with members of different groups, and educating the public about crime and safety issues. They survey residences known to have security troubles, do follow-up visits of victimized households, and frequently inspect problem areas. Both foot patrol officers and EU officers respond to emergencies; the foot patrol officers handle routine emergencies and EU officers take the lead in responding to serious emergencies. EU officers can be regarded as an intentional overlap to beat patrol and provide assistance to patrol officers when needed. For specific crime problems, uniformed patrol officers and Crime Branch officers work closely together. Although uniformed officers do not play a major role in crime investigation, they are regularly briefed about criminal cases by investigation team leaders. Patrol officers usually handle the initial stage of the investigation and crime investigators take over the subsequent investigation if it is determined that a crime has occurred. Beat patrol officers also initiate and make a significant proportion of arrests as first responders.

Effective police operations also depend on a unified working relationship among members of the same unit. To this end, police managers play an active role in bringing together officers with diverse backgrounds and facilitating their communications and understanding of each other. Oftentimes there are different types of officers working in the same unit due to different levels of education, years of service, and ages. Officers with a college education tend to have more academic knowledge and better communication skills, and thus may develop a friction with veteran officers who do not possess the same educational credentials. In such a situation, the police managers make sure that higher education does not create a gap between younger and older officers. They are careful in sending a consistent message about the relationship between academic knowledge and desired qualities of a good officer. Albeit higher education is important, it remains an element of the critical characteristics of an effective officer, including common sense, attitude, and commitment. Higher education and experience in police work are both valuable backgrounds and cannot replace each other. In this light, a police manager stresses the duty of all officers to work together to achieve their common goals and appreciates the contributions of all officers to his or her unit.

Effective police structure and operations must also be built on a positive vertical relationship between superior and subordinate officers. Street and management officers tend to have diverse perspectives on police duties due to differences in their positions, responsibilities, experiences, and working environments. They may hold different values and world outlooks and see police problems in contrasting lights. The police managers deal with various administrative, organizational, and personnel issues such as officer schedules, report writing, human resources, policies, planning, and meetings. They need to ensure that they have adequate manpower to cover all beats in their areas. They need to take time for developing the officers including their training, self-learning, and career advancement. They contend with officers' personal and work-related problems such as debt management and public complaints. Street officers in contrast are free from these administrative and managerial duties, have more direct contact with the public, and work on practical problems on the street. They spend most of their time patrolling the street or investigating crime. But management and street officers are also similar and share certain views about the police profession. They both joined the police because of a strong sense of justice and social responsibility. They both tend to be more conservative about social and crime issues than the general public. And they both are family-oriented and hold strong moral values. They believe in law and order, respect professionalism, and care about the Force reputation.

To ensure that they reach their common objectives, the lower and higher ranks must highlight their commonalities and bridge their differences by increasing their communications. For example, both street officers and police managers understand the importance of visibility, stop-and-search, rapid response to calls, and order maintenance during their routine operations. They believe that by being visible the police can prevent crime and disorder in the community and, by conducting stop-and-search, police officers contribute to crime prevention. These common viewpoints about operational priorities allow the police managers to pay more attention to the substance of officer activities rather than statistical figures and to give officers the needed discretion to address problems and prevent crime in their specific areas. One of the areas that they tend to differ in is the Service Quality Initiatives as police managers have a vantage point to see the rationale for a service orientation and street officers at the street level find it difficult to reconcile the service aspect of police work with their traditional duties. Realizing this difference, the police management has increased communication and training to the officers. A police manager takes advantage of a wider purview of his or her unit, regularly shares his or her vision, and provides direction and motivation to the officers. In return, the officers develop a stronger commitment to the organization and higher dedication to their duties. As a result, a more open and transparent relationship between superior and subordinate officers has developed. Many officers, for instance, have expressed the view that their superiors have improved significantly or have become more professionalized in recent years. Due to improved quality of police management, many officers also come to understand the Force priorities better and appreciate the way their superiors handle their problems. The Hong Kong Police has also been effective in controlling police corruption and misconduct. Due to various measures taken to address these problems in the past few decades, the seriousness and magnitude of police corruption have been significantly reduced. Syndicated corruption is widely believed to be under control and no longer plagues the Force. Bribery cases and officer involvement in vice, drugs, and organized crime, especially those that are serious, occur very rarely today and the vast majority of public complaints are related to neglect of duty or misconduct and improper manner. The police therefore have been able to shift their attention to malfeasance. Causes of malfeasance vary for individual officers. But many police commanders believe that a direct relationship exists between poor personal financial management and officer misconduct. They cite officer debt as one of the most serious concerns for police management and believe that financial problems not only impair officers' operational efficiency but also lead to emotional difficulties and illegal behaviors. Indebtedness and associated gambling habit are viewed as a time bomb that may cause officers to commit corrupt acts and even crimes. Police misconducts in the form of officer debt and gambling, however, remain insignificant Force-wide. Although the complaint figures in recent years have been on the rise, they remain also within a tolerable range considering the number of cases proportionate to Force size. Most police officers are able to perform their duties professionally and the majority of the public remain highly respectful of the police. What is different now is that the police management is taking a far more serious stance toward public complaints.

Mechanisms against police corruption and misconduct in Hong Kong fall generally under two categories: internal measures involving Hong Kong Police's own efforts and external measures independent from the Force. Internally the Hong Kong Police has a zero tolerance policy against misconduct and has developed tough disciplinary measures and preventative strategies for controlling police misbehaviors. The disciplinary unit and complaint investigation activities within the Force represent the reactive or punitive approach. In this regard, the police have devoted significant resources for investigating complaints related to misconduct. Elaborate rules and procedures have been established for handling police problems from abuse of authority to unmanageable debt. In case of officer debt, the police investigate if there are any violations of disciplines and may establish a disciplinary hearing committee to address officer bankruptcy. According to the Force policy, all officers filing for bankruptcy are subject to police investigation. In contrast to these investigative, disciplinary, and supervisory measures, the police also promote certain cultures and values such as integrity and honesty and monitor officer performances in order to achieve a long-term effect on officer behavior. Such activities are part of the proactive or preventative approach to controlling police corruption and misconduct. The areas that are appropriate for this approach include recruitment, training, and socialization activities. Recruitment programs in recent years have been modified to ensure that new recruits have sound judgment and ethics. In-service training programs such as the Living-the-Values workshop have been used to reinforce positive officer values and instill the spirit of service. The police management has also integrated value training and quality service ideas into a Healthy Lifestyle campaign. Commanders at all levels promote a culture of prudent financial management and are vigilant in identifying officers with financial problems to allow timely assistance including debt restructuring to be offered.

The most significant external body for controlling police corruption is the Independent Commission against Corruption (ICAC). Its organization and operations follow three enabling ordinances: the ICAC Ordinance, Prevention Ordinance, and Corruption Ordinance. The establishment of the ICAC in the 1970's reflected the public's detestation of corruption and its acceptance of the government's coercive maintenance of public order at the time. There has been a strong legislative backing and public support for corruption control in Hong Kong since then. The ICAC remains a well-funded anti-corruption agency and its independence is stipulated in the Basic Law, a mini-constitution of Hong Kong after the change of sovereignty. As an agency vested with extensive powers, the ICAC also has a comprehensive system of checks and balances to ensure that its agents act within the requirements of the law. The ICAC has practiced a well-known three-pronged approach to fighting corruption, i.e., detection, prevention, and education. This approach has become a model for corruption control for many other anti-graft agencies around the world. It is reflected in the three departments of the ICAC: the Operations, Corruption Prevention, and Community Relations Department. The Operations Department is the investigative arm and the largest department of the Commission. The Corruption Prevention Department is responsible for identifying loopholes in the practices and procedures of government departments and public bodies. The Community Relations Department is in charge of educating the public against the evils of corruption and harnessing support for the ICAC. The ICAC has enjoyed an unblemished reputation in Hong Kong and the three-pronged approach has been widely regarded as a success. It is believed that public trust, good management, accountability, and proactive investigation have contributed to its success.

Among the various control measures against corruption and misconduct, the officers tend to regard those involving the efforts of the Hong Kong Police and ICAC as the most effective. Both are professional law enforcement agencies and the officers hold them in higher regard than civilian oversight mechanisms. Many senior officials from the Hong Kong Police and ICAC believe that effective control of police corruption should be founded on a partnership relationship between the police and the ICAC and a strong culture against corruption. As two of the largest law enforcement agencies in Hong Kong, the police and ICAC have had their share of tensions and frictions in history. But disagreements between them are extremely rare and should not be used to characterize their relationship. On a routine basis, they collaborate and cooperate with each other and are able to resolve their differences through existing channels. Over the years they have developed a coordinated partnership approach to investigating and reducing opportunities for police corruption. In fact, the partnership approach has been an official policy for the Hong Kong Police and ICAC for many years. The leadership and management of these two organizations understand also the importance of fostering a culture against corruption and have been committed to creating this culture, which in turn has become the foundation for better police-ICAC cooperation. A partnership relationship plus a culture against corruption have become the cornerstone for the successful control of corruption in the Hong Kong Police.

Overall, a mixed approach that encompasses a variety of measures aimed at controlling corruption and misconduct has achieved both an immediate and long-term effect on police misbehavior. These measures include reducing opportunities, increasing material benefits, strengthening deterrence, improving internal management, and cultivating an anti-corruption culture. Reduced opportunities have an immediate effect on officer behaviors by blocking existing channels for corruption. Increased material benefits may also have an immediate effect because they reduce the temptation of officers to seek trivial gains. Strong deterrence, which involves punitive measures designed for investigating and punishing corrupt and wrongful behaviors, can have both an immediate and long-term effect on corruption. The idea for improving internal management, which is based on the concept of total quality management, is aimed at creating a transparent and inspiring working environment to allow career-minded officers to grow and advance and in turn to cultivate a lasting force against corruption. Lastly, an anti-corruption culture creates an attitude among officers against corruption and makes it difficult for corrupt behaviors to exist at the outset. As officers internalize values of integrity, professionalism, and quality service, they will speak up against corrupt behaviors and channel their colleagues to ethical conducts.

Organizational and Institutional Dimensions

A major police force with a long history often has a life of its own despite dramatic changes in its external environment. With a history that goes back to the mid-19th Century, the Hong Kong Police maintains many of its earlier principles and practices. Notwithstanding major socio-political changes under the British rule and after the change of sovereignty, the Hong Kong Police has always been relied upon for maintaining law and order. With a mandate to protect the economic interest of the business elites, the colonial government in Hong Kong in history had had no agenda to open up the political arena and develop the colony's democracy. This tradition means that the Hong Kong Police has enjoyed a prominent role in the political, economic, and social life that is rarely seen in municipal policing in other parts of the world. It is responsible not only for traditional police duties such as crime control and law enforcement, but also for internal and border security, public order management, counter smuggling activities, and anti-illegal immigration. Its role in the economic life of Hong Kong is well recognized because its effectiveness is believed to be directly linked to the economic stability of the territory. Due to the colonial tradition, public order management has been institutionalized as a primordial mission of the Hong Kong Police. This priority endures at present even though crime and law enforcement have been raised to a higher level of emphasis since the 1980s. An important measure of the high premium placed on public order management is the policy that every officer is mandated to serve in the Police Tactical Unit (PTU). The PTU is charged with the responsibility for managing large-scale public events such as demonstrations, ceremonies, civil disobedience, riots, and disasters. As part of its public order management tradition, the Hong Kong Police has also been actively engaged in anti-illegal immigration activities. Hong Kong is now a part of China and continuing to treat Chinese citizens as illegal immigrants beats logics. But, due to "the one-country, two systems" formula, there has been no change in the Hong Kong Police in its anti-illegal immigration operations.

A paramilitary capability, coupled with the "effective policing model," is regarded essential for public order management and remains a dominant feature of the Hong Kong Police. Like many Western colonies in the world, the Hong Kong Police developed a paramilitary structure and public order emphasis early on both to defend the colony from the Chinese mainland and to control the local population. Despite some reviews and realignment aimed at higher efficiency and greater effectiveness, the paramilitary structure and operations endure. It is to a great extent the history of the Hong Kong Police that has shaped this character. And the wide powers bestowed by the colonial government have made it possible for the police to employ the effective policing model. The continuity of such a character and model in Hong Kong policing demonstrates not only the strength of the colonial police tradition, but also the resilience of the military concepts, identified by both the police and civilians alike. Consequently, the police are paramilitary in nature and their structure and operations model after the military. As a large public organization, the Hong Kong Police is also powerful in influencing its institutional environment's perceptions. The public therefore has grown accustomed to the character of the Hong Kong Police believing that it represents the quality of a legitimate police organization. Many members of the public, in turn, accept and demand effective policing, particularly for the purpose of maintaining political stability and economic prosperity in the territory. Economically related issues associated with fears about social unrest dominate personal concerns in Hong Kong pressuring the police to keep public order management a top priority.

The strong traditions in public order management and effective crime control in the Hong Kong Police do not preclude possibilities for change, however. The police as a public organization must develop and evolve in a way that reflects changes in the society. They adopt strategies in response to transformations in their political and social environment. They serve as an immediate link between politics and citizens, affect citizen life, and provide feedback to the government they represent (Bayley, 1991). To the extent that the police protect public order and meet citizens' demand, they represent the orientation of the government and reflect the changes of the society simultaneously. Their practices in general mirror the political ideology, economic thinking, and cultural traits of the time they find themselves. As a police organization experiencing major political and social transformations, the Hong Kong Police will change inevitably. Its changes can be traced to new governmental reforms, new public demands, and new trends in the police profession. As the political and economic policy of a society changes in a way that widens the role of the government, the power of the police tends to narrow and become circumscribed. As the society becomes more open and the citizens more right-conscious, the police must strive to maintain public confidence. As the police profession advocates fairness and impartiality in all its dealings with the public, the police tend to become more professionalized. They reflect the demographics of the community they serve, take a strong stance against racism and bigotry, and engage in public service. The colonial police function of controlling the local population in the interest of colonial rulers in the old days must give way to a priority of maintaining law and order in the interest of the public according to the rule of the law.

Changes in policing do not take place by themselves. They are usually a result of a struggle between a conservative police force that by nature protects the status quo and a progressive civil society that by instinct demands more openness. Changes in the Hong Kong Police have occurred due to such interplay between internal forces and external impetuses. As police everywhere, the police in Hong Kong have a strong tendency to protect their domain, comprising of certain core traditional police practices. Powerful as the traditions may be, the police cannot ignore forces for change both from within the police profession and from the public. As much as they treasure and identify with their traditional practices, the police follow the contemporary development in the police profession. The public, while demanding effective policing, also wants the police to trim their powers and become more service-oriented. The development in the field of policing and the demand from the general public essentially mean that the police must fulfill their traditional functions with a more professional and communitarian orientation.

The development of the Hong Kong Police in history and at present demonstrates that there exists a direct relationship between securing the legitimacy of governance and professionalization of policing. At a time of dramatic social changes, the police must maintain public confidence in order to achieve effective governance. To this end, the Hong Kong Police has endeavored to understand and address the sources of public discontent, including underlying, intermediate, and immediate causes over the years. It has fought corruption and misconduct, reviewed its performances, and evaluated its relationships with the public. Changes and development of the Hong Kong Police have also occurred in such areas as modernization, professionalization, and service quality. After the anti-corruption years of the 1970s, the police have engaged in modernizing themselves with better equipment and technology, upgrading officer training and education, and enhancing the efficiency and effectives of police operations. More recently the police have embarked on the Service Quality Initiatives to improve their services to the public and to make the police more open and transparent.

Although it makes no sense to trace artificially the specific changes to the 1997 handover, it cannot be denied that the change of sovereignty has brought immense psychological pressure to the police for change and the steps for change have quickened toward the end of the colonial rule and after the handover. The transition from a colonial system to a sovereign part of China requires first and foremost that the police maintain stability both within the Force and in the society. To fulfill this mission, the Hong Kong Police has proactively prepared for the change and judiciously executed a series of transition strategies. It has stabilized the police internally and addressed public concerns in a new social and political environment. The issues touched upon by the change are wide-ranging, including organizational structure, human resources, communication, professional relationships, officer morale, and public confidence. Looking back, it can be concluded that the police have been well prepared to handle both tangible issues and psychological impact resulting from the transition. Their careful planning and implementation strategies have paid dividends in the form of a smooth transition in the Force and a stable society.

The gathered materials suggest that the Hong Kong Police has been committed to building a culture of quality service over the past decade. This culture is consistent with the development in the police profession and sentiment in the Hong Kong society, once a Western colony and now a world class city as a part of China. The rationale for creating this culture is that the police must keep pace with and respond to changes in the society and secure legitimacy in the eye of the public in order to function effectively. The police in Hong Kong are at a special time and a special place. No longer a colonial force, they must develop new values and attitudes and new organizational knowledge. While they do not have to abandon their traditional structure and operations, they do need to carry out their duties with a new character, a service orientation. It is also natural that certain traditional colonial practices may need to be reevaluated as the Hong Kong Police enters a new era. The Anti-II activities, for example, are clearly a part of the colonial tradition. Since Hong Kong is now a sovereign part of China, anti-II activities are used mostly for the purpose of keeping the "one-country, two-systems" promise. As Hong Kong and mainland China become more integrated economically, politically, and culturally, government policies on IIs and cost-effectiveness of anti-II operations may need to be reevaluated. A related but separate issue is a bias against immigrants in general and minority immigrants in particular resulting from the anti-II tradition, which is not conducive to the development of a civil and service orientation in the Hong Kong Police.

The service-oriented policing as envisioned by the Hong Kong police leadership revolves around a series of Service Quality Initiatives and the idea that the public are customers of the police. The police believe that these initiatives represent a global trend and reflect the values and best practices of professional organizations. The concept of service quality is a many-splendored thing. It means that the police not only need to provide better services to the public but also improve internal management. To achieve these goals, the police have developed performance pledges that describe the services they deliver, performance standards, and monitoring methods. Performance audits are used to support the management process, provide checks and balances, and facilitate informed operational and managerial decisions. Due to the Service Quality Initiatives, communication, community relations, and a customer orientation have received a stronger emphasis in recent years. The management officers now communicate more, listen more, and seek more input from their lower ranks and the communities they serve and are committed to building a transparent working environment.

Service-oriented policing, as a police orientation, is based on a set of coherent and logically linked theoretical assumptions, organizational principles, and characteristic activities. The theoretical assumptions are that in a free society, the police operate with consent and trust, i.e., legitimacy; as a politically sensitive public organization, the police are responsive to the need of and demand from the public; and as a professional organization, the police engage in developing and improving themselves in pursuit of excellence. The organizational principles in this orientation include openness and trust, customerization, continuous improvement, and professionalism. The characteristic activities under this orientation include the use of social skills and technology, courteous and respectful service, effective and efficient communication, and life-long learning and development. As the police stand between their responsibility to maintain order and protect civil right, the service orientation helps reduce the inherent tension and bridge the gap between diverse police goals and functions. As a rationally conceived and politically insightful reform program, the Service Quality Initiatives that undergirds the service orientation is appropriate for balancing different police orientations, including the paramilitary tradition, public order management, police professionalism, and community policing. As years go by, the service orientation will also facilitate the police effort to acquire new knowledge and technology and to become more efficient and effective. Ultimately, the realization of the service orientation requires that the police move away from window-dressing in its public relation activities and institutionalize far-reaching policies and cultural changes that emphasize serving the people and the community.

The Service Quality Initiatives marks the most significant effort of police management in Hong Kong to build a culture of service and raise the standard of service to the public. To reach this goal, service-oriented and value-based training, workshops, and seminars have been provided to the entire Force. The commitment to serving the people of Hong Kong has been vigorously promoted in three areas in particular, i.e., enhancement of the Complaints against Police Office (CAPO), improvement of police report rooms, and public opinion surveys. Key areas identified for the police to work on include working in partnership with the community to prevent crime, providing the public with a high quality of service, improving communications within the Force and with the public, and living the values the police have publicly declared to uphold. A significant effort aimed at bringing about a change of culture and values is a one-day workshop called Living-the-Values provided to the entire Force on a yearly basis by the Service Quality Wing.

As a part of the overall police reform strategy, the Hong Kong Police has also been committed to developing a learning culture. This culture in essence embodies the use of cutting-edge training curricula and promotion of knowledge-based practices. Such a culture is now permeating throughout the Force from recruitment and selection, to academy and in-service training, and to police policies at the senior management level. The police have reviewed their Recruitment and Selection Programs on an annual basis to reflect changes in the field and the society. They have raised the exposure of their recruitment program to the public, increased the size of the application pool, and increased the minimum educational standard for all officers. In the process, they look for people that are career-minded and committed to the police profession and try to screen out those that seek police work only as a job. In their basic and in-service training programs, the police have given greater emphasis to integrity and other Force values in recent years. The recruit training syllabus has been redesigned to provide new recruits with a foundation to build their career, to establish a training continuum, and foster the concept of career and a sense of dedication. The training strategy follows a purpose-driven curriculum in line with the Force Strategic Directions and is aimed at fulfilling the Force Values among all officers. Developmental, continuation, and promotion courses are also offered with the same principles to reinforce officers' knowledge and values.

To maintain the most advanced training programs, the police directors at the Training Wing are actively engaged in updating, revising, and developing in-service training courses according to changes in the society and new information in the profession. Three in-service training programs, the Junior Command Course (JCC), the Intermediate Command Course (ICC), and the Advanced Command Course (ACC) are provided to officers newly promoted to various ranks. These programs are organized into modules that cover a variety of subjects including information management, language, communication, human resources, stress and counseling, negotiation, resource and financial management, strategic management, public order management, and police ethics. These courses also emphasize Force values such as professionalism, protection of civil right, and service quality. Training modules developed in such a manner are on the cutting edge of contemporary management and human resource research. Geared to opening the horizon of the trainees, they are above and beyond the traditional content of in-service training and reflect a new learning culture the police try to cultivate. The trainees' inputs as to how well the aims of the modules are addressed are taken seriously and many of the courses are redesigned on the basis of feedback from the trainees. To move to a higher level of knowledge and learning, the Hong Kong Police has also developed a knowledge-based program and has established a Research Division and a Police College. Because knowledge-based practices represent a cultural change, officers associated with this initiative are responsible also for advocating and marketing the program within the Force. The success of the program eventually depends on the extent of officers' contributions and consumptions of police-related knowledge.

The Service Quality Initiatives is an ambitious reform program in response to changes in the society and require a sweeping change of police character and an institutional transformation. It demands new budgetary allocation and substantial investment in training the officers. A reform of such magnitude and complexity naturally is confronted with challenges and obstacles of various kinds and calls for application of knowledge in organizational change and social relations. Understanding that they must adapt to their new external environment by engaging in internal institutional development, the police have actively involved themselves in an organizational learning and development process to expand the officers' horizon, promote new policing philosophies, and support best practices in consistency with the changed social and political environment. As a result of the Service Quality Initiatives, the Hong Kong Police has been evolving from an authoritarian and paramilitary force to a more service-oriented and community-oriented organization. A new character has gradually emerged in the Hong Kong Police demonstrated by officers' positive attitude toward the public and their strong professionalism.

Challenges and Strategies for the Future

The Hong Kong Police still faces many challenges internally and externally in the area of police management, public order management, community policing, and in institutionalizing the service orientation. In terms of police management, the police have a clear division of labor and a tall hierarchy. While such a structure is indispensable for a large police force to achieve efficiency, it may stifle initiatives and reduce police effectiveness. A bureaucracy characterized by too many rules and procedures also hampers integration and coordination, reducing its efficiency. The Hong Kong Police, therefore, as any large public organization, will continue to find room for higher efficiency and greater effectiveness. The Crime Unit, Uniformed Branch, and Tactical Unit, for example, are all horizontal but highly specialized units, and need to find a way to work more closely together. More incentive for coordination may need to be provided to encourage more collaborative efforts and programs. Hierarchically, the Hong Kong Police has fourteen ranks and four major levels from the Headquarters, to regions, to districts, and to divisions. Although ridding any rank or level would affect the entire Force and the Force's relationship with the public, the police at a certain time and a certain place may be required to reanalyze its cost-effectiveness and find a way to achieve greater efficiency.

The challenge for managing public order is rooted in some inherent contradictions in the police priorities and in the lopsided development of the Hong Kong society. As a modern and professional police agency, the police priorities should be crime control, law enforcement, and public service. Public order is important only when a society is in danger of drifting into serious chaos and, therefore, requires police intervention. But in case of the Hong Kong Police, public order management has been treated as a top priority due to both the colonial police tradition and the trepidations at a time of political and social transitions, not due to major disorders in the Hong Kong society. The lopsided development in the society lies in the fact that Hong Kong has developed its economy, education, information, and communication system to a world-class level, but has remained politically undemocratic where the public is unable to elect its political leaders directly. The Hong Kong people have shown greater interest in politics and are more actively involved in demanding for a representative government in recent years. Hong Kong is also a convenient place for local and international groups to organize issue-oriented protests due to the liberal media in the city. Facing these inherent and societal contradictions, the police face the challenge of reprioritizing and changing their traditional mentality to better fit the law and order reality in Hong Kong on the one hand and preparing for large-scale disorders related to the society's quest for democracy and the territory's exposure to the media on the other.

Building a community partnership relationship remains a challenge due to the social, cultural, and economic characteristics of the Hong Kong society as well as the traditional mentality of police officers. The population in Hong Kong is infamous for its high mobility as many Hong Kong people consider the city a place of transition rather than permanent residence. They live here as an option and are ready to move elsewhere once life becomes undesirable. This sentiment can lead to a weak sense of community, which is often considered detrimental to community policing. Although the police are willing to listen to public suggestions, the community does not always provide direct input or tells the police exactly what it wants. Where the community does voice its preferences, it seldom provides a consistent idea. The community is apparently not monolithic, and the police often find it difficult to balance different community interests. Many officers themselves also remain dubious about community policing or distrustful of public involvement in policing. The traditional mentality of "police know police business the best" remains with these officers. Some of them even view community involvement in police business as inappropriate as they question the extent of public involvement in police work and prefer that the community work with the police when requested only.

Certain other areas the police need to work on that are related to community policing include equity in service, civil right protection, and domestic violence intervention. The police need to address the needs of people in all social strata and ethnic and racial backgrounds. As a city with a significant income gap between the rich and poor and without a strong middle class, it is easy for some officers to develop the idea that people in different social strata deserve being treated differently. Some officers may abuse their authority and violate due process rules and procedures due to their negative attitude or insensitivity toward members of certain disadvantaged groups. A related emerging issue is concerned with social policies such as civil right protection, anti-discrimination laws, and multiculturalism. As a society where certain groups of people experience discriminatory treatment because of their race and ethnicity, the government needs to legislate against such practices and the police need to develop a stronger awareness of such behaviors. There has been a clear gap in this area in Hong Kong policing because many officers view socially motivated laws and legislations as only remotely related to their profession. Bias, bigotry, and racism have received scant attention from the police management as well as other government agencies. Frontline officers need to move away from their negative stereotypes of mainlanders, South Asians, South East Asians, and Africans. The police management can have an impact in this process by providing sensitivity and diversity training to police officers to help them work more effectively with people from different backgrounds. Such training can perhaps be integrated into the Service Quality Initiatives being implemented in the Hong Kong Police. It should make sure that police officers understand the significance of civil right policies and multiculturalism as part of community policing and police effort in maintaining public confidence. Community policing also demands that the government and the police intervene in certain areas that are traditionally and culturally viewed as personal or family matters such as domestic violence. Domestic violence rate has increased significantly in recent years in Hong Kong indicating that family solidarity may be deteriorating. Multiple factors have been blamed for the problem: poor economy, financial hardship, unemployment, work-related pressure, family and personal-relationship problems, and lack of communication and understanding. Hong Kong police officers need to abandon their traditional view that family affairs are private matters that they should stay out of and the government needs to be more aggressive in legislating against domestic violence.

There has been a significant change in the Hong Kong Police to a service orientation. But the change process is not straight-forward as the effort made in this regard has been met with serious challenges. Changes are also oftentimes superficial and related police policies and programs are only selectively and ceremonially presented to the public in a way commonly found in policing (Manning, 1977; 1997). The constraints in carrying out fundamental reforms are mainly due to continued priorities given to institutionalized "real" or "core" police duties such as public order management and tactical activities. The paramilitary traditions of the Hong Kong Police have always been influential in the later stages of its development. Due to its origins and the developed structures and processes such as the Emergency Unit, the Police Tactical Unit, and quasi-military training, police officers are effectively socialized into traditional police values and practices. Officers, especially those at the rank-and-file level, therefore, have resisted the transformation of the Hong Kong Police to a service-oriented organization. They remain more committed to public order and crime control and view these tasks as their core duties.

Due to the influence of traditional practices, the officers do not favor a social role for the police and view moral preaching or shaping social development antithetical to the police function. With the exception of youth-programs, they do not view themselves as having a social impact on the community. Part of the effort to promote service is geared to changing officers' traditional mentality. But the promulgated Force values such as integrity, professionalism, and law and order are not necessarily different from their traditional values and moral standards. Service quality is perhaps the only value that does not fit the tradi-tional police structure and practices. Although it was introduced in response to changes in the Hong Kong society and in the police profession, many rank-and-file officers view it as incompatible with their traditional values and feel challenged to adjust to a service orientation. Even among officers believing in the importance of service, they still see the Service Quality Initiatives as inconsistent with the police role. As they embrace traditional law enforcement values, they find it difficult to identify with social aspect of police work. From an institutional perspective, the police tend to change when the changes do not conflict with their core values and traditions. Where changes are against their core knowledge and principles, it will be more difficult for them to materialize.

The police officers' lack of identification with service aspect of police work is exacerbated by their perceived lack of cooperation from the public. As street-level bureaucrats, police officers represent the most direct contact the public has with the government. In turn police officers may become the target for the public to vent its dissatisfaction with anything that may go wrong with the government and experience first-hand the uncertainties and difficulties of a society in transition. The public has expressed a growing dissatisfaction with the police in recent years, which can be seen as a result of a higher expectation of the police after the handover. Since more people in Hong Kong consider Hong Kong their home and the police, once colonial and run largely by foreigners, their own as well, they have dramatically increased their expectations of the police. In this process, many officers have negative experiences with members of the public and view them as becoming more disrespectful and uncooperative. The increased complaints have added to the pressure for change as many officers view them as unreasonable demands. The changed attitudes and behaviors of the public have also made it more difficult for them to engage in service aspect of police work. As the public complaints have increased, some officers have also become more vocal about their dissatisfaction with the public. They complain about more stress on the job due to increased demand and decreased respect from the public. With this mindset, some officers, instead of trying to improve their service quality to the public, try to avoid complaints in order to reduce their workload.

The issue of increased complaints is also related to the creation of an independent body for handling public complaints. The police by nature seldom view the creation of an external oversight body as desirable even though it is inevitable. In the same way as the Hong Kong Police rejected the ICAC in history, it has been successful in keeping the CAPO an internal function. Its success is due largely to the timeframe in which the Independent Police Complaint Council (IPCC) was originally proposed, which was immediately after the 1997 change of sovereignty, when the priority of the Hong Kong Government was to maintain social stability and public order. Social stability and public order require first and foremost a stable and orderly police force. At a potentially chaotic historic period, it was a concern that the IPCC, which grants the power of complaint investigation to an external body, would be damaging to police morale and therefore was unacceptable. It has been many years since the handover and the Hong Kong Government has been able to maintain a stable and orderly society. The time may have come for the government to focus its attention to creating an independent body for investigating public complaints against the police and to further improve the quality of police service. The flipside of this issue is that this external body may be viewed as a further interference in the officers' daily work and therefore create more trouble-avoiding behaviors on the street.

The change of a police force the size of the Hong Kong Police cannot be accomplished without institutionalized effort both internally and externally. The police leadership must address both internal officer morale and external citizen satisfaction and engage in a balancing act between police traditions and public expectations, between the inertia of a paramilitary force of the past and a vision of a progressive and service-oriented organization of the future. As many officers claim to have suffered from a low morale in recent years due to changes in the society and within the Force, the police management has tried to walk a fine line between addressing malfeasance and boosting officer morale. To do so, the police need to strike a balance between strengthening public confidence and maintaining police autonomy. To strengthen public confidence, the police have continued to target officer misbehaviors such as bad manners and attitudes that cause most of the public complaints. To uphold police autonomy, they have continued to give emphases to their traditional law enforcement functions and their political neutrality and voiced criticism when the public and other government agencies cross their boundaries in dealing with the police. The Hong Kong Police, therefore, will continue to balance between the public demand for a more open and transparent force and the internal desire for traditional and professional practices.

The police must continue to develop individual officers as well as the organization to bring about a service culture among the rank-and-file. Officer resistance to the Service Quality Initiatives represents the pain before the birth of a new culture. The evolution and transformation of the police to a service orientation is a part of the global trend and stands for the wave of the future in policing. The process is never meant to be straightforward. Although the police management sees the need to change the culture in response to changes in the society and in the profession, the balance of public and organizational interests lies ultimately on the shoulder of individual officers during their routine activities. Street officers inevitably face the struggle between service and traditional police duties. There is therefore a gap between the police management and street officers regarding the service aspect of police work. Police management strongly believes that effective policing comes with strong public confidence and genuine reduction in police misbehaviors. The police managers accept the dual responsibility for reducing crime and improving service quality. The street-level officers however often find it difficult to reconcile these two aspects of police work in their daily activities. They also complain about the way public complaints are handled by their superiors and the lack of support from the police management in general. Some even view the increased complaints as caused by the Service Quality Initiatives and the pro-community behaviors of management officers. They express a desire for more management support and understanding. Although such perceptions are far from the truth, the burden of bridging differences between management and street officers ultimately lies with the management. The police management needs to have a clear assessment of officer morale and performances and understand the causes of officer frustrations for better training and management purposes. First, the low morale can be a misinterpretation of officers' stress and frustrations, which should not be viewed as equivalent to low performances. The street officers in fact have continued to demonstrate a high level of professionalism and dedication and improved significantly their quality of service to the public in recent years. It should be understood also that police officers work in a profession that is quasi-military in nature and often requires a firm stance toward the public. In such a working environment, they do not enjoy as much "democracy" with their management as those in other professions and frequently face public dissatisfaction and disrespect. They are routinely in contact with the dark, ugly, and tragic side of society and may easily develop a negative world outlook. This working environment is clearly a source of stress and burnout and may create a sense of disenfranchisement. Such feelings should not be interpreted as equivalent to low morale, however. Second, several factors explain the officers' stress and frustrations including difficulty in adjustment to change, perceived lack of respect from the public, and perceived lack of support from the management. The adjustment to changes due to changes in the Force and in the Hong Kong society is an add-on to the officers' routine responsibilities. The officers also expect respect from the public when they provide services but do not always get it. When this happens on a daily basis, they may feel the public is not on their side and in turn become less motivated to engage in serve-related activities. Complaining about their difficulties is also a way to shift the burden of responsibility to police management so they can gain more support and understanding from their superior officers.

Senior management officers also experience challenges and difficulties in this change process as they themselves need to change their traditional management approach and develop new organizational knowledge in order to function in a service-oriented culture. They need to cultivate new values and behaviors among their officers and improve their relations with the public and the community. Due to their vantage point, they have a better understanding of the importance of keeping pace with changes in the profession and their environment. But to create genuine changes, they need to consult with members of the Force, conduct research on social, economic, political, and technological trends in Hong Kong and the mainland, develop Force-wide strategies, and examine and consider various models on future policing. Police commanders in charge of local jurisdictions need to communicate more, rectify problems in their areas, align local operations with Force directions, and focus more on developing their subordinate officers. They need to pay attention to the service standard and remind their officers regularly about expected behaviors. Some police managers, however, find it difficult to convince themselves about the change and therefore are not committed to service quality. Some see the service orientation as a threat to their traditional priorities and to their autonomy and authority. They question the overall value of the service policy and the general direction in which the police are heading. The cultivation of the service culture, therefore, is a difficult process and requires the development of the organization from senior police administrators to middle managers and to the frontline.

In a large organization like the Hong Kong Police, there are apparently different values among the officers and ideas about what should be the priorities for the police. In the police profession, different policing styles have also been developed for serving the public. There is a need, therefore, to balance different orientations for the Hong Kong Police. This means that a police commander at the divisional level should balance various functions in his or her area. This is necessary especially when police officers need to perform different tasks designed in light of diverse values and principles. There are tensions, for example, between the need to maintain order and follow the rule, to control crime and protect civil right, to enforce the law and provide service. Such tensions have become more significant in recent years due to the Service Quality Initiatives and are a sticking point among different groups in the Hong Kong Police, particularly between senior management and street officers. On the one hand, many police commanders expect the officers to resolve the tensions arising from different values and orientations. On the other hand, many street officers find it difficult to balance them in their daily activities. Police management should consider the inherent friction between law enforcement and service while recognizing that this strain is not necessarily negative. The police, in maintaining order and fighting crime, must follow due process rules and procedures and treat the public with respect and courtesy. The stress in this process is conducive to developing a more professionalized police force.

As the society has changed and public expectation for the police is higher, the Hong Kong Police need to respond to changes in its environment and develop an organizational character based upon an equilibrium between law enforcement and service. This balance should not only be discussed rhetorically but also be reflected in all police functions, tasks, trainings, and officer behaviors. Several specific measures can be taken to achieve this balance. Values and ethics such as professionalism and honesty can be used to cultivate a sense of fair law enforcement and public service. Training and education programs can be used to help officers develop better judgment and communication skills. Police managers should play a more active role in communicating with the rank-and-file about police professionalism, civil right, and service quality. There is no question that the Hong Kong Police is a highly advanced professional law enforcement organization and is poised to forge ahead with best knowledge and practices in policing. It can be expected to continue the programs and strategies that have proven successful and are looked upon as models by many police forces in the world. It can also be expected to develop new initiatives and break new grounds in raising the standard of service for the public. With such efforts, it has the potential to become the best police organization in the world.

A Conceptual Framework

As the first systematic inquiry of the changes and development of the Hong Kong Police after 1997, this book provides a description and analysis of the colonial past, the 1997 handover, the changes and continuities, the structure and operation, the learning culture, the impact of the Bill of Rights, the street officer behavior, the management officer behavior, the crime problems, and the control of corruption and misconduct in the Hong Kong Police. These issues are examined from several theoretical or conceptual perspectives arrived at inductively rather than deductively. The theme of this book, as stated in the Preface, is arrived at through the same process, which is: the police change and develop and eventually progress by counterbalancing various forces within and outside the organization and interacting with key groups or sovereigns in their institutional environment. This theme is made deliberately broad to cover the wide-ranging issues and complex change processes associated with the Hong Kong Police. But, two words, "counterbalancing" and "interacting," are the key to understanding the Hong Kong Police. It has been illustrated, throughout this book, that the Hong Kong Police has transformed itself over several historical periods and advanced to a highly professional and overall better force through balancing different police orientations and interactions with its institutional environment.

The theme of counterbalancing and interactions in policing in order to make progress has been informed by several theoretical frameworks developed by police and organizational scholars as well as my field experience in Hong Kong. These include Wilson (1972)'s concept of police styles, Bourdieu (1990)'s concepts of "habitus" and "field," Sackmann (1991)'s "organizational knowledge," Skolnick (1994)'s "law" and "order," Manning (1977)'s "dramatic metaphor," and the more general but closely related cultural and institutional perspectives (Brint and Karabel, 1991; DiMaggio and Powell, 1991; March and Olsen, 1984; and Meyer and Rowan, 1991). These concepts, as a whole, form the basis of the theme of this work as they fill many gaps in the analysis and interpretation of gathered materials. The gathered materials, conversely, lend further support to these concepts.

Wilson (1972)'s three police styles (i.e., watchmen, legalistic, and service), originally used to describe patterns of police behavior in eight American communities, provide a theoretical base for explaining the evolution of police in Hong Kong as the Hong Kong Police has shown certain elements of each style during different stages in its historical development, watchmen during the colonial period and most of the administrative state period, legalistic during the last decade of the administrative state period and the democratic period, and service during the post-colonial period. Different from findings in Wilson's study, however, the Hong Kong Police experience demonstrates that a single police organization may go through each of these styles one by one as it evolves and progresses, although all the elements associated with the styles as described by Wilson are not fully displayed and the journey of this evolution is far from complete. This journey of police evolution can be interpreted as a process of counterbalancing different police orientations.

Bourdieu's "habitus" and "field" provides an understanding of the interaction between police professional know-how and their political and social environment. This interaction is further explained by Skolnick (1994)'s idea of "tensions" between law and order and Manning (1977)'s concept of "dramatic metaphor." Through interactions, tensions, and dramatic presentations, the police become more transparent and professionalized. The cultural perspective can also be used to examine the interaction, in the context of Hong Kong, between two different cultural orientations, the Western and Chinese, resulting from the official mandate to follow Western law enforcement principles and the grass-root, Chinese cultural disposition among the rank-and-file. The institutional perspective provides further insight into the interplay or linkage between the past and present in policing and the influence of institutionalized policies and practices on contemporary policing. Such an influence has been demonstrated mainly through traditional police culture's restrictive effect on police reforms and police thinking in Hong Kong. The police, therefore, develop through contradictions and interactions, at both macro- and micro-levels, and progress toward and come to terms with the most balanced or rational approach, often a compromise between their traditional knowledge and the changing social political environment.

References

Alderson, J. C. 1981. "Hong Kong, Tokyo, Peking: Three Police Systems Observed." *Police Studies* 3(4):3-13.

Anderson, D. M., and D. Killingray. 1992. *Policing and Decolonization: Politics, Nationalism and the Police 1917-65*. Manchester: Manchester University Press.

Annual Report by the Commissioner of the ICAC, 2000, Hong Kong Special Administrative Region Government.

Annual Report of the Singapore Police Force 1997-98; 1998-99. Singapore Police Force (http:www.spinet.gov.sg)

Apple Daily, May 25 and 26, 2002, Hong Kong News section.

Bayley, D. H. 1985. *Patterns of Policing: A Comparative International Analysis*. New Brunswick, NJ: Rutgers University Press.

Bayley, D. H. 1991. *Forces of Order: Policing Modern Japan*. Berkeley, CA: University of California Press.

Bayley, D. H. 1992. "Comparative Organization of the Police in English-speaking Countries." In *Crime and Justice: A Review of Research*, edited by M. Tonry and N. Morris. Chicago: University of Chicago Press.

Bayley, D. H., and C. D. Shearing. 2001. "The Structure of Policing: Description, Conceptualization, and Research Agenda." Research Report. Washington, D.C.: National Institute of Justice, U.S. Department of Justice.

Beazer, W. F. 1978. *The Commercial Future of Hong Kong*. New York: Praeger Publishers.

Bourdieu, P. 1990. *In other Words: Essays towards a Reflexive Sociology* (Translated by Matthew Adamson). Standard, CA: Stanford University Press.

Briefing Note for Regional Command and Control Center HKI, 1999, Hong Kong Police Force.

Brint, S., and J. Karabel. 1991. "Institutional Origins and Transformations: The Case of American Community Colleges." In *The New Institutionalism in Organizational Analysis*, edited by W. W. Powell and P. J. DiMaggio. Chicago: University of Chicago Press.

Broadhurst, R. 2000. "Crime Trends in Hong Kong." Working paper prepared in part for the Hong Kong Social Services Council – Social Indicators Project 2000, Center for Criminology, University of Hong Kong (www.hku.hk/crime).

Brogden, M., and R. W. K. Lau. 2001. "The Hong Kong Context: The Development of the Hong Kong Police." In *Core Issues in Policing*, Unit 8, coordinated by R. W. K. Lau. Hong Kong: Open University of Hong Kong.

Burns, J. P. 2002. "Accountability and the Senior Civil Service in Hong Kong." Paper presented at the Government Accountability Forum of the Department of Politics and Public Administration, University of Hong Kong, June 3.

CAPO Annual Report, 1995, 2000, Hong Kong Police Force.

Census and Statistics Department. 2005a. "Hong Kong in Figures." Hong Kong: Census and Statistics Department of the Hong Kong Government.

———. 2005b. "Census and Statistics Department." The Hong Kong Government Website (http://www.info.gov.hk/censtatd).

Chan, C. L. L. 1998. "Community Policing in Hong Kong: A Case Study of the Community Awareness Programs in Tin Sui Wai, Yuen Long." M.Soc.Sc. Dissertation, Sociology Department, University of Hong Kong.

Chan, J. 1996. "Changing Police Culture." British Journal of Criminology 36:109-34.

Chan, P. Y. 1989. "A Review of the Recruitment Process of Police Constables in the RHKPF." Master's Thesis, Department of Public and Social Administration, City University of Hong Kong.

Chan, W. S. 1998. "An Assessment of the Police Superintendent's Discretion Scheme." Master's Thesis, Department of Politics and Public Administration, University of Hong Kong.

Chen, A. H. Y. 1988. "The Development of Immigration Law and Policy: The Hong Kong Experience." McGill Law Journal 33:631-75.

———. 1999. "Continuity and Change in the Legal System." In The Other Hong Kong Report: 1998, edited by L. C. H. Chow and Y. K. Fan. Hong Kong: Chinese University Press.

Cheung, A. K. C. 1996. "The Impact of Bill of Rights on Law Enforcement of the Hong Kong Police." Hong Kong Public Administration: A Journal of Policy and Administration in the Asia-Pacific 5(2):153-70.

Cheung, J. 2002. "Hardened Views 'Aid Squeeze on Rights.'" South China Morning Post, June 3.

———. 2003. "Draft of Security Law Goes Before Exco Today." South China Morning Post, February 11.

Cheung, M., and N. M. Boutte-Queen. 2000. "Emotional Responses to Child Sexual Abuse: A Comparison between Police and Social Workers in Hong Kong." Child Abuse and Neglect 24(12):1613-621.

Cheung, T. S., and C. C. Lau. 1981. "A Profile of Syndicate Corruption in the Police Force." In Corruption and Its Control in Hong Kong, edited by R.P.L. Lee. Hong Kong: Chinese University Press.

Chinoy, M. 2003. "Shock Reversal for Hong Kong Vote." CNN.com/World, July 7.

Chow, M. 2002. "Police Promotion Ban Challenged." South China Morning Post, June 5.

Chui, L. P. C. 1991. "A Study of the Role and Structure of RHKPF in the Transitional Period." Master's Thesis, Department of Politics and Public Administration, University of Hong Kong.

Chung, R. T. Y., M. C. F. Tong, and R. K. M. Lui. 1992. "Public Opinion Programme Poll 30 April-2 May 1992: Hong Kong People's Opinion on Law and Order." Summary Report, Social Sciences Research Center, University of Hong Kong.

Clarke, R. V. 1992. Situational Crime Prevention: Successful Case Studies. Albany, NY: Harrow and Heston.

Coopers and Lybrand. 1992. "Review of the Top Management Structure of the Royal Hong Kong Police: Final Report." Hong Kong: Coopers & Lybrand Management Consultants Limited.

Crank, J. P., and R. Langworthy. 1992. "An Institutional Perspective of Policing." The Journal of Criminal Law and Criminology 83(2):338-63.

Davis, M. C. 1995. "Adopting International Standards of Human Rights in Hong Kong." In Human Rights and Chinese Values: Legal, Philosophical, and Political Perspectives, edited by M. C. Davis. Hong Kong: Oxford University Press.

DiMaggio, P. J., and W. W. Powell. 1991. "Introduction." In *The New Institutionalism in Organizational Analysis*, edited by W. W. Powell and P. J. DiMaggio. Chicago, IL: University of Chicago Press.

Editorial. 1997a. "Cause for Complaint." *South China Morning Post*, May 22.

————. 1997b. "Closing Ranks." *South China Morning Post*, June 25.

Edwards, R., L. Henkin, and A. Nathan. 1986. *Human Rights in Contemporary China*. New York: Columbia University Press.

Endacott, G. B., and A. Hinton. 1968. *Fragrant Harbour: A Short History of Hong Kong*. Hong Kong: Oxford University Press.

Gaylord, M. S., and H. Traver. 1994. "The Hong Kong Criminal Justice System." In *Introduction to the Hong Kong Criminal Justice System*, edited by M. S. Gaylord and H. Traver. Hong Kong: Hong Kong University Press.

————. 1995. "Colonial Policing and the Demise of British Rule in Hong Kong." *International Journal of the Sociology of Law* 23:23-43.

Grant, I. C. 1992. "1997: The Implications for Community Policing in Hong Kong." Master's Thesis, Center for Police and Criminal Justice Studies, Exeter University.

Guangdong Police Studies Association. 2001. "Cross-border Crimes Involving Hong Kong and Macaw Black Society." In *Crime Prevention Symposium Proceeding*, Central Police University, Taipei.

Ho, S. W. M. 1989. "Administrative Reform in the Royal Hong Kong Police." Master's Thesis, Department of Politics and Public Administration, University of Hong Kong.

Hodson, D. 1995. "Law Enforcement and the Bill of Rights." In *Hong Kong's Bill of Rights: 1991-1994 and Beyond*, edited by G. Edwards and A. Byrnes. Hong Kong: University of Hong Kong.

Home Affairs Bureau. 1997. "Equal Opportunities: A Study on Discrimination on the Ground of Race, A Consultation Paper." Hong Kong Government, February.

Hong Kong Annual Report. 1966. Hong Kong: Government Printer.

Hong Kong Baptist College. 1993. "Public Opinion Poll Result." *South China Morning Post*, September 17.

Hong Kong iMail, September 11, 2001; April 25-26, 2002, Hong Kong section.

Hong Kong Police Force. 2000. "Police in Figures."

Hong Kong Police Review, 1996, 1997, 2000, 2004. Hong Kong Police Force.

Hong Kong Police Statistics. 2005. Hong Kong Police Force (www.info.gov.hk/police).

Hong Kong Transition Project. 2001. "Becoming China: The Public State of Mind on Hong Kong's Integration with the Mainland." Government and International Studies, Hong Kong Baptist University,

————. 2002. "Winter of Despair: Confidence and Legitimacy in Crisis in the Hong Kong SAR." Government and International Studies, Hong Kong Baptist University.

Hui, E. K. O. 1997. "Statement of Strategic Directions." Hong Kong Police Force.

————. 2002. "Management Reforms in the Police Force." In *Public Sector Reform in Hong Kong: Into the 21st Century*, edited by A. B. L. Cheung and J. C. Y. Lee. Hong Kong: Chinese University Press.

Huntington, S. P. 1994. *The Clash of Civilizations?* New York: Foreign Affairs.

ICAC Advisory Committees. 2000. "Reports of ICAC Advisory Committees." Hong Kong: Government Printing Department.

ICAC Complaints Committee. 2000-2001. "Annual Report of ICAC Complaints Committee." Hong Kong: Government Printing Department.

ICAC Operations Department Review. 1998-1999. Hong Kong: Government Printing Department.

Information Office of the State Council. 1991. *Human Rights in China*. Beijing: Information Office of the State Council.

Jiao, A. Y. 2002. "Organizational Behaviors and Political Sensitivities: Policing Hong Kong After 1997." *Public Administration and Policy: A Hong Kong & Asia-Pacific Journal* 11(1):41-60.

Jiao, A. Y., R. W. K. Lau, and P. Lui. 2005. An Institutional Perspective of Organizational Change: The Case of the Hong Kong Police. *International Criminal Justice Review* 15(1): 38-57.

Jung, C. G. 1976. *Psychological Types.* Princeton, NJ: Princeton University Press.

Keenan, F. 1995. "The Right Stuff: Clean Cops Harder to Find As 1997 Looms." *Far Eastern Economic Review*158, Oct. 19.

Kwok, M. W. 2001. "Opening Address." 2nd Annual Symposium on Crime and Its Control in Greater China, the Center for Criminology, Hong Kong University.

Kwok, Y. M. 1999. "An Analysis of the PC to SGT Promotion System of the HKPF." Master's Thesis, Department of Politics and Public Administration, University of Hong Kong.

Langworthy, R. H., and L. F. Travis III. 2003. *Policing in America: A Balance of Forces.* Upper Saddle River, NJ: Prentice-Hall.

Lau, E. 1988a. "Policing the Police: Critics Want Sweeping Powers to Be Curbed by 1997." *Far Eastern Economic Review* 141:31, July 14.

Lau, N. K. 2002. "Police Spat with ICAC Sign of HK's Ugly Mood." *South China Morning Post,* May 27.

Lau, R. W. K. 2004. "History As Obstacle to Change: A Neo-Institutionalist Analysis of Police Reform in Hong Kong." *International Journal of the Sociology of Law* 32:1-15.

Lau, S. K, and H. C. Kuan. 1988b. *The Ethos of the Hong Kong Chinese.* Hong Kong: The Chinese University Press.

Lau, S. 2002. "Deserted Charter Garden Is Graveyard of Broken Dreams." *South China Morning Post,* April 26.

Lee, E. 2002. "Families Suffer amid Social Change: Index Shows Improvement for HK in Key Areas, But Worsening Rates of Divorce and Domestic Violence." *South China Morning Post,* May 29.

Lee, E. W. M. 1991. "An Investigation into the Prevailing Morale and Personnel Problems Facing the Royal Hong Kong Police Force." Master's Thesis, Department of Public and Social Administration, City Polytechnic of Hong Kong.

Lee, S. 1997. "Twin Moves Set To Make Police More Accountable." *South China Morning Post,* 11 May.

———. 2002a. "Rethink Urged on Tough Rules for Police Bankruptcy." *South China Morning Post,* June 3.

———. 2002b. "ICAC Hurt Our Reputation, Says Defiant Police Chief." *South China Morning Post,* May 25.

Lee, S. and S. Lau. 2002. "Police Swoop on Abode Protesters." *South China Morning Post,* April 26.

Liu, C. F. 1988. *A Chief Inspector's Diary.* Hong Kong: Bo Yi Publications.

Lo, C. 2003. "The Authority of Officers Is Challenged on the Streets, Security Staff Order Police Out of Hotel." *South China Morning Post,* February 27.

Lo, S. H. 2001. "The Politics of Triads in Greater South China: Hong Kong, Macau and the Pearl River Delta." Paper presented at the 2001 Symposium of Crime Control in Greater China, University of Hong Kong.

Lo, T. W. 1993. *Corruption and Politics in Hong Kong and China.* UK: Open University Press.

Loper, K. 2001. "Cultivating A Multicultural Society and Combating Racial Discrimination in Hong Kong." A paper prepared for government policy makers in Hong Kong. Hong Kong: Civic Exchange.

Lowe, K., and E. McLaughlin. 1994. "An El Dorado of Riches and A Place of Unpunished Crime: The Politics of Penal Reform in Hong Kong, 1877-1882." In *Criminal Justice History: An International Annual*, vol. 14, edited by L. A. Knafla. Westport, CT: Greenwood Press.

MacWilliams, B. 2003. "Sex Trafficking, Forced into Prostitution." *The Chronicle of Higher Education*, L(6):A34-A36.

Mah, E. F. H. 1993. "An Analysis of Hong Kong Government's Localization Policy in Legal Department and the Police Force: Progress and Obstacles." Master's Thesis, Department of Public and Social Administration, City Polytechnic of Hong Kong.

Manning, P. K. 1977. *Police Work: The Social Organization of Policing*. Cambridge, MA: MIT Press.

———. 1997. *Police Work: The Social Organization of Policing*. 2nd ed. Prospect Heights: Waveland Press.

March, J., and J. Olsen. 1984. "The New Institutionalism: Organizational Factors in Political Life." *The American Political Science Review* 78:734-49.

Marketing Decision Research Limited (MDR). 1997. "Customer Satisfaction Survey for the Royal Hong Kong Police: Topline Report." Report prepared for the Royal Hong Kong Police.

———. 1997. "Opinion Survey on the Quality of Police Services: A Report." Report prepared for the Hong Kong Police Force.

Masttofski, S. D., R. R. Ritti, and D. Hoffmaster. 1987. "Organizational Determinants of Police Discretion: The case of Drinking-Driving." *Journal of Criminal Justice* 15: 387-402.

Meyer, J. W., and B. Rowan. 1991. "Institutionalized Organizations: Formal Structure As Myth and Ceremony." In *The New Institutionalism in Organizational Analysis*, edited by W. W. Powell and P. J. DiMaggio. Chicago, IL: University of Chicago Press.

Ming Pao, September 6, 1989; August 1, 2001; May 8, 25, and 26, 2002, Daily News section.

Mitchell, T. 2002. "Fragments Fuse into Economic Giant: Massive Investment by Hong Kong in the Region Is Beginning to Pay Huge Dividends for all the Players." *South China Morning Post*, January 29.

Moy, P. 2003. "Alarm at Drastic Rise in Number of Battered Spouses." *South China Morning Post*, February 11.

Mukherjee, S., C. Carcach, and K. Higgins. 1997. *A Statistical Profile of Crime in Australia*. Canberra: Australian Institute of Criminology.

Newman, G., ed. 1999. *Global Report on Crime and Justice*. New York: Oxford University Press.

Naughton, B. 1997. "The Future of the China Circle." In *The China Circle: Economics and Technology in the PRC, Taiwan, and Hong Kong*, edited by B. Naughton. Washington, D.C.: Brookings Institution Press.

Ng, M. 1995. "Are Rights Culture-Bound?" In *Human Rights and Chinese Values: Legal, Philosophical, and Political Perspectives*, edited by M. C. Davis. Hong Kong: Oxford University Press.

Ng-Quinn, M. 1991. "Bureaucratic Response to Political Change: Theoretical Use of the Atypical Case of the Hong Kong Police." Hong Kong Institute of Asia-Pacific Studies, Chinese University of Hong Kong.

Offbeat - The Newsletter of the Hong Kong Police Force. 2001. Issue 711, September 12 to 25, News section.

———. 2002a. "Kudos for the Force." Issue 723, March 13.

———. 2002b. "Crime Prevention Campaign in Tuen Mun." February 27-March 12.

———. 2002c. "Understanding Public Perception of Police." February 27-March 12.

———. 2002d. "Force to Tackle Indebtedness Problem Evenhandedly." March 26-April 8.

Open Magazine. 2001. "Special Topic: China's Entry into WTO." Issue 180:35, December.

Oriental Daily News, September 8, 2001; May 25-26, 2002, Hong Kong News section.

Pang, T. Y. 1999. "An Analysis of the Legitimization of Police Powers in Hong Kong." Master's Thesis, Department of Politics and Public Administration, University of Hong Kong.

PayScale. 2005. "Salary Survey by Country/City" (http://www.payscale.com/salary-survey).

Porter, M. E., J. D. Sachs, A. M. Warner, C. Moore, J. M. Tudor, D. Vasquez, K. Schwab, P. K. Cornelius, M. Levinson, and B. Ryder. 2000. *The Global Competitiveness Report 2000*. New York: Oxford University Press.

Porter, M. E., K. Schwab, X. Sala-i-Martin, and A. Lopez-Carlos. 2004. *The Global Competitiveness Report 2003-2004*. New York: Oxford University Press.

Powell, W.W. 1991. "Expanding the Scope of Institutional Analysis." In *The New Institutionalism in Organizational Analysis*, edited by W.W. Powell and P.J. DiMaggio. Chicago, IL: University of Chicago Press.

Pritchard, S. 2002. "Dealing with A Frontier Mentality: Hong Kong Is Well Placed To Become the PRD's Nerve Center." *South China Morning Post*, January 29.

Rabushka, A. 1973. *The Changing Face of Hong Kong: New Departures in Public Policy*. Washington, D.C.: American Enterprise Institute for Public Policy Research and Stanford, CA: Hoover Institution on War, Revolution and Peace.

Rear, J. 1971. "The Law of the Constitution." In *Hong Kong: The Industrial Colony: A Political, Social and Economic Survey*, edited by K. Hopkins. Hong Kong: Oxford University Press.

Reichel, P. L. 2002. *Comparative Criminal Justice System: A Topical Approach*. Upper Saddle River, NJ: Prentice-Hall.

———. 2005. *Comparative Criminal Justice Systems: A Topical Approach*. 4th ed. Upper Saddle River, NJ: Pearson Prentice Hall.

Rosi, A. 2002. "Handle with Care." *South China Morning Post*, June 5.

Sackmann, S. A. 1991. *Cultural Knowledge in Organizations: Exploring the Collective Mind*. Newbury Park, CA: Sage.

Sai, B. H. H. 1998. "An Analysis of the Policy on Investigating Complaints against the Police Force." Master's Thesis, Department of Politics and Public Administration, University of Hong Kong.

Scott, I. 1989. *Political Change and the Crisis of Legitimacy in Hong Kong*. Hong Kong: Oxford University Press.

Shamdasani, R. 2003. "Article 23 Scuffles As Bill Receives Its First Reading." *South China Morning Post*, February 27.

Sinclair, K. 1983. *Asia's Finest: An Illustrated Account of the Royal Hong Kong Police*. Hong Kong: Unicorn.

Sinclair, K., and N. K. Ng. 1997. *Asia's Finest Marches On: Policing Hong Kong from 1841 into the 21st Century*. Hong Kong: Kevin Sinclair Associates.

Skolnick, J. H. 1994. *Justice without Trial: Law Enforcement in Democratic Society*. New York: Macmillan College Publishing.

Smith, B.J., and D. Lawley. 2003. "Police Initiatives to Combat Juvenile Crime." Seminar given at the Center for Criminology, University of Hong Kong.

So, A., and C. F. Cheung. 2002. "Mainlanders Put Strain on Prisons." *Sunday Morning Post*, May 19.

South China Morning Post, May 14, 20-23, 2002, Hong Kong News section.

Starr, J. B. 2001. *Understanding China: A Guide to China's Economy, History, and Political Culture*. New York: Hill and Wang.

State Council. 1991. *Human Rights in China*. Beijing: Information Office of the State Council.

Sum, I. N. L. 1989. "The Changing Nature of Colonial Bureaucratic Authoritarianism in Hong Kong and Its Implications for Public Policies." Master's Thesis, Department of Politics and Public Administration, University of Hong Kong.

Sung, Y. W. 1997. "Hong Kong and the Economic Integration of the China Circle." In *The China Circle: Economics and Technology in the PRC, Taiwan, and Hong Kong*, edited by B. Naughton. Washington, D.C.: Brookings Institution Press.

Ta Kung Pao, September 9 and 11, October 7, 2001; May 14, 2002, Hong Kong News section.

The Sun, February 24, 2002, Front Page section.

Tolbert, P.S., and L.G. Zucker. 1996. The Institutionalization of Institutional Theory. In *Handbook of Organization Studies*, edited by S. Clegg, C. Hardy, and W. R. Nord. Thousand Oaks, CA: Sage.

Traver, H., and J. Vagg, eds. 1991. *Crime and Justice in Hong Kong*. Hong Kong: Oxford University Press.

Tsang, Y. P. 2002. "Letter to Hong Kong." Radio broadcast on RTHK, January 27.

Tung, C. H. 2003. "Tung Chi-Hua's First Policy Address of His Second Term as Chief Executive of the Hong Kong Special Administrative Region," January 8.

University of Hong Kong. 1998. "Staff Opinion Survey Results 1998." The Poon Kam Kai Institute of Management, University of Hong Kong.

———. 1999. "Public Opinion Survey on the Public Image of the Hong Kong Police Force: Survey Report." The Poon Kam Kai Institute of Management, University of Hong Kong.

———. 2001a. "Key Findings: Customer Satisfaction Survey 2000." The Poon Kam Kai Institute of Management, University of Hong Kong.

———. 2001b. "Key Findings: Staff Opinion Survey 2000." The Poon Kam Kai Institute of Management, University of Hong Kong.

———. 2002a. "Key Findings: 2001 Public Opinion Survey." The Poon Kam Kai Institute of Management, University of Hong Kong.

———. 2002b. "Key Findings: 2001 Staff Opinion Survey." The Poon Kam Kai Institute of Management, University of Hong Kong.

Vagg, J. 1993. Sometimes a Crime: Illegal Immigration and Hong Kong. *Crime and Delinquency* 39(3):355-372.

Vines, S. 2002. "Policing the Police: Tung Needs to Put A Stop to Bickering between the Force and the ICAC." *Hong Kong iMail*, May 27.

Washington Street Journal. 2002. "Hong Kong's Lack of Progress: The Local Pro-China Elite Is More Dangerous than Beijing." Opinion section, July 1.

Wilson, J. Q. 1972. *Varieties of Police Behavior: The Management of Law and Order in Eight Communities*. New York: Atheneum.

Wong, B. H. K. 1991. "To What Extent the British Nationality Package Can Solve the Brain Drain Problem in the Government Sector: A Case Study of Royal Hong Kong Police Force." Master's Thesis, Department of Public and Social Administration, City Polytechnic of Hong Kong.

Wu, A. 1995. "Why Hong Kong Should Have Equal Opportunities Legislation and a Human Right Commission?" In *Human Rights and Chinese Values: Legal, Philoso-*

phical, and Political Perspectives, edited by M. C. Davis. Hong Kong: Oxford University Press.

Yu, H. 1995. "On Human Rights and Their Guarantee by Law." In *Human Rights and Chinese Values: Legal, Philosophical, and Political Perspectives*, edited by M. C. Davis. Hong Kong: Oxford University Press.

Index

About the Author

Allan Y. Jiao is currently Chair and Professor of Criminal Justice in the Department of Law and Justice Studies at Rowan University in New Jersey, U.S.A. He holds a Master's Degree in Public Administration (1991) from Lewis & Clark College and a Ph.D. in Criminal Justice (1996) from Rutgers University. Working for years at the undergraduate and graduate level, he has taught courses that span various academic disciplines including English, Economics, Sociology, Public Administration, and Criminal justice. Jiao has published extensively in the field of policing and criminal justice including refereed journal articles, book chapters, and books. His current research interests include policing, public policy, and comparative criminal justice issues. Jiao spent one academic year in 2001-02 as a Fulbright Scholar in Hong Kong and traveled to mainland China, Macaw, and Taiwan during the same time. He loves traveling and has been to many countries in Asia, Europe, and South America while giving presentations on his research. He plans to venture into countries in Africa and the Middle East in the near future. Jiao enjoys communicating and collaborating with practitioners, scholars, and students from all over the world.

Made in the USA
Middletown, DE
27 December 2018